50 Hikes in North Florida

50 *Hikes*

In North Florida

**Walks, Hikes, and Backpacking Trips in
the Northern Florida Peninsula**

First Edition

SANDRA FRIEND

BACK COUNTRY

Backcountry Guides
Woodstock, Vermont

AN INVITATION TO THE READER

Over time trails can be rerouted and signs and landmarks altered. If you find that changes have occurred on the routes described in this book, please let us know so that corrections may be made in future editions. The author and publisher also welcome other comments and suggestions. Address all correspondence to:

Editor
50 Hikes™ Series
Backcountry Guides
PO Box 748
Woodstock, VT 05091

LIBRARY OF CONGRESS CATALOGING-IN-PUBLICATION DATA

Friend, Sandra.
  50 hikes in north Florida : walks, hikes, and backpacking trips in the Northern Florida penin- sula / Sandra Friend. -- 1st ed.
    p. cm.
  Includes index.
  ISBN 0-88150-530-7
    1. Hiking--Florida--Guidebooks. 2. Trails-- Florida--Guidebooks. 3. Backpacking--Florida-- Guidebooks. 4. Florida--Guidebooks. I. Title: Fifty hikes in north Florida. II. Title.

GV199.42.F6F75 2003
917.59--dc21
                    2002043893

Cover and interior design by Glenn Suokko
Cover and interior photographs by Sandra Friend
Maps by Mapping Specialists Ltd., Madison, WI

Copyright © 2003 by Sandra Friend

First Edition

Published by Backcountry Guides,
a division of The Countryman Press
P.O. Box 748
Woodstock, VT 05091
www.countrymanpress.com

Distributed by W. W. Norton & Company, Inc.
500 Fifth Avenue
New York, NY 10110

Printed in the United States of America
10 9 8 7 6 5 4 3 2 1

"For inspiration, I look to the power, the mystery, and the beauty of nature."

—David Muench

DEDICATION

To Rich Evans, who helped me rediscover Florida's outdoors: The journey of a thousand miles began with a single step.

50 Hikes at a Glance

HIKE	LOCATION
1. Suwannee River State Park	Ellaville
2. Anderson Springs Loop	Ellaville
3. Swift Creek Conservation Area	White Springs
4. Big Shoals	White Springs
5. Fanning Springs State Park	Fanning Springs
6. Andrews Wildlife Management Area	Fanning Springs
7. Manatee Springs State Park	Chiefland
8. Lower Suwannee National Wildlife Refuge	Chiefland
9. Cedar Key Scrub State Preserve	Cedar Key
10. Atsena Otie Key	Cedar Key
11. Big Gum Swamp Wilderness	Deep Creek
12. Olustee Battlefield Historical State Park	Olustee
13. Alligator Lake Recreation Area	Lake City
14. O'Leno State Park	High Springs
15. Ichetucknee Springs State Park	Fort White
16. Devil's Millhopper Geological State Park	Gainesville
17. San Felasco Hammock Preserve State Park	Gainesville
18. Morningside Nature Center	Gainesville
19. Gum Root Swamp Conservation Area	Gainesville
20. Paynes Prairie Preserve State Park	Micanopy
21. Goethe State Forest	Dunnellon
22. Ravine Gardens State Park	Palatka
23. St. Johns Loop	Rodman
24. Salt Springs Loop Trail	Salt Springs
25. Silver Glen Springs	Silver Glen Springs

DISTANCE (miles)	FEATURES	GOOD FOR KIDS	CAMPING	NOTES
15.3	H		B, D	Confluence of the Suwannee and Withlacoochee Rivers
5.2	G		B	Riverside hike within Twin Rivers State Forest
4.5	F			Meander along high bluffs in historic White Springs
7.3	G			Extensive hike along Florida's only Class III white water
1.6	G	★		Short loop through karst along the Suwannee River
12.4	F			Impressive number of Grand Champion trees
6.0	G	★	D	A first-magnitude spring, sinkholes, and shady forests for hiking
2.4	H	★	D	Massive shell midden on the tidal marsh
8.9	W			Coastal scrub community hosting rare Florida scrub-jay
2.0	H	★		End of John Muir's thousand-mile walk to the Gulf of Mexico
4.9	F		B	Remote and rugged wilderness trek for intrepid hikers
1.1	H	★	D	Florida's most significant Civil War battlefield
6.3	W	★		Great bird-watching on the wetlands
14.4	G		B, D	The Santa Fe River plays peek-a-boo through karst
4.0	G	★		Stunning blue spring feeds a clear, healthy run
0.9	G	★		Waterfalls and lush vegetation in a 120-foot-deep sinkhole
12.2	F			Deeply wooded hammock on karst with diverse and rare flora
2.6	F	★		Family-oriented interpretive trails through a variety of ecosystems
2.6	H	★		Dark cypress swamp hides ancient secrets
22.1	W	★	D	North Florida's largest open prairie
14.9	W		B	Significant red-cockaded woodpecker population
2.1	G	★		Unusual landscape of deeply eroded ravines and bubbling springs
3.6	H			A variety of habitats along the St. Johns River
1.9	F	★	D	Scrub forests along Salt Springs Run
3.1	G	★		Beautiful waterfront walk along Lake George

50 Hikes at a Glance

HIKE	LOCATION
26. The Yearling Trail	Silver Glen Springs
27. Juniper Run Nature Trail	Juniper Springs
28. Lake Eaton Trails	Lake Eaton
29. Silver River Connector Trail	Nuby's Corners
30. Dunns Creek Conservation Area	San Mateo
31. Welaka State Forest	Welaka
32. Ralph E. Simmons Memorial State Forest	Boulogne
33. Cary Nature Trail	Bryceville
34. Fort Clinch State Park	Fernandina Beach
35. Talbot Islands	Fort George
36. Fort George Island	Fort George
37. Timucuan Ecological and Historical Preserve	Jacksonville
38. Kathryn Abbey Hanna Park	Mayport
39. Jennings State Forest	Middleburg
40. Black Creek Ravines Conservation Area	Middleburg
41. John P. Hall Sr. Nature Preserve	Green Cove Springs
42. Stokes Landing Conservation Area	St. Augustine
43. Guana River State Park	Ponte Vedra Beach
44. Anastasia State Park	Anastasia Island
45. Moses Creek Conservation Area	Dupont Center
46. Princess Place Preserve	Colfax
47. Washington Oaks Gardens State Park	Hammock
48. Graham Swamp Conservation Area	Palm Coast
49. Haw Creek Preserve	Bunnell
50. Bulow Creek Trail	Ormond

DISTANCE (miles)	FEATURES	GOOD FOR KIDS	CAMPING	NOTES
5.5	H	★	B	Remnants of historic community featured in the novel *The Yearling*
1.4	G	★	D	Walk through subtropical forest along a glassy stream
4.1	G	★	D	A massive sinkhole punctures the sand pine scrub
3.6	F	★		Hike through an unusual floodplain forest to the Silver River
3.0	F		B	Vivid and varied wildflowers; large sundew population
7.4	G	★	B	Panoramic views from riverside campsites; pristine Mud Spring
9.3	F		B	Beautiful campsites on the St. Marys River
1.4	F	★	B	Features a boardwalk through a titi swamp
11.6	H	★	D	A classic 1800s masonry fortress at Florida's northern tip
11.1	W	★	D	Painted buntings nest in maritime hammocks
4.2	H	★		Layers of history from Timucuan middens to 1700s plantation
5.5	H	★		First French settlement in the Americas
2.7	W	★	B, D	Oceanfront park with heavily forested trail
6.7	F		B	Rugged hikes through pine flatwoods and sandhills
7.8	G		B	Scenic views of Black Creek, fabulous wildflowers
7.0	W		B	Camp along the wilds of the St. Johns River
2.7	W	★	B	Sweeping panoramas of salt marshes
9.0	F			Extensive trail system through a variety of habitats
10.8	H	★	D	North Florida's longest and most enjoyable beach hike
12.9	F		B	Great campsites along the salt marshes of the Matanzas River
4.1	H	★	D	Historic Cherokee lodge sits along Pellicer Creek
4.2	G	★		Coquina rock beach with unusual formations
1.0	W	★	B	Rare freshwater marsh just 2 miles from the sea
1.6	W	★	B	Watch wildlife from the boardwalk along Haw Creek
7.8	H		B	1820s sugar mill ruins and 2,000-year-old live oak

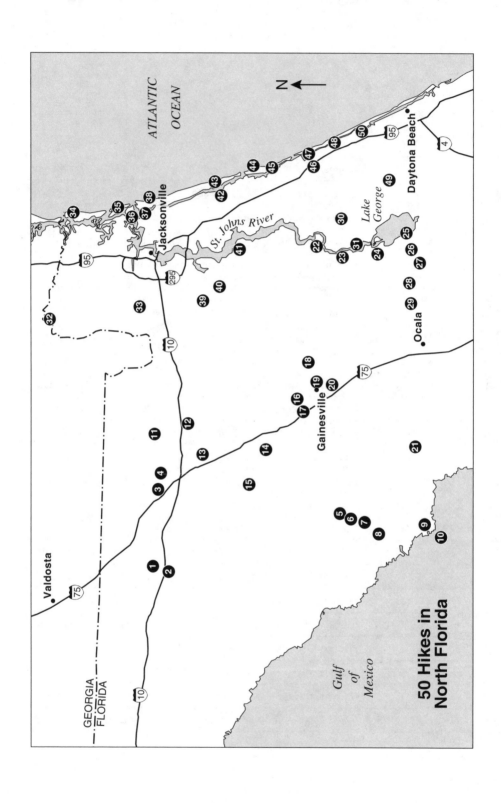

**50 Hikes in
North Florida**

CONTENTS

Acknowledgments 13
Introduction 15

I. Suwannee River

1. Suwannee River State Park 33
2. Anderson Springs Loop 43
3. Swift Creek Conservation Area 48
4. Big Shoals 54
5. Fanning Springs State Park 61
6. Andrews Wildlife Management Area.........................66
7. Manatee Springs State Park 73
8. Lower Suwannee National Wildlife Refuge 79
9. Cedar Key Scrub State Reserve 86
10. Atsena Otie Key...92

II. Central Highlands

11. Big Gum Swamp Wilderness 100
12. Olustee Battlefield Historical State Park 105
13. Alligator Lake Recreation Area 110
14. O'Leno State Park 115
15. Ichetucknee Springs State Park 122
16. Devil's Millhopper Geological State Park 129
17. San Felasco Hammock Preserve State Park 133
18. Morningside Nature Center 140
19. Gum Root Swamp Conservation Area 146
20. Paynes Prairie Preserve State Park 151
21. Goethe State Forest 162

III. Ocala National Forest

22. Ravine Gardens State Park 174
23. St. Johns Loop..179
24. Salt Springs Loop Trail 184
25. Silver Glen Springs 189
26. The Yearling Trail 194
27. Juniper Run Nature Trail.......................................200
28. Lake Eaton Trails..204
29. Silver River Connector Trail 209
30. Dunns Creek Conservation Area 214
31. Welaka State Forest 218

IV. Jacksonville Metro

32. Ralph E. Simmons Memorial State Forest 224
33. Cary Nature Trail 231
34. Fort Clinch State Park 236
35. Talbot Islands 245
36. Fort George Island 253
37. Timucuan Ecological and Historical Preserve 260
38. Kathryn Abbey Hanna Park 267
39. Jennings State Forest 272
40. Black Creek Ravines Conservation Area 277

V. Atlantic Coast

41. John P. Hall Sr. Nature Preserve......................286
42. Stokes Landing Conservation Area 292
43. Guana River State Park 296
44. Anastasia State Park 303
45. Moses Creek Conservation Area 309
46. Princess Place Preserve 315
47. Washington Oaks Gardens State Park 321
48. Graham Swamp Conservation Area 328
49. Haw Creek Preserve 332
50. Bulow Creek Trail 337

Index 345

Acknowledgments

Thanks to friends and family who joined me on both short walks and long, difficult treks through some of Florida's most beautiful landscapes—Deb Blick, Rich Evans, Phil and Linda Friend, Joan Jarvis, Deborah Kent Stewart, Annette Rao, Sandy Hubbard Trouba, Susan Schmidt, Paula Snellgrove, Elizabeth VanMierop, and John White.

For their help with my field research, my sincere thanks to Susan and David Roquemore in Cedar Key; John White of Silver Springs; Judy Johnson with the Cedar Key Area Chamber of Commerce; Captain Dan, Doris, Janice, and Vernie with the Island Hopper; Ranger Paula Lewis at the Salt Springs Visitors Center, Ocala National Forest; Ranger Frank Mooney at Suwannee River State Park; Ranger Gene McCoy at O'Leno State Park; Ranger Aaron Rodriguez at Little Talbot Island State Park; Phyllis Houston, Suwannee Chapter, Florida Trail Association; Donna and Winn Horton, North Florida Trailblazers; L. Arthur Bellot Jr., County Coordinator, Dixie County; Mark Gluckman and Edwin McCook, Suwannee River Water Management District; Patrick McSweeney, St. John & Partners Advertising & Public Relations; Ranger Jill Howard, Timucuan Preserve; Ben Harris, Marketing Director, Florida State Parks; and Kenneth Meyer of the Avian Research and Conservation Institute.

Hiking North Florida meant a lot of overnight stays to start hikes in the cool early morning hours, so I appreciated the lodgings provided by friends and fellow outdoors enthusiasts. Thanks to Deb Blick; Susan and Tom Schmidt of Summer Haven; Jaymie and Joe Brunofsky, owners of the Gulf Side Motel in Cedar Key; Jessica, Kevin, and Pat at the Suwannee Valley Campground in White Springs; and Laura Healan, Public Relations Manager, and the courteous staff at Amelia Island Plantation. And a big thanks to my friend Gweneeth Conklin for a quiet writer's retreat in a cabin in the mountains of North Carolina while I assembled my field notes into this book.

Introduction

With a limited population base, numerous state parks, and expansive state and national forests, north Florida provides the hiker with an extensive array of natural communities to explore. Vast expanses of longleaf and slash pine flatwoods create habitats for vanishing species, such as the Florida black bear and the red-cockaded woodpecker. Coastal hammocks protect the painted bunting, Florida's most colorful bird, and the least tern, North America's smallest tern. The dry, desertlike scrub of the Ocala National Forest provides shelter for the threatened Florida scrub-jay and the Florida scrub lizard; mergansers, green herons, and yellow-crowned night herons take up residence in the floodplain forests of the St. Johns, Ocklawaha, Suwannee, and St. Marys Rivers. Trails follow in the footsteps of William Bartram, John Muir, and John James Audubon, exposing hikers to rare plants, like Bartram's ixia, and unusual birds, like the wood stork.

The human occupation of north Florida started more than three thousand years ago. The Timucua lived along the shores of the St. Johns River, leaving behind burial mounds and middens to mark their passing. In 1562 French Huguenots claimed Florida for France, establishing a settlement next to a Timucuan village near the mouth of the St. Johns River. By 1565 the Spanish had founded a permanent colony at St. Augustine, the nation's oldest continuously occupied city. Building missions on the coast and in the interior, they attempted to convert the Timucua to Catholicism. British pirates raided the coastal islands and the newly formed cities, leaving behind myths of buried treasure. During the Civil War, most of Florida's battles and skirmishes centered in north Florida, from Fort Clinch on the St. Marys River to the Cedar Keys. Hiking trails explore the unique history and culture of the region, from the Spanish coquina quarries used to build the Castillo de San Marcos, America's oldest masonry fortress, to Florida's largest Civil War battle, at Olustee.

North Florida's geology differs greatly from the rest of the peninsula, offering more physical challenges for the hiker: deep ravines, rough riverside trails along steep bluffs, and giant sinkholes. Formed by the steady erosion of the limestone bedrock, karst topography creates geologic oddities such as sinkholes, natural bridges, disappearing rivers, and dozens of enormous crystal-clear springs. Along the Atlantic coastline, outcroppings of coquina form caves and arches etched by the sea, delicate landscapes in miniature.

The rugged delights and panoramic views available on north Florida's hiking trails offset their typically short lengths. Hiking in north Florida allows the opportunity to camp along the state's broadest rivers, to clamber in and out of ravines and up and over relict dunes, to walk to the edge of sweeping vistas across prairies and salt marshes, and to hike along vast lakes and bubbling springs. Subtle delights charm as well. Be on the lookout for the small wonders of the forest, from the delicate red clusters of the carnivorous sundew

Oak scrub along the Salt Springs Loop Trail

plant to the bright orange cones of wild bachelor's button. Due to fewer people in this part of the state, you're bound to see more wildlife. Scout for bison and wild horses on Paynes Prairie, watch for wintering manatees in Manatee Springs, and see playful dolphins in the Atlantic surf off Anastasia Island.

When winter snows fall from northern skies, it's prime hiking season in Florida. Between October and March temperatures become comfortable, and the insect population declines. Fall color appears in north Florida's deciduous forests in November. Seasonally out of synch with most of the rest of the nation, Florida provides a perfect winter playground for the active hiker.

HOW TO USE THIS BOOK

For purposes of this book, I've designated north Florida as the counties north of FL 40 (which runs from Dunnellon east through Ocala to Daytona Beach) to the Georgia border and east of the Panhandle, including Alachua, Baker, Bradford, Clay, Columbia, Dixie, Duval, Flagler, Gilchrist, Hamilton, Lafayette, Levy, Nassau, Putnam, St. Johns, Suwannee, and Union Counties, and the northern half of Marion County.

Hikes in this book vary from short interpretive boardwalks to overnight backpacking trips. I have avoided paved trails, except where they are used to access longer hikes. I have also excluded hikes along the Florida National Scenic Trail, as they will be covered in a separate book; however, several of the hikes in this book utilize short segments of the Florida National Scenic Trail as a part of a loop.

In many of the parks, forests, and wilderness areas I visited, there are multiple alternatives for hikes. I have shown all alternatives on the maps, but each discussion and mileage focuses on a particular preferred route. Most of these hikes were measured using a Rolatape 415 surveyor's measuring wheel. For beach walks and remote islands, I relied on a Garmin Etrex GPS.

All attempts at habitat and plant identification are my own, using a variety of references. When there were multiple possibilities for a plant's name, I chose the one most commonly used in the local vernacular, such as "cabbage palm" for our state tree rather than the more regal "sabal palm" preferred by botanists.

KEY FEATURES

Each hike highlights a particular key feature—flora, geology, history, or wildlife.

Flora

Florida's varied habitats, lush with wildflowers, trees, and shrubs, are one of the best reasons to get out on the trail. Of more than 4,000 types of plants, 3,600 are native to this state. Only California and Texas surpass Florida in botanical diversity. Naturalists William Bartram, John James Audubon, and John Muir all expressed their delight at the variety of plants and flowers found in Florida. Every season coaxes forth colorful wildflowers. Many trails are established to show off specific plant communities—boardwalks through titi swamps, trails past bogs filled with pitcher plants, climbs along dunes covered with morning glories, and walks through colorful sandhill habitats.

Geology

Florida's karst geology provides an interesting look at an unusual landscape. Karst is the name for any type of terrain where the bedrock dissolves easily. In Florida, limestone forms the "basement" of the state, studded with fossils from millions of years ago. Since limestone dissolves easily, the karst landscape is full of cracks, crevices, and caves. Sinkholes form, allowing natural waterfalls to trickle down into their depths. North Florida is well known for its bounty of first-magnitude springs, gushing forth out of the Floridan Aquifer to form rivers and streams. Some trails focus on springs, sinkholes, and other karst landforms; others follow the steep bluffs and ravines associated with the erosion of streams flowing into north Florida's rivers. Expect to see more surface limestone in the northern part of the state than in the rest of the Florida peninsula.

History

Many hikes focus on features of historic interest. Florida's human habitation dates back thousands of years; reminders of these settlements can be seen trailside. More recent events occurred over the past five hundred years, from the waves of European settlements starting in 1562 to the many conflicts, including the Seminole Wars, the Civil War, the Spanish American War, and both World Wars. Fortresses, ghost towns, and living-history demonstrations are just a few of the delights to be discovered along Florida's trails.

Florida's extensive turpentine industry thrived during the late 1800s and early 1900s since wooden sailing ships relied on the products of the pine tree, called naval stores (tar, pitch, rosin, and turpentine), to protect them from the harsh effects of salt water. Crockery turpentine cups were hung on trees that had been **catfaced**—a line of bark stripped, and deep V-shaped gashes cut into the wood, faced with metal strips. The sap would slowly drip into the cup, to be collected and emptied into larger containers for further processing. Artifacts of this time can be seen along many of the trails described in this book.

Wildlife

Florida's diversity of wildlife can be enjoyed on many trails through lands set aside for wildlife preservation, such as the wetlands of Alligator Lake Recreation Area, protecting nesting colonies of herons and egrets; the sandhills of Black Creek Ravines Conservation Area, home to dozens of gopher tortoises; and the Cedar Key Scrub State Reserve, with its growing population of Florida scrub-jays. Walk quietly, and you'll be rewarded with wildlife sightings: barred owls and red-cockaded woodpeckers in the trees, bald eagles and red-shouldered hawks circling overhead, West Indian manatees and river otters gliding up crystal-clear rivers.

HABITATS

Since Florida's topography doesn't easily lend clues as to where you are on a trail, hike descriptions focus on the changes in habitat that occur as a trail gains or loses elevation. There are many variations in habitat across north Florida, and different sources use different names for the same general habitat. The following summary explains the habitat designations used in this book.

COASTAL HABITATS

With more than 1,200 miles of coastline, Florida's habitats include many communities adapted to life along the sea, where wind and salt spray shape the environment. **Coastal strands** are created by wind-blown sand and anchored by deep-rooted grasses such as sea oats. In the **maritime hammock,** windswept live oaks create a canopy above lush thickets of saw palmetto. Brittle grasses and succulent plants such as glasswort and sea purslane grow along the edges of **salt flats** and **salt marshes,** where herons, egrets, and ibises stride through the shallows. **Estuaries** and **coastal savannas**

A great blue heron in flight at Anastasia State Park

are extensive grassy salt marshes punctuated by islands of cabbage palms, typically found between barrier islands and the mainland. **Mangrove swamps** form along the edges of tidal basins.

FORESTS

Hardwood hammock is a catchall term for a forest of mixed hardwoods, such as sweetgum, hickory, and ironwood, often interspersed with oaks and pines. The **oak hammock,** usually made up of live oak and laurel oak, is Florida's climax forest. **Pine flatwoods** are the state's largest natural community, covering nearly half the land. With acidic, poorly drained soils supporting ferns, gallberry, saw palmetto, and a high canopy of tall pine trees, pine flatwoods feel very open. Historically dominated by longleaf pine, which has been logged out of most of Florida's forests, the pine canopy varies according to the soil drainage. Longleaf and loblolly pines prefer the high ground, while slash pine prefers some

dampness. Pond pine tolerates seasonal flooding. A clay layer beneath the soil holds in rainfall, causing flatwoods to stay flooded for a few days after a rainstorm—leaving the trail, the low spot, full of water. **Cabbage palm flatwoods** intersperse cabbage palms through a canopy of pond or slash pines and occur in floodplain areas. **Scrubby flatwoods** have better drainage than most pine flatwoods, but the pines have more space between them, forming breaks in the canopy. **Upland hardwood forests** are a dense canopy of beech, elm, hickory, and southern magnolia, where azaleas and dogwoods may grow. The unique microclimates created by **bluffs** and **ravines** increase Florida's plant diversity; certain species, such as spleenwort and green dragon, prefer cool, shady spots with exposed limestone.

PRAIRIES

Treeless and open, prairies are extensive dry grasslands that can be seasonally inundated with water. Wildflower enthusiasts seek out prairies for their unusual and colorful flowers, such as the pine lily, pale meadow beauty, and elephant's root. Prairies may contain islands of oak hammocks or cabbage palm flatwoods and are host to bayheads, cypress domes, and freshwater marshes. Less than 20 percent of Florida's prairies are under state protection; most have been converted to cattle ranches, sod farms, and citrus groves.

SANDHILLS

These gently rolling pine-topped hills of white to orange sand have suffered more than any other natural community from Florida's ongoing development because of their dryness. Prior to logging, longleaf pine was the dominant species; slash pine now provides most sandhill shade. Many varieties of oaks flourish in the dry, well-drained soil. Forming a protective layer over karst, sandhills allow rainfall to trickle through and recharge the Floridan Aquifer, the state's most crucial source of fresh water. A related habitat, **clayhills,** hosts the same types of plants on a base of thick red clay.

SCRUB

Scrubs form on well-drained, loose "sugar sand," deposited along ancient shorelines. They are thought to be Florida's oldest plant communities, in existence for more than 20 million years. A limited number of plants tolerate the extreme dryness of the scrub environment. In a **sand pine scrub,** tall sand pines dominate the forest, with an understory of oak scrub, rosemary scrub, and saw or scrub palmetto. A **rosemary scrub** is an unusual place, where rosemary bushes up to 8 feet tall grow out of a white-sand base; the ground may be covered in lichens. **Oak scrub** is dominated by sand live oak, wax myrtle, Chapman oak, and myrtle oak, with

the highest diversity of scrub plant and animal life.

SWAMP FORESTS

Red maple, sweetgum, red bay, bay magnolia, loblolly bay, and water oak are common residents of the **floodplain forest,** created by rivers that seasonally overflow their banks, scouring adjoining channels higher than the normal river level. Thick with bald cypress, pond cypress, and cabbage palms, the low-lying **hydric hammock** occurs along river and lake floodplains, experiencing flooding whenever water levels are slightly above normal. **Palm hammocks** provide slight elevation over the surrounding marshes. A basin, or **bay,** is a swampy interior forest of cypress, bay, and mixed hardwoods. Looking like a dome from a distance, the **cypress dome** forms in a low depression in a prairie, fed by seeping water. Similarly, **bayheads** receive their watery base from seepage, encouraging dahoon holly, bay magnolia, and loblolly bay to grow. Unless a boardwalk is available, don't expect to keep your shoes dry when hiking through a swamp forest.

WETLANDS

In addition to coastal marshes, mangrove swamps, and swamp forests, Florida's moist habitats include **freshwater marshes,** which form along lake and river drainages; **ephemeral ponds,** which occur in low spots during the rainy season; **flatwoods ponds,** created from the trickling runoff in the pine flatwoods; and **wetlands,** shallow grassy basins in pine flatwoods, scrub, and prairies. Rare **seepage slopes** happen primarily in scrub and sandhill, where an elevation change allows water to trickle slowly out of the side of a hill, nourishing moist meadows where carnivorous plants thrive.

Narrow-leaf pawpaw at Morningside Nature Center

ADVICE AND PRECAUTIONS

Alligators

Alligators are rarely a problem for a hiker, unless humans have fed the alligator. If an alligator is habituated to human presence, it won't get out of your way. If an alligator fearlessly blocks the trail, do not approach it or try to walk around it. Make noise, stomp your feet, and let *it* move before you continue. Never feed or touch an alligator.

Bears

Consider yourself fortunate if you see a Florida black bear. Mostly active in the early morning hours, this elusive mammal teases you with scat and tracks left on hiking trails. A full-grown Florida black bear weighs no more than 350 pounds and will quickly move out of your way if it sees you. No one has ever been attacked by a Florida black bear.

Camping

Tent camping (backpacking or car camping) in Florida is best enjoyed between October and March, when the muggy nights with high temperatures yield to a cool evening chill. Wildfires spark easily in Florida, so please refrain from building a campfire unless a fire ring is available—use a camp stove for cooking. Pack out all waste materials from your campsite. Where privies are available, use them; otherwise, dig a hole at least 400 feet from any campsite or water source. When camping in a primitive campsite, particularly an undeveloped site, follow Leave No Trace ethics: Leave the site as pristine as when you entered it. Eliminate any signs of a campfire unless there is an established fire ring. To protect your food supply, use a bear bag in bear territory, not just to foil the bears, but also to outwit the wily raccoons that congregate near established campsites. If you camp on the banks of a river, stream, or lake, keep in mind that alligators roam at night.

Deforestation

Even in protected areas such as state parks, state forests, and wilderness areas, a hiker is bound to come across gaping gaps in the forest: hammocks charred by wildfires, pine forests felled by loggers, and trees fallen like scattered matchsticks, victims of the southern pine beetle. State and national forests issue permits to logging companies for regular harvesting of timber, and care is not always taken to leave a corridor of trees around a hiking trail. Sandhill and scrub habitats require wildfire to regenerate new growth. Logging frequently occurs to help restore these fragile habitats with fresh growth.

Most insidious, however, is the spread of the southern pine beetle southward into Florida. These minute beetles primarily infest loblolly pine trees, exhibiting termite-like behavior as they tunnel through the soft inner tissue of the pines. In 2001 alone, beetles infested more than 14,000 acres of Florida's forest, forcing forest rangers to chop down the affected trees to attempt to prevent the spread of the menacing creatures.

If you come across an area where blazes are missing, use your best judgment in crossing an open area. Look carefully for telltale blazes on the distant tree line. If the trail has been following jeep roads, look for alternate routes around the clear-cut. Make sure that you know where you entered the open area in case you need to backtrack.

Heat and Dehydration

When hiking in Florida, it is very easy to become dehydrated without realizing it. The warm temperatures and sunshine will sometimes prompt you to drink, but not often enough. Dehydration and long exposure to the sun can lead to heat exhaustion, which starts with nausea, chills, and dizziness and can lead to deadly heatstroke. If you feel any of these symptoms, stop hiking. Drink as much fluid as possible, and rest a while before attempting any further exertion. Always carry enough water for your hike. I carry a minimum of 1 liter per 4 miles, and twice that when temperatures are more than 80 degrees.

Hunting

Florida's prime hiking season is also the state's prime hunting season, which can lead to conflicts on certain state lands, such as Wildlife Management Areas, Water Management District lands, state preserves, and state forests. During deer season, wear a lightweight blaze-orange vest when hiking these lands. Hunting is *not* permitted in county parks, state parks, or state recre-ation areas. Backpackers should be aware that certain lands are closed to overnight camping during general gun season; some trails (particularly in state forests and WMAs) are entirely closed to hiking during the gun season, due to the perceived risk to hikers. For full details on hunting dates and restrictions in specific state lands, check the Florida Fish and Wildlife Conservation Commission's web site at http://floridacon-servation.org.

Insects

Thanks to the warm weather, Florida's insects enjoy longer lives than in most states. As a result, your hike will not be entirely insect-free until the first serious chill hits, usually by mid-November. Bug-free bliss continues through March. For the rest of the year, keep a long-lasting sportsman's insect repellent in your pack and apply liberally to keep disease-bearing mosquitoes away.

To keep off ticks and chiggers (also known as red bugs), spray your hiking clothing beforehand with permethrin. To minimize bug problems when you sit, carry a plastic garbage bag to sit on when you take your breaks. Spray yourself with repellent before starting out on the trail. Longtime Florida hikers recommend wearing long pants to beat the mosquitoes and dusting your socks with sulfur powder (available over-the-counter from a pharmacist, who has to grind it) to fend off chiggers, microscopic bugs that attach themselves to your skin to feed. If your legs feel itchy after a hike, take a 15-minute plunge in a hot tub or a hot bath to ward off any further affects from chiggers. Check yourself carefully for ticks.

Spiders can be problematic to Florida hikers between March and November as they tend to build large webs across the trail. Most commonly, you'll see the large golden orb spider in its sticky yellow web and the crab spider, smaller but obvious because of the shell on its back. Be proactive. Pick up a stick (the stalk of a saw palmetto frond works well) and hold it tilted in front of you to catch any human-height webs. Try to duck under webs that you can see, as a spider's web is a masterpiece of nature—and the spider is helping to rid the forest of pesky bugs.

Marine Life

Enjoying a barefoot hike along Florida's beaches means keeping your eyes open for the marine life that washes ashore, particularly clear, glassy blobs of jellyfish. Stepping on a jellyfish means hours of intense pain. If you decide to enjoy a dip in the sea, bear in mind that Florida leads the world in shark attacks on bathers. Most attacks occur along the central Atlantic Coast. On the Gulf of Mexico, wading in the sea calls for the "stingray shuffle." Set each foot down on the ocean floor with a resounding *stomp*, which alerts the stingrays to stay clear.

Mountain Bikes and Equestrians

On multiuse trails, mountain bikes and equestrians may share the trail. Allow them the right of way so they don't further tear up the edges of the footpath. You're more likely to see riders on horseback than bikers, since horse farms dominate the landscape of the Central Highlands. Multiuse trails are indicated in the text.

Plants

No matter how far south you travel in the United States, there's no escaping poison ivy. Be particularly alert to the poison ivy vine that grows up trees along some boardwalk trails. Tread softly, also known as stinging nettle, has a beautiful white flower atop a tall stem; its leaves are covered with tiny stinging nettles. Avoid brushing bare skin

against it. Many trails are not maintained between the months of April and September since most hiking occurs in the fall and winter. An overgrown trail can be painful when burrs and nettles dig into your socks. Consider purchasing a pair of low gaiters to cover your socks and shoes, or do as the experienced hikers do—wear long lightweight pants when hiking, even in summer.

Proper Clothing and Equipment

Always carry rain gear! Storm clouds come up suddenly and unexpectedly and can easily put a damper on your hike if you're not prepared. Find a jacket that will fold down small enough to attach to a fanny pack or fit inside your daypack. If you are hiking more than a couple of miles, carry some sort of small pack. At a minimum, your pack should contain water, a first-aid kit, a flashlight, a compass, and emergency food. To beat the heat, a sturdy fanny pack with water-bottle holsters is a good choice. A hat is essential to keep your head cool.

Because Florida's terrain is often sandy or wet, your footwear need not be the rugged mountain-climbing gear you see at most outfitters. Avoid heavy leather boots and "waterproof" lined boots—your feet *will* sweat, and to minimize blisters, you need your feet to breathe. Look for a lightweight hiking shoe, a trail running shoe, or even comfortable running shoes. Some Florida hikers use sports sandals with socks, although sandals are a poor choice for the more rugged of north Florida's rocky riverside hiking trails. When your shoes get waterlogged, you want them to be able to dry.

Wear two layers of socks—a good hiking sock on the outside, and a thin polypropylene or silk/nylon sock on the inside. Instead of rubbing against your skin, the socks will rub against each other. Avoid cotton socks. When they get damp, they abrade your feet.

If you do feel a hot spot or a blister coming on, treat it immediately. Cover it with a piece of moleskin (found in the foot-care section of most drugstores) and apply a small piece of duct tape over the moleskin to keep it water- and sweat-proof.

Interested in backpacking? Many of the trails in this book feature backcountry camp-sites, some along relatively short trails. The Florida Trail Association offers several be-ginners' backpacking workshops each year, which is a great way to try out gear (and the whole concept of backpacking) before you spend any money on the hobby. While a hands-on workshop is your best bet, you may not have the time—so read one of the many excellent books on backpacking, in-cluding *Backpacking* (Adrienne Hall), *Backpacking: One Step at a Time* (Harvey Manning), *The Complete Walker IV* (Colin Fletcher), and *Hiking & Backpacking: A Complete Guide* (Karen Berger). For spe-cifics on backpacking in Florida, seek out *From Here to There on the Florida Trail* (Susan Roquemore and Joan Hobson), by two Florida Trail Association members who backpacked the entire Florida National Scenic Trail.

Snakes

Central Florida's poisonous snakes include the southern copperhead, the cottonmouth moccasin (sometimes called water moc-casin), the eastern coral snake, and three types of rattlesnake: timber, eastern dia-mondback, and pygmy. Although nonpoiso-nous, the black racer can be aggressive. In areas where the trail is overgrown, be wary of where you set your feet. Never han-dle a snake.

Sun

When hiking under the bright Florida sun, use a high-strength sports sunblock lotion and wear a hat to protect your face. Depending on the habitats you'll be hiking through, you may want sunglasses as well—sun glinting off white-sand beaches and open scrub makes it hard to see.

Unattended Vehicles

Use common sense when leaving your vehi-cle at a trailhead. Don't leave valuables in plain sight, and lock the vehicle. If a permit is required to enter the land or to hike the trail, be sure the permit shows inside the front windshield.

Water

Florida's trails run the gamut on water sup-plies—either they have plenty of it, or they have none. Because of drainage from citrus groves and cattle pastures into rivers and creeks, you cannot trust water sources to be pristine, with the exception of free-flowing artesian wells and springs along the trail. Even these can have an unpleasant taste due to a high sulfur or salt content and can require filtering. Not all water sources can be easily reached—a flatwoods pond, for in-stance, may require some slogging through muck before you reach water. I mention water sources for backpackers but suggest you carry your own supply whenever day hiking. Always use a water filter or chemical treatment such as iodine before drinking "wild" water. Do *not* drink the water in mine reclamation areas.

Weather

While the average hiker wouldn't stray out-side in a hurricane, the frequency of after-noon thunderstorms in the summertime doesn't always keep a person off the trail. But darkening skies are no laughing matter. Violent thunderstorms can spawn fierce wind gusts and, occasionally, tornadoes. If you are caught out in the open during a storm, attempt to reach cover as quickly as possible.

FLORIDA STATE PARKS

Florida's State Parks, State Reserves, and State Recreation Areas all require an entry fee, varying from location to location. Residents can save themselves some money by picking up an annual Florida State Parks entrance pass ($30 individual, $60 family), covering all entrance fees for a year. The family pass is good for up to eight people entering in a single vehicle. Visitors can also invest in a Florida State Parks vacation pass, available in increments of a week at a time for $10 per week. State parks, reserves, and recreation areas are generally open 8 AM to sunset. Many provide camping facilities, which can now be reserved online through Reserve America at http://www.reserveamerica.com.

For more information on the state park system, including links to information for specific state parks, visit http://www.dep. state.fl.us/parks/information/index.htm, or call 850-488-9872 for a free Florida State Parks guide.

FLORIDA TRAIL ASSOCIATION

Founded in 1964 to promote the creation of a 1,300-mile footpath from Pensacola to the Everglades, the statewide Florida Trail Association (FTA) encourages hikers to build, maintain, and enjoy Florida's trails. Volunteers from the FTA maintain many loop hikes across the state. Although all FTA-maintained loops are blazed orange, the FTA does not maintain all of the orange-blazed trails in the state. In 1998 the state Department of Environmental Protection adopted orange as the standard color for blazing all hiking trails. Look for the FT sign at the trailhead for trails built and maintained by the Florida Trail Association.

Local chapters hold monthly outdoors-focused meetings and sponsor frequent hiking, backpacking, and trail-work activities to introduce Floridians and visitors alike to the great outdoors, Florida-style. For information on a chapter near you, contact the Florida Trail Association, 5415 SW 13th Street, Gainesville, FL 32608, call 877-HIKE-FLA, or visit http://www.florida-trail.org.

FLORIDA STATE FORESTS/TRAILWALKER PROGRAM

All Florida State Forests require a permit for camping, available through the office of the particular forest. Check the Florida State Forests web site at http://www.fl-dof.com for details. The Florida Division of Forestry Trailwalker Program encourages you to get out and hike specially designated trails in Florida's state forests. As you complete each hike, send in a postcard to the program. After 10 hikes, the state awards you a Trailwalker patch and certificate. There are nine Trailwalker trails covered in this book. For a Trailwalker application, visit any of the designated Trailwalker trailheads for a brochure, call 850-414-0871, or visit the web site at http://www.fl-dof.com/Recreation/Trailwalker.

SUGGESTED READING AND FIELD GUIDES

Alden, Peter, Rich Cech, and Gil Nelson. *National Audubon Society Field Guide to Florida*. New York: Alfred A. Knopf, 1998.

Andersen, Lars. *Paynes Prairie: A History of the Great Savanna*. Sarasota, FL: Pineapple Press, 2001.

Bartram, William; Mark Van Doren, ed. *Travels of William Bartram*. New York: Dover Publications, 1955.

Bell, C. Richie, and Bryan J. Taylor. *Florida Wild Flowers and Roadside Plants*.

Chapel Hill, NC: Laurel Hill Press, 1982.

Belleville, Bill. *River of Lakes: A Journey on Florida's St Johns River.* Athens, GA: University of Georgia Press, 2000.

Brown, Paul Martin. *Wild Orchids of Florida.* Gainesville, FL: University Press of Florida, 2002.

Carr, Archie. *A Naturalist in Florida: A Celebration of Eden.* New Haven, CT: Yale University Press, 1994.

Comfort, Iris Tracy. *Florida's Geological Treasures.* Baldwin Park, CA: Gem Guides Book Co., 1998.

Dietz, Tim. *Call of the Siren: Manatees and Dugongs.* Golden, CO: Fulcrum Publishing, 1992.

Derr, Mark. *Some Kind of Paradise: A Chronicle of Man and the Land in Florida.* Gainesville, FL: University Press of Florida, 1998.

D'Orso, Michael. *Like Judgment Day: The Ruin and Redemption of a Town Called Rosewood.* New York: Boulevard Books, 1996.

Friend, Sandra. *Florida in the Civil War: A State in Turmoil.* Brookfield, CT: Twenty First Century Books, 2001.

____. *Sinkholes.* Sarasota, FL: Pineapple Press, 2002.

Muir, John. *A Thousand-Mile Walk to the Gulf.* Boston, MA: Houghton-Mifflin Company, 1981.

Nelson, Gil. *The Ferns of Florida.* Sarasota, FL: Pineapple Press, 2000.

____. *The Shrubs and Woody Vines of Florida.* Sarasota, FL: Pineapple Press, 1996.

____. *The Trees of Florida.* Sarasota, FL: Pineapple Press, 1994.

Ripple, Jeff, and Susan Cerulean, editors. *The Wild Heart of Florida: Florida Writers on Florida's Wildlands.* Gainesville, FL: University Press of Florida, 1999.

Rawlings, Marjorie Kinnan. *Cross Creek.* Atlanta, GA: Mockingbird Books, 1969.

____. *South Moon Under.* Atlanta, GA: Mockingbird Books, 1977.

____. *The Yearling.* Atlanta, GA: Mockingbird Books, 1969.

Sanger, Marjory Bartlett. *Forest in the Sand.* New York: Atheneum, 1983.

Stamm, Doug. *The Springs of Florida.* Sarasota, FL: Pineapple Press, 1994.

Stowe, Harriet Beecher. *Palmetto Leaves.* Gainesville, FL: University Press of Florida, 1999.

Taylor, Walter Kingsley. *Florida Wildflowers in their Natural Communities.* Gainesville, FL: University Press of Florida, 1998.

Tekiela, Stan. *Birds of Florida Field Guide.* Cambridge, MN: Adventure Publications, Inc., 2001.

ADDRESSES

Hike 1
Suwannee River State Park
20185 CR 132
Live Oak, FL 32060
386-362-2746

Hike 2
Florida Division of Forestry
Live Oak Work Center
7620 133rd Road
Live Oak, FL 32060
386-208-1462

Hike 3
Suwannee River Water Management District
9225 CR 49
Live Oak, FL 32060
386-362-1001
1-800-226-1066 (within Florida only)

Hike 4
Big Shoals Public Lands

P.O. Drawer G
White Springs, FL 32096
386-397-2733

Hike 5
Fanning Springs State Park
c/o Manatee Springs State Park
NW 115th Street
Chiefland, FL 32626
352-463-3420

Hikes 6, 9
Florida Fish and Wildlife Conservation
Commission
9550 NW 160th Street
Fanning Springs, FL 32693
352-493-6020
http://floridaconservation.org

Hike 7
Manatee Springs State Park
NW 115th Street
Chiefland, FL 32626
352-493-6072

Hike 8
Lower Suwannee National Wildlife
Refuge
16450 NW 31st Place
Chiefland, FL 32626
352-493-0238

Hike 10
Cedar Keys National Wildlife Refuge
16450 NW 31st Place
Chiefland, FL 32626
352-493-0238

Hike 11
Osceola Ranger District Office
P.O. Box 70
Olustee, FL 32072
386-752-2577

Hike 12
Olustee Battlefield Historic State Park
P.O. Box 40
Olustee, FL 32072
386-758-0400

Hike 13
Columbia County Parks and Recreation
P.O. Drawer 1529
Lake City, FL 32055
386-755-4100

Hike 14
O'Leno State Park
Route 2, Box 1010
High Springs, FL 32643
386-454-1853

Hike 15
Ichetucknee Springs State Park
Route 2, Box 5355
Fort White, FL 32038
386-497-2511

Hike 16
Devil's Millhopper Geological State Park
4732 Millhopper Road
Gainesville, FL 32653
352-955-2008

Hike 17
San Felasco Hammock State Preserve
c/o Devil's Millhopper Geological State Park
4732 Millhopper Road
Gainesville, FL 32653
352-955-2008

Hikes 18, 19
Gainesville Recreation and Parks
Department
Station 24, Box 490
Gainesville, FL 32602-0490
352-334-5067
http://www.natureoperations.org

Hike 20
Paynes Prairie Preserve State Park
100 Savannah Boulevard
Micanopy, FL 32667
352-466-3397

Hike 21
Division of Forestry
Goethe State Forest
8250 SE CR 336
Dunnellon, FL 34431
352-447-2202

Hike 22
Ravine Gardens State Park
P.O. Box 1096
Palatka, FL 32712
386-329-3721

Hike 23
Florida Department of Environmental
Protection
Office of Greenways and Trails
8282 SE Highway 314
Ocala, FL 34470
352-236-7143

Hikes 24, 25, 26, 27, 28, 29
Ocala National Forest
Lake George Ranger District
17147 East Highway 40
Silver Springs, FL 34488
352-625-2520

Hikes 30, 40, 41, 42, 45, 48
St. Johns River Water Management District
P.O. Box 1429
Palatka, FL 32178-1429
904-676-6614
http://sjr.state.fl.us

Hike 31
Florida Division of Forestry
Welaka State Forest

P.O. Box 174
Welaka, FL 32193-0174
386-467-2388

Hike 32
Florida Division of Forestry
Ralph E. Simmons State Forest
Route 3, Box 299
Hillard, FL 32046
904-845-3597

Hike 33
Florida Division of Forestry
Cary State Forest
Route 2, Box 60
Bryceville, FL 32209
904-266-5021

Hike 34
Fort Clinch State Park
2601 Atlantic Avenue
Fernandina Beach, FL 32034
904-277-7274

**Hikes 35, 36 (Fort George Island
Cultural State Park)**
Little Talbot Island State Park
12157 Heckscher Drive
Jacksonville, FL 32226
904-251-2320

Hikes 36 (Kingsley Plantation), 37
National Park Service
12713 Fort Caroline Road
Jacksonville, FL 32225
904-251-3537

Hike 38
Kathryn Abbey Hanna Park
500 Wonderwood Drive
Jacksonville, FL 32233
904-249-4700
http://www.coj.net/fun

Hike 39
Jennings State Forest
1337 Long Horn Road
Middleburg, FL 32068
904-291-5530

Hike 43
Guana River State Park
2690 South Ponte Vedra Boulevard
Ponte Vedra Beach, FL 32082
904-825-5071

Hike 44
Anastasia State Park
1340A A1A South Street
St. Augustine, FL 32080
904-461-2033

Hikes 46, 49
Flagler County Parks and Recreation
1200 East Moody Boulevard, #3
Bunnell, FL 32110
386-437-7490

Hike 47
Washington Oaks Gardens State Park
6400 Oceanside Boulevard
Palm Coast, FL 32137
386-446-6780

Hike 50
Bulow Plantation Ruins State Park
P.O. Box 655
Bunnell, FL 32110
386-517-2084

I

Suwannee River

Knarled oaks at Atsena Otie Key

1

Suwannee River State Park

Total distance (3 circuits): 15.3 miles

Hiking time: 9 hours or overnight trip

Habitats: Hardwood hammock, bluffs and ravines, sandhills, sinkholes

Maps: USGS 7½' Ellaville, park map, Florida Trail Association map PH-5

Situated where the Withlacoochee and Suwannee Rivers meet, Suwannee River State Park is one of those don't-miss Florida outdoors experiences, with two ghost towns and three very different hiking loops to explore. On the southern side of the Suwannee River, the park encompasses a developed campground, picnic area, historic site, and gentle but interesting hiking trails suitable for the entire family. The remote northern side of the park can be reached only by hiking the Big Oak Trail, best enjoyed by experienced hikers as an overnight backpacking trip to a primitive campsite on a peninsula formed by the confluence of the Suwannee and Withlacoochee Rivers. All trails in the park are marked with yellow footprints painted on a diagonally cut post.

To get to Suwannee River State Park, you have several choices. If you're on I-75 north of I-10, take exit 460, Jasper/Madison. Follow FL 6 east for 3.5 miles. Turn south on CR 751, at the sign 15 MILES SUWANNEE RIVER STATE PARK. The road turns into CR 249 after crossing the Suwannee River. After 8.4 miles you reach a stop sign. Turn right on CR 132, following it 6.6 miles to a stop sign. The park entrance is on the right. From I-75 south of I-10, exit onto I-10 toward Tallahassee. From I-10 westbound take exit 275, Live Oak/Lee. Follow US 90 for 5.1 miles west to the park entrance, on the right. From I-10 eastbound from Tallahassee, use exit 262, Lee. Head north on CR 255 for 2.9 miles to US 90. Turn

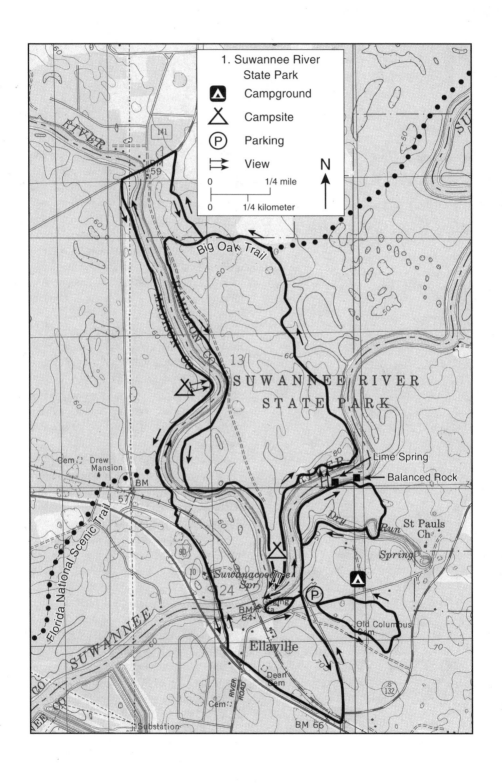

1. Suwannee River State Park

🛆 Campground

⋀ Campsite

Ⓟ Parking

⇨ View

N

0   1/4 mile

0   1/4 kilometer

Big Oak Trail

SUWANNEE RIVER
STATE PARK

Lime Spring

Balanced Rock

Drew Mansion

Cem

BM

St Pauls
Ch

Dry Run

Spring

Florida National Scenic Trail

Suwanacoochee Spr

BM Sta
64

Old Columbus
Cem

SUWANNEE

Ellaville

Dean
Cem

Cem

RIVER ROAD

132

Substation

BM 66

right. Follow US 90 east for 8.9 miles, to the park entrance on the left just after the bridge over the Suwannee River.

After paying your State Parks fee at the self-service pay station, drive up to the parking lot and park in one of the first few spaces. Just behind you are the trailheads for the Sandhill Trail and the Live Oak Trail, and the rest rooms are in the nearby ranger station. Trail maps are available at a kiosk on the other side of the parking lot, toward the river.

EARTHWORKS TRAIL AND SANDHILLS TRAIL

To learn about the history of the ghost town of Columbus, start your hike by turning left and walking through the picnic area, passing in front of the ranger station. Watch for the machinery and boardwalk. A boomtown during the mid to late 1800s, Columbus encompassed scattered houses and plantations built here at the confluence of the Withlacoochee and the Suwannee Rivers. More than five hundred people lived in the town during its heyday, making their fortunes from the virgin pine and hardwood forests around them. They cut trees for lumber and set up turpentine operations. As you come up to the sign HISTORICAL AREA, RIVER OVERLOOK, continue straight ahead past the skeleton of a paddle-wheeler steamboat shaft. Steamboats made Columbus, and they contributed to its demise. Long before automobiles and the advent of a good road system in Florida, steamboats provided reliable transportation from Columbus (and its sister city, Ellaville, across the river) to the Cedar Keys, allowing merchants to ship their goods to distant ports. When the steamboats stopped running in the 1920s, supplanted by the railroad, the boomtown faded away.

Columbus's strategic location made it a prime target during the Civil War. If Union forces could destroy the railroad bridge crossing the Suwannee, shipments of desperately needed food from plantations in western Florida would be prevented from reaching Confederate troops stationed in Georgia. Confederate soldiers built a large earthen fort to hold the position against a Union attack. That invasion was ultimately stopped at the Battle of Olustee (Hike 12). Cross the boardwalk over the fortress and continue into the forest. The trail curves to the right, following the river, becoming a boardwalk again. Look down. That deep spot below you was once Florida's only east-west highway, dropping down a roadcut that let wagons trundle down to a ferry at the river. Once at the river, drivers had their choice taking a ferry to the far shore of either river. Now that the roadcut is filled with trees, it's hard to imagine that it was once Florida's busiest highway.

The boardwalk ends at a viewing platform with benches, giving you a sweeping view of the confluence of the Withlacoochee and Suwannee Rivers. Not to be confused with the north-flowing Withlacoochee River in central Florida, *this* Withlacoochee River starts in the swamps of Georgia and flows south to this point. Echoing the past, the railroad bridge to the left is still the main line through north Florida. Turn around and walk down the boardwalk, stepping down to the side trail on the right. Hidden in the forest are the remaining pilings of the original railroad, the one that the Confederate troops protected. The trail turns to the left and heads up the slope. At the fork, keep to the right. When you emerge at a T on a jeep road, turn left. Follow the jeep road down past the rangers' residences to the entrance road at the pay station. Cross the entrance road and step over the low cable gate. Turn right to start your walk on the Sandhills Trail, after 0.5 mile.

Lime Spring

The Sandhills Trail is an interpretive trail, winding through sandhill habitat. Under the tall longleaf pines, the understory is mostly young oaks and longleaf pines in their candle stage. Wildflowers abound. Look for the broad purple blooms of butterfly-pea and the waxy ivory blossoms of the sandhill milkweed. On the left, a short spur trail leads to a deep sinkhole choked with small oaks. Sinkholes, springs, and disappearing streams are all a part of the underlying topography here, an ever-changing landscape known as karst. Karst happens when groundwater picks up the acid in the oak leaves and etches pathways through the bedrock below—in Florida's case, limestone.

Continuing along the main trail, you cross a firebreak and pipeline. You can see a structure up ahead in the forest: the outer walls of the Columbus cemetery, marking the far edge of the town that once stretched from the confluence of the river to here. Fences or walls demarcate several family plots. Most unusual is the lone grave of Thomas E. Swift, who died July 11, 1893. Atop his gravestone is a row of six large and very weathered conch shells, perhaps indicating that he was a native of Key West, the Conch Republic. A lone butterfly-pea rises up between the wrought-iron fence posts.

The trail meanders out of the graveyard between scattered clumps of lady lupine, resplendent in their tall spring blooms. Young white oaks reach for the sky between the gopher tortoise burrows. At 1 mile, turn right at the arrow. Walk along the firebreak to the next arrow; turn left. You're now walking beneath a power line, but this route has a greater significance: This was once the original road through north Florida, the stagecoach trail that passed through Columbus and Ellaville on its way to Pensacola. A narrow-leaved pawpaw groans under the weight of its long, skinny greenish-white blooms. At the end of the loop, you're facing the pay station and the cable gate. Turn right down a corridor of pines to return to the parking lot, emerging at the trailhead sign after 1.7 miles.

SUWANNEE RIVER TRAIL SYSTEM

Crossing the parking lot again, continue past the trail kiosk to the NATURE TRAIL sign. The Suwannee River Trail System encompasses three short but interesting nature trails: the Suwannee River Trail, the Balanced Rock Trail, and the Lime Sink Run Trail. Turning right, you walk down along the edge of the river through a dense hardwood hammock with sweetgum and water oak, white oak and pignut hickory. The trail crosses the road to the boat ramp. Follow the footprint markers across to the wide path through the forest. A large pileated woodpecker swoops past.

At 0.2 mile you reach a sign for the SUWANNEE RIVER TRAIL SYSTEM at the bridge over Lime Sink Run, indicating the junction of trails. Cross the bridge, looking down at the massive chunks of limestone and the grand old cypresses and maples. The staircase to the right leads to the Suwannee River Trail loop; continue straight. You're walking on a natural levee above the Suwannee River, carved out of thick sand by the sporadic floods that shape the river's floodplain. Benches allow you to sit and relax, watching the river flow by. Don't stray off the footpath—poison ivy dominates the forest floor. Short spur trails lead to the side of the bluff for open scenic views.

The sound of bubbling water echoes in your ears as you reach a staircase leading down to the left. Walk down it to the observation platform over Lime Spring. Although the spring isn't much larger than a child's wading pool, it sits above the river on a terrace of limestone, pumping its flow

Bluestar

down a small waterfall that tumbles into the Suwannee. Two separate spring vents at the waterfall's base push water upward, mounding on the river surface. Over its 206-mile course, more than 70 named springs feed the Suwannee River. Hundreds of smaller spring vents add to the flow. Under natural hydraulic pressure, the water wells up from the Floridan Aquifer, a network of water-filled caverns and crevices deep within the karst.

When you reach the junction of the Suwannee River Trail and the Balanced Rock Trail at 0.5 mile, continue straight, following the river. After walking across a pipeline crossing, you reenter the shady forest. American holly predominates, showing off its glossy, pointy-tipped leaves. Keep alert for the balanced rock—a limestone formation jutting out over the river, standing on a ledge that's balancing over the void. Once you pass it, the trail turns to the right, away

from the river. A thick blanket of Virginia creeper covers the forest floor. Look for jack-in-the-pulpit and green dragon poking out of the underbrush. Found in north Florida and the Panhandle, these two related species contain a significant amount of calcium oxalate crystals, which easily irritate mucous membranes. Jack-in-the-pulpit sports its distinct "pulpit," while green dragon shows off long, thin radiating leaves.

At 0.9 mile you come to a trail junction. Turn left to start the Lime Sink Run Trail. The trail curves to the right at a cable gate. The deep sinkhole off to your right is Lime Sink, suffering these days from the overall drop of the water level in the Floridan Aquifer over the past decade. When the water rises high enough, it spills out along Lime Sink Run. A couple of side trails let you walk along bluffs above the sink for a better view—but mind the poison ivy. The trail circles around the sink to follow the run down to the river. Without its full complement of water, Lime Sink Run provides a unique perspective on the nature of karst. The rocks are full of cracks, crevices, and holes, soaking up the water as it attempts to flow downstream, creating a series of disconnected basins edged by jagged limestone. You descend to a bridge to cross one of the sinks. Notice the enormous bald cypresses towering above, reflected in the dark water below.

A staircase leads upwards from the bridge. Turn right at the top of the stairs, passing a RETURN TO PARKING LOT sign and a footprint blaze to confirm your route. Walking along another segment of the run, you wander through a forest of giant cypresses, their knees rising up to 5 feet tall. After you pass a stone wall holding back a portion of the run, the trail reaches a fork at 1.2 miles. Up to the left you can see rest rooms in the developed campground. Take the right fork, the narrower path, following the stream. Ducking through a dark forest, you emerge back along the stream channel, with views of small caverns within the limestone sides of the channel. The trail turns to the left. Crossing a broad open area, you pass through another section of forest. Returning to the bridge over Lime Sink Run, you've completed the 1.4-mile loop. Turn left to walk back through the forest, crossing the boat ramp to retrace your path along the river back to the parking lot, completing the Suwannee River Trail System after 1.7 miles.

BIG OAK TRAIL

Starting at the ranger station, just across the entrance road from the trailhead to the Sandhills Trail, the Big Oak Trail ranges outside the park boundary to access a remote section of the park on the north side of the Suwannee River. Although this 12.5-mile hike can be done as a very long day hike, this is rugged terrain for Florida, so you may want to consider tackling this as an overnight trip, enjoying the primitive campsite with its stunning river views. Even if you're just headed out on a day hike, register at the ranger station before beginning your hike. If you're day hiking, expect to spend seven hours on the trail. Bring adequate water (or a filtration device), and start your hike early enough to ensure you return to your car before the park gates close at sunset. Because of the strenuous nature of this trail, it is not recommended for young children. Although the footpath is posted for hiking only, don't be surprised to see mountain bikers on the trail.

Pick up a map at the kiosk behind the ranger station. Walk down the park entrance road—following the blue blazes—and through the park gate, carefully crossing the railroad tracks on your way to US 90. When you reach US 90, turn right and stay along the shoulder of the road. Walk through the agricultural station and wave to the inspector. Turn right at the YIELD sign onto old US 90, where the old bridge over the Suwannee River still provides passage for hikers. Squeeze between the guardrails and cross the bridge. Where the guardrails end at the far end of the bridge, turn right at the historical marker and follow the blue blazes through the edge of an old picnic area with stone picnic benches and fireplaces. You've hiked 1.5 miles. Just upriver from this site was the former estate of Governor George F. Drew, Florida's governor during the post–Civil War Reconstruction period, an elegant landmark in the former town of Ellaville.

Watch carefully for the blue blazes as the trail dives left into the forest since the footpath is obscured. Loggers removed the pines due to beetle infestation, so this first section of woods is a jumble of downed logs and southern magnolias. The trail enters the cool shade of untrammeled forest, its understory dense with Virginia creeper, poison ivy, and slender limestone-loving ferns, ebony spleenwort. Ironwood and hickory trees rise overhead. An alluring aroma fills the air, filtering from the white and yellow blooms of honeysuckle. Pinkish-red roots dangle from thick grapevines. At 1.8 miles, you reach a T intersection with the Florida National Scenic Trail, a 1,300-mile footpath that runs from Pensacola to the Everglades. You'll be following its route for the next couple of miles to access the northern end of Suwannee River State Park. Turn right, following the orange blazes.

Climbing up an embankment, you come to the railroad tracks again. Cross here with extreme caution—this is a busy route with frequent trains. The trail drops down a steep embankment on the other side into the forest, crossing a jeep trail. Just beyond the jeep trail, watch for scattered turpentine-camp debris—broken clay pots and singed chunks of limestone—on the left side. You're entering the ghost town of Ellaville. With the town in decline after the steamboats stopped in the 1920s, the townspeople scattered when the sawmill shut down, the forests stripped of their virgin yellow pine. When the post office closed in 1942, Ellaville became a ghost town.

As you look down a deep ravine, you catch your first glimpse of the Withlacoochee River. The trail winds out to the edge of the river bluff, and then turns to follow it north. As in the Suwannee, tannins stain the waters of the Withlacoochee River, giving it a murky appearance from a distance. Close-up, the water is perfectly transparent, the color of iced tea. When you see massive limestone boulders in the woods, keep alert for some building foundations hidden by the tangle of vines in the underbrush. A tree grows out of one brick enclosure. On the far shore, you can see the remains of an old pier from when the ferryboats crossed the river.

When the trail turns away from the river, it passes through another area where the pines have been logged out, leaving young sweetgum and oak to fill in the forest. At 2.6 miles you reach a campsite with a picnic table and fire pit, and a trail leading down to the river for water access. This is *not* the backpacker's campsite for the Big Oak Trail, but it is one of many riverside campsites along this section of the Florida National Scenic Trail. A forest road that leads to the campsite parallels the trail for a while, and the trail eventually joins it at 2.9 miles. After another 0.4 mile, the trail turns right, again becoming a narrow path into the forest. It pops out into an open area along a corridor for a high-tension power line, weaving back and forth between the open and the forest on the river's bluff before coming to the foot of a large embankment. Look to the left and you can see a FLORIDA NATIONAL SCENIC TRAIL sign at the top of the embankment. Make your way up the steep slope, turning right at the sign to walk along CR 141, crossing the Withlacoochee River on the highway bridge. There is a lane for hikers on the right side of the bridge, but be alert for passing traffic. Once you cross the bridge, continue along the guardrail until it ends, at 3.8 miles. Head down the embankment to meet the jeep road, and follow it around back toward the river, continuing along the orange blazes. When you reach the gate, continue straight down the easement for the gas pipeline.

At 4.2 miles you reach the BIG OAK TRAIL sign. The Florida Trail, blazed orange, continues straight down the pipeline; the Big Oak Trail, blazed blue, turns right. If you're hiking in late April or early May, watch for fat raspberries ripening down low in the middle of the broad jeep trail. Keep alert for the double blaze where the trail turns right, and then makes an almost-immediate turn to the left, off the jeep trail and into the woods. The trail skirts the first of several chains of deep sinkholes along this peninsula before emerging along the edge of the river. You hear the sound of rushing water rising from a series of small rapids in a broad bend in the river before the trail turns into the forest again, winding its way to an old road. Turn right. This narrow track once allowed stagecoaches and riders on horseback to head toward Georgia from the town of Columbus after they'd crossed the river ferry.

The trail turns away from the road and toward the river at 5 miles, winding past massive bluff oaks and tall yellow pines. One yellow pine sports a broad canopy more than 130 feet above the forest floor. Giant pinecones litter the footpath. A broadhead skink, its foot-long golden body glistening in the sun, scampers out of the debris pile of a rotting pine and climbs up a nearby holly, its rusty head standing out against a halo of leaves. Keep alert for gnawed-off cedar stumps, the handiwork of beavers.

The levee broadens as the trail continues, and a river floodplain parallels you off to the left. The trail turns away from the river and crosses the floodplain, skirting the edge of another system of sinkholes. The deepest sink is nearest the trail, dropping down with sheer rocky sides to an inky pool, a window to the watery confines of the Floridan Aquifer. As with Lime Sink Run, the aquifer remains too low to feed the channel, which winds around through several sinkholes before reaching the river. The trail drops down into the channel at the river's edge, affording you a sweeping view of the next bend in the river.

After the trail rejoins the woods road, you walk right in to the backpacker's campsite for Suwannee River State Park, 6.2 miles into the hike. It sits high above the confluence of the two rivers, providing a constant, cooling breeze across the flat sand surfaces where you can pitch your tent. A fire ring and two picnic tables provide your kitchen and dining room, and you can work your way down a steep trail to the river's edge to gather water. Hear the sound of splashing water? A short side trail leads upriver along the Withlacoochee to a view of Suwanacoochee Spring, which pours out of a containment area—an old brick wall for a spring house—on the far side of the river, another remnant of the town of Ellaville. Another side trail leads to the very end of the peninsula, where you look across to the observation platform by the Confederate earthworks. As the crow flies,

you're less than 0.25 mile away from the trailhead at the ranger station. It's a beautiful campsite, but be aware that you're within maximum range of the sound of the trains crossing the trestle over the Suwannee. Look closely at the pines growing along the bluff's edge. They look similar to sand pines, with hexagonally patterned bark and clusters of small pinecones, but they are spruce pines, a species rarely found in Florida. These pines thrive on limestone bluffs along rivers.

The Big Oak Trail exits the campsite and continues its loop by following the Suwannee River upstream. Swamp chestnut oak, bluff oak, and large American holly shade this portion of the trail, and you can see the boat ramp on the far side of the river. When the trail turns into the forest, it winds past the tall skeleton of an old bluff oak tree. With the core of the oak rotted away, three people can fit in the space encompassed by its still-standing outer layer. After skirting an extensive floodplain, the trail drops down into it and makes a beeline to the river. There is no double blaze, so take caution not to miss the turn to the right. As you walk along the river, look carefully at the water's surface to notice the upwelling from numerous small spring vents. Scan the far shore and listen for the sound of flowing water, and you'll eventually notice Lime Spring. From this shore, you can more clearly see the constant cascade of water from the spring's pool down into the river.

At 6.8 miles you cross the gas pipeline corridor. Star rush peeks out of the taller grasses, and wild indigo grows in large clumps, enjoying the full sun. Once you enter the forest again, keep alert for the Big Oak, the namesake of this trail. There are many large oaks along this stretch of the trail, but the Big Oak towers over them all, a live oak formerly holding Grand

Champion record status for its height and canopy spread. It would take eight people holding hands to span the circumference of its gnarled, knobby base. If you aren't sure which tree it is (there is no sign), look carefully at the footpath. Trail maintainers cut a walkway through a fallen log just in front of the Big Oak, carving diagonal lines into the remaining layer of wood.

As the trail turns away from the Suwannee for the last time, it enters the deeply shaded hardwood hammock. Shallow karst depressions and deeper sinkholes pockmark the leaf-strewn forest floor, including one very deep sinkhole at 7.3 miles. Barren limestone reflects in the water at the bottom. The trail drops down into an area that was once clear-cut of its yellow pines, but it has grown back with a crowded understory of oaks, sweetgum, and young pines in the disturbed clay-rich soil. Turning a corner, the trail reenters the denser forest and comes to a large sign—you've reached the Florida Trail again. Despite what this older sign says (3.5 miles), you still have 4.5 miles to go to return to the Suwannee River State Park parking lot. Be alert when you reach this sign—turn *left* and follow the orange blazes, passing another series of deep sinkholes. The trail emerges at the gas pipeline clearing. Turn right. When you come up and over the rise, you'll reach the sign at the beginning of the Big Oak Trail loop. You've walked 8.3 miles.

From this point on, you're retracing the route you walked along the Withlacoochee River and the roads. Pass back through the gate and walk along the cattle fence to CR 149. Turn left, and cross the river on the bridge, staying to the left side of the road. When you reach the FLORIDA NATIONAL SCENIC TRAIL sign, turn left and head downhill and into the forest, following the orange blazes along the Withlacoochee River. Just after you cross the railroad tracks, keep alert for the trail sign marking where the blue-blazed connector trail back to the state park turns off to the left, at 10.7 miles. Following the blue blazes through the forest, out past the picnic area, and over the old highway bridge over the Suwannee, pass through the agricultural inspection station and keep to the broad shoulder of US 90 as you walk back to the turnoff for the park. Turn left at CR 132, and walk down the park entrance road to return to the ranger station and parking lot. You've completed a strenuous but satisfyingly scenic hike of 12.5 miles.

2

Anderson Springs Loop

Total distance (circuit): 5.2 miles

Hiking time: 2.5 hours

Habitats: Hardwood hammock, ravines and bluffs, upland hardwood forest, sink-holes, oak hammock

Maps: USGS 7½' Falmouth

One of the most pleasant hiking trails in the Florida State Forest Trailwalker program, the Anderson Springs Loop in Twin Rivers State Forest runs a scenic 5.2-mile circuit through shady forests along the undulating bluffs of the Suwannee River. Deep sinkholes, steep ravines, and rocky shorelines add to the fascinating scenery. The hard-packed footpath affords a strenuous workout as you hike along the river's edge. Primitive camping is permitted—bring your gear and head down the trail, picking out a sweet spot on a river bluff for the night. One word of caution: These woods have a healthy population of poison ivy. Dress appropriately; hiking in sandals is *not* recommended.

To get to Anderson Springs, take I-10 westbound to exit 275, Live Oak/Lee, and drive west 5.6 miles. You'll pass the entrance to Suwannee River State Park (Hike 1) before reaching River Road, on the left across from the agricultural inspection station. Eastbound on I-10, use exit 262, Lee. Go north on CR 255 for 2.9 miles. Turn right and follow US 90 east 8.4 miles to River Road, turning right just after the bridge over the Suwannee River. Drive south on River Road for 2.1 miles to a sign for Twin Rivers State Forest, Anderson Springs Tract. Turn right. Follow the narrow gravel track for 0.2 mile to the trail kiosk, and park on the left. If no parking spaces are available, drive a little farther to the main parking area above the spring, with a picnic table and grill at the trailhead. A short trail leads down from the parking lot to Anderson Spring, a popular site for cave

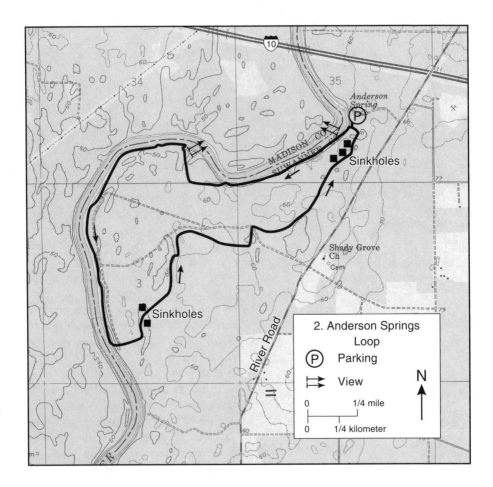

2. Anderson Springs Loop

(P) Parking

⊢→ View

N

0   1/4 mile

0   1/4 kilometer

divers. Kayakers can launch at the put-in. The area is open from 8 AM until dusk.

Starting from either the kiosk or the main parking area, follow the blue blazes as they skirt a deep ravine. The approach trails join together and immediately reach the edge of the river under a canopy of hardwoods— hickory, white oak, American holly, and basswood. You catch a glimpse of one of the Suwannee's famed sand beaches on the far shore, formed around the sweep of a river bend. At 0.1 mile you reach a junction with a yellow-blazed route from the left, your return trail. Continue straight, following the

blue blazes. Shaggy-barked bluff oaks tower overhead. That gigantic splash in the river wasn't a tree limb falling—it was the sound of an alligator sliding in off a rock. Don't be surprised if you see hikers on the far bluffs. The Florida National Scenic Trail runs for nearly 100 miles along the northern shore of Suwannee River, with several trailheads and loop trails in Twin Rivers State Forest providing access.

As the trail climbs up and over the natural levees along the river, carved out of the hills during floods, you realize this isn't your average Florida hike. Your muscles quickly feel the strain. The dense upland hardwood forest provides a constant canopy of shade. Stay to the well-defined footpath, as a mix of poison ivy and Virginia creeper carpets the forest floor. On the far side of the river, you see limestone shelves and fallen boulders. The many cavernous spaces under the limestone ledges on the far shore provide hiding places for river otter, water moccasin, and a rare breed of turtle, the Suwannee cooter, *pseudemys concinna suwanniensis.* It's a species confined to the Suwannee River and other rivers and streams feeding into the Gulf of Mexico down to the Hillsborough River, in Tampa. With vivid yellow stripes on its head and front legs, the Suwannee cooter stands out from other turtles. According to naturalist Archie Carr, "it swims faster than any freshwater turtle I know." Once hunted for its meat, the Suwannee cooter is now a protected species. The name "cooter" comes from *kuta,* the word for turtle in some African languages.

As the trail drops down into a floodplain channel, you walk amid a stand of towering white oaks and Florida maples. The immense tree dead ahead, with a base of more than 12 feet around, is a swamp chestnut oak. Live oaks lean over the river, their adornments of Spanish moss reflecting in the placid water. The far shore shows signs of collapse into the river, with numerous solution holes—pathways etched through the karst by steady erosion caused by acidic rainwater seeping down and breaking apart the limestone. It makes you wonder what the ground beneath your feet rests on. Are you on a limestone ledge, or solid ground? As if to give you an answer, surface limestone appears, and the trail heads down one of those wonderful little jogs that hikes along the Suwannee are well known for: drop down off the levee into the

old channel, and zoom back uphill again. It's these sudden steep grades that will give your leg muscles a serious workout.

At 0.8 mile the blue blazes lead right onto a short stretch of an old jeep trail to work around a small piece of private property along the river. At the T intersection, turn right. Intersecting with a jeep trail, continue straight. The gate to the right is posted NO TRESPASSING. You're walking through a dense forest of American holly, loblolly pine, and laurel oak. Two white-tailed deer pause in the footpath and bolt into a thicket of highbush blueberries. Beyond the trees on the left, you see open sky—an open field carved out of the forest. As you work your way through this forest, keep alert to the twists and turns of the trail. Follow the blazes carefully. At 1.2 miles the trail makes a sudden right turn that's easy to miss. It winds around a dense stand of saw palmetto in a floodplain channel before emerging back out along the river on a high levee. Down below, two scuba divers sit in a boat, adjusting their gear, and they toss a buoy with a diver's flag into the water. They're about to go cave diving in one of the Suwannee River's many spring vents. Caves formed by solution holes line the far shore of the river. A pretty forest of loblolly pine and saw palmetto fills the dry floodplain channel to your left.

The levee you're on is terraced, with the trail sticking to the highest terrace. As it narrows, you're balanced between the drop to the river on the right and the drop into the floodplain channel on the left. The trail drops down through another classic Suwannee roller coaster, popping back up to the top of the levee. After 1.6 miles the levee broadens, creating a spot for a potential campsite high on the bluff. A sinkhole on the left has a cabbage palm sprouting out of it. As you come back out along the very

Suwannee River

edge of the bluff, notice how the sun sparkles on the underside of the dangling live oak limbs, the river's surface acting as a mirror to reflect light to the underside of the trees. Swinging over to the channel side of the levee, you walk through a corridor of saw palmettos. The trail turns down into the floodplain, wandering amid the saw palmetto and deerberry for another 0.5 mile before returning to the river bluffs. Saw palmetto fronds frame views of the swift dark water rushing past.

After 2.8 miles you reach a sign: LOOP TRAIL 1. The blue blazes continue straight ahead, leading bikers on a longer route. Off to the right, a broad bluff with a sweeping river view would make a great campsite. Turn left onto the loop trail, for hikers only, blazed in yellow. A common yellowthroat flits past, showing off its bright yellow breast. Keep alert, as the trail makes a quick turn to the right, into the forest, rounding a large open field. Poison ivy creeps into the footpath, which isn't very distinct. Be sure to follow the blazes carefully. Along the right side of the trail, look for a catfaced snag—a now-dead pine that was once carved into for its sap. With the metal strips still embedded in it, the tree is a remnant of the turpentining era. Florida's turpentine industry was once its second largest industry, after logging. Logging took precedence here, feeding the sawmill up at Ellaville with the native yellow pine until the pine forests were gone. Around you are second- and third-growth pines, mostly loblolly, dropping a shaggy carpet of needles onto the footpath. Carved from a sea of saw palmettos, this part of the footpath took some serious effort to build.

As you walk by a couple of sinkholes, look for the strange orange blobs rising from the oak leaves, orange jelly mold looking like curled-up pieces of shrimp. Stalks of white wild indigo bloom show off their pealike white flowers; look closely, and you'll see the deep veins of indigo deep inside each blossom. At 3.3 miles you cross a jeep trail. Another big sinkhole lies just beyond the jeep trail. The small undulations underfoot come from plow lines, indicating this property was once a farm. Follow the yellow blazes carefully as the footpath is buried in oak leaves. Walking past a stand of dogwood, you come to an old oak arching low over the trail. Duck!

At 3.7 miles you emerge into a clear-cut area, which is filling back in with small trees and shrubs. Marked by fence posts painted with yellow blazes, the trail crosses it. You swerve around a spiky devil's-walkingstick. These shrubby trees show off huge clusters of small white flowers all summer. Although poisonous, its berries were used by early settlers in medicinal compounds to ease toothache pain and rheumatism. Because of the newly emerging undergrowth, take care to scout your route to the next post—the line of sight isn't always clear, and the footpath is not obvious. You briefly return to the cool shade of an oak hammock before emerging into another, shorter section of clear-cut. Crossing a jeep road at 4.2 miles, the trail reenters a hardwood hammock. Follow the blazes! The route twists and turns through tunnels of oaks and deerberry, going up and over a steep dirt pile, skirting around plow lines. You reach another broad open clear-cut at 4.5 miles. Crossing another jeep road, you reenter the forest for good. The oak canopy lifts high overhead; young hickory trees struggle to reach the sun. A limestone-loving fern, the ebony spleenwort, begins to appear en masse. Poison ivy weaves its way across the forest floor. Look for both jack-in-the-pulpit and green dragon rising out of thick beds of Virginia creeper. Although they cannot be eaten raw, both plants have been used as herbal remedies. American Indians aged and dried the roots of green dragon to treat menstrual cramps, and they boiled or dried the roots of jack-in-the-pulpit to provide treatments for respiratory problems.

Several sinkholes lie off to the left, appearing in quick succession. All of them are old, stable sinkholes with significantly large trees growing out of them. Based on their location, they may have formed above the underground stream that leads to Anderson Spring. The trail rejoins the river route at 5.1 miles, completing the loop. Turn right and follow the blue blazes back to the parking area, finishing your hike of 5.2 miles. Be sure to stop by the kiosk and pick up a Trailwalker postcard to mail in—let the Division of Forestry know your opinion of this trail.

3

Swift Creek Conservation Area

Total distance (circuit): 4.5 miles

Hiking time: 2 hours, 15 minutes

Habitats: Scrubby flatwoods, bluffs and ravines, oak hammock

Maps: USGS 7½' White Springs East, Suwannee River Water Management District map, Suwannee Bicycle Association map

It's not often that hikers will go out of their way to tromp down a single-track mountain-bike trail, but the trail through the Swift Creek Conservation Area is worth making an exception, with its fascinating exploration of the bluffs above the Suwannee River. Lightly used and extremely scenic, these public lands sit within walking distance of downtown White Springs. This is by no means an easy trek—you're in for some serious exertion as you scramble up and down the floodplain channels of the Suwannee River.

From I-75 exit 439, White Springs, head east on FL 136 for 3 miles. After you cross the Suwannee River, turn right at the blinker onto US 41 south. Just past the next blinker, after 0.5 mile, turn right on Adams Memorial Drive. Since the trailhead has limited parking and a rough approach road, you may want to park in the ball field parking lot and walk down the hill, adding 0.25 mile (round-trip) to your hike. The trailhead kiosk sits down a deeply eroded jeep road to the right off a curve around the cemetery.

After you walk around the cable gate, stop at the kiosk to look at the map, and then head down the jeep road into the pine forest. The once-vast pine forests surrounding the Suwannee River have been logged several times in the past century, but since this land is now protected, the young slash and loblolly pines around you have the opportunity to grow to full maturity. The trail starts off as a broad needle-strewn road, curving off to the right between the stands of pine. Royal and bracken fern crowd the

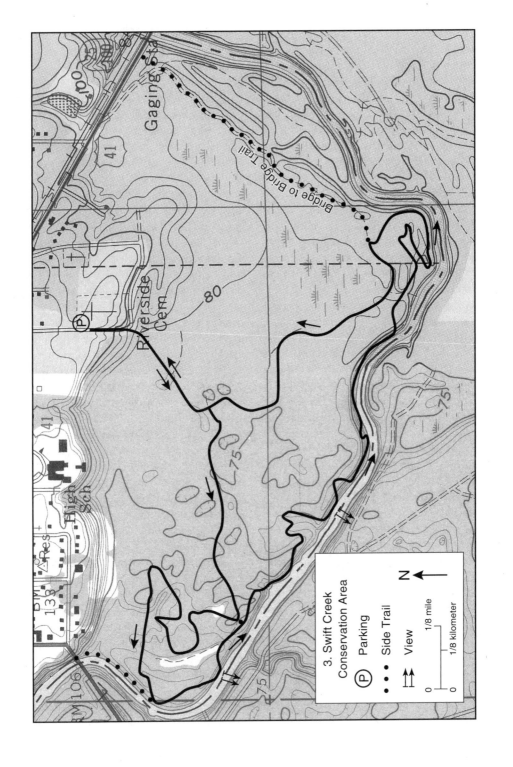

3. Swift Creek
Conservation Area

P Parking
••• Side Trail
⇈ View

N

0 ___ 1/8 mile
0 ___ 1/8 kilometer

understory. After 0.3 mile you arrive at a fork with the BRIDGE TO BRIDGE TRAIL sign. The Bridge to Bridge Trail is a bicycle trail running from the FL 136 bridge over the Suwannee at one end of White Springs to the US 41 bridge at the other end. Turn right to start your loop hike. Blue blazes mark the trail route, maintained by the Suwannee Bicycle Association.

Notice the strange low tones filling the air, like distant church bells? Those are the bells of the carillon tower at the Stephen Foster Folk Center State Park on the other side of White Springs. Stephen Foster's song "The Swanee River" spotlighted this little town, a popular spa at the turn of the 20th century. Visitors would "take the waters" in a building just below the present-day site of the Florida Nature & Heritage Tourism Center (where you can pick up a map of this trail). The Stephen Foster Folk Center State Park provides access to the Florida National Scenic Trail and hosts a permanent village of shops where folk artists weave pine-needle baskets, dip candles, and make thatch from palmettos. Every May the center hosts the State Folk Festival.

The undergrowth under the pines becomes a dense thicket of greenbrier, young oaks, and various shrubs, including blueberries. A monarch butterfly rests on a honeysuckle bloom. At 0.6 mile the forest road ends. The trail continues as a single-track hard-packed bicycle route, starting out under a large live oak draped in Spanish moss. Especially on weekends, when most mountain bikers hit the woods, be alert and courteous to bikers by stepping off the narrow track to let them pass. Unless you're out here on a weekend or late afternoon, you'll meet few bicycles and fewer hikers.

The trail winds through scrubby flatwoods, but the plants aren't just the usual scrubby stuff you see in other parts of Florida. Myrtle oak, sand live oak, and gallberry thrive in the sandy banks here, but the extra moisture from fogs over the river basin allows additional species to flourish, such as sweetgum, sparkleberry, deerberry, flame azalea, ogeehee tupelo, and highbush blueberry. Here, the blueberry bushes grow to incredible heights, with some gnarled old specimens topping 10 feet. Given how prolific they are in this forest, you can just imagine them weighed down with plump fruits in late May, a berry feaster's delight.

After 0.7 mile a low fence sits to the left side of the trail, with a trail going around it. This marks a shortcut out to the river. If you take the shortcut, you'll miss some of the prettier parts of the interior forest and some of the river views, but it will shave 1.2 miles off your hike. If necessary, you can also use this shortcut as a "ditch" point later on in the hike to save some return miles by retracing this part of your route. To stick with the main loop, continue straight. The tree canopy rises, thanks to taller live oaks and sweetgum shading the saw palmettos below. As the trail turns through a stand of young slash pines, notice the lone bald cypress rising above the pines. Normally, cypresses prefer to have their roots submerged. The flood of 1998 was this tree's last chance to sit in a puddle, when the Suwannee rose more than 25 feet above flood stage.

Ditches slice across floodplain channels, the legacy of loggers and turpentiners trying to keep the forests dry in times of high water. The trail jogs along a ditch, which broadens out into an old floodplain channel, and banks sharply as it drops down and across the channel. This is the area that the bikers call the "Rollercoaster"—for the next mile, you'll be following ditches and clambering in and out of floodplain channels, some with pretty steep inclines, as the trail

The Bridge to Bridge Trail

winds its way toward the river. Although there are a few soft sand spots where the bikes come off the inclines, the footpath is generally in excellent shape. Watch for more healthy stands of highbush blueberries. A red-shouldered hawk swoops under the branches of a live oak, a mouse dangling from its talons.

At 1.3 miles you reach a T that marks the intersection of the Bridge to Bridge Trail and the River Bluffs Trail. Turn left to continue your loop, following the River Bluffs Trail into a tunnel of young sand live oaks. The trail drops down a slope, away from the oaks into a forest of larger trees, and rises up a small bluff into an oak hammock. Dropping down a couple of bluffs later, you climb up a rise under broad live oaks and catch your first glimpse of the Suwannee River channel, the open area just beyond the next bluff. The trail swings to the left to follow the river upstream. Although the river is hidden from view, you can take the opportunity to scramble up a side trail at 1.8 miles over to the side of the bluff. It's a sheer drop down to the swift dark water, 40 feet or more below. A massive sandbar blocks half the channel, and the water flowing over it looks transparent but tea-stained from tannic acids—all these oak trees along the river *do* make a difference! Despite the large number of springs feeding the Suwannee with crystal-clear water, tannins leach out of oak leaves and acorns, imparting the black hue to the river.

Defined by saw palmettos and partially shaded by live oaks, the trail continues along the back side of the bluff, reaching the shortcut at 1.9 miles. If you need to make a quick return to the trailhead, turn left on this trail, and then immediately right onto the Bridge to Bridge Trail, following it back past the sign (take the left fork) to the trailhead, wrapping up a 2.6-mile hike.

However, you haven't seen the best of the river yet—so stick with the River Bluffs Trail. Past the shortcut, take a moment to explore the right fork, which ends up on the edge of the bluff. Looking down, you can see white-sand beaches on the far side and cypresses along the shore. A small landing comes down from the forest from a private residence. Returning to the main trail, turn right.

After 2 miles the trail reaches a section where you have an unobstructed view of the river as you walk along. Despite the panorama, you can't help but notice the blue blaze on an unusually large loblolly pine, almost 5 feet around. Down along the river, however, the far shore changes from white sand to white rock—limestone ledges littered with loose limestone boulders and smaller, water-rounded rocks caught on the ledges, looking like a shoreline from the Great Lakes. It's an unexpected sight, a rocky beach on a Florida river. Then the forest fills the gap again, shutting off the view to simple glimpses of the river channel. The trail turns to the left to loop around a deep ravine spilling into the Suwannee. Past the WALK BIKES sign, notice how cypress knees crowd the ravine. Tree roots trap dirt to provide stairs for the trail, in and out of the bottom of the gorge. At the top of the bluff, the trail turns again to return to the river, passing through a corridor of flame azalea. Visit the trail in early March to enjoy its fragrant blooms.

Your first river view on this side of the gorge is that of the terraced observation platforms of the Suwannee Valley Campground on the far shore. As the view opens up after 2.5 miles, you can see the sand beaches again. The water runs deep and dark through this part of the river, with numerous bald cypresses at the base of this bluff. Wizened sparkleberry shades the trail. Also known as farkleberry or huckleberry, this tall member of the blueberry family has crooked limbs and a distinctively smooth reddish-brown bark that always seems to be peeling. On the left, a catfaced pine has almost healed over its turpentine scar. The bark wraps around the V-shaped metal flashing used to collect the resin 40 years ago or more, giving a hint as to the age of this still-prospering tree.

Turning away from the river, twisting and turning over floodplain channels, the trail makes its way over to an old forest road. Along one curve of the trail, the patterns of bracken ferns and saw palmettos under the pines look like a quilt strewn across the forest floor. When you come to an interpretive sign, RATTLESNAKES, the trail merges onto the forest road, which comes in from the right at 3.2 miles. Continue straight, following the blue blazes. As the trail rises up into an oak hammock, you catch a glimpse of rocky walls and a deep channel. You're paralleling the Suwannee for one last stretch and can walk out on a short spur trail to take a look at the narrowing channel. See how cleanly the fast-moving water of the river scours the limestone base of the bluffs—they look like poured concrete.

At 3.5 miles you reach a T with the Bridge to Bridge Trail. Turn left to continue your loop hike—the trail to the right leads to a roadside park at the Suwannee River Bridge on US 41. You're back on a broad jeep trail through the scrubby flatwoods, decorated with the spring blooms of the highbush blueberries. As the trail rises up, it enters the dense forest of young slash pines that will surround you for the remainder of the hike. An armadillo roots around in the underbrush, digging for grubs. Notice the chunks of granite in the footpath? Florida has no native granite, but railroad companies imported Georgia stone for use in rail beds for logging camps. Given the granite, this road may follow the track of an old logging railway.

After 4.2 miles you complete the loop by returning to the fork with the BRIDGE TO BRIDGE TRAIL sign. To return to the trailhead, head straight. You complete your hike of 4.5 miles as you walk around the cable gate.

4

Big Shoals

Total distance (2 circuits): 7.3 miles

Hiking time: 4.5 hours

Habitats: River bluffs, pine flatwoods, scrubby flatwoods, oak hammock, hardwood hammock, floodplain forest

Maps: USGS 7½' White Springs East, Suwannee Bicycle Association map

Class III whitewater . . . in Florida? Only the Big Shoals of the Suwannee River can boast this designation, with more than a mile of rocky rapids capable of tearing holes in the bottoms of canoes. Canoeists portage around the roughest section; kayakers go for the holes. The Big Shoals Trail provides access for hikers to enjoy this rugged stretch of river, unlike any other in Florida.

From I-75 exit 439, White Springs, head east on FL 136 for 3 miles. After you cross the Suwannee River, turn right at the blinker onto US 41 south. Continue 0.5 mile to the next blinker, turning left onto CR 135 at the BIG SHOALS sign. After 1.5 miles you'll pass the entrance to the Little Shoals tract of Big Shoals Public Lands. At some future date the Woodpecker Trail will connect this area with the hiking trails at Big Shoals. Continue another 2.3 miles, turning right on SE 94th Street. Drive 1.7 miles down this dirt road to the Big Shoals main entrance. The park is open from 8 AM to dusk daily and provides rest rooms and picnic tables at the trail-head. During hunting season, use caution walking the trails in this park; wear blaze orange, and avoid the forest roads.

The eastern end of the preserve has two trails: the Big Shoals Trail, a 2.2-mile round trip leading out to the river rapids, which can be extended into a 4.9-mile loop, and the Long Branch Trail, heading upriver on the Suwannee for a 2.5-mile loop through hardwood hammocks and river bottom forest. Both start from the parking area.

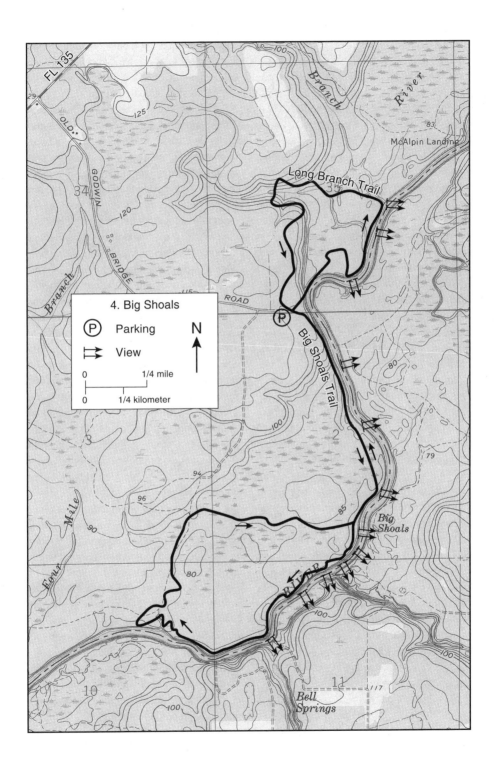

4. Big Shoals

Ⓟ Parking

→ View

N

0 ——————— 1/4 mile
0 ——————— 1/4 kilometer

BIG SHOALS LOOP

Look for the TRAILWALKER sign at the beginning of the Big Shoals Trail. Yellow blazes lead you downriver through the picnic area and into an oak hammock dense with laurel oaks. The river channel parallels off to the left, thick with ghostly mist early in the morning. Turning right, the trail crosses a bridge, then makes a left onto a broad path. Watch for the enormous gopher tortoise burrow on the left. These slow-moving creatures like to dig five or more burrows in an area, inhabiting one while the others become home for armadillos, rat snakes, field mice, and hundreds of other species.

The trail curves to the left through the old road cut for Godwin Bridge, with the bridge piers directly in front of you. Turning right, it then follows the river along the bluff, providing great views through the dense hardwood forest. Sphagnum moss and resurrection fern grow thickly on the trunks of live oaks. At 0.3 mile turn left at the arrow, indicating a reroute of the trail to a more scenic route along the river. A sign claims 20 MINUTES TO BIG SHOALS, and the claim is right on if you hike 2 miles per hour. Climbing up atop the river bluff, you have a view of the river framed by oaks and saw palmettos. Turn right to follow the trail as it weaves through the saw palmetto at the top of the bluff, providing sporadic panoramas of the calm black water below. A gnarled canopy of sparkleberry and sand live oak shades your walk. The trail jogs to the right when it rejoins the rerouted section, with an overlook off to the left to look down on the dark water. After you pass the BIG SHOALS 10 MINUTES sign, the trail winds back close to the river's edge again. You start to hear the muffled rumble of the rapids echoing upriver.

An overlook gives you a glimpse of the CANOE PORTAGE sign and pathway on the far shore. The sound of rushing water increases with each footfall down the trail. At 1 mile you reach an overlook where the water below seems to be increasing in speed, flowing over submerged rocks. The air feels thick, saturated with water droplets kicked up by the rapids. Another overlook provides a glimpse of water flowing through small chutes. The trail jogs to the right, going through a floodplain channel, and then turns to the left, approaching the roar of the rapids. Healthy growths of aquatic grasses, clinging to their limestone perches, create the green patches you see in the river. A flock of white ibises picks through the shallows, searching for small fish.

A slender young sassafras tree struggles to stay rooted in the eroding sand bluff at the next overlook, where you have a sweeping view of the rapids of the Big Shoals. At the base of the bluff, the largest rapid bubbles like cola being poured as it tumbles over the rock ledges, creating hydraulics. Farther out in the river, water spills through a series of chutes in the limestone ledge. With so much exposed rock, there is no good route for canoes or kayaks to pass through this section of river, except when water levels are at flood stage. The constant splash of water creates a microclimate at the base of the largest rapid, where netted chain, royal fern, and cinnamon fern grow in profusion along the otherwise dry, sandy wall of the bluff.

Continuing down the yellow-blazed trail, you reach a T intersection with a blue-blazed trail, and the sign BIG SHOALS. This marks the start of a biking loop, which you can use to walk a loop down to the end of the rapids and back around through the forest to this point. Turn left. This section of trail is maintained by the Suwannee Bicycle Association; be courteous to

Whitewater at Big Shoals

oncoming bikers, and step off the trail to allow them to pass. Blazes are one-way in the opposite direction of your hike.

Framed by a Spanish moss–draped oak, the next overlook provides a look at the second set of rapids, created where the water flows over a limestone escarpment. At certain times of the year and in drought, the river may be so low that it can't pass over the escarpment, so it flows through tight channels hugging this shoreline. The sound of whitewater fades as you continue down the trail, and the blazes soon end, but it's easy to follow the well-defined footpath. Watch for the next overlook access at 1.2 miles, a faint trace of a spur trail leading through the saw palmetto to the side of the bluff. From here it's a steep but moderate climb down to a broad white-sand beach in the calm area below the main rapids, a spot where canoeists and kayakers camp on their multiday trips down the Suwannee. Frothy root beer–colored foam drifts by, a bubbly byproduct of the rapids. A series of flowerpots rise tall on the far shore, limestone pillars that are narrow at the bottom and broad at the top. These formations occur when fluctuating water levels erode different layers of the limestone at different speeds. If you do scramble down to the beach, be sure to follow your footprints in the sand back up the slope to the climb up to the trail.

When the main trail forks, the left fork, a short spur, provides access to an overlook with a good clear view of the flowerpots. Continue down the right fork, enjoying the sporadic river vistas from the bluff forest of sparkleberry, laurel oak, and rusty lyonia. In early spring, Florida azalea flaunts its large, fragrant pink blooms. Jogging off to the right, the trail circumvents a large sinkhole before coming back out to the bluff. You hear the sound of whitewater again and can see grass-covered rocks dotting the river, creating a minor set of rapids. One overlook lets you look straight down at the rapids. You've hiked 1.5 miles.

Continuing downriver, the trail winds in and out of floodplains on the bluffs, always coming back to views of the river; stretches of jagged, eroded limestone; and beaches of soft white sand. Along the trail's rim, saw palmettos cluster en masse in enormous sculpted bowls, shaded by live oaks and cypresses. Keep alert for a small memorial to the area's history: a display of almost-intact turpentine cups on the right. At 2 miles you pass the standing remains of a catfaced pine, rotted through its core so you can see right through it.

One more stretch along the bluff's edge allows you to take in another panorama of the Suwannee, broken up by limestone ledges coated in the spring green of aquatic grasses, the green patches a stark contrast against the black water. Zigzagging off the floodplain channel, the trail turns away from the river to cross a bridge, meeting a forest road at a T intersection at 2.5 miles. During hunting season (generally November–December; check at the information kiosk for specific dates) you'll want to turn around and walk back the way you came; at all other times you can use the forest roads to make a loop back to Big Shoals. Turn right. Almost immediately, you come to another T intersection with a blue arrow pointing in the direction from which you just came. Turn right to follow Forest Road 2, which is blazed with orange bands and shared with equestrians and bikers.

A broad path through the tall loblolly pine flatwoods, the forest road is the legacy of turpentine companies that came through and crisscrossed the forest with many roads to access the dense groves of pines. Saw palmetto creates an unbroken understory. Just beyond the pine trees lies an extensive floodplain forest of hardwoods, a mix of cypress and sweetgum, tupelo and hickory, maple and oak. The trail drops down into the hardwood forest before reaching the ROAD 18 sign at 3 miles. Turn right, walking down the road through the pine flatwoods until the road ends abruptly at 3.6 miles. Starting at a "No Horses" symbol, the narrow blue-blazed bike trail (with blazes in the opposite direction of your hike) leads into the forest, curving along the edge of a cypress swamp and crossing it on a long bridge, rising back up into a dense thicket of saw palmetto.

After 3.8 miles you complete the loop, returning to the junction of the blue-blazed trail and the yellow-blazed trail. Turn left to walk back past Big Shoals, retracing the next mile along the Suwannee River back to the parking area. After you pass the Godwin Bridge piers, you'll notice your heart rate increasing as you follow the trail up the slope. Keep alert on the broad jeep trail so you don't miss the right turn into the oak hammock. Walking back along the river and through the picnic area, you complete your hike of 4.9 miles at the TRAILWALKER sign.

LONG BRANCH TRAIL

Providing a different look at the Suwannee River and its environs, the Long Branch Trail starts on the other side of the parking lot, across from the handicapped spaces in front of the rest rooms. Walking past the handicapped-accessible picnic area, follow the fence along the bluff to the broad earthen steps down to the canoe launch. A LONG BRANCH TRAIL sign sits at the bottom of the steps. Take a moment to walk down to the canoe launch, on the right. Here, the Suwannee shows its placid side, black water surrounding the steps leading into the water.

Backtracking to the fork, take the left fork to start the trail. Blazed in blue, it leads you straight into a hardwood hammock of sweetgum and hickory, cypress and azalea, with roots breaking up the footpath. Rising up to a view of the river, the trail then parallels the river upstream just behind the bluff, winding back and forth across the bluffs. Two of the bluffs shelter cypress swamps, which the trail crosses on bridges. Watch for the many colorful dragonflies that hover around the cypress knees, including the variable dancer, a dragonfly with an iridescent electric blue or green body and black wings shaped like maple seeds. Dropping down into a low spot between cypress knees, the trail climbs up and into the bowl of a bluff and follows it, surrounded by sand live oaks and highbush blueberries, making a U-turn to climb up the bluff to the river.

At 0.5 mile a short spur trail leads to the river's edge, where you can walk down to a sandy beach under a cypress tree and admire the tranquil scene. Dark water reflects the tall frames of cypresses and the green leaves of the water tupelos that dangle out from the river's edge. A lone titi grows between the knees of the pond cypress, grazing its bottlebrush blooms against the river's surface. Returning to the trail, you continue along a nice open section with sweeping views. The trail jogs on and off the bluffs again, leading into a corridor of highbush blueberries shading the trail. At 0.9 mile you reach an interpretive marker about water snakes. The spur trail off to the right is your last view of the Suwannee along this hike as the trail now turns inland, paralleling a cypress floodplain forest.

As the terrain changes, so does the habitat. River bluffs give way to scrubby flatwoods of loblolly pines and oaks, growing out of old deposits of river sand. The trail quickly drops down into a deciduous bottomland forest, a floodplain of hickory, sweetgum, and elm, cypress and maple, showing off a parade of crimson, purple, and gold in the late fall. At 1.1 miles two railings define an area where a seasonal creek flows through the forest. Walk down and take a look at the deeply scoured channel. Just up the trail from the railings, two grand old loblolly pines tower over the rest of the forest, rising nearly 100 feet tall. The trail curves to the right, paralleling a distant fence separating the forest from the open fields of an adjoining cattle farm. Keep alert on the right for a natural sculpture; the thick base of a damaged but living live oak, the trunk strangely warped and gnarled as if the wood were carved into fantastic shapes.

The understory opens up, with large-leafed swamp chestnut oaks and southern magnolias burying the footpath under their huge crunchy leaves. The trail twists and turns up to the edge of the farmer's field, crossing a couple of small drainage channels before it rises up into an oak hammock. The massive amounts of pine duff and leaves underfoot obscure the footpath, so keep alert for blazes. The crimson blooms of a coral bean stand out against the surrounding green leaves of young oaks. After dropping down into another section of mixed hardwood hammock and cabbage palms, the trail rises back into the oak hammock.

At 1.8 miles you reach a T intersection. An interpretive marker stands off to the right, in front of a stand of loblolly pines. The trail, however, turns to the left. Just after you make the turn, notice the young sassafras tree with its mittenlike leaves. The roots of the aromatic sassafras, a relative of the red bay, are used to brew a strong tea. Heading downhill, the trail curves past a couple of railings and heads down a corridor of bluejack, laurel, and live oak. Given the size of these trees, it's easy to believe that this land was cleared, a farmer's field, approximately 30 years ago. The oaks, which tend to take over disturbed habitats, stretch down to the line of saw palmettos that delineate the edge of the hardwood bottom swamp. Passing under an arching Florida maple around 2 miles, the trail begins a long downhill to the hardwood bottom, and then rises up a long strenuous slope back into the oak hammock.

Keep alert to the twists and turns of the trail as it comes to a T intersection with an old firebreak from the old farm, at 2.1 miles, in front of a stand of loblolly pines. Turn left, following the ditchlike firebreak as it parallels the pines, forming a barrier between the pine forest and the hardwood hammock. Reaching another T intersection, turn left on the old woods road. Several white-tailed deer leap off the road and into the pine forest. Up ahead, you see pavement—the parking-lot loop at Big Shoals. The trail ends at the pavement. Turn left and walk back along the road to return to your car, completing your loop hike of 2.4 miles.

5

Fanning Springs State Park

Total distance (circuit): 1.6 miles

Hiking time: 1 hour

Habitats: Floodplain forest, hardwood hammock, sinkholes, spring

Maps: USGS 7½' Fanning Springs, park map

Although the hikes are brief at Fanning Springs State Park, the venue is worth the visit. Centrally located in Fanning Springs on US 19, just south of the Suwannee River bridge, this tiny state park encompasses one of the Suwannee River's largest swimming holes. Two short walks comprise the hiking at this park: a journey around the swimming area and spring, following a boardwalk down to the river, and a nature-trail loop that takes you past some of the large sinkholes that formed upstream from the spring vent.

Look for the entrance on the western side of the highway, less than a mile north of the junction of US 19 and FL 26. A new entrance station is under construction. If it's not yet open, enter and drive around to the parking lot. Pay the $1 per-person fee at the gate leading into the swimming area. Once a popular private spa and swimming resort, the park included a water slide and Ferris wheel in the 1940s. Check out the interpretive kiosks for period photos of Fanning Springs's heyday. Now the only day you're apt to see a huge crowd is during the annual "Red Belly Day," held every May. During this folk festival that celebrates the town's favorite member of the bream family from the Suwannee River, which makes for a great fish fry, you'll see families participating in sack races, melon chunking, and the ever-popular belly-flop contest.

Start your hike with a walk around the spring. Pouring out of a deep sinkhole on the edge of a cove, the aquamarine waters surrounding the spring vent are striking.

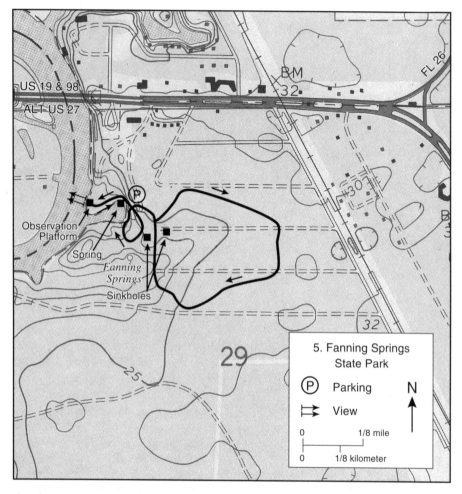

US 19 & 98
ALT US 27
BM
32
FL 26
BM
3
Observation Platform
Spring
Fanning Springs
Sinkholes
30
29
32
25

5. Fanning Springs State Park

Ⓟ Parking

⊢→ View

N

0   1/8 mile

0   1/8 kilometer

Divers can plunge straight into the first-magnitude spring, one of 27 major springs in Florida. Most visitors prefer to bask in the constant 72-degree waters of the shallow cove. A floating dock allows foot traffic across the swimming area. Like many of the larger springs along the Suwannee River, Fanning Springs is separated from the main watercourse by a short spring run. In the winter, manatees nose their way up the spring run for immersion in the warm water.

Walk down the terraces for an up-close look down into the spring vent, and then around the low terrace to the end, where a boardwalk climbs up the hill from the swimming area. Surrounded by bald cypresses, a small floodplain forest fits in one corner of the cove. Woods ferns drape over a rugged limestone boulder. Bare karst is every-where—exactly what you'd expect along the Suwannee River, where sinkholes and springs are an integral part of the terrain. As you walk along the boardwalk, you get nice views of the cypress forest marching down the slope to meet the cove. Stopping to pause on a bench, you can sit and marvel at

Fanning Springs

the juxtaposition of cypress knees and chunks of limestone, listening to river traffic steam by just over the rise. A short staircase to the left leads to the canoe concession; the canoes are stored under the boardwalk and available for rent for a paddle up or down the river.

As the boardwalk curves to meet the river, you can see a few old houses on the far shore. Three Florida counties meet at this junction in the river: Gilchrist, Levy, and Dixie. Back in 1838, U.S. troops fighting the Second Seminole War built and manned a small wooden fortress at this spot, Palmetto. Renamed Fort Fannin in honor of Col. Alexander Fannin, the name became corrupted over time to Fanning Springs. As the war raged on and Fannin attempted to round up Seminoles for deportation to the West, the garrison grew from a dozen men to nearly two hundred in 1843. Yellow fever ravaged the troops. The remains of the fort,

which was abandoned in 1849, vanished back into the forest. After the wars, commerce thrived in Fanning Springs as steamboats traveled up from Cedar Key to the cities of Ellaville and Columbus (Hike 1). The very last of the Suwannee River steamboats, the *City of Hawkinsville* was sunk offshore here in 1922. It's now a designated underwater archaeological preserve, open for divers to explore.

The boardwalk ends at an observation deck with seating on the river, next to an unusual double-trunked cypress. Look out over the bend, and watch the sun sparkle on the river. If you look straight down, the tannic water lapping at the base of the cypresses shows a gradient of hues, deepening from yellow to sienna to dark black as the water gets deeper. Turn around and follow the boardwalk back to the swimming area. Climb up the terraces to the park gate. You've walked 0.5 mile.

Walking out the park gate, follow the chain-link fence around to the right to a kiosk labeled FANNING SPRINGS HIKING TRAIL. It shows a rough map of the trail route through the lush hardwood hammock. As you wander into the woods, keep alert for bicyclists who share the trail. Within a few moments you come to a set of four signs that say HIKING at a trail junction, the top of the loop. Turn left. Cross over the service road, continuing into the forest on the other side.

Notice the towering grayish shaggy-barked oaks. These are bluff oaks, a species limited to a handful of Florida counties. It only thrives in regions where karst is close to the surface. Nearby Andrews Wildlife Management Area (Hike 6) has one of the state's largest bluff oaks. Southern magnolias sprinkle their leathery leaves across the footpath. Gray squirrels scamper to and fro, in search of the bounty of acorns that falls on the forest floor. When you reach the arrow, turn right. The trail becomes a relatively straight track through the forest, a mixed upland hardwood hammock with lots of hickories, southern magnolias, and oaks. A cedar waxwing perches in a small southern red cedar, picking at the tiny white berries. Fresh tracks lead out of a gopher tortoise burrow on the edge of the trail. Chunks of limestone are scattered throughout the forest.

The trail turns to the right to zigzag between saw palmettos, coming up to a tall sugarberry tree. Also known as hackberry, this tree has a very distinctive bark, its smooth, gray surface broken up by pimply protrusions. A cardinal alights on a saw palmetto frond, a strong contrast of red against green. Riddled by holes of many shapes and sizes, a tall snag shows evidence of a variety of woodpeckers picking at it for insects. Look carefully, and you'll see coontie growing in the underbrush, half-hidden by drifts of oak leaves. Also known as Florida arrowroot, these endangered plants are fairly uncommon in the forests of Florida's west coast. Coontie is the only member of the cycad family native to Florida.

Crossing an old forest road, you've walked 1 mile. A lone slash pine rises to the right. Watch your feet as you step over the gatorbacks, the long knobby saw palmetto trunks lying in the trail. Obscured by clumps of saw palmetto, a southern magnolia reaches for the sky from the bottom of a rocky sinkhole. A Florida maple shades the trail. This species of maple thrives in ravines and on rocky slopes in karst areas. As the trail curves, notice the long fallen log on the right. The shelf fungus growing from it looks as fragile as parchment, growing in sheets parallel to each other. As you continue to walk through the dark shady woods, the trail winds through the trees, crossing an abandoned path blocked off by tree debris on the right and thick poles on the left. A grove of southern magnolias surrounds you, leaves glistening in the sun. Young cabbage palms sprout from the forest floor, their fronds filling the understory. Notice the slender ferns with rounded fronds: ebony spleenwort. It's another species that thrives best in karst environments.

At 1.4 miles you come up to the lip of a large sinkhole. Ferns cascade down one rocky face into the rounded, leaf-filled bowl. This is the first in a series of four large sinkholes, a chain stretching to the right and left above an underground stream, in a direct line with the spring vent at Fanning Springs. As water levels rise and fall in caverns, it causes tremendous pressure on the limestone above. High water erodes the soluble limestone roof of the cavern more quickly, and low water removes a crucial part of the support available for the cavern roof. When the cavern roof collapses inward, these collapse sinkholes happen.

As you walk past another broad, empty sinkhole bowl on the left, sweetgum balls carpet the footpath. A trail arrow marker points to the right, blocking off an older trail down to the spring vent. The older trail is now fenced off, but if you look off to the left, you can see sunlight streaming in above the spring. Turn right. Spleenwort competes for space with the grassy ground cover. Crossing the service road again, you can see a playground off to the left, within the park's chain-link fence. The trail zigzags through the forest to complete the loop. At the trail junction, turn left to walk back out to the kiosk and to the parking lot, completing your 1.6-mile hike.

Andrews Wildlife Management Area

Total distance (2 circuits): 12.4 miles

Hiking time: 6 hours

Habitats: Upland hardwood forests, sandhill, river bluffs, floodplain forest, hardwood hammock

Maps: USGS 7½' Fanning Springs, park map

Imagine a persimmon tree so tall that you can't see its leaves, and a maple that dwarfs the forest around it. Sitting high above the bluffs of the Suwannee River, the dense, dark hammocks of Andrews Wildlife Management Area harbor these trees of distinction and others–registered Florida Champion trees, growing to incredible heights in the last large tract of untouched hardwood forest along the Suwannee River. To guide hikers to these incredible trees, the Florida Fish and Wildlife Commission created six hiking trails within Andrews Wildlife Management Area, which is primarily managed for hunting and fishing. Camping is not permitted within the preserve. The trails themselves are very short, ranging from 0.2 mile to 1 mile one-way. However, since few people drive the preserve's many shaded forest roads, the roads provide pleasant connectors to create longer loop hikes, as described here. One particular caution for this hike: It's well known to local hikers as a seriously tick-infested area. Wear light-colored clothing, and use copious amounts of insect repellent.

Andrews Wildlife Management Area sits 1 mile off US 19, just south of Fanning Springs. From the junction of FL 26 and US 19 in Fanning Springs, drive 1.9 miles south and turn right on NW 160th Street. If you are headed northbound on US 19 from Chiefland, drive 5.1 miles north of FL 320 and turn left onto NW 160th Street at the brown park sign. Drive 1 mile, crossing the Nature Coast Rail Trail en route. The road enters the park gate. Stop at the check

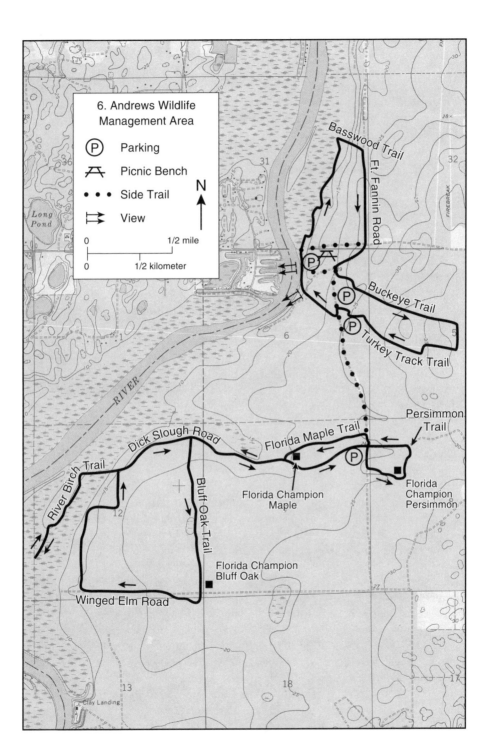

6. Andrews Wildlife
Management Area

(P) Parking

🛆 Picnic Bench

• • • Side Trail

⊢→ View

N

0 _____ 1/2 mile
0 _____ 1/2 kilometer

Basswood Trail

Ft. Fannin Road

Long
Pond

FIREBREAK

Buckeye Trail

Turkey Track Trail

RIVER

Persimmon
Trail

Dick Slough Road

Florida Maple Trail

River Birch Trail

Florida Champion
Maple

Bluff Oak Trail

Florida
Champion
Persimmon

Florida Champion
Bluff Oak

Winged Elm Road

Clay Landing

station and ask for a map. Drive up to the entrance gate and drop your $3 per-person fee in the self-pay station.

From the entrance gate, drive 0.8 mile down to a fork; turn left at the sign RIVER LANDING ROAD. When you reach the SUWANNEE RIVER sign, turn right. The road soon ends at a clearing along the Suwannee River, with a shaded picnic table and barbecue grill. Don't be surprised to see folks fishing down on the banks of the river—this is a popular spot for anglers, especially on weekends.

Loop 1: Andrews Road, Basswood Trail, Buckeye Trail, and Turkey Track Trail

This loop encompasses three trails and several forest roads to lead you 4.5 miles through the woods, returning to this parking area on the Suwannee River. Facing the river, turn right and walk down to the yellow gate, which protects the "wild" portion of Andrews Road. Heading away from the gate, with the blue water of the river beside you, continue on the clearly defined path until it opens up into a forest road along a narrow island of pine and cabbage palm. You catch the sun sparkling off the river; turtles sun on logs. As you walk, be mindful to follow the distinct path—there are no blazes on Andrews Road. Tucked away between the cypresses are small mucky ponds created by receding river waters, ringed with cypress knees. Their shallow water attracts alligators looking for a place to keep cool. The trail curves to the left to pass through a sandy clearing. At 0.2 mile a broad, canopied forest road takes off to the left. Continue straight, following Andrews Road as it winds along the edge of the floodplain forest. The peeling bark of sparkleberry trees catches your eye. As the trail rounds a bend to the right, it threads between

clumps of saw palmettos with long trunks. Veering to the left past a loblolly pine, you skirt a large sinkhole, dropping down into the shade along the cypress swamp. As the trail sweeps upwards to the right, watch for the BASSWOOD TRAIL sign on your right.

At 0.9 mile turn right to start the Basswood Trail, next to a solution hole. It's a narrow trail, not much wider than a game trail, blazed sporadically with white rectangles. American basswood and red bay dominate the forest around you. The empty post next to a rotting stump is the only clue that a Florida Champion American basswood once stood along this trail. Also known as linden, American basswood has a heart-shaped leaf, similar in nature to a white mulberry. Its drooping yellowish-white flowers open in early summer, attracting bees with their extremely fragrant blooms. Basswood honey is considered one of the choicest grades of honey.

After passing under a stand of southern magnolias, the Basswood Trail ends at a T intersection with a jeep trail. Turn right. When you walk around the gate, you're on Ft. Fannin Road. Continue straight, passing an open meadow with a green bat box. A tiny yellow gopher tortoise cowers in its shell. As the tortoise grows older, its shell will darken to a light gray. Gopher tortoises build their burrows in these open areas, managed as food plots for the resident deer and wild turkeys.

When you come to the fork, stay right to reach River Landing Road. Turn right. This is the only busy section of road in the preserve, so keep alert for cars. Follow the road down along the power line. After it crosses under the power line, watch for the SUWANNEE RIVER sign on the right. You've walked 2.2 miles. Look to your left for the BUCKEYE TRAIL sign. This Buckeye Trail starts along the edge of a sinkhole, just behind the gate.

A massive live oak at Andrews WMA

Turn left to follow the trail. It's a wide old woods road through the shady upland hardwood forest. Tall American hollies drop their jagged leaves on the trail. An armadillo shuffles through the underbrush. The mix of trees in the forest changes slightly with each change in elevation. Watch for small coonties peeking out of the leaves.

When the trail starts sweeping to the left, watch for the TURKEY TRACK TRAIL sign on the right. Turn right. The trail curves slightly to the right past an area with an open canopy of forest, scattered loblolly pines through a sandhill habitat on the edge of the hardwood forest. Passing snags riddled with woodpecker holes, the trail curves to the right to enter a shadier upland forest. At 3.3 miles, turn right. Gnarled sand live oaks spread their branches overhead. Oak leaves crunch like cornflakes underfoot. Longleaf pines signal their presence by large pinecones scattered across the trail. You notice a deer scrape, a spot in the leaves where a deer rolled around to indicate its presence to other deer. Walk carefully around the lip of a sinkhole in the road. Gray squirrels dash across the fallen leaves to gather hickory nuts.

At 4 miles you come to a yellow gate at Ft. Fannin Road. Cross the road, and walk around the yellow gate with the ZONE D sign. The forest road continues on to the Suwannee River through a botanically diverse hardwood hammock, where you'll spot rusty lyonia, highbush blueberry, hickory, basswood, American holly, southern magnolia, and dozens of other trees. As you walk under a power line, the bright blue water of the Suwannee River beckons. Passing in front of an abandoned cabin, turn right to rejoin Andrews Road along the river. Skirt around the gate and continue to walk along the road. Several spots provide places to scramble down to the water's edge. Watch out for the rocks! Although they look like limestone, they're actually slippery sculpted formations of hard-packed sand. From this vantage point you can take in the sweep of a bend in the river. Several private landings and homes dot the far shore; this shore remains pristine, the domain of tall bald cypresses. Returning to Andrews Road, continue to the parking area, completing your 4.5-mile loop.

Loop 2: Persimmon Trail, Florida Maple Trail, Bluff Oak Trail, Winged Elm Road, River Birch Trail

From your parking place along the Suwannee River, head back up along River Landing Road to the junction with Ft. Fannin Road. Turn right. Drive 1 mile, passing the trailhead signs for the Turkey Track Trail and the Florida Maple Trail. At the T intersection, turn right, passing the DICK SLOUGH ROAD sign. On your left is the parking area for this loop. Do not block the gate.

Using the forest roads as connectors, you can hike a loop of up to 7.9 miles to join together the four blazed trails in this section of the preserve. First on your route is the Persimmon Trail. Walk around the gate and head down the forest road, paralleling a broad meadow. When you see the green bat box, turn left and walk over to the PERSIMMON TRAIL sign, following the trail into the shady hammock. It's marked with faded yellow blazes, but the footpath is distinct despite the heavy leaf cover. After 0.4 mile the trail turns sharply left around the star of this trail. Look for the FLORIDA CHAMPION PERSIMMON sign at the base of a tree with deeply grooved black bark, a tree so tall that you can't make out its crown. When registered, this particular tree rose 90 feet and had a crown spread of 39 feet. The common persimmon grows throughout Florida but is generally no more than 20 feet tall, loaded with small orange fruits in late fall. If you sample a freshly fallen fruit, watch out! The astringent flavor of a wild persimmon creates a serious pucker-mouth. Let the fruit ripen for a few days, and it will take on a sweeter flavor.

As you wind through the dark shady hammock, watch for scattered coonties. Hearing your footsteps crackling through the leaves, several deer flee through the open understory. When you come to a T intersection with Randall Road, turn left. At 0.8 mile you reach the fork in the road at the FT. FANNIN ROAD sign. You can see your car off to the left. Turning right, head for the sign on the opposite side of the road—FLORIDA MAPLE TRAIL. Follow the yellow blazes along the indistinct footpath into a dense uplands hardwood forest, a true walk in the woods beneath tall laurel oak and hickory, bluff oak and American holly. Caught in the act of picking apart a mouse, a great horned owl rises up from its perch on a rotted log and alights in a southern magnolia. As the trail curves left, you round a large sinkhole. Maples and sweetgum grow out of its bottom. It's the beginning of a series of long, low-slung sinkhole bowls stretching out through the forest, an indication of an underground stream. Asleep at the base of a winged elm, a tiny spotted fawn rises up out of its bed of leaves and gambols away in search of its mother.

Follow the yellow blazes closely, as the path becomes more leaf-strewn and indistinct, easy to lose in the open understory. Overhead, a downy woodpecker rattles the trunk of a laurel oak. Tangled vines hang down, swinging in the breeze. A fence lizard clambers up a snag, its scaly gray skin almost lost against the gray bark. At 1.4 miles you reach a tangle of brush blocking the trail. The FLORIDA CHAMPION MAPLE sign is knocked over by the fallen tree. This Florida maple, on the left, rises more than 85 feet above the forest floor, its trunk more than 82 inches around at the base.

To get around the brush, work your way around to the right. Continue following the yellow blazes through the stand of maples, likely descendents of the Florida Champion tree. After 1.5 miles the blazes stop at Dick Slough Road, signaling the end of the Florida Maple Trail. This is your last chance to bail out on the full loop. If you turn left, you'll return to your car after a 2-mile hike. To enjoy the full 7.9-mile circuit, turn right. Dick Slough Road is a pleasant walk, shaded by the old-growth forest. Dropping down past a large sinkhole on the left, it continues to lose elevation as you draw closer to the Suwannee River. At 2.6 miles you reach the trailhead on the left with the BLUFF OAK TRAIL sign.

The Bluff Oak Trail starts out as a firebreak, creating a difficult footpath to start. It quickly eases up as you walk through the forest of young red bay and grapevines. The trail curves left to follow the edge of a meadow. A flood of tiny piglets, orange and black, squeals as it streams across the open grass. Their parents follow closely behind. Keep to the edge of the meadow, and watch for the yellow blazes as they swing to the right, into the forest. The trail becomes a narrow track between the hardwoods, hickory and mulberry, southern magnolia and live oak, rounding numerous broad sinkholes. Walking through a stand of southern magnolia, you come to a grove of shaggy barked trees—the bluff oak. Growing only in karst areas, where limestone nears the surface, the bluff oak's gray shaggy bark makes it easy to identify. Its leaves are similar to a white oak but are more sharply pointed at the ends. Bluff oaks have an extremely limited range, restricted to only a few Florida counties along the Big Bend and up into the Panhandle.

After you pass the CLOSED TO HUNTING AND TRAPPING signs, watch for the FLORIDA CHAMPION BLUFF OAK sign at the base of the prize oak, at 3.3 miles. It towers above an equally impressive dogwood. This Champion tree rises more than 105 feet and has a circumference of nearly 9 feet at its base. Continuing along the trail, you walk past a loblolly pine with a good 6-foot circumference. Keep alert to the yellow blazes as the path twists and turns through the forest. Under the shade of a tall swamp chestnut oak with enormous leaves, water collects seasonally in a low depression, attracting deer. You reach a T intersection with Winged Elm Road at 3.5 miles. Turn right.

A narrow grassy jeep track under a tall tree canopy, Winged Elm Road leads you into hunting Zone F. A tall green bat box marks a fork in the road. Keep right. The corridor opens up, paralleling a long, thin meadow planted to attract deer. Since the road is roughed up through this area, keep to the left, where the ground is firmer. The hardwoods yield to a dark cypress forest. Becoming a causeway, the road comes up to a gate at the end of Dick Slough Road at 4.8 miles. Watch for the old wooden cattle corral as the road curves to the left. Cattle ranching and cypress logging were the primary uses of this land during the early 1900s.

After 5.1 miles you reach the RIVER BIRCH TRAIL sign, another decision point. The trail is an out-and-back trek to the remains of the Florida Champion river birch; the tree is long gone, felled by lightning. However, the trail meanders along a bluff island among many impressive oaks and gives you a few glimpses of the Suwannee River through the floodplain forest. To follow it, turn left, passing another old corral. Yellow blazes lead up a causeway through a tall stand of pond cypresses. Cypress knees poke out of the footpath. The humid air encourages air plants, particularly wild pine, to grow in the tall trees. As you rise up into a mixed hardwood forest, the streak of blue off to your right is the Suwannee River, beyond the cypresses. The trail curves away from it and to the left, staying on the dry bluff island.

As you pass another corral, the trail becomes indistinct and hard to follow. If you want to plunge ahead, the faded blazes are no great help—follow the DESIGNATED TRAIL signs. There is no footpath. As long as you stay out of the cypresses, you can't get too lost—you're on an island. Massive live oaks rise overhead. Gigantic loblolly pines brush the sky. The floodplain forest is a dark and woolly place, with sun dappling through a gradation of a million shades of green, from light to black. After 6 miles the trail ends at the RIVER BIRCH sign at the edge of the floodplain forest. Turn around and carefully retrace your path, using the reverse sides of the signs to navigate your way back.

When you return to the beginning of the River Birch Trail, turn left to walk up Dick Slough Road. Across from the ZONE D sign, you'll pass a rare cluster of needle palms. As you head up Dick Slough Road, you'll see many older saw palmettos, rising tall on their long, slender trunks. At 7.3 miles you reach the BLUFF OAK TRAIL sign. Continue on up the road, passing the FLORIDA MAPLE TRAIL sign as the road climbs upward under the dense shade of the hardwood forest. When you reach the parking area near the beginning of Dick Slough Road, you've completed a 7.9-mile loop.

7

Manatee Springs State Park

*Total distance (2 circuits, 1 round trip):
6 miles*

Hiking time: 3.5 hours

*Habitats: Pine flatwoods, hardwood
hammock, scrubby flatwoods, sinkholes,
floodplain forest*

*Maps: USGS 7½' Fanning Springs,
park map*

During his travels in the summer of 1774, naturalist William Bartram visited the grand Creek village of Talahasochte along the Suwannee River. Traveling downriver by canoe, he and his party came to Manatee Springs. "The ebullition is astonishing, and continual," Bartram wrote, " . . . a lucid sea green color . . . throwing up small particles or pieces of white shells, which subside with the waters . . . " Although it was the wrong time of year to see manatees in the spring, Bartram saw "part of a skeleton of one, which the Indians had killed last winter . . . the Indians call them by a name which signifies the big beaver."

Look into the brilliant boil of Manatee Springs and step back into the past. Although the popular state park that surrounds it has added campgrounds, concessions, and trails, the spring and the spring run are timeless, as crystalline as when Bartram first paddled across its surface. From US 19 in Chiefland, follow FL 320 west for 6 miles. The road leads straight into the park entrance. Pick up a map at the entrance gate when you pay your Florida State Parks entrance fee. Manatee Springs State Park provides three distinct hiking experiences: a gentle boardwalk along Manatee Springs Run out to the Suwannee River, the short Sink Trail Loop, and the extensive North End Trail System. Bring a swimsuit—except in winter, when the manatees take residence, the spring is open to swimming. Two developed campgrounds cater to campers, and visitors can enjoy cave diving, canoeing, and biking on the North End Trail

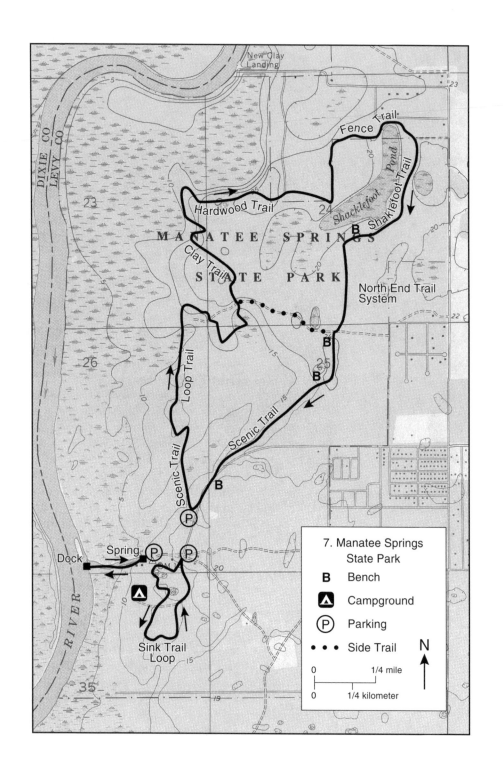

New Clay Landing

DIXIE CO
LEVY CO

Fence Trail

Shacklefoot Pond

Shacklefoot Trail

Hardwood Trail

B

M A N A T E E   S P R I N G S

24

Clay Trail

S T A T E   P A R K

North End Trail System

26

Loop Trail

B

25

B

Scenic Trail

Scenic Trail

15

Scenic Trail

B

P

Spring

P   P

Dock

RIVER

Sink Trail Loop

35

7. Manatee Springs
State Park

B   Bench

▲   Campground

Ⓟ   Parking

• • •   Side Trail

N

0   1/4 mile

0   1/4 kilometer

System. One precaution: Except in the dead of winter, ticks are prevalent in these bottomlands. Before you hike, spray yourself thoroughly with insect repellent, and wear light-colored clothing to make it easier to catch and destroy these nasty insects.

As you drive in on the park entrance road, watch for a parking-area sign on the right for the North End Trail System. Although the trail system is an 8.5-mile network of old forest roads, this 4.7-mile hike leads you along the perimeter, utilizing a portion of a marked interpretive trail. All trails are named and signposted, making navigation simple if you carry the park map with you.

NORTH END TRAIL SYSTEM

Starting at the parking-area kiosk, pick up a copy of the interpretive brochure. Begin your hike on the Scenic Trail, walking through the shady upland forest of hickory, southern magnolia, and American holly. The numbered signs correspond to the interpretive brochure. Where you pass a low sink, a twisted, charred snag rises like a sculpture from the center of a clump of saw palmetto. At the junction with the Loop Trail, take the left fork. The leathery leaves of tall southern magnolias glisten in the sun. Notice the post oak, with its distinctively scalloped, thick, leathery leaves. Post oaks thrive in poor sandy soils. You pass an active gopher tortoise burrow, with fresh tracks in the soft sand. At 0.5 mile saw palmettos encircle a sinkhole. After the trail swings away from the sinkhole, it approaches a T intersection with the Scenic Trail. Turn left. Listen carefully, and you'll hear armadillos scrabbling around through the leaves and needles, looking for insects. Coontie sprouts between the pines. You're walking through a second-growth forest of loblolly pines, the site of the Hardee Plantation in the 1860s.

The plantation owner's wife died in 1860 and is buried at Clay's Landing. When you come to a junction with the Clay Trail at 1 mile, continue straight. Despite its name, the western end of the Clay Trail dead-ends long before it reaches Clay's Landing. Unless you're simply looking to extend your hiking miles, skip the dead-end trails in this trail system—none of them make it to the Suwannee River.

At the next trail junction, the Hardwood Trail, turn left. Keep alert, and you'll see a rusted old chain looped around a set of rotted logs—perhaps hitched together to be pulled by oxen down to the river landing. Rusty lyonia and sand live oak form a low canopy overhead. At the fork, keep right, staying on the Hardwood Trail. You come to a T intersection at 1.6 miles. Turn right, walking up a straight, long path under the trees, reminiscent of an old road leading to the river landing. When you reach the FENCE TRAIL sign at the corner of a rusty barbed wire–topped fence, continue straight along the fence line, walking through the oak hammock. At 2.2 miles the Fence Trail and the Hornet Trail meet at a T intersection. Turn left to follow the fence line to reach the hidden gem of this trail system, Shacklefoot Pond. When the fence makes a sharp right turn, follow it. Numerous gopher tortoise burrows riddle the soft sand.

As you walk along, the forest transitions to a taller, more open canopy of laurel oak, loblolly pine, and live oak. The ground on the right slopes down from several directions into a broad, shallow sinkhole. Sand cordgrass grows along its edge. Massive Spanish bayonets rise from the forest floor. On the other side of the park boundary fence, you see some homes. The trail drops through a floodplain forest, becoming a causeway with bald cypresses on both sides. Wild pine thrives up on the cypress

Manatee Run

limbs. The trail rises up, and you see blue sky ahead. When you reach the intersection of the Fence Trail and the Shacklefoot Trail, turn right. On the left, the ground slopes down to Graveyard Pond, a murky duck-weed-covered cypress swamp. At 3 miles you pass a SHACKLEFOOT sign on the left, walking into a zone where most of the loblolly pines have been logged out, victims of the southern pine beetle. Keep alert on the right for access to Shacklefoot Pond. Walk down and examine this primeval cy-press swamp. Royal ferns sprout out of the stumps of ancient cypresses, logged long ago to be made into citrus crates and shin-gles. A wild turkey picks its way along the water's edge. Nosing through the duck-weed, an alligator lifts its snout out of water. A herd of white-tailed deer dashes off into the forest, startled from their drink-ing hole. Shacklefoot Pond is a glimpse of ancient Florida, a place for quiet reflection on how humans have altered the land.

Returning to the main trail, turn right. Walk through the clear-cut until you reach an intersection with the Spur Trail at 3.5 miles. Continue straight, rising up into an upland forest. The trail jogs off to the left, re-turning moments later to its arrow-straight path. More coontie pokes up through the leaf litter. You walk past a bowl surrounded by saw palmettos, another solution hole, be-fore reaching a major trail junction at 3.7 miles. Trails come in from four directions, and a large map sign stands off to the right. Walk up to the map and make a left to con-tinue on the Shacklefoot Trail, rejoining the inner interpretive loop. A stand of young candle-stage longleaf pines grow across from a bench by Marker 19. You walk past another large solution hole at 4.2 miles. Traveling here from the Alachua Savanna (Hike 20), William Bartram was amazed at the complexity of limestone formations he found in the Central Highlands. "The land is rocky and hollow, abounding with wells and cavities." During one exploration of a sink-hole, Bartram had a close call. "I was sur-prised, and providentially stopped in my career, at the ground sounding hollow under my feet . . . I quickly drew back, and returning with a pole with which I beat the earth, to my astonishment and dread ap-peared the mouth of a well through the rocks, and I observed water glimmering at the bottom."

When you reach the gate at 4.6 miles, walk around it and turn right. A connector trail leads over to the parking area, tightly winding between the bushes, rounding a cypress swamp. A broad, curving sinkhole sits off to the left, a leaf-filled bowl with rocks at the bottom. The trail ends at the parking lot after 4.7 miles. Straight ahead of you is a sign for the SPRINGS AND PICNIC AREA trail, connecting this trail system with the campground. Unless you've walked up here from the campground, jump in your car and head on to the next trailhead.

SINK TRAIL LOOP

As you leave the North End Trail System parking area, turn left. Drive up the park road and watch for the SINK TRAIL LOOP sign on the left, at a small parking area just be-fore the campground turnoff. Start this 0.6-mile interpretive loop by following the trail into the forest, walking past a tall bluff oak. These stately oaks only grow around lime-stone outcrops. As the narrow path mean-ders through the forest, it passes under an archway of deerberry in bloom.

The trail forks in front of a large live oak. Keep to the right, rising up through a corridor of wax myrtle. A strangely shaped southern magnolia drops its giant flower cones on the forest floor. A side trail off to the left leads to the brink of a pocket-shaped sinkhole with a rocky bottom, long and narrow. Return to the main trail and turn left. Sand live oak knits a low canopy above the saw palmetto. Passing a bench, you see another side trail at 0.4 mile. Turn left and walk down to the lip of the sinkhole, a broad bowl with large pines rising out of it. Returning to the main trail, turn left. As the trail turns left at an arrow sign, you approach an interpretive sign about sinkholes on the edge of a large sinkhole at 0.5 mile. This is the first in a chain of sinkholes that the trail continues to parallel on the right. When sinkholes form in a chain like this, they are typically above an underground stream. As the level of the stream fell, it no longer supported the cavern ceiling—and the earth above caved in. Each sinkhole is separated by a little ridge of limestone yet is distinctively bowl-shaped.

Returning to the beginning of the loop, turn right. You pass a side trail on the left, which leads to the campground. Reaching the parking area, you complete the 0.6-mile hike.

SUWANNEE RIVER BOARDWALK

Drive down the remainder of the park road, which ends in a parking lot within sight of a picnic area. You can do a lot of rambling around the spring, but it's an easy 0.7-mile hike to see the spring and walk down to the Suwannee River. From the parking lot, follow the sidewalk to the concession area and rest rooms. Turn right at the building to walk up to Manatee Springs. Feast your eyes on its breathtaking aquamarine hue, caused by suspended limestone particles in the water. Walk down the stairs to the edge of the natural rock ledge and peer into the

blue infinity. Although most Floridians find the spring's constant 72-degree temperature too chilly, it suits tourists and manatees just fine. Every winter, West Indian manatees make their way up the Suwannee River from the Gulf of Mexico to bask in the spring, feeding on the aquatic plants. The warmer temperature is essential for their survival—they can't stay in the open sea when it dips below 68 degrees. Winter is the only time you see manatees in groups. Solitary creatures, they range along Florida's coastline and its rivers, with a population estimated at 3,200 in the southeastern United States in 2001.

Turn around and walk down along the spring run to the SUWANNEE RIVER BOARDWALK sign, just past the canoe rental. The boardwalk zigzags through the floodplain forest of tall bald cypresses. Wandering softly between cypress knees that rise over their heads, deer browse in the late afternoon shade. Walk out to the overlook and take a look down into the spring run, which Bartram described as "the crystal stream; the current swift." Tapegrass waves along the bottom as schools of sheepshead drift by. At the second overlook, sit and watch a mud turtle propelling itself along the glistening bottom. Suwannee cooters bask on fallen logs. The boardwalk ends at a platform on the Suwannee River at 0.4 mile. Black vultures cluster in the cypresses, fussing at each other as they tend to their nests. After taking in the river view, return back up the boardwalk to the canoe concession. Turn right and follow the sidewalk up to the parking lot, completing your 0.7-mile tour of Manatee Springs.

8

Lower Suwannee National Wildlife Refuge

Total distance (1 circuit, 2 round trips, 1 one-way): 2.4 miles

Hiking time: 1 hour, 45 minutes

Habitats: Coastal savanna, maritime hammock, salt marsh, salt flats, floodplain forest, hardwood hammock, pine flatwoods, bayhead

Maps: USGS 7½' Vista, USGS 7½' Cedar Key

Protecting more than fifty-two thousand acres where the Suwannee River meets the Gulf of Mexico, the Lower Suwannee National Wildlife Refuge provides a quiet refuge for bald eagles and manatees, sea turtles and swallow-tailed kites. Thousands of species pack the extensive floodplain forest that flanks the Suwannee River, from Fowler's Bluff to the California Swamp. With 26 miles of coastline, the refuge includes coastal savannas, salt flats, and a singularly significant archaeological site—an ancient shell mound covering nearly five acres.

As befits a National Wildlife Refuge, access is limited, the sites remote. Many miles of hard-packed limestone roads meander through the eastern side of the refuge, open for hiking and biking. Three marked trail systems invite visitors to stroll and explore this wild corner of Florida: the Shell Mound Unit, the Suwannee River Boardwalk Trail, and the Dixie Mainline Trail. All are far-flung but worth the time and effort to seek out and enjoy.

SHELL MOUND UNIT

At the most southerly site in the refuge, the Shell Mound Unit, your trek strings together three short but interesting trails for a total hike of 1.6 miles. From Cedar Key (the nearest town) drive east 3.3 miles on FL 24 to C-347. Turn left, following the road 2.3 miles to the turnoff for C-326, on the left. Turn left and follow C-326 until the pavement ends, passing the developed campground at

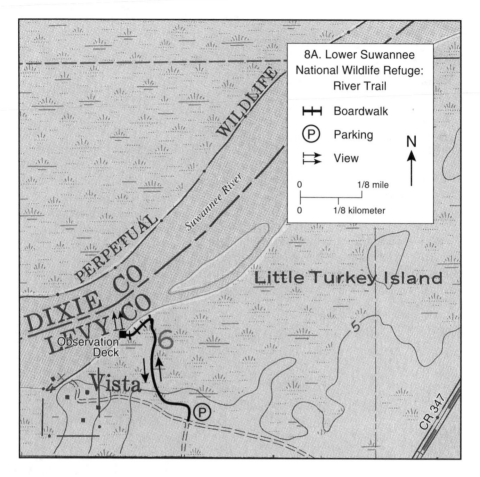

8A. Lower Suwannee National Wildlife Refuge: River Trail

⊢⊣ Boardwalk

Ⓟ Parking

⇨ View

N

0   1/8 mile

0   1/8 kilometer

PERPETUAL

WILDLIFE

Suwannee River

Little Turkey Island

DIXIE CO

LEVY CO

Observation Deck

Vista

6

5

CR 347

Ⓟ

Shell Mound County Park. Continue on the dirt road for a short distance to the trailhead parking, on the left under the large oak trees, at 3.4 miles.

Starting at the parking lot, turn toward the DENNIS CREEK LOOP TRAIL sign and follow the footpath down into the maritime hammock under the spreading live oaks. Saw palmettos line the trail. Looking off to the right through the trees, you see the sweep of the tidal marsh, the open coastal savanna that characterizes the Gulf coast north of Tarpon Springs. Black needlerush sticks its spiky points out into the trail. When you come to the trail junction, turn right to cross a boardwalk over the salt flats. Channel markers in the distance indicate how close you are to the Gulf of Mexico. It's a prairie made of needlerush, broken up with clumps of sea purslane and bounded by cedars. To the left, the marsh flows inland between isles of pines. Fiddler crabs scurry about, the earth balls they disgorge while feeding indicating the locations of their holes. The boardwalk ends, and you're on an island of pine flatwoods. Just ahead is a tidal pond, where a pair of Louisiana herons stalks the shallows and a willet picks at the mud.

Salt marshes along the Dennis Creek Loop

Two belted kingfishers wheel overhead, warbling to each other as they perform a mating display.

The trail turns to the right and follows the edge of the island. You walk past an armadillo hole tucked between the roots of a slash pine. Crossing another boardwalk over the salt flats, you reach another island. Gnarled sand live oaks knit a canopy overhead. Passing an arrow pointing in the opposite direction, you walk by a tidal pond. A slightly overgrown trail leads to the right toward Dennis Creek, branching out into a network of narrow paths along the tidal marsh.

On the main trail, you reach a bench in an oak hammock at 0.5 mile. It's situated to give you a fine view of Dennis Creek. A brown pelican roosts on a piling of an old dock, while a great blue heron fusses over an oyster bed. Periwinkle snails lay their eggs on the black needlerush. The trail heads directly away from water back into an oak scrub, which yields to taller pines. A flock of ibises flies overhead in formation. Underfoot, it seems like the remnants of an old limestone road, hard packed with chunks of rock, perhaps leading to the abandoned landing.

Walking across a small shell mound, you take another boardwalk over the salt flats. You reach a TRAIL sign at 0.6 mile, at a trail junction. The narrow trail straight ahead of you heads to the campground at Shell Mound County Park. Turn left to finish your loop back around to the parking lot. When you pass the beginning of the loop, continue straight. At the parking lot, turn left along the sand road and walk a short distance to the trailhead sign for the Shell Mound Loop Trail. This short trail takes you to the most significant archaeological

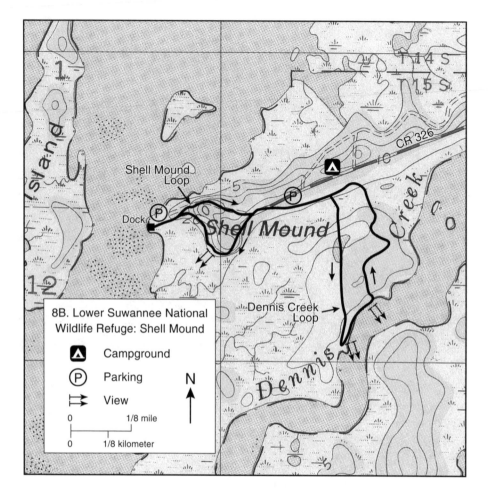

8B. Lower Suwannee National
Wildlife Refuge: Shell Mound

🅰 Campground

🅿 Parking   N

⊢→ View

0   1/8 mile
├─────────┤
0   1/8 kilometer

feature in this region, a 28-foot-tall shell midden created between 2500 B.C. and A.D. 1000 by the ancestors of the Timucuan tribes who once inhabited this coastline.

Turn left and follow the trail into another shady maritime hammock, crowded with cedar and red bay. As you approach the midden, notice how much it looks like a landfill–which is exactly what it was in pre-historic times. The trail swings to the left to make a steep ascent to the top of the mound, passing by a lone coontie. Many unauthorized trails run off in all directions–stick to the broad main trail to avoid further

degradation of the midden. At 1.1 miles you reach a bench with a sweeping view of the estuary. At 1.2 miles turn left to follow a broad unmarked trail down the side of the midden. The trail emerges in the parking area at the end of C-326. Walk across it to access the Al Georges Boardwalk, and wander out to the end for a close-up view of wading birds in the salt flats and the chance to see dolphins in the open water.

Return back across the parking area and up the slope of the mound, turning left when you meet the main trail. The trail steadily drops downhill to reach the road. When you reach the road, look off to the right and you can see the parking area. Walk over to it, completing a 1.6-mile circuit.

SUWANNEE RIVER BOARDWALK TRAIL

The refuge's sole trail along the Suwannee River is only 0.6 mile long and starts near the park headquarters. From the Shell Mound Unit, follow C-326 out to C-347. Drive north 14.7 miles. Turn left at the park headquarters sign. The parking area is on the right. Take a look at the kiosk before you start; it contains maps and brochures about the refuge. The trail starts out from the gravel parking lot, down a path edge with railroad ties along a floodplain forest bordering the Suwannee River. Royal ferns rise up from the damp ground. The path turns right onto a broader trail covered with pine needles, dropping into a bottomland forest of red maple, sugarberry, hickory, and sweetgum. Bald cypress becomes the dominant tree, and the trail turns into a causeway through the cypress swamp. The blooms of golden aster add a splash of yellow to the green backdrop. The trail rises up into a hardwood forest, passing an ironwood with its trunk stippled pink and white from lichens.

Coming to a bench under a stand of oaks, the trail turns left onto a boardwalk, winding through the floodplain forest on the river's edge. Be cautious of the climbing poison ivy vines that grow to immense proportions, their leaves mimicking hickory leaves. You can see glimpses of water between the sweetgum and willow oak. After 0.3 mile the trail ends at a double-decked observation platform on the Suwannee, a great place to sit and watch wading birds in the shallows or ospreys soaring overhead. Within 10 miles of where it empties into the Gulf of Mexico, the Suwannee is a broad, swift-moving river bounded by unbroken floodplain forests on both sides. Smooth patches of water alternate with ripples, catching reflections of the sky. Watch closely, and you may see a manatee slide by on its way upstream or an alligator breaking the surface with its knobby tail.

Leaving the platform, retrace your steps back along the trail, turning right at the bench and left when you see the gate ahead of you. When you reach the parking lot, you've hiked 0.6 mile.

DIXIE MAINLINE TRAIL

In the most remote corner of the refuge, the Dixie Mainline Trail isn't technically a trail—it's a 9-mile, one-lane, hard-packed limestone road through the wilds of the California Swamp, serving as an interpretive drive. With a short stop at Salt Creek, it provides an immersion into cypress swamp and coastal hammock. Traffic is low enough that you might consider hiking or biking it, but swarms of mosquitoes and yellow flies will dog your steps in all but the dead of winter.

Since the California Swamp sits on the west side of the Suwannee River, it takes quite a few miles to get from refuge headquarters over to the Dixie Mainline Trail. Follow C-326 north 6 miles to C-330. Continue on C-330 for 11 miles to C-345, coming to a traffic light at US 19. Turn left and drive up through Chiefland to C-320, the turnoff for Manatee Springs (Hike 7). Continue north on US 19 for 11.7 miles, passing the turnoffs to Andrews Wildlife Management Area (Hike 6) and Fanning Springs State Park (Hike 5) on your way to Old Town in Dixie County. At Old Town, turn left at the light to head south on CR 349. After 9.6 miles on CR 349, you enter the Lower Suwannee National Wildlife Refuge. Keep alert for the small brown LOWER SUWANNEE NATIONAL WILDLIFE REFUGE sign at

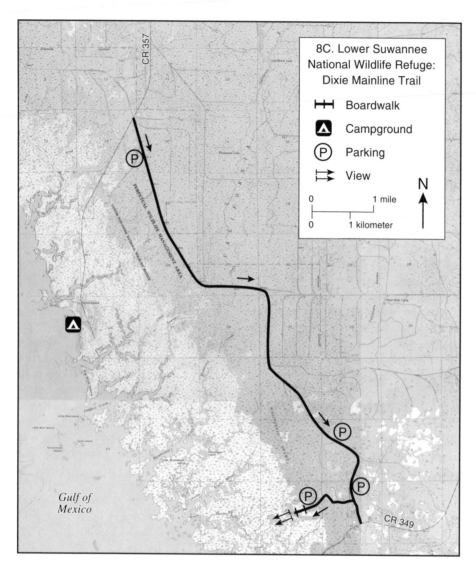

8C. Lower Suwannee National Wildlife Refuge: Dixie Mainline Trail

H—H Boardwalk

△ Campground

Ⓟ Parking

⇥ View

N

0 — 1 mile
0 — 1 kilometer

CR 357

Gulf of Mexico

CR 349

21.7 miles. Turn right onto the limestone road with the DIXIE MAINLINE ROAD GUIDED TRAIL sign and pick up an interpretive guide at the roadside kiosk. As you drive, don't expect to go more than 20 miles per hour, and keep alert for oncoming traffic. Pull-offs allow vehicles to pass, and several parking spots let you get out and explore along the swamp on foot.

After 0.3 mile on the Dixie Mainline, a SALT CREEK POINT sign points to the left. Turn left to drive down through wet flatwoods and salt marshes to the very edge of the coastal savanna, where black needlerush flows around saline creeks and islands of slash pines, cedars, and cabbage palms. At 1.5 miles the road ends in a small open area; park and continue on foot on a 0.2-mile round trip along a causeway to the boardwalk for a sweeping view of the coastal savanna along Salt Creek. The houses off to the distance on the left are the coastal community of Suwannee, where the Suwannee River flows into the Gulf of Mexico.

Turn around and drive back to the Dixie Mainline, and turn left. The habitat transitions from pine plantations to bayhead to floodplain forest as you enter the California Swamp, dominated by large bald cypress, sweetgum, and red maple, after 5 miles. A blackwater slough parallels the road, water lilies drifting across its surface. A young alligator lazes on a log above the dark water. Look up, and you'll notice epiphytes sprouting in hairy bunches from tree trunks. Passing through a gate at 5.7 miles, you're now fully immersed in the refuge. A parking area sits off to the right. At 6.1 miles a road comes in from the right. Continue straight, passing another parking area on the right. After the next gate, the habitat shifts to coastal savanna at 7.7 miles as you cross a

series of one-lane bridges over Sanders Creek, surrounded by islands of cabbage palms within the salt marsh. Fiddler crabs scuttle across the road. You reenter the cypress floodplain, passing through another slice of coastal savanna at Shired Creek after 9.1 miles. After the next gate, keep alert for a large grassy pull-off on the left side of the road, at 10.5 miles. Although there are no marked trails, old logging tramways lead away from the parking spot to provide foot access to an older slash pine forest. After 10.9 miles the Dixie Mainline Trail ends at CR 357. To return to US 19, turn right and drive 7.7 miles to a T intersection. Turn right, and continue another 8 miles to Cross City to reach US 19. If you're interested in camping along the Gulf of Mexico, Dixie County maintains a rustic seaside campground near the end of CR 357; turn left at the end of the Dixie Mainline Trail and drive 3.5 miles to Shired Island, making a right turn one road after the BOAT LAUNCH sign.

9

Cedar Key Scrub State Reserve

Total distance (2 circuits): 8.9 miles

Hiking time: 4.5 hours

Habitats: Scrubby flatwoods, pine flatwoods, salt marsh, coastal scrub, coastal savanna, maritime hammock, freshwater marsh, prairie, cypress dome

Maps: USGS 7½' Cedar Key, park map

With two separate trails and a family of Florida scrub-jays to keep you company, the Cedar Key Scrub State Reserve provides an interesting hiking experience through an uncommon Gulf Coast coastal scrub. You'll walk along part of the massive coastal savanna called Gulf Hammock, a place of salt marshes and scattered islands that stretches for miles out to the Gulf of Mexico. Located on FL 24 between Cedar Key and Otter Creek, the eastern trailhead is the one folks see on their way to Cedar Key. Of the two loops, the 5.9-mile hike from the western trailhead is more scenic and provides a better chance of spying the reserve's most important resident, the Florida scrub-jay. Both areas are open 8 AM to sunset, and both trails are shared with bicycles.

From I-75 exit 384 in Gainesville, head east on FL 24 for 48 miles, passing through the town of Bronson before you cross US 19 at Otter Creek. Continue on through Rosewood and Sumner before you see the sign for the eastern trailhead of the reserve, on the right. If you're coming from accommodations in Cedar Key, drive west 6 miles on FL 24 to the trailhead entrance on the left. This trailhead provides parking and a small picnic area, as well as a composting toilet. It's the gateway to a 3-mile loop, primarily in oak scrub and pine flatwoods. For the western trailhead, drive 3 miles west on FL 24 to C-347. Turn right. Continue 1 mile north to the small parking area set off the road on the left, signposted as the CEDAR KEY SCRUB WMA.

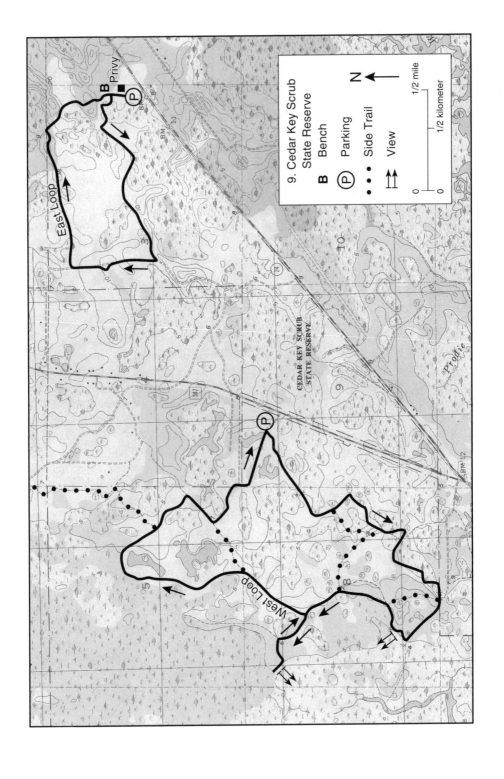

East Loop

Privy

B

Ⓟ

West Loop

Ⓟ

CEDAR KEY SCRUB
STATE RESERVE

Prdie

WESTERN LOOP

The Wildlife Management Area sign says it all: Since these lands are designated a "reserve" rather than a "preserve," hunters roam the woods during the fall and winter. Check the Florida Fish and Wildlife Conservation Commission web site before hiking here during hunting season; if you're visiting between late September and November, wear safety orange. The kiosk shows a detailed trail map, the trail system an interconnected set of forest roads that creates the loops. Your 5.9-mile hike will utilize several different trails.

You start out on an open grassy jeep track into an oak scrub. Most of the myrtle oaks and sand live oaks stand 3 or 4 feet high, providing a perfect habitat for the Florida scrub-jay. Endemic to Florida, these rare birds feast on acorns, insects, and lizards. They prefer the low scrub forests, an uncommon habitat that is threatened by the never-ending development of the state. Statewide, there are about ten thousand scrub-jays.

At the TRAIL 10 sign turn left, following the white blazes. A high canopy of loblolly pines rises above the scrub: second-growth forest, just filling in. In the early 1900s, loggers from the nearby towns of Rosewood and Sumner worked these woods, feeding the busy Cummer and Sons sawmill with pine and cypress until the forests were laid bare. Inflamed by racial tensions over a suspected rape, an angry mob burned the all-black town of Rosewood in 1923. Its residents fled, never to return.

Notice the large wetlands off to the right, forming a wet prairie with tufts of bushy-beard bluestem along its edges. The trail drops down, and you step over flowing water, which feeds the arrowroot and Virginia willow on the edge of the marsh. As the trail rises up, you enter scrubby flat-woods, meandering through stands of cabbage palm and pine. Passing through an area dense with saw palmetto, the trail rises again into scrub. At 1.1 miles you reach the junction of the red and white blazes. Turn left, following the red-blazed trail. This is a high-water trail with deep ruts that can flood, so don't use it if you've already had to wade along the trail—stick with the white blazes. You see the quick flash of a scrub-jay landing in a myrtle oak. Unlike most jays, the Florida scrub-jay travels in a family group, ranging over a 25-acre territory. When you see one land, expect to see more. Each pair mates for life, raising its family with the aid of their older children, who delay their own breeding to help their parents raise another brood.

When you come to a T intersection, turn right. Rising up, the trail parallels a prairie bounded by a line of pines and saw palmettos, heading down an ecotone the division between prairie and scrub. A gopher tortoise ambles along, stopping every few moments to take a bite out of the vegetation in the middle of the trail. Curving up along the edge of an ancient sand dune, the trail drops back down to a fence line. You meet blue blazes coming in from the right. Continue straight, following the blue blazes up to a cable gate. Turn right at the TRAIL 6 sign, following the trail away from the fence. Within a few moments, you catch your first sweeping view of the savanna, cabbage palms waving on tiny islands in the endless salt marsh. After 2 miles the trail curves around a dark maritime hammock of red bay and live oak along the edge of the salt marsh. Turning inland, it rises into a sand pine scrub. You meet the loop junction for the blue-blazed trail; continue straight. At 2.4 miles the blue blazes end at a T intersection. Turn left to follow the white blazes. When you see blue blazes turning off to the

The edge of the salt marsh

left, follow them. A broken chunk of a turpentine cup juts out of the sand, another reminder of the olden days. Ships sailing into the Cedar Keys were eager for naval stores, and a local industry sprung up to supply turpentine, rosin, and pitch. Keep alert, and you'll notice catfaces on some of the older pines.

After 3 miles the trail comes to a dead-end on the edge of the salt marsh. Cabbage palms and cedars frame a view of the lazy salt rivers that flow through the needlerush. Out on these edges of this forest, a cottage industry thrived during the Civil War—salt making. Boiling off the salt water in massive iron kettles, local residents would pack up the encrusted salt and send it off with blockade runners, who sailed their skiffs where the Union Blockading Squadron couldn't go. Salt sold for as much as $50 a bushel in 1864, well worth the risk to both parties. Used to preserve meat, it was an essential commodity for the Confederate commissary.

Turn around and retrace your path. At the fork keep left, rejoining the white blazes at the TRAIL 6 sign. Scattered throughout the scrub, Florida rosemary grows tall. After crossing a boggy area where a concrete base keeps the trail from washing away when the marsh floods, you soon come to a junction with an orange-blazed cross trail. If you want to shorten your hike by 1.5 miles, take the cross trail. Otherwise, turn left to follow the white blazes out into the pine flatwoods. Orange bachelor's buttons poke their noses out of the grass. Watch for a small stand of coontie on the right, shaded by scrub oaks. You're looping around a broad prairie. At 4.7 miles you pass a blue-blazed trail to the left—a dead-end leading into Black Point Swamp. Stay with the white blazes unless you want to add a few miles of out-and-back exploration into the swamp.

Pause for a moment and notice the silence—no road noise and no airplanes, just the chirps of birds and the sound of the wind rustling palmetto fronds.

At 5 miles you come to a T intersection with a TRAIL 7 sign—the junction with the orange-blazed shortcut. Turn left. Keep alert—a family of scrub-jays lives in this vicinity. Stand quietly, and you'll be rewarded with a sighting of this hard-to-find bird. A sentinel will perch high in a pine, surveying the territory. Other curious family members will flit from oak to oak. Their bright blue and gray plumage makes them easy to spot.

Just after you pass the scrub-jay territory, a road comes in from the right, making a fork in reverse. Another comes in from the left. Keep walking straight ahead, following the white blazes. You walk along a pine plantation with a warning sign regarding hunting, since there is a residence beyond the pines. Keep alert to the blazes through this section, since indistinct trails come in from all directions. Crossing over a concrete bridge, you come to the end of the loop. Continue straight ahead to the parking lot, completing a hike of 5.9 miles.

EASTERN LOOP

From the developed trailhead off FL 24, start your hike at the kiosk. Pick up a map and follow the white blazes. This 3-mile loop will take one and a half hours. Although it does not have the same picturesque appeal as the lesser-known western trail, it's an important habitat for the Florida scrub-jay and the gopher tortoise. As you walk down the grassy track, take a moment to look at the interpretive sign FLORIDA'S DESERT, which explains the uniqueness and value of the scrub. You come to a TRAIL 3 sign and a bench, signaling the beginning of the loop. Turn left, following the white blazes down a jeep track into the scrub. Sand pines shake their wispy needles in the wind; wiregrass, blueberry, and saw palmetto jut of out the impenetrable mat of scrub oaks forming the scrub on the right. Oak and rusty lyonia grow in heaping mounds, graduated in size. Gopher apple thrives along the trail's edge. After 1 mile you see a gopher tortoise burrow, with bright orange sand dug from the hole splayed across the white sand of the scrub.

You reach a T intersection at the TRAIL 4 sign. Turn right, rising up into an oak hammock. Virginia willow and loblolly bay fill a marshy area surrounded by cinnamon fern. Passing a trail coming in from the left, the trail rises up into blinding white sand surrounded by scrub. Another side trail comes in from the left. Keep going straight, and you'll come to a T intersection at another TRAIL 4 sign, with a TRAIL 5 sign just beyond it. Turn right. You rise back up into the low scrub, walking along the short sand live oaks. The trail drops down and circles left around a wet prairie; spider lilies grow in a damp spot. Entering a shady pine forest, you arrive at another T intersection, the junction of Trail 5 and Trail 2. Turn right, dropping into deeper shade. Keep alert as the blazes leave the forest road to make a beeline through the woods for a short stretch. Straight ahead is a line of posts leading off into a wet prairie; the trail curves off to the right. A wall of scrub oaks stretches off to right to the far line of pines. In a blur, a six-lined race runner scurries back into the scrub. These colorful skinks enjoy sunbathing on the hot sand.

The walking gets a bit difficult as the trail curves past a property boundary with a NO TRESPASSING sign. You're on the edge of the reserve, walking along a fence line outside a private residence. The trail climbs up and over the undulating ancient dunes through broad stretches of desertlike open sand.

Wild bachelor's button

Watch for the orange sand, and you'll spot the many gopher tortoise holes. After you pass a road to the left, straight ahead is a cypress dome, the young pond cypresses decked out in their feathery needles. You pass a TRAIL 2 sign and veer around the cypresses. At 2.5 miles you reach a side trail, blazed blue, leading to the left. The side trail is a 1.4-mile round trip around another stretch of scrub and is worth it only if you feel like taking a longer hike. Continue straight, walking along the edge of the scrub. The charred forms of gnarled sand live oaks rise above green saw palmettos. When you reach the beginning of the loop, the bench is off to the right. Walk straight ahead to the parking area, completing a 3-mile hike.

10

Atsena Otie Key

Total distance (round trip): 2 miles

Hiking time: 1.5 hours

Habitats: Maritime hammock, coastal scrub, salt marsh, beach

Maps: USGS 7½' Seahorse Key

Pronounced AT-senna AWE-tee, this barrier island in the Cedar Keys National Wildlife Refuge hosted the first American settlers in this region. Drawn to the newly dedicated state of Florida in the 1850s, fishermen and entrepreneurs flocked to the Gulf Coast, accessible via David Yulee's brand-new Florida Railroad from Fernandina. They discovered a bounty of cedar trees along the thousands of small islands that make up the Cedar Keys and set about building an industry—pencil making.

From the waterfront of the present-day town of Cedar Key, Atsena Otie Key fills the horizon, blocking the island's clear view of the Gulf of Mexico. When speculators thought to fill that horizon with condos, the residents of this quiet fishing village fought the plan—and won. In 1997 Atsena Otie Key, abandoned a century earlier by most of its settlers after an 1896 hurricane-driven storm surge, became a permanent part of the Cedar Keys National Wildlife Refuge. The refuge had been established in 1929 to protect the designated wilderness areas of Snake Key—according to naturalist Archie Carr, a breeding ground for cottonmouth moccasins—along with Bird Key, North Key, and Seahorse Key, all important rookeries for colonial nesting birds such as cormorants, herons, and pelicans. In acquiring Atsena Otie Key, the state ended up with one big plus from the developer: a lengthy dock with multiple slips, at which boaters can now tie up and wander the island or kick back and fish from the dock.

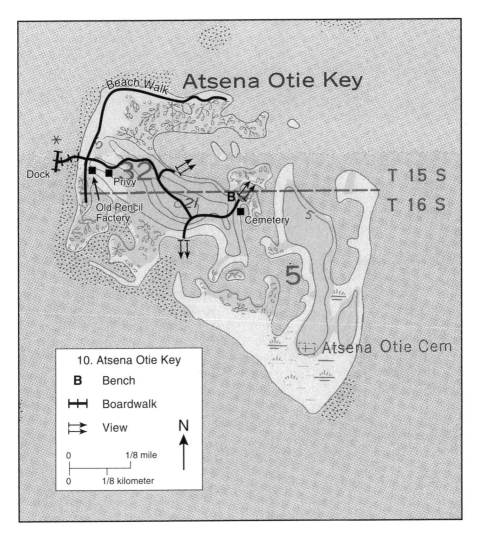

Getting to Atsena Otie Key takes a little bit of effort. From I-75 exit 384 in Gainesville, head east on FL 24. It's a 54-mile drive from the city to the end of the road at the quiet fishing village of Cedar Key. Once in town, you have a few options: You can launch your own canoe, kayak, or private boat at the public marina and make your way across the channel; you can stop by one of the local outfitters (Fishbonz, 352-543-9922; Nature Coast Expeditions, 352-543-6463) and rent a canoe or kayak for day trip; or you can plunk down some cash with one of the tour-boat operators (Island Hopper, 352-543-5904; Lady Pirate Tours, 352-543-5141) and be dropped off on the island for several hours, free to explore. In any case, you'll be launching from the point of land that naturalist John Muir reached in October 1867, ending his 1,000-mile walk to the Gulf of Mexico from his home in Indiana. "For nineteen years my vision was bounded by forests," writes Muir, "but today, emerging from a multitude of tropical plants, I beheld the Gulf of Mexico stretching away unbounded, except by the sky." Collapsing a few days later from yellow fever, Muir spent the next several months here recuperating. Once he regained his strength, he sailed from island to island to explore their botanical wonders.

After beaching your kayak or embarking at the dock, walk on up to the big ATSENA OTIE KEY sign to start your hike. The name Atsena Otie, appropriately enough, means "Cedar Island." Buried under cover of the maritime hammock, around you lay reminders that this was the original town of Cedar Key. The bricks scattered around a deep hole on the left are all that's left of the Eberhard Faber Pencil Mill, which washed away in the tidal surge of 1896, leaving the townspeople suddenly unemployed. The deep hole contained the machinery of the mill, driven by water flowing through a sluice. Workers sawed cedars into the small slats required for making pencils. In an ironic twist of nature, a grand cedar now crowns the spot.

Across from a composting toilet, several interpretive signs give the historical background of the town, as well as information on the Cedar Keys National Wildlife Refuge. A word of caution for this hike: The island's interior is rife with mosquitoes. Spray yourself well with insect repellent before proceeding any farther. The trail heads down a shaded needle-strewn path, flanked by longleaf pine and red bay, saw palmetto and cedar. After the trail makes a sharp right, it heads up through a dense grove of red bay and cedar, arriving at a high spot with a water cistern. Although the bricks are covered with concrete, a spout sticks out of

one side. In 1839 the U.S. Army established a supply depot and a hospital on this island, calling it Depot Key. A thriving town grew, jumping from 47 people in 1850 to 297 people in 1860. This cistern is one of the scattered reminders of homesteads on the island. Despite the destruction of the pencil mill, 35 homes survived the terrible storm of 1896. The families stayed on this island, turning to oystering and fishing for their livelihood, until 1904, when the company houses were bought and moved by barge to the mainland.

Walking a little farther, you reach the remains of a windmill. The blade has fallen and is twisted on the ground, but the metal tower still stands. Rising up into a grove of windswept sand live oaks waving streamers of Spanish moss, you see the bright red blooms of coral beans. The trail winds down past the town's cemetery, set on a bluff overlooking the salt marshes. The marble tombstones date back to 1882, some fallen, some as clean as the day they were erected. A wrought-iron fence cordons off one tiny corner, a private family plot under the windswept oaks. Paths meander between the grave sites. Judging from the inscriptions and dates on the tombstones, most of those buried here lived brief, harsh lives. Life on the Florida coast was no picnic in the days before air-conditioning and tourism. The residents of this island wrested a life from the sea, hoping to sell their catches to buyers headed to distant ports. They fought off plagues of fleas, as well as mosquitoes that bore yellow fever and malaria. They worked hard in the blazing heat, all year long.

Keep to the left of the cemetery to follow the trail downhill to the salt marsh. A bench provides a sweeping view of the marshes that separate the two halves of Atsena Otie Key. Below it, the trail ends at the very edge

The graveyard at Atsena Otie Key

of the water, at 0.5 mile. Gentle waves lap at the glasswort, saltwort, and bitter panicum. Across the marsh, the far northern end of Atsena Otie Key is populated primarily by ospreys, seen cruising over the water, searching for mullet. Black mangroves grow along the tidal basin, here at the northern extent of their range. The bench is a great place for bird-watching—sit tight long enough, and you might see a bald eagle wing past on its way to Snake Key.

Retrace your path up into and through the old cemetery. Returning back along the same path, keep alert for a side trail on the left before you get in sight of the windmill. It's a broad path across a stretch of coastal scrub, out in the open, with gleaming white sand. Take note of the prickly pear cactus in bloom. Before the yellow flower is fully open, the flower bud sports a peach hue. The footpath drops down into the coastal

hammock along the edge of the salt marsh, with a clear view of Snake Key. After describing his initial visit to Snake Key as yielding several cottonmouth specimens, naturalist Archie Carr, an avid herpetologist, catches "ten more cottonmouths. We didn't go out of our way to search for them—we merely avoided stepping on them." Studying the abnormally high snake population on these islands, Carr postulated that the snakes enjoyed a healthy diet from the heron rookeries.

Retrace your path from the edge of the salt marsh back up the hill to the main trail. Turn left. Just after passing the windmill structure, turn right on a side trail that winds between scattered bricks. The trail heads downhill through a coastal scrub, with aromatic silk bay and red bay trees, prickly pear, and scattered deer moss. Dropping down to the edge of the salt marsh, it

Cormorants

nating. "Woe to the luckless wanderer who dares to urge his way through these armed gardens," he wrote. "By one of these leaves a man might be as seriously stabbed as by an army bayonet."

Half buried in the beach are the remains of a rusting rounded object, which looks like half of an old steam boiler. The Union Navy steamed straight to the Cedar Keys because of its strategic position at the end of the railroad, wresting it from Confederate forces in January 1862. But many residents kept up their profitable salt-making operations, relying on local sailors who had adapted their skiffs to the shallow waters in order to run the blockade and deliver the salt to Confederate buyers. Salt making took just a few ingredients: seawater, a boiler, firewood, and time. As the water boiled off, it left behind a dark brown salt that would be scraped up and, if time allowed, left to dry to a cleaner white, suitable for preserving meat.

As you round the point, the wind picks up. A foot-long horseshoe crab lies stranded on the beach. The sand is rippled by wind, the grass and trees windblown to the northeast, no longer protected by Cedar Key's waterfront from the steady winds whipping off the Gulf's open waters. Dozens of white sulfur butterflies flit back and forth between big circles of sea purslane, attracted to the tiny flowers that bloom all summer. The beach yields to a stand of black mangroves, their finger roots poking out of the sand. Behind them is a sandy strip you can walk along for sweeping views of the salt marshes out to the tall longleaf pines on the far end of the island. You see the windmill tower up on the bluff, off to the right. A little blue heron fusses at your approach, taking to the sky. At 1.5 miles along your hike, the beach peters out into the grassy marsh. Turn around and walk back to the dock.

affords another view over to the docks of Cedar Key. Several huge prickly pears sit at the base of the bluff. Turn around and make your way back to the windmill. Turn right and follow the trail back through the maritime hammock, past the kiosk and composting toilet, and out to where the dock meets the beach. You've walked 1.2 miles. Step down on your right and head up the beach. Oyster shells and clumps of seaweed lay strewn across the ivory sand. Poke around, and you'll find all sorts of things—large conch shells, bits of rock, rusted metal, hunks of bricks covered with barnacles, and pieces of glass being turned by the waves, remnants of the former town. Half hidden by the cedars, healthy Spanish bayonets grow above the high-tide line, in the shade. Muir found these members of the lily family fasci-

If you have time, continue along the beach on the other side of the dock out to the western salt marshes. Bearing multiple trunks and multiple layers, a grand old cedar tree rises from the sand bluff. Two types of cedars grow on the islands: the common southern red cedar, found throughout the state, and the lesser-known white cedar. They're hard to distinguish as there are only slight differences in their needles. Continue out along the narrow sand path into the salt marsh. Fiddler crabs squat by little earth balls next to their holes, scuttling away as you approach. This little spit of land is bounded by salt marshes on either side. Pelicans skim low on the water. Look for more remnants of the town: scattered chunks of brick and railroad ties, half-buried in the mud. The trail ends at a tidal pond, where blue crabs scuttle in the shallows. Turn around and return to the dock, completing 2 miles of walking on Atsena Otie Key.

No matter whether you kayaked to the island or you're waiting for a boat to pick you up, take some time to watch the shallows for manatees. During spring and summer they commonly cruise the channel between here and the mainland, grazing on the thick beds of sea grasses that foul propellers on a regular basis. Bottle-nosed dolphins are sighted daily, playing in the wake of motorboats. Royal terns, pelicans, and cormorants come and go from the dock's pilings.

During the Civil War, the Union Blockading Squadron occupied this island along with the neighboring keys, all of which are now part of the Cedar Keys National Wildlife Refuge. The Civil War–era lighthouse still stands on Seahorse Key, along with a cemetery in which several Union naval men are buried. Seahorse Key is also home to a particularly rare type of rookery, a nesting ground for brown pelicans. Although its shores are closed March 1 through June 30 to protect the breeding population, the University of Florida opens up the lighthouse to the public two days each year, on the first Saturday in July and the Saturday during the Cedar Key Seafood Festival in October. If you have the opportunity, take the trip out to the island to walk its extensive beaches, visit the lighthouse, see the cemetery, and in July, catch a rare glimpse of gawky young pelicans at the end of the nesting season.

II

Central Highlands

River Sink at O'Leno State Park

11

Big Gum Swamp Wilderness

Total distance (circuit): 4.9 miles

Hiking time: 2 hours, 45 minutes

Habitats: Pine flatwoods, cypress dome, bayhead, freshwater marsh, bay

Maps: USGS 7½' Big Gum Swamp, park map

It's a silent place, a land left to the white-tailed deer and the Florida black bear, the red-tailed hawk and the coyote, its core a blackwater swamp, untrammeled by humans. One of Florida's rare designated wilderness areas, the 13,600-acre Big Gum Swamp Wilderness lies northeast of Lake City within Osceola National Forest, a dark boggy forest of cypress and sweetgum ringed by pine flatwoods. This is an adventure hike for folks who like to get off the beaten path and don't mind their shoes getting wet. Expect to bushwhack, although a safety net of blazes will help keep you on the right track. Primitive camping is permitted in the National Forest, so bring your gear if you really want to get away from it all.

From I-10 exit 303, Lake City/Fargo, follow US 441 north 11.5 miles to Deep Creek. Turn right on NE Drew Road. Beyond the OSCEOLA WILDLIFE MANAGEMENT AREA sign, Drew Road turns to dirt, passing the Deep Creek Trailhead of the Florida National Scenic Trail. Crossing a creek, the road narrows down to a single-lane jeep track, signposted as FR 262. After 9.2 miles FR 262 ends at a T intersection with FR 232. Turn left and immediately park in the cleared grassy area on the right. Although no sign indicates the trailhead, the Big Gum Swamp Wilderness trail starts here, indicated by a silver-dot blaze on a longleaf pine.

Starting behind the WILDLIFE MANAGEMENT AREA sign, follow the silver dots along a raised old railroad grade into the longleaf pine flatwoods. The flatwoods surrounding

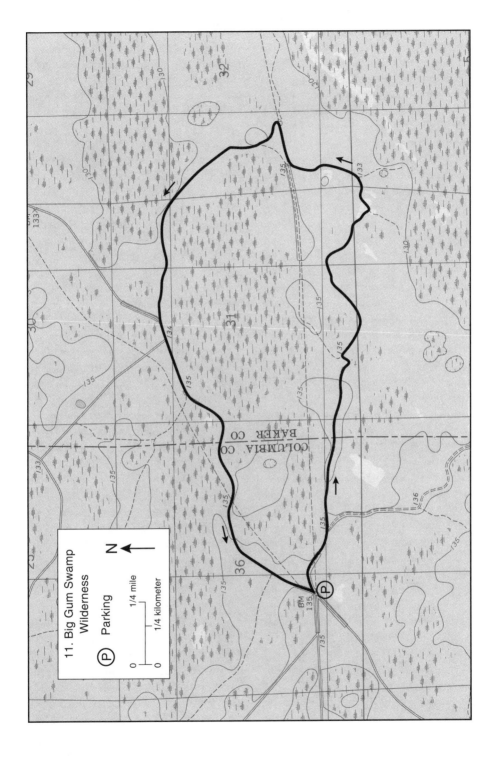

11. Big Gum Swamp
Wilderness

Ⓟ Parking

N

0 ____ 1/4 mile
0 ____ 1/4 kilometer

COLUMBIA CO
BAKER CO

the swamp succumbed to both logging and turpentining over the decades, well before this land became Osceola National Forest. This railroad grade and the vanishing forest roads that the trail follows are what little remains of the signs of human activity. You pass a post charred by a forest fire, etched with the code P4 A12 57. All of the typical pine flatwoods plants are here: bracken fern, gallberry, and shiny blueberry. Saw palmettos weave a solid understory beneath the pines. At 0.3 mile you reach a fork. Keep left as the trail leaves the railroad grade to follow an overgrown forest road. Swamp lilies rise out of a damp spot in the trail. Off to the right you see a nice flat area with a thick carpet of pine needles, a perfect place to pitch a tent. Although there is no water nearby, the woods ferns surrounding the spot are large and healthy. Tiny blooms of yellow-eyed grass rise on tall, slender dark stems. A big chunk of a turpentine pot sits in the footpath, a reminder of the history of this region.

At 0.9 mile the trail narrows down to an almost indiscernible track. Here's where the fun begins. Follow the blazes *very* carefully, always scouting ahead for the next blaze, because you can easily be misled by game trails leading off the overgrown forest road. The footpath is not maintained regularly, and it may be very overgrown when you hike. Keep those blazes in sight! Pushing through dense stands of loblolly bay, the trail opens back up briefly to drop into a boggy grassland. Coated with dew, the bright pink blooms of pale meadow beauty glisten in the morning sun. After 1.2 miles the trail veers steadily to the left. You find yourself pushing through the vegetation, wading through a forest of wax myrtle and bay over your head. Don't lose sight of the blazes! Surrounded by the calls of birds, you look up. A nuthatch clings tightly to the bark of a longleaf pine trunk. Most of the pines around you are too young to be from the turpentine era, but watch for one grand old giant rising 70 feet or more over the forest floor, a silver blaze decorating its side. It's the type of tree a red-cockaded woodpecker would choose for a home. These endangered woodpeckers thrive in the old-growth longleaf pines of Osceola National Forest, with nearly 60 clusters of birds counted in 1999. Several woodpecker nests can be seen near Olustee Battlefield (Hike 12), the trees banded in white to indicate the existence of a nest.

Peering over an unbroken sea of saw palmetto, you notice the subtle dappling of sunlight through the palmetto fronds, the leaves showing variations of color: orange and yellow from drought, shades of green from lime to dark olive, and the creamy tan of dead fronds. At 1.6 miles a bayhead lies to the right of the trail, blending into a cypress dome. Large white blooms decorate the sweetbay magnolias. Where the trail works its way around the dome, swamp lily grows in the footpath. As the trail returns to a more clearly defined forest road, it curves to the left. You walk through an area charred by forest fire, a ghost forest of snags above the live understory. Making a hard left at 1.9 miles, the trail rises up into a damp, open area. Sphagnum moss squishes underfoot. Keep alert as the trail curves to the left at an indistinct fork.

At 2.2 miles you make a sharp right onto an old tramway. Murky sloughs line both sides, their edges lush with woods ferns. A red-tailed hawk launches from a high branch, letting out a mournful cry. Step carefully—there are holes in the footpath from where stumps burned out during the forest fire. Sandhill wireweed dangles its long bottlebrush blooms, and dog banana flaunts thick ivory blossoms. Just as you

Cannas in Big Gum Swamp

push through a stand of young oaks at 2.4 miles, the trail turns left, dropping down off the tramway and into the forest. Turning farther left, it almost doubles back on itself—you can see the pines that define the route of the tramway paralleling you on the left. Winding through a thicket of gallberry, the trail reaches a grassy spot edged with ferns. It curves to the right into a thicket of winged sumac and tall bracken fern. A damp, furry smell wafts across the trail, like the stink of a dog caught in the rain. The bushes rustle as a creature retreats away from the trail—a Florida black bear. The black bear prefers pine flatwoods as its habitat, where it can gobble up berries, dig insects out of rotted logs, and tear open the hearts of saw palmettos. Encounters with this endangered species are rare, but your chances of seeing one in the wilderness increase if you hike in the morning—and walk quietly.

Swamp hyacinth

When you reach the trace of an old forest road, turn right. Exhausted from fighting an overnight storm, a zebra swallowtail lies still on the mat of grass that covers the footpath. Colloquially known as "frog hair"—since it's "as fine as the hair on the belly of a frog"—this grass creates soft thick mats through the pine flatwoods. Off to the left, the croaks of frogs echo from the dark heart of a cypress dome. A little flicker rests in a low branch of a pine. The footpath is well defined through this section: just follow the open corridor. At 3 miles the trail drops down into a marsh along a creek. Tall canna with yellow blooms fills the floodplain, which drains a portion of the Big Gum Swamp. Turn right to follow the creek channel on the edge of the swamp forest. Pond cypresses rise tall above the green needlerush. The forest of sweetgum and cypress is cool and inviting. If the swamp is dry, a hummocky spot covered with pine needles would make a great campsite. Follow the creek past a marshy area, where the huge pinkish-white blooms of swamp hibiscus wave in the breeze. A ground skink slips deep into the pine duff.

As you walk through the broad, open grassy area between the pines, watch for silver blazes to lead you down the correct path since there are many open spaces and crisscrossing game trails. The trail twists and turns between clumps of saw palmetto. You emerge at FR 232 after 3.5 miles. Turn left to walk down the open road, back to where your car is parked. You pass FR 272, which comes in from the left. Old longleaf pines line the road but provide little shade. Around 4 miles, pond cypress and sweetgum crowd close to the road in a cool, wet basin. Startled, a wild turkey bursts into flight, winging its way to the high branches of a longleaf pine. As the road turns a corner, you see your car. You complete your hike after 4.9 miles.

12

Olustee Battlefield Historical State Park

Total distance (circuit): 1.1 miles

Hiking time: 45 minutes

Habitats: Pine flatwoods, scrubby flatwoods, bayheads

Maps: USGS 7½' Olustee, park map

In early 1864 the stage was set. Deep in the Confederate states, Union forces held most of Florida's significant seaports: Fernandina, St. Augustine, Key West, Cedar Keys, and Pensacola. The Union Blockading Squadron sailed up and down the coastlines and into Florida's rivers, crippling maritime commerce, raiding plantations, and breaking up salt-making operations. On February 7, 1864, Gen. Truman A. Seymour landed in Jacksonville with his troops, meeting no resistance from the war-weary city. With him was John Hay, President Lincoln's personal secretary. Despite Florida's secession from the Union in 1861, if Hay could convince at least 7,800 Floridians to sign an oath of allegiance to the Union, he could represent Florida's electoral vote in the upcoming presidential election. Within days of landing, Seymour's troops overran Confederate positions at Camp Finegan and Ten Mile Run, capturing the strategic railroad crossroads at Baldwin. Before contacting his superior officer, Maj. Gen. Quincy Gillmore, Seymour ordered troops to push farther west along the railroad. Their target: the railroad bridge at the confluence of the Suwannee and Withlacoochee Rivers, in Columbus (Hike 1). If they succeeded in destroying the bridge, Tallahassee would be cut off from the rest of the state. But this time—unlike the many other invasions of Florida over the past few years—the Confederacy was ready. Florida had become too valuable, providing a steady stream of desperately needed beef

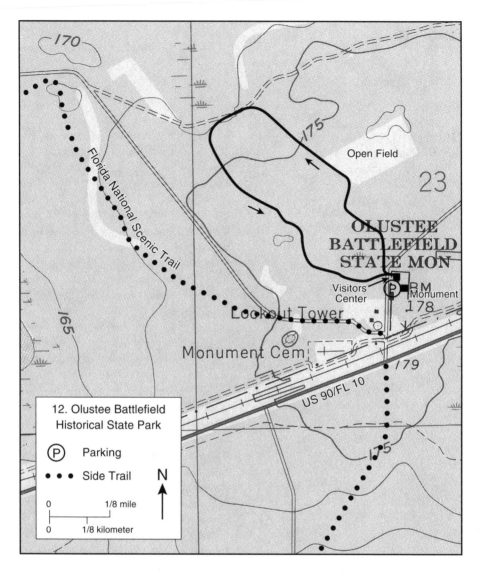

12. Olustee Battlefield
Historical State Park

(P) Parking

• • • Side Trail

N

0   1/8 mile

0   1/8 kilometer

and other provisions to the Confederate Army. Troops gathered near Lake City. Gen. Joseph Finegan, who had ordered his troops to retreat from Jacksonville, chose a defensible spot along the railroad to make their stand, just east of Ocean Pond. On February 20, 1864, Confederate and Union forces met in the pine forests near Olustee.

From I-75 exit 427, Lake City, drive 18.6 miles east on US 90 east to Olustee Battlefield Historical State Park. On the way, you'll enter the Osceola National Forest and pass turnoffs to Olustee Beach (a swimming area on Ocean Pond) and the Ocean Pond Campground. The entrance to the historic site is on the left. If you're traveling on I-10 westbound, use exit 324 and follow US 90 west for 5.5 miles to the park entrance. There is no entrance fee, except during special events.

As you enter the park, you pass a parking area on the left for the Florida National Scenic Trail, which crosses in front of the fire tower. Continue straight and park in front of the interpretive center, either in one of the few parking spots or across the road in the grass. The center is open 9 AM to 5 PM Thursday through Monday and features a 20-minute film on the battle as well as numerous exhibits about Florida's role in the Civil War. Take the time to visit the center before your hike to gain a better understanding of the magnitude of this battle.

The hike through Olustee Battlefield is short, but its historical significance is great. More than two thousand men died in this forest that fateful winter afternoon, casualties of the bloodiest battle on Florida soil. Start directly across the road from the interpretive center, at the kiosk explaining the scene of the battle. Although this is an interpretive trail, it's not like any other in Florida—as you walk around the loop, the signs explain how the battle unfolded. Continue past the kiosk to the first bench and interpretive marker, which marks the start of the loop. Turn right, following the wide, open path (a "barrier-free" trail, accessible to wheelchairs with assistance) into the pine flatwoods. A downy woodpecker swoops past. The rat-a-tat of another woodpecker catches your attention. These tall longleaf pines provide havens for many species of woodpeckers, including the endangered red-cockaded woodpecker. In the surrounding Osceola National Forest, rangers work toward a goal of quadrupling the existing population. Pines with white bands indicate woodpecker nests.

A red arrow on a silver diamond marks the trail route. When you reach the first T intersection, turn left, passing an interpretive marker. Walking through the pines, hearing the whisper of the wind through the treetops, it's hard to imagine this forest as a battlefield. Yet this same expanse, thick with saw palmetto under the tall pines, provided little shelter when the armies met. Off to the right of this side of the trail, the Union troops set up their lines. Behind them was an old open field, broken up by fences, and an impenetrable bayhead that blocked their retreat. In front of them, a marshy pond blocked the advance of the Union troops. Continuing down the broad needle-strewn path, you come to a fork at 0.2 mile. Stay to the left, walking toward the bench. Just before you get to the bench, look up at the pine next to the one with the trail marker; it's growing up through the tangled embrace of a sand live oak. An eastern fence lizard scurries up its jagged bark. Off to the right you can see the open field, kept in the same condition it was when the armies met. The bloodiest charges of the battle, cavalry meeting cavalry, occurred across that patch of open land.

After you pass the bench, you walk across the cross trail through the battlefield, used by reenactors as they ride their horses from their encampment to the open field. Sets of bleachers attest to the interest in watching the annual reenactment. Held the third weekend of February (Friday, Saturday, and Sunday), the Battle of Olustee is the largest Civil War reenactment in the southeastern United States, drawing up to ten thousand participants. Period encampments add living history to the mix.

A stretch of scrubby flatwoods lines the north edge of the field, where prickly pear cacti show off their bright yellow blooms in

The interpretive trail at Olustee Battlefield

spring. Continuing past the field, the trail walks the edge between the scrubby flatwoods and pine flatwoods. Bracken fern fills in a vast open space devoid of saw palmetto. Just beyond the interpretive sign past the open field, the 48th New York lined up in the woods just shy of the bayhead. As the wind picks up, it rattles the saw palmetto fronds, and you hear the clash of bayonets. "Grape and canister swept by with hideous music, and shell after shell tore through our ranks and burst amid heaps of our wounded heroes," wrote a survivor of the 115th New York.

Coming up to a bench at 0.5 mile, the trail turns to the left. Look across the expanse of pines. Even in the middle of the day, you can see a fine mist. Although the chemistry of tree transpiration causes "smokes" and "fogs" in dense deciduous forests, the mist that perpetually hangs in this particular pine forest has an otherworldly feel. Like Gettysburg, this battlefield harbors its own ghosts. A bayhead forms the thick wall of vegetation behind the pines to the right. This dense swamp proved fatal for many, blocking off the soldiers' retreat.

As the trail rounds a curve to the left, it heads along the line of the Confederate positions. The railroad to their backs, they came in from the vicinity of Ocean Pond, where they had built a temporary earthen fortress. When the advance guard of the Union troops met the Confederate scouts in this forest, the earthworks were abandoned, and the Confederates moved forward to meet the Union troops at this point. A small bridge elevates the trail over occasional drainage flows. At 0.9 mile a bench sits at an intersection with a jeep trail from the right. Continue straight toward the next interpretive marker. Blackroot and narrow-leaf pawpaw poke out of the dense pine straw on the forest floor. The delicate bright yellow blooms of a saw palmetto attract the attention of a zebra swallowtail.

Blackjack oaks take over the pines' understory as you approach the cross trail. Continue straight, following the red arrow. Given the age of the pines in this forest, it's interesting that you see no catfaces from the turpentine industry that flourished in this area. The 1899 Florida legislature raised the funds to purchase this land and protect it as a historic site in order to honor the men who died here. As you continue to walk, you can see the flags flying behind the interpretive center, flanking a memorial monument that dates back to 1912. The loop ends at a bench. Turn right to walk back past the kiosk and over to the parking lot, completing your hike of 1.1 miles.

13

Alligator Lake Recreation Area

Total distance (circuit): 6.3 miles

Hiking time: 3 hours

Habitats: Freshwater marsh, floodplain forest, oak hammock, hardwood hammock, prairie

Maps: USGS 7½' Lake City East

For a park smack dab in the middle of Lake City, Alligator Lake Recreation Area packs a powerful amount of hiking into a small space. Restored from an agricultural area to wetlands, this Columbia County park opened in April 2002 with hiking as its primary recreational focus. Visitors can also enjoy the picnic area and playground or launch a canoe or kayak into the wetlands for a close-up view of heron rookeries.

To find the Alligator Lake Recreation Area, take I-75 exit 427, Lake City. Follow US 90 east for 2.4 miles to SW Baya Drive (FL 10A). Turn right. Follow Baya Drive for 2.6 miles, crossing US 41 and US 441 before you reach the traffic light at SE Country Club Road. Turn right and drive 1.2 miles to the park entrance, on the right. The park has limited hours: 11 AM to 7 PM Wednesday through Friday and 8 AM to 7 PM Saturday and Sunday. Stop at the main parking area by the rest rooms to check out the kiosk with its trail map, and then head down to the end of the road, by the canoe launch, to start your hike at the JAMES H. MONTGOMERY TRAIL trailhead sign. A network of trails covers the preserve, open to both hikers and bikers, and is signposted at both ends with an estimated hike time. Color-coded trail signs match the colors on the main map.

Starting out on the Montgomery Trail, the footpath leads through an overgrown meadow, steering you to the shade of the live oaks. Blackberries grow plump and juicy, enticing local families to pick bucketsful in May. Spoil piles rise to the right, cutting off your view of an open pasture. To the

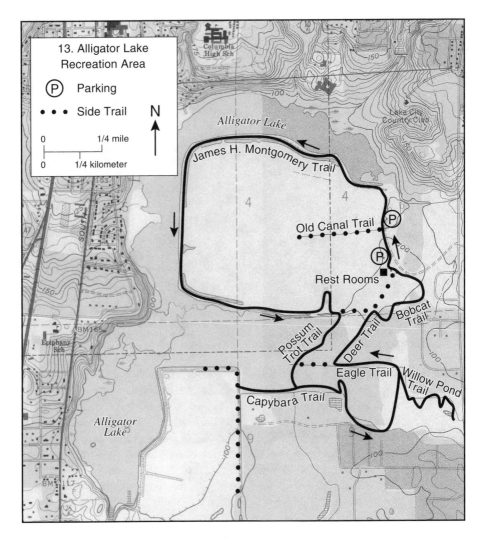

13. Alligator Lake
Recreation Area

P Parking

• • • Side Trail   N

0   1/4 mile

0   1/4 kilometer

Columbia
High Sch

Lake City
Country Club

Alligator Lake

James H. Montgomery Trail

Old Canal Trail   P

P

Rest Rooms

Bobcat
Trail

Possum
Trot Trail

Deer Trail

Eagle Trail   Willow Pond
Trail

Capybara Trail

*Alligator
Lake*

Epiphany
Sch

left is a broad expanse of marsh—the crowning achievement of this preserve, turning the open fields back into their natural habitat. The wading birds appreciate the change. Watch carefully, and you'll see great blue herons poking through the shallows, green herons preening themselves, and snowy egrets fussing over snails. Following the white arrow on a green background, you turn left onto a dike. Look closely at the herons as you approach. The blue heron with a white belly is the Louisiana heron, also known as the tri-colored heron.

Keep alert for movement to the right as a trio of ostriches bobs their heads above the elderberry. Bison and their calves lay in the marsh muck, keeping cool. Both species wander the adjoining private land along Alligator Lake. Trumpet flowers cascade over the Virginia willows growing out the sides of the dike. At 0.5 mile a bridge

Alligator Lake

carries you over the drainage of the marsh into Alligator Lake. An eastern redbud rises from the marsh, cloaked in crimson. Green needlerush crowds against the base of the dike. The marsh is a mirror, reflecting clouds and blue sky in its still water. A coot splashes away with the chatter of a monkey. Off in the distance, you see several islands covered with birds—nesting colonies of cattle egrets. Exploding out of the cattails in tandem, two red-winged blackbirds chase a white heron away from their nesting area; it seeks safety in the high branches of a pond cypress. At 1.1 miles you pass a directional arrow, and the dike starts to curve left to follow the sweep of the marsh, allowing you a better view of the nesting colonies.

As you draw close to the marshy Alligator Lake, cattle egrets squeak and squawk. Watch your head! Overhead, it's a busy flyway for the egrets as they explode out of the marsh grasses to head for their nests. At 1.5 miles a sign on the left says DO NOT LEAVE DIKE. Not that it's possible—unless you want to swim, a bad idea in this prime alligator habitat. Across the water, you see the end of the Old Canal Trail, where cattle egrets cluster in the trees. The exploded soft shells of turtle eggs lie strewn across the path, the slider hatchlings now enjoying life in the marsh. As the dike curves left, the marsh becomes more open. You cross another bridge at 1.8 miles, enjoying the cool breeze across the open water. A cypress swamp parallels the dike after 2 miles. Water the color of café au lait laps at the broad buttresses and knees of bald cypresses. Notice the high water mark on the trees—nearly even with the top of the dike. Virginia willows and red maples shield your view of the marsh on the left. You pass another directional arrow at a broad grassy strip leading down to the marsh on the left. The dike narrows, becoming a slim corridor

Buttonbush

under the shade of bald cypress and cherry laurel, skirting around a floodplain forest of sweetgum, maple, and cypress. Watch on the left for a massive mound of wild roses, their sweet fragrance drifting across the trail.

At 2.5 miles you reach the POSSUM TROT TRAIL sign. Turn right. The Possum Trot Trail follows a faded jeep road through a grassy meadow, weaving between scattered live oaks. A small freshwater marsh fills a borrow pit. After 2.8 miles you reach the junction with the Eagle Trail. It comes in from the left on top of a low dike. Continue straight, crossing a bridge over a small creek. You walk along a fence line, but trees lean over the fence to provide shade. Coming to a T intersection at 2.9 miles, turn right on the Capybara Trail, blazed in black. It's a broad jeep trail that parallels Price Creek and is shaded by sweetgum and hickory. A dry cypress swamp sits off to the left, broad stumps betraying the logging activity of long ago. The creek has that same coffee-with-cream color you've seen before—and as you cross a bridge, you find out why. The creek drains into the cypress swamp you walked by earlier. At the far end of the bridge, you reach another T intersection with a dike. Since neither direction is signposted nor maintained, turn around and head back up the Capybara Trail, back to the junction with

the Possum Trot Trail. Continue straight at the junction, meandering along Price Creek through the shade of the hardwood hammock. As the trail curves to the right, it becomes a dike between the creek and the old cypress swamp. Royal ferns gain a foothold in the crevices of cypress stumps. A forest of bamboo rises tall, putting out tender young shoots. A water oak is caught in a grapevine's embrace. You see houses across the creek, reminding you that you're still in Lake City.

A set of white arrows on black signs catches your attention: The Capybara Trail turns off the dike and drops into a small open prairie. Turn left, walking through the splendor of a variety of grasses, from sand cordgrass and bushybeard bluestem to yellow Indiangrass and sawgrass. At the far end of the prairie, you reach a trail junction at 4.2 miles. Turn right to walk to Willow Pond, ducking into the deep shade of red maple and sweetgum growing along a slough. Startled, several white-tailed deer dash off into the adjacent floodplain forest, zigzagging between scattered clumps of saw palmetto. An Allegheny chinquapin provides a perch for a red-shouldered hawk as it scans for mice. Draped in Spanish moss, a lone sand pine leans across the trail. Underfoot, the trail becomes hummocky. Beware of the small holes that can catch a toe. You start to hear the sounds of traffic. The trail ends within sight of Country Club Road, at 4.6 miles, at the edge of the willow-choked pond. Turn around and retrace your steps back to the trail junction. At the junction, walk straight across to start the Eagle Trail. In the shade of the hardwood hammock, you parallel a dark slough covered in duckweed so thick that sphagnum moss grows atop it. Occasionally the carpet of moss bounces—the movement of a turtle, the flick of an alligator's tail.

At 5.3 miles you reach the DEER TRAIL sign. Turn right. Like the Possum Trot Trail, the Deer Trail follows a faint jeep track through an open meadow with scattered live oaks. As you cross over a slough, you can see a portable classroom up ahead. At the junction with the Bobcat Trail, turn right. An American beautyberry shows off its brilliant purple berries. Following another slough through the woods, you emerge in a grassy area. Turn left to follow the jeep track. Watch for the yellow arrow as the Bobcat Trail quickly turns off the jeep track and curves away on a faint mower track through an open area, headed for a stand of live oaks and southern magnolia. Reaching a fence line, the trail turns left, dropping through a small drainage. An arrow points in the direction from which you came. Turn left to follow a short dike through a hardwood hammock. As you emerge from the forest, you're walking parallel to the park entrance road. You reach the rest rooms and main parking lot at 6.1 miles.

Cross the parking lot and continue past a log cabin with a FUTURE ENVIRONMENTAL EDUCATION CENTER sign. Walking on the edge of the entrance road, you pass the Old Canal Trail. If you have time, wander out on this out-and-back dike; the sign estimates a 30-minute walk, adding an extra mile to your hike. Otherwise, continue straight. You end your hike at the canoe launch, back at your car, after 6.3 miles of hiking.

14

O'Leno State Park

Total distance (2 circuits): 14.4 miles

Hiking time: 7 hours or overnight trip

Habitats: Floodplain forest, hardwood hammock, oak hammock, sandhill, oak scrub, scrubby flatwoods, sinkholes

Maps: USGS 7½' Mikesville, park map

If you've never seen a disappearing river before, O'Leno State Park will fascinate you. Few rivers behave as the Santa Fe does along this hike—it disappears and reappears numerous times through forests underlaid by karst, a type of landscape that forms in any bedrock, such as limestone, that is both porous and permeable. Water seeps into the cracks and crevices, filling up the spaces like a sponge. At River Sink, the Santa Fe River soaks down into the karst but continues to flow south within it, emerging in places as long, thin lakes. Eventually, it reaches River Rise and resumes its aboveground flow. The main hike stitches together a network of trails to lead you along a 13.8-mile route from River Sink to River Rise and back again. A primitive campsite along a quiet lake allows you to make this an overnight trip.

If you're driving northbound on I-75, take exit 399. Follow US 441 north for 5.4 miles to the traffic light at the intersection with US 41 in High Springs. Continue north on US 441/41 for an additional 6.2 miles, passing the gated entrance to River Rise Preserve State Park. Turn right at the O'Leno State Park sign, and then right again into the park entrance road. Southbound drivers should use I-75 exit 414. Follow US 441/41 south, passing CR 18 (the turnoff for Hike 15, Ichetucknee Springs) after 4.5 miles. After another 0.5 mile, turn left at the O'Leno State Park sign. Follow SE Sprite Loop for 0.7 mile, turning left into the park entrance road.

If you plan to backpack this hike, alert

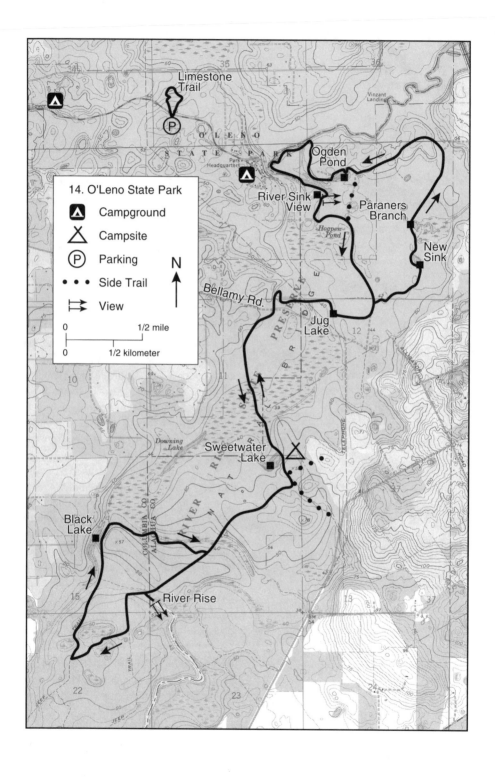

Limestone
Trail

O'LENO

STATE · · · PARK

Park
Headquarters

Ogden
Pond

Vinzant
Landing

River Sink
View

Paraners
Branch

Hogpen
Pond

New
Sink

14. O'Leno State Park

▲ Campground

△ Campsite

Ⓟ Parking

••• Side Trail

⇥ View

N

| 0 | 1/2 mile |
| 0 | 1/2 kilometer |

Bellamy Rd.

Jug
Lake

PRESERVE

Downing
Lake

Sweetwater
Lake

RIVER

NATURE

BRIDGE

TELEPHONE

Black
Lake

COLUMBIA CO.
ALACHUA CO.

River Rise

BM
54

JEEP

TRAIL

the ranger at the entrance so you can pick up a permit for the primitive campground. Ask for a map of the hiking trails. After you stop at the ranger station and pay your Florida State Parks day-use fee, continue down the entrance road. You'll pass the Dogwood Campground on the left. The 1.4-mile linear Dogwood Trail meanders through deep forest to connect the campground to the river and is primarily used by campers.

Stop and park for a quick stroll down the Limestone Trail, which starts across the road from a small parking spot where the Dogwood Trail crosses the entrance road. It takes 15 minutes to walk this 0.6-mile trail, which winds through a representative section of the sort of hardwood hammock you'll see along the longer hiking route—dark and leafy, strewn with pignuts and sweetgum balls. The limestone boulders in the forest and chunks of rock in the footpath are part of the karst landscape. As you come up to the edge of a large sinkhole, watch for a limestone overhang at the RESTRICTED AREA BOUNDARY sign. Below it, you can see the smooth walls of a small quarry, where settlers once carved out limestone blocks for their buildings and fireplaces. As the trail curves right, away from the sinkhole, it loops back around past a smaller sinkhole and under large dogwood trees, which show off their white blossoms in March. After you complete the loop, turn left and cross the road to reach your car.

At 2.6 miles down the entrance road, you reach the parking lot for the swimming area and the turnoff for the Magnolia Campground. The two campgrounds contain a total of 64 spaces, and 17 cabins are nestled along the river, a stone-and-log legacy of the 1930s Civilian Conservation Corps, which managed what's now the group camping area as a summer forestry

camp and training center. This is one of only nine parks in Florida where the CCC performed its great feats of engineering—not just the cabins, but also the long suspension bridge over the Santa Fe River. The site of the camp was once the frontier town of Keno, established in the mid-1800s. Settlers came this way because the breaks in the river afforded them a natural bridge to head west. As the logging industry grew, so did the town of Keno. Its name changed to Leno, and it became the terminus of the first telegraph line in Florida. But when the new railroad came into the area, it bypassed Leno. Businesses moved to be closer to the railroad, and the town faded away, vanishing by the early 1900s.

From the end of the parking area, follow the bark-chip path past the warning sign about alligators in the river, past the rest rooms and downhill into the picnic area. Turn right to walk the bluff along the Santa Fe River. When you reach the swinging suspension bridge, continue straight, following the River Trail. At times of low flow, the river appears to be a jumble of rocks and grass with scattered puddles, but belowground, in the karst, it continues to flow. You walk past the group campground with its frontier-style log buildings. At the trail intersection a WIRE ROAD sign points to the right. Continue straight, following the River Trail down to River Sink. Peer closely at the tannic water, and you'll see white circles where water bubbles up from springs near the far shore. Although stairs lead to the water's edge, a sign warns NO SWIMMING. Pause at the observation deck to look out over the shallows, watching river cooters crowded on fallen logs at the base of the floodplain levee filled with cypresses.

A second observation deck provides a sweeping view of river sink, where the river simply ends. Water hyacinths float across

River Rise in River Rise Preserve State Park

its placid surface, giving no clue as to where the river goes. Following the edge of the sink, the trail comes up to a short fence. If you continue straight, you can walk down a series of boardwalks above the deep floodplain channels of the river—best done when the water is high. That section of the trail continues on to form a 1.5-mile loop back to the suspension bridge. You'll be using part of that loop on your return trip. For now, turn right, following the jeep trail behind the fence down to Wire Road. Paralleling a floodplain channel, the trail crosses it and turns left to parallel the channel downstream. The jeep trail merges into another one coming in from the left. Continue straight. When you meet Wire Road at the T intersection, turn left, passing Bench 8. Keep alert for bikers, who share these broad old forest roads. Crossing a bridge over a cypress-lined floodplain chan-

nel, Wire Road rises up into sandhills. The trail becomes open and sunny, with little shade. Keep alert for yellow footprints on brown posts, which mark the trail routes. You walk past clear-cut areas, the pines victims of Southern pine beetle infestation. After you pass Bench 7, sand live oaks provide tiny snatches of shade. When you see the PARANERS BRANCH TRAIL sign, watch for the next forest road on the right. Turn right. At Bench 6 you emerge at a trail junction, where the east side of the Paraners Branch Trail comes in. You've hiked 1.7 miles. Turn right at the trail mileage sign to follow a narrow path into scrubby flatwoods, walking through tiny stretches of scrub. Scattered pieces of limestone surround reindeer lichen like a rock garden, where prickly pear cacti display their bright yellow blooms. Streamers of old man's beard dangle from sand live oaks. The trail winds to the left and enters an oak and pine hammock along the edge of a cypress floodplain. Off to the right is Jug Lake—a long, narrow karst window providing your first peek into the underground flow of the Santa Fe River. Massive reddish limestone slabs sit at the bases of grand old cypresses, whose tall forms reflect in the inky water. You see swirls of oily water at both ends of the lake, where the river sinks and rises. If you step to the edge of the lake, you'll notice the water is dark but clear.

The trail rises away from Jug Lake through a stand of tall loblolly pines, entering a dense hardwood hammock. The footpath narrows, winding between clumps of saw palmetto. You cross another floodplain forest and see more channels to the left—an unusual sight in the middle of the forest. Each of these marks a place where the Santa Fe River can rise up through the ground in times of high water. Climbing up into an oak scrub, the trail meets Bellamy Road at 2.3 miles. This sand path was a wagon trail, the original road used by settlers to cross this broad natural bridge over the Santa Fe River. Continue straight across into the hardwood hammock. You emerge into the bright sun of scrubby flatwoods, the understory a thick oak scrub. The trail curves to the left down a corridor edged by slender loblolly pines. Walking through the pine forest, watch your step—roots make the trail rough in places. As you skirt the edge of another floodplain forest, cypress knees poke out of the footpath. The trail plunges into a dark hardwood hammock, the ironwoods covered in lichens, the bases of bluff oaks fuzzy with mosses. Dark black earth forms the footpath. You rise up through a grassy area, skirting boulders in the trail, including one smoothly scalloped slab of chert, a form of limestone used for flint-knapping. Passing an outhouse, you

come to a clearing with boulders scattered around a fire ring and a sweeping view of a lake—the Sweetwater primitive campsite, at 3.5 miles. If you're spending the night, pitch your tent here and leave the bulk of your gear behind before heading down the trail to River Rise. Steps lead down to the edge of Sweetwater Lake, another emergence of the Santa Fe River. Take a moment to enjoy the view, but be mindful of alligators—no swimming is allowed. A large Florida softshell turtle paddles past, poking its snout out of the duckweed.

As you leave the campsite, the trail becomes broader, meandering through a shady hardwood hammock. A red fox leaps over a fallen log, disappearing into the dense forest. Passing the back side of a sign, you come to a loop trail leading both forward and left, blazed as a horse trail with yellow diamonds but shared with hikers and bikers. Continue straight, walking through a more open forest. At the next trail junction the horse trail goes straight. Turn right to continue to River Rise on a forest road shared with horses and bikers. Mounds parallel the road, covered in thick forest growth. The dark hardwood hammock yields to floodplain forest as the trail becomes a causeway between the cypresses. Notice an important difference between these floodplain forests and the ones you see along Florida's rivers: There are no air plants. These cypresses flourish only because their roots are tapping into the water flowing through the karst, out of sight. The lack of standing water on the surface means there is less humidity in the forest, leading to an absence of epiphytes.

At 4.6 miles you reach a junction with the Black Lake Trail coming in from the right. This will be your return route on the loop through River Rise Preserve State Park. Continue straight, walking through an oak hammock with a high canopy. The trail curves off to the right, and you pass the back of a hiker-symbol sign before coming to a T intersection with a bench off to the left. Turn left. Walk around the low fence, following the trail down to the water—River Rise, at 5.2 miles. As you approach the emergence of the Santa Fe River, it's like walking to the edge of a large lake—spectacular because of the river's sudden appearance in a broad, clear sweep, with no sign of a spring boil. The limestone perches make a pleasant place for a picnic, but no camping is permitted along the River Rise. Sun shimmers on the waves pushed by the wind across the water. A little blue heron picks through the pennywort in the shallows. A solution hole sits off to the left, like a natural well at the base of the trail. From here the river flows down to High Springs, eventually pouring into the Suwannee River. Poke around the rocky walls on the left, and you'll find another solution hole, thickly coated in duckweed.

Turn around and retrace your steps back to the trail junction at the last bench. Continue straight, walking through more hardwood hammock on the shaded forest road. Keep alert, and you'll notice many sinkholes along the trail. Standing in the middle of the road, a white-tailed deer pauses and stares before it takes off into the forest. At 6.1 miles you come to a sign with a horse symbol and the word *barn* under it. Turn right, walking around a cable gate to follow a forest road toward Black Lake. The shady hardwood hammock parallels an expanse of cypress swamp, where cypress knees grow in thick clusters around the towering bald cypresses. As the trail curves right, it rises away from the floodplain into an upland hardwood forest of elm and ironwood, laurel oak and southern magnolia. A fallen tree blocks the road, but hik-

ers have trampled a permanent path around it on the left. The path pops out onto the spur trail down to Black Lake. Walk down to the water's edge. Oddly enough, Black Lake is less dark than the other karst windows along the Santa Fe River. Healthy, dense mats of aquatic plants drift across its surface. A young alligator cruises past, its eyes and snout barely above the surface of the water. As it moves, small fish leap out of the lake, shimmering in the sun.

Walking back up the spur trail, you immediately reach the trailhead of the Black Lake Trail on the other side of the forest road. Continue straight. Following the Black Lake Trail requires constant vigilance. The faint footpath is often obscured by a fresh fall of leaves and needles, and many of the trail markers, the short brown posts with yellow footprints, have rotted away or fallen over. Keep alert to the many twists and turns, confirming the route with the trail markers. Fallen logs and branches can throw you off the right track. Curving around a large patch of saw palmetto, the trail emerges into an area with many tall loblolly pines. Stay along the edge of the open understory, following the saw palmetto. As you drop down toward a floodplain forest, another footprint blaze indicates a right turn to follow the upper edge of a channel. Swamp chestnut oaks tower overhead, and several deer gather around a waterhole in the floodplain. A massive southern magnolia drops leaves covered in a pattern like polished burled wood, outlined in deep dark brown. As you pass a rotted log, the trail becomes hard to find. Keep toward the edge of the floodplain until you find the footpath. Royal ferns grow at the bases of cypresses. Watch for when the trail swings to the right, climbing up into a corridor through scrubby flatwoods, the footpath becoming sandy underfoot.

At 7.9 miles the Black Lake Trail ends at a

T intersection on the road to River Rise. Turn left to retrace your path back up to Sweetwater Lake. At the next T intersection you see a sign, O'LENO 3.2 MILES, pointing to the left. Don't believe it—your return route is longer. Turn left, passing the horse-trail loop on your right before you enter the clearing at the primitive campsite. Take a moment to pause and relax, enjoying the cool breeze off the lake before pressing on. All of the footprint markers along the next section of trail face the opposite direction, so keep alert to the twists and turns of the footpath. At 10.2 miles you cross Bellamy Road. At 10.7 miles you reach Jug Lake. The trail curves around it to the left, emerging back out at a jeep road. Turn left. You're back at the bottom of the loop at the north end of the park. Take the right fork (you came in on the left fork) to hike the eastern side of the Paraners Branch Trail loop. At the next forest road intersection you cross Wire Road. Continue straight. Hardwood hammock yields to scrubby flatwoods and sandhills as the trail curves toward the east. You reach Jim Sink, a duckweed-covered sinkhole with a small patch of open water beneath a towering bald cypress. A side trail leads down a bluff to an open view across the water. Continue along Paraners Branch Trail, passing a squared-off borrow pit on the left. The cones of button snakeroot poke out of the pine straw beneath the loblolly pines. The Timucua used the leaves of this member of the carrot family to treat dysentery; chewing on the leaf increases saliva flow.

Dropping down into another area of sinks, you see water-filled New Sink, with a short trail leading down to it. Limestone boulders frame its edges. A banded water snake works its way across the duckweed. Your last view into a karst window on the Santa Fe River is at 11.6 miles, at Paraners Branch, the river's first emergence

south of River Sink. Pond cypresses line the far shore of this lake, many with cypress knees rising up to 4 feet tall. Sit down and relax on Bench 4, admiring the sparkling clear water, before you continue along the trail. After meandering through the dense hardwood hammock, the trail eventually enters a mile-long stretch of oak hammock dominated by laurel oaks. You pass a jeep trail leading off to the right. At Bench 3 another jeep trail leads to the right. Continue straight. At Bench 2 a trail comes in from the left. Continue straight, walking along the edge of the sandhills. Turkey oaks shade the candle-stage growth of young longleaf pines.

After 12.8 miles you come to another PARANERS BRANCH TRAIL sign. You've reached the north end of this trail's loop. Turn right. As you pass Ogden Lake, take the time to look for waterfowl—little blue herons hang out here, stalking frogs through the water hyacinths. Watch the water closely, and you'll probably see a small alligator or two. At the RIVER TRAIL sign, turn right for a pleasant walk through the shade of the hardwood hammock. You pass a spur trail to the left, leading down to another segment of the river sink, and round a floodplain forest before emerging along the edge of the regenerating sandhills. The trail turns to the left, crossing a bridge over a side channel. Sparkleberry grows lushly along the river basin. Pignut hickory towers overhead. The trail parallels a natural levee hosting a floodplain forest of cypresses. Since there are few plants in the understory, you have a nice view of the Santa Fe River. As the trail curves to the left, you see the suspension bridge. Turn right and cross it. Follow the pathway back past the swimming area, up between the picnic tables and past the rest room to the parking lot, completing your 13.8-mile hike.

15

Ichetucknee Springs State Park

Total distance (round-trip and circuit): 4.0 miles

Hiking time: 2.5 hours

Habitats: Hardwood hammock, floodplain forest, springs, sandhills

Maps: USGS 7½' Hildreth, park map

Deep beneath thick limestone karst, waters flow. The contents of Cannon Creek, Clay Hole, and Rose Creek vanish underground, dropping into sinkholes to merge together in a network of caverns. Natural hydraulic pressure pushes the water along, and it emerges in one of the state's most stunning springs: Ichetucknee, where the spring vent glows an ethereal robin's-egg blue, and the clear waters flow away to create one of Florida's most popular tubing destinations, Ichetucknee Run.

Tucked away outside the small community of Fort White, Ichetucknee Springs State Park is a popular summer weekend destination. To approach the park from the north, take I-75 exit 414, Lake City/High Springs. Drive south on US 41/441 for 4.3 miles. Turn right at CR 18, at the ICHETUCKNEE SPRINGS sign. (Hike 14, O'Leno State Park, lies straight ahead on US 41/441.) After 6.4 miles you reach a stop sign at US 27. Turn right, entering Fort White.

If you're driving northbound on I-75, take exit 399, Alachua/High Springs. Turn north on US 441 and drive 15 miles. As the highway narrows and swings right into High Springs, turn left at a TO US 27 sign. This 0.6-mile connector takes you to a traffic light in downtown High Springs, intersecting with US 27. Cross the intersection. After 2.5 miles you pass River Rise Preserve State Park (part of Hike 14). Continue another 7.5 miles to First Street in downtown Fort White.

At the intersection of US 27 and First Street (FL 47), turn right. Drive 2.2 miles,

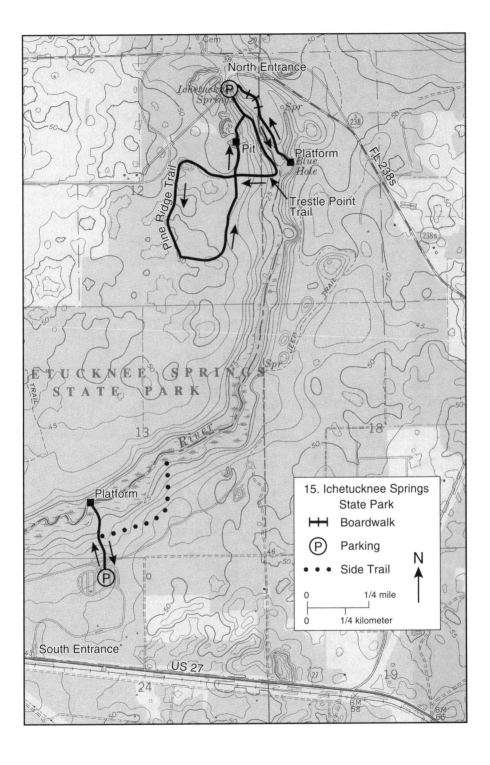

North Entrance

Ichetucknee
Spring

Spr

S
238

FL 238s

Pit

Platform
Blue
Hole

Pine Ridge Trail

Trestle Point
Trail

12

TRAIL

ETUCKNEE SPRINGS
STATE PARK

Spr

JEEP

TRAIL

45

50

238s

50

45

13

River

18

50

Platform

46
50

55

P

50

South Entrance

US 27

27

19

24

BM
58

BM
66

50

50

15. Ichetucknee Springs
State Park

⊢⊢ Boardwalk

Ⓟ   Parking

● ● ●   Side Trail

N

0   1/4 mile

0   1/4 kilometer

and then turn left on CR 238. If you're considering tubing after your hike, grab a rental tube (average price of $2) from one of the many roadside vendors, who pick up their tubes after your float from a corral at the south end of the run. Continue another 3.7 miles to the state park's north entrance, on the left. As you pay your Florida State Parks entry fee, ask the ranger for a trail map. It contains the interpretive brochure corresponding to the markers on the main loop trail. Drive to the far end of the parking lot, parking near the TO LAUNCH, HEAD SPRINGS, NATURE TRAIL sign.

Your hike starts at the BLUE HOLE SPRING sign. This 1-mile round-trip trail leads you to a deep spring that serves as one of the park's two natural swimming holes. Starting out on a boardwalk that crosses a floodplain forest, the trail meets a T intersection with a jeep trail. Turn right. There's a healthy growth of poison ivy on the forest floor, so stick to the footpath. In the spring, look for sandspur, showing off a reddish flower not unlike a small trillium, and coral bean, with its bright red blooms towering well above the forest floor. A thick canopy of hickory, elm, sweetgum, southern magnolia, red maple, and deerberry shades the trail. Dense growths of vines choke the understory. Off to the right you catch a glimpse of a narrow stream run, half covered in duckweed. The woods are alive with birdsong in the morning; a pileated woodpecker drums in the distance.

After you pass a bench, a narrow side trail on the right leads down to Ichetucknee Run. Picking your way over the roots and rocks, you pause at the edge of the run. Cypress knees rise out of the crystal-clear water, which teems with the activity of tiny fish. Tapegrass waves with the current. The swirls and whorls of water bugs make the water's surface shimmer like liquid glass.

Returning to the main trail, turn right. Another short side trail to the right leads to bent and twisted oak tree with unusually large gall and a thick undergrowth of cinnamon ferns beneath it. Deer trails lead in all directions along the spring run. As you continue on the main trail, you see the glimmer of water and a boardwalk up ahead. Keep alert for a small side trail leading off to the left that gives you an up-close view of a small spring run flowing from Cedar Head Spring into Blue Hole Spring. A small mud turtle floats on the bottom amid a cloud of decaying leaves, basking in a spotlight of sun. As the leaves part, you see a shimmer of white sand underneath.

At 0.5 mile the short boardwalk ends at a swimming platform for Blue Hole Spring. Notice how the water welling up from the deep vent makes the smooth surface of the swimming hole bulge. Watch shellcrackers and bluegill drift by, suspended in their aquatic garden of waving tapegrass. A fence at the far end of the run keeps swimmers in and tubers out; between October 1 and March 31, registered cave divers are permitted to explore the spring vent and its network of water-filled caverns. Turn around and retrace your steps along the trail. Southern red cedars shed streamers of shaggy bark. When you reach the trail intersection with the boardwalk, turn right. Titi grows in this floodplain basin, showing off its bottlebrush blooms. At the end of the boardwalk, turn left and head down past the picnic tables and rest rooms to the NATURE TRAILS sign. Take a moment to wander down the stone stairs to the park's showcase attraction, Ichetucknee Spring. Your first glimpse will take your breath away as you admire the chalky blue color of the spring vent. Unfortunately, this is considered one of Florida's most endangered springs. In karst, everything is interconnected under

Ichetucknee Spring

the ground. The Sierra Club has not been able to convince the Florida legislature to revoke a permit for a new mining operation nearby, despite the danger that blasting in the mine could change the underground water flow in this region, potentially drying up this beautiful spring forever.

Continuing past a state park map sign after 1 mile, walk down a stone walkway past the spring and into the forest. A gigantic southern magnolia looms to the right, shading your path as you walk past the spring. Large boulders lie scattered along the trail, a reminder of the karst beneath your feet. The red trumpet flowers of the cross vine rain down from the forest canopy. When you reach a fork, keep left, staying with the broader trail. At the second fork, note the signs: TUBE LAUNCH to the left, NATURE TRAIL straight ahead. Take a moment to walk down and see the tube launch. Tubers start here in the 72-degree water, floating down the narrow run.

Back at the top of the boardwalk, turn left. A short path leads over to the start of the nature trail, past some canoes stored off to right. Turn left, walking past a kiosk with information about aquatic plants and the sandhill habitat. At 1.2 miles you come to the trailhead sign and map for the Trestle Point Trail. Turn left, following the white blazes along the spring run, atop a terraced bluff. At Marker 2 you get a nice view of the stream down a short spur trail to the left. The footpath becomes a narrow corridor between tall cinnamon ferns, with frequent exposures of bare limestone. After you pass another overlook the trail curves right, around a large bowl of floodplain forest along the run. At 1.5 miles you're across from Blue Hole Spring; listen for the sounds of splashing bathers in the chilly water. Don't be surprised to see the gnawed remains of slender tree trunks along the

water's edge. Few people associate beavers with Florida, but visitors report sightings of both beavers and otters along the run. Ichetucknee Run may be the southernmost extent of their habitat; the name "Ichetucknee" means "Pond of the Beaver."

When you come to a T intersection, turn left to walk down to the water's edge. Two benches flank Trestle Point, where a railroad line ran in the early 1900s from nearby phosphate mines to the main line, crossing the run at this point. Look carefully at the far side of the run. Ironwood trees balance carefully off the tops of deeply scoured solution holes, natural pipes leading from the forest floor into the stream, formed by the erosion of limestone into karst. Duck down, and you can look up into the largest solution hole to see how water has carved the rock. Turning around, walk back past the trail junction and continue down the broad, straight trail—the old rail line for the phosphate mine. You're headed straight to the mines. A yellow pine and a tall dogwood grow across from a towering southern magnolia, dwarfed by the shade of a hickory rising more than 60 feet tall.

At 1.7 miles you reach another trail junction. The Trestle Point Trail turns right, leading back to Ichetucknee Spring; the Pine Ridge Loop starts straight ahead. Continue straight, crossing a service road and walking past a NATURE TRAIL sign. Longleaf pines and cedars are scattered amid this hardwood forest. The shady forest closes in tightly on the trail as you pass a footprint marker—the blazing for this trail. Passing a fresh sinkhole, you reach a fork. Stay to the right. You won't miss the mining bucket, used on a steam shovel to excavate phosphate ore. With a tree growing through its maw, it's an unexpected sight. A bench perches on the edge of the adjoining phosphate pit, a former part of the mining operation. Florida's phosphate boom started in the late 1890s, just after a big freeze killed off the commercial citrus industry. This pit and several others scattered throughout the park are the remnants of a commercial open-pit mining operation that ran during the early 1900s. The early boom went bust during World War I, when the European countries that relied on Florida's phosphate could no longer ship it safely. Decades later, large-scale open-pit mining rebounded, ranking Florida as one of the nation's top states in mining production.

The trail turns to the left and goes up a small set of stairs, wandering along the edge of the phosphate pit. It's a long, rectangular pit with squared-off edges that make it obvious that it's not just a sinkhole in this land of karst. From this vantage point you get the perspective of the impressive length of the pit, now filled in with forest. Hardwood hammock yields to sandhill as you continue along. Emerging into full sun, you traverse the sandhills, with wiregrass so thick and lush it looks like a mist between the scattered oaks and longleaf pines. A lizard with black stripes and an aquamarine tail zips across the trail: the southeastern five-lined skink. Brilliant blooms peep out of the grass: butterfly pea, daisy fleabane, and roserush. Watch for the shadow cast by an American kestrel in flight. Marker 9 points out a kestrel nesting box high in a longleaf pine, in constant use since 1994. Kestrels normally nest in abandoned woodpecker cavities, but there are few snags in this sandhill that suit that purpose.

As you meander through the open sandhill, you see many wildflowers. Roseling, an herb found only in Florida, lifts its fragile three-petaled pink blooms above grasslike leaves. The slim flowers of slender beard tongue point in many directions from its tall hairy stem. The trail turns left, back toward the hardwood hammock, as it passes woodlands phlox thick with pink blooms and small Allegheny chinquapins—saplings with thick, deeply ribbed leaves and soft fluffy flowers like white tails. Passing a bench marking the ecotone transition at 2.4 miles, you enter the cool shade of a hickory grove, wandering into an oak hammock that has taken over the sandhills as the climax forest. Redheaded and gold bodied, a massive broadhead skink dashes under a fallen log. Several white-tailed deer race into the hardwood forest. You come to a fork. The left fork is a spur trail that leads to Marker 13, a catfaced pine from the turpentining era. Continue along the right fork, walking under a large post oak. At the T intersection you complete the Pine Ridge Loop after 2.8 miles. Turn right. White jelly fungi spill out of a crevice in a laurel oak's trunk. Cross the service road. At the junction with the Trestle Point Trail, turn left.

After 3 miles you come to a T intersection. A sign—OVERLOOK—points to the left. Turn left and walk down the spur trail to a bench overlooking a deep phosphate pit filled with a bounty of trees and ferns, from longleaf pines rising up to 70 feet tall to immense stands of Hercules'-club. These unusual members of the lime family have compound, fernlike clusters of leaves—looking down on them, they seem to be arranged in a square pattern. Returning to the T intersection, continue straight. A side trail under a dogwood tree leads to another view of the pit from the north end. A redheaded woodpecker picks at a laurel oak, grubbing for insects. The loop ends at a sign, TRAIL'S END, at the map. Turn left, retracing your walk past the informational kiosks and outdoor classroom. Take the left fork of the two forest paths to walk past the tubing-put in toward the main spring. With one last peek at Ichetucknee Spring, wrap up your hike at the parking lot, completing a 3.4-mile loop.

Although there are no official hiking trails at the south end of Ichetucknee Springs State Park, your chances of seeing river otters increases dramatically if you take a trip down to the south entrance. To drive to the south entrance (no footpath connects the two ends of the park—yet), turn right out of the north entrance and drive 3.7 miles to FL 47. Turn right and continue 2.2 miles to US 27 in Fort White. Turn right at the stoplight and drive another 4.4 miles. The park entrance is on the right. Be sure to show your receipt (which should be taped to your windshield) so you are not asked to pay another entrance fee. Park in front of the visitors center and walk through it to access a 0.6-mile round-trip paved path. Past the rest rooms and into the forest, the trail passes a turnoff to the Mid-Point Takeout. Open only during tubing season, this 1-mile round-trip trail affords tubers access to the run and allows hikers a chance to wander through the hardwood hammock to another scenic view. The trail you are following turns into a boardwalk leading to Dampier's Landing and ends at a swimming platform on the run. Stately cypresses line the crystal-clear water. Watch the tapegrass wave on the bottom like an impressionist painting. From the far end of the swimming platform you can see Devil's Den, an unusual karst formation along a bend in the river, where a perfectly round solution hole cuts down through the rocky cliffs into an open cave below. Keep alert for the shimmering form of a river otter, its long, sleek body following the edge of the shore as it searches for food.

If you'd like to try a float trip down the Ichetucknee, it takes about three hours. Tubing season runs from May 1 through early September. Arrive early on weekends—no more than 750 people are allowed on the run each day. Visitors may snorkel in the northern part of the run between Memorial Day and Labor Day. Canoeing is encouraged year-round, but it is best to go on weekdays or during the off-season to avoid collisions with tubers. During the summer tubing season, park employees will shuttle you from the south entrance to the north entrance. Rental canoes are available at the north end of the park.

16

Devil's Millhopper Geological State Park

Total distance (circuit): 0.9 mile

Hiking time: 45 minutes

Habitats: Hardwood hammock, oak scrub, sandhill, ravines, sinkhole, freshwater marsh

Maps: USGS 7½' Gainesville West, park map

Ancient tribes feared it. In the 1890s tourists climbed down its steep slopes to pose for pictures. Today, you can immerse yourself in it, walking down a series of landings connecting 232 steps to the very bottom. Surrounded by waterfalls cascading behind thick foliage, you feel like you've stepped into the Amazon. But it's a just a quirk of geology, one of Florida's most fascinating sinkholes–the Devil's Millhopper.

As one of only two state parks dedicated to geological exploration, Devil's Millhopper Geological State Park provides a short hike that's long on scenery. Sitting in the middle of suburban Gainesville, Devil's Millhopper is but one of thousands of sinkholes in a thick belt of karst running through the Central Highlands, a landscape formed by the steady erosion of limestone bedrock by acidic rainwater trickling down to the Floridan Aquifer. However, this sinkhole is a whopper–500 feet across and 120 feet deep–with a profound affect on the forests surrounding it.

To drive to Devil's Millhopper Geological State Park, take I-75 exit 390, Gainesville, and head east into Gainesville on FL 222 for 3.4 miles. Turn left at the traffic light for NW 43rd Street. Drive 1 mile to NW 53rd Ave (Millhopper Road) and turn left. Within 0.3 mile the park entrance is on the right. Drop your Florida State Parks fee in the self-pay station before hitting the trail. A paved path leads from the parking lot to the visitors center. If you arrive on a Saturday morning, plan to take a guided tour with the resident ranger at 10 AM. Otherwise, you're on your own. Pick up information sheets and a map at the visitors center, and take the time to watch the short movie that explains the history and geology of this massive sinkhole.

The hiking trail starts at the back of the visitors center, near the rest rooms. Pavement quickly yields to a hard sand path winding through scattered limestone boulders. Florida violets peep out of drifts of oak leaves; poison ivy climbs up the trunk of a loblolly pine. A gray squirrel sits in the shade of a pignut hickory, nibbling on an enormous double-hulled nut. When you reach the T intersection at the lip of the sinkhole, turn right. You can hear the sound of water splashing and voices carrying from far below. Only in winter and early spring can you actually see visitors clambering down the stairs—the deciduous trees are quick to put on their new sets of leaves, shading the sinkhole from view. The trail circles around the sinkhole into the sandhills, passing behind a housing development and a communications tower. Many of the larger loblolly pines lay fallen, victims of the southern pine beetle. Sand live oaks cluster around a small patch of oak scrub, where you see the dark shiny green leaves of a silk bay tree. Look underneath for confirmation— the leaves have silky-haired red undersides. If you crush one, it emits the strong aromatic smell of bay leaves used in Italian cooking. This tree is a close relative of the red bay but grows only in Florida's scrub.

As you continue to circle the sinkhole, you reach a bridge at 0.5 mile. It spans a ravine that looks like it's been dropped here out of the Appalachian Mountains, with a rocky stream flowing downhill into the sinkhole. The trail crosses the bridge, turning left to follow the edge of the ravine. You emerge in a clearing, with a staircase leading down into the sinkhole to your left. It's a

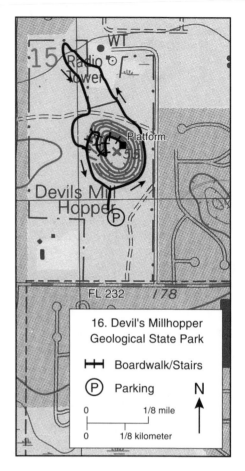

16. Devil's Millhopper
Geological State Park

⊢⊣ Boardwalk/Stairs

Ⓟ Parking

N

0   1/8 mile

0   1/8 kilometer

strenuous climb down and back but one you shouldn't miss. Turn left and start down the staircase, which was completed in 1976. An earlier version existed in the 1930s, but visitors persisted in climbing down the slopes, which damaged the fragile vegetation, until the land became a state park in 1974. To your left, the stream trickles down out of the ravine, forming waterfalls that vanish under limestone boulders and reappear, momentarily, before vanishing again. You hear a constant echo, the rush of water under the rock. As you reach the third landing, look off to the right to see a tall cascade dropping into the sinkhole. The sound

Staircase into Devil's Millhopper

of water echoes off the rocks as it tumbles down the sinkhole's steep slopes. Tiny springs feed this constant flow, fed by groundwater trapped above a clay cap in the forest. The sinkhole cuts through the cap. As the water trickles across buried limestone sheets, it emerges at the edges of the sinkhole and flows down the walls in numerous cascades.

Reaching the bottom, you go across a boardwalk past a cool hollow on the left with exposed moss-covered rocks, where a steady torrent flows down, down, down into the marsh at the very base of the sinkhole. Since the swallow hole is ringed by Virginia willow, it's tough to see—but rest assured, all of this water keeps flowing downward into the natural plumbing system of the karst, ending up in the Floridan Aquifer. This cool, damp environment encourages unusual plants to thrive down here, such as cutleaf spleenwort, jack-in-the-pulpit, and wakerobin, a variety of trillium with deep ma-

roon blooms in late winter. The boardwalk comes to an end at a platform overlooking the swampy bottom of the sinkhole, with a cluster of needle palms growing above you on the slope. These hardy palms are distinguished from saw palmetto by their more delicate fronds that do not join together like a fan at the stem. Preferring surface limestone and floodplain forests, the needle palm is right at home in this habitat. It's thought to be one of the world's most cold-hardy palms, surviving brief temperature drops down to -20 degrees.

Take your time as you climb back up the stairs, resting on the landings to catch your breath and take in the view. When you reach the top, turn left. A scenic overlook lets you get one last look down into the Devil's Millhopper before you depart. As you complete the loop, you come to the trail junction. Turn right to walk past the visitors center and back out to the parking lot, completing your 0.9-mile walk.

17

San Felasco Hammock Preserve State Park

Total distance (3 circuits): 12.2 miles

Hiking time: 6 hours

Habitats: Sandhills, hardwood hammock, ravines, freshwater marsh, sinkholes

Maps: USGS 7½' Gainesville West, park map

Just up the road from Devil's Millhopper, the San Felasco Hammock Preserve State Park provides another look at north Florida's fabulous karst landscapes with two separate hikes that dip past sinkholes and follow disappearing streams. South of Millhopper Road, a 1.5-mile nature trail winds around several broad sinkholes, paralleling Moonshine Creek through a lush hardwood forest full of unusual species of plants. North of Millhopper Road, two longer loops allow hikers to put in some miles while enjoying the rolling karst hills.

From I-75 take Gainesville exit 390 and head east into Gainesville on FL 222 for 3.4 miles. Turn left at the traffic light for NW 43rd Street. Drive 1 mile to NW 53rd Avenue (Millhopper Road) and turn left. You'll pass the Devil's Millhopper Geological State Park (Hike 16) as you drive 4.5 miles to the small parking area for San Felasco Hammock Preserve State Park, on the left. Local runners and folks walking their dogs tend to hit the trails during late afternoons and weekends, so you may have trouble finding a parking space at those times. The park is open 8 AM to sunset. Before heading out on the trail, stop by the self-pay kiosk to pay your Florida State Parks entrance fee. If you plan to hike the longer trails and no maps are available at the trail kiosk in the picnic area, drive back to Devil's Millhopper Geological State Park and ask the ranger for a map of San Felasco's hiking trails. Ask about the upcoming schedule of ranger-led hikes, which include overnight camping opportunities—

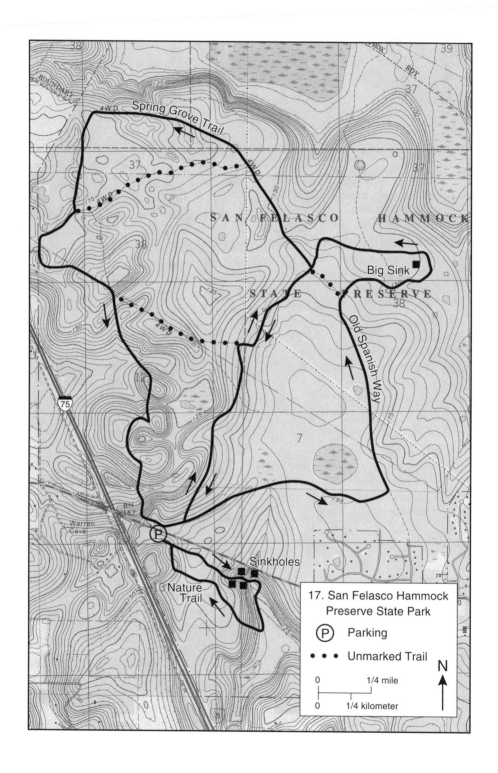

Spring Grove Trail

SAN FELASCO HAMMOCK

Big Sink

STATE PRESERVE

Old Spanish Way

BOUNDARY

4WD

75

Warren
Cave

BM
157

P

Sinkholes

Nature
Trail

17. San Felasco Hammock
Preserve State Park

(P) Parking

• • • Unmarked Trail

N

0   1/4 mile

0   1/4 kilometer

individuals are not permitted to backpack the trails alone.

SAN FELASCO NATURE TRAIL

Starting at the parking lot, walk in through the picnic grove with its latrine and up to a kiosk with the park map. The Nature Trail starts here. Follow the footpath to a jeep road and turn right. At the next fork the trail turns left to continue through the sandhills, a lush savanna of longleaf pine, turkey oak, and bluejack oak. You see mounds of orange sand in the trail—the telltale sign of pocket gophers, rodents that dwell underground. The trail drops down into an oak hammock, curving away from an older trail. When you come to the yellow arrow, turn left to follow the footpath as it descends toward Moonshine Creek. Purple violets bloom along the edges of the footpath. The karst landscape is immediately evident as you skirt a large sinkhole. Plants that love cool, damp places thrive here, including the trillium-like wakerobin, rain-lily, and woodbine. Sundial lupine, identified by its unusual pinwheel-like radiating leaves and its spiky bluish blooms in early spring, carpets the forest slopes. After 0.4 mile you come to a spur trail that leads left into the sinkhole. Take a moment to peer down into this broad, multichambered sink. A cluster of needle palms rises from the bottom, and American holly grows along the edge. Returning to the main trail, you pass another sinkhole on the left as you continue downhill. A spur on the right leads to a broad bowl of a sinkhole filled with needle palms. Take a look, and then continue down the main trail.

When the trail reaches Moonshine Creek, it meanders in parallel with the creek's oxbow curves, twisting and winding through the hardwood hammock. Crossing a small bridge over the creek, the trail swings away from it, and you hear a chorus of frogs. Walk-ing under a swamp chestnut oak, you notice small crevices in the karst walls of the creek, exposed by the low water. You cross another bridge and see a sinkhole off to the left, filled with stagnant water and rotting duckweed—the source of the frog sounds. All around you the forest slopes down, reminiscent of a walk through an Appalachian forest. A patch of bamboo grows in front of the next bridge over the creek, at 0.8 mile. Look up. Ages ago, a southern magnolia fell and rested on a tall swamp chestnut oak; now, the oak's trunk surrounds the still-living magnolia. These trees, and the others around you, rise more than 60 feet above the forest floor, creating a solid canopy. As you rise up away from the creek, the trail winds uphill. Dense thickets of greenbrier spill over the forest floor, choking off the wildflowers as the trail levels out. The trail parallels the eastern edge of a clear-cut pine forest, another casualty of the southern pine beetle. A lone Florida dogwood shows off its intensely white blooms. You return to the beginning of the loop at 1.2 miles. Continue straight back through the sandhills. When you get to the park gate, turn left and walk back past the kiosk to the parking lot, completing the 1.5-mile trek.

If you plan to tackle the more extensive trail system across the street, carry an adequate supply of water for the 10.7 miles of trail, which is broken into two loops: the yellow-blazed Spring Grove Trail (5.7 miles) and the blue-blazed Old Spanish Way (5 miles). Both loops share 1.7 miles of trail in the middle, so most visitors choose to hike one or the other of the trails during a day hike.

SPRING GROVE TRAIL

From the parking lot, carefully cross Millhopper Road to access the entrance trail,

Moonshine Creek

which leads up to a kiosk with a park map. Check the "Notices to Hikers" before hitting the trail. At the kiosk, turn right. Both blue and yellow blazes lead you down the shared section of the trail, starting out through a healthy sandhill forest with longleaf and loblolly pine. Although equestrians have their own extensive trail system in the north half of this park, don't be surprised to see that horses have torn up this soft sandy section of the hiking trail. For good footing, stay to either side of the main track.

At 0.3 mile you reach a fork. The Old Spanish Way heads left; keep to the right to follow the shared section of the loop. You immediately enter a shady forest of tall laurel oaks, transitioning into a hardwood hammock of hickory, elm, sweetgum, dogwood, and basswood. After 0.8 mile you notice the ground sloping off to the left into a big sinkhole. Several signs say CLOSED AREA due to the fragile nature of sinkhole slopes and the plants that grow there. The karst environment within this park shelters a large number of rare plants, so many sections of the park are off-limits unless you join one of the many ranger-led tours, including overnight backpacking trips. Then you'll visit places like the blowing cave hidden between the roots of a huge old tree, or Bromeliad Lake, an area in the forest where rare varieties of bromeliads thrive. When hiking on your own, stick to the blazed trails.

The bright space off to the right is a large sinkhole pond covered in duckweed. Notice the black and white stripe painted on the tree—a mile marker, indicating you've hiked 1 mile. Watch for these as you continue around the loop. The trail curves off to the right away from an unmarked trail, where the forest slopes down into a karst valley. You emerge into sunlight, walking through a more open forest as you cross under a power line, where a swallow-tailed kite glides overhead. Off to the right is a wild plum tree, which drowns under a cascade of bright blooms each February. Although its plums are ripe in May, you'll find them too astringent for a snack.

Continuing through the forest, you see the sloping bowl of a sinkhole on the right. Much of the pine forest has been logged to destroy infested trees. Look closely at a fallen tree, where its bark has peeled off, and you can see the devastation that the southern pine beetle causes, turning wood to sawdust. A coral bean flaunts its crimson blooms between the soft green wax myrtles. You reach the second junction of the yellow and blue loops at 1.7 miles. Turn left to continue on the yellow-blazed Spring Grove Trail. Somewhere in this area, lost to history, is the ghost town of Spring Grove, established in the early 1800s as the original county seat of Alachua County.

A tall canopy of oaks and hickories shades this portion of the trail as you pass the 2-mile mark. Coming out of the loblolly forest, you pass back under the power line, heading west. The forest flows down into a large rounded sinkhole on the left. Covering the sandhills, the pine forest around you contains tall loblolly pines and scattered turkey oaks, with a dense understory of wax myrtle and blueberry. Notice the unusually tall white flowers off on the right—white wild indigo. Their leaves and pods are reminiscent of cowpeas, each blossom white but showing off its deep indigo coloring where it attaches to the stem. Indigo was one of the first major European crops in Florida, sought after for its use as a blue dye. Raised as crops on large plantations, the plants were cut in the late summer and fermented before being mashed and distilled into bricks thick with dye. Indigo remained a cash crop in the

southeastern United States until 1905, when German scientist Adolf von Baeyer won the Nobel Prize for unlocking the molecular structure of indigo, allowing the color to be reproduced synthetically.

At 2.7 miles the trail splits and flows around a little island of vegetation. Keep alert for deer, as hikers report sighting albino deer along this section of trail. After you pass the triple-stripe marker, the trail turns left at a double blaze. A stand of red buckeye shades the trail, its bright red blooms rising tall overhead. The trail follows the ecotone between dense oak hammock on the right and the sandhills sweeping off to the left. The waxy blooms of sandhill milkweed peep up from variegated leaves. A duckweed-choked sinkhole sits off in the oak hammock, the sounds of frogs echoing off its walls. At 3.7 miles you reach a fork. Stay left, passing a little white house off to the right in the woods; the trail turns left, away from the house, and you hear the hum of traffic from I-75. It's a long downslope through the pines. Poppy mallow grows along the edges of the trail. At 4 miles you make a right turn at a double blaze, passing another section where ailing loblolly pines have been logged. Sweetgum and American beautyberry fill in the gaps. Strewn with pine needles, the hard-packed footpath rises back into rolling hills covered in elm, sweetgum, and bluejack oak. Decked out in their purple four-petaled flowers, several woodland phlox add an unexpected splash of color. After an uphill climb you enter a corridor of low oaks under tall loblolly pines. Watch for young sassafras trees growing in the shade, at the southernmost boundary of their range.

As you drop downhill on a slick skid of pine duff, the sound of traffic increases. You come to a T intersection at 5.4 miles. Turn left. Caught napping, a white-tailed deer rises from its leafy bed and flees into the thicket. Rounding a bend, you head up a steep slope, the footpath deeply eroded by rain. When it reaches a bluff above Millhopper Road, the trail swings to the left. You pass an unmarked trail on the left before returning to the kiosk, completing the 5.7-mile loop. To exit the park, turn right. To hike the Old Spanish Way, continue straight.

OLD SPANISH WAY

From the kiosk follow the blue and yellow blazes forward, retracing part of the Spring Grove Trail through the sandhills. At the trail junction, take the right fork to walk counterclockwise around the blue loop. You start out along the ecotone between the oak hammock and the sandhills. Judging from the number of gopher tortoise burrows under the turkey oaks, it seems a healthy population of young tortoises is increasing. The blue blazes are a little hard to see on darker tree trunks, so watch for them carefully. The trail enters a hardwood hammock, surrounded by dogwood, mature laurel oak, scattered sweetgum, and pignut hickory. Through the trees on the left you can see a broad open area flanked by persimmon trees and Virginia willow—a large sinkhole pond, inhabited by river otters. Growing up to 4 feet long, otters are the only aquatic mammals to have a lining of fur instead of blubber. They prefer living in marshes along wooded streams, rivers, and lakes, where they build their dens.

At 0.6 mile the blue blazes lead you left off the jeep road and onto a narrow trail into the forest. Look for ebony spleenwort growing under tall bluff oaks as you walk through the dark hammock, a dense forest of ironwood, hickory, and elm. You pass the 4-mile marker, zebra stripes painted on a tree. On this hike, use the markers to count down the number of miles remaining. After 1.2 miles

of winding through the forest, the trail empties out onto a jeep road. Turn left. White wild indigo and dog banana thrive in the deep shade. You pass a lone needle palm and walk under towering southern magnolias. After crossing under a power line at 1.5 miles, continue straight into a young forest. In 1993 the "Storm of the Century" felled the older growth, leaving the forest to slowly recover. Most of the trees are less than 15 feet high, attracting an incredible number of birds—the woods resonate with song. Wildflowers, especially indigo, fill the low spots, tempting bumblebees and butterflies with a variety of fragrant blooms. Entering a mixed oak and pine forest, you pass the 3-mile marker. A little way beyond, just past a stand of dogwoods that arches over the trail, keep alert for a blue arrow and a double blaze as the trail turns to the right to once again become a narrow path through the woods. A fat eastern fence lizard lies still, assuming invisibility against the thick carpet of pine needles on the trail. The loblolly pines show char marks up their trunks from a fire. A broad bowl of a sinkhole slopes off to the right; sweetgum trees take root in its bottom. Winding through a dark forest, the trail makes several sharp turns, coming back around a pond. Chunks of limestone break through the trail. An aroma like alfalfa hay rises from the seedpods of elm trees, stringy bits of fluff fallen on the footpath.

The trail drops down to parallel one of the ponds, veering left so you can see a marshy plateau—acres of dog fennel, but no visible open water. A needle palm grows where the trail dips down to meet the marsh. In every direction you see sinkholes. They drain the overflow from the pond and create the undulating terrain under the thick hardwood canopy. You pass Big Sink, a large water-filled sink on the left, thought to be at least 75 feet deep. A southern magnolia stretches out over its duckweed-covered surface; a river cooter lies sunning on a log. At 2.8 miles you reach an intersection of trails. Straight ahead is a RESTRICTED AREA . . . DO NOT ENTER sign. This is another fragile karst zone, accessible only during a ranger-led tour. Turn left, walking along the lip of Big Sink to stay on the blue loop as you continue down a jeep trail. Hidden in these woods is the site of the San Francisco de Potano mission, one of the first Spanish missions in the New World. Established as early as 1608, it was one in a string of missions created to instruct the Timucua in the ways of Christianity. In 1703 the mission and neighboring Timucuan village were attacked and burned by a British-led force from South Carolina, seeking to loosen Spain's grip on Florida, which they saw as a threat to their new American colonies. Jesuit priests returned and rebuilt the mission, but they finally abandoned the post in 1706, tiring of the constant raids. They retreated to their only remaining stronghold, St. Augustine.

Passing many more sinkholes, all in various stages of formation, the trail continues through the hardwood hammock. Seven deer bound off through the forest in fluid, graceful motion, the sound of leaves rustling as they run. You reach the 2-mile stripe after 3 miles of hiking, and the forest changes character, becoming more open. Just beyond the marker you meet a road coming in from the right. Continue straight as the footpath becomes crushed limestone. When you reach a fork at 3.3 miles, keep to the left. You've met back up with the Spring Grove Trail. Turn left to walk back down the combined yellow- and blue-blazed path. At the next fork, keep right. After you pass under the power line, the trail curves left, away from an unmarked trail on the right. You return to the beginning of the Old Spanish Way loop at 4.8 miles. Continue straight. When you reach the kiosk, you've hiked 5 miles. Turn left and cross Millhopper Road to return to the parking lot.

18

Morningside Nature Center

Total distance (circuit): 2.6 miles

Hiking time: 1 hour, 15 minutes

Habitats: Pine flatwoods, sandhills, freshwater marsh, cypress dome, bayhead

Maps: USGS 7½' Gainesville East, park map

With its meandering trails, educational center, picnic grove, and living-history farm, the Morningside Nature Center provides a great outing for families with small children. Older hikers will appreciate the thousands of wildflowers that bloom throughout this 278-acre remnant of the longleaf pine savanna that once covered the sandhills of the Central Highlands. Open 9 AM to 5 PM daily, the center is located to the east of downtown Gainesville. From I-75 take exit 382, Gainesville/Williston. Head north to the first traffic light and continue straight on FL 331 for 2.2 miles. After crossing US 441, keep to right as the road splits, and continue on FL 331 (Waldo Road) for 3.3 miles to the traffic light at FL 24/26/20 (University Drive). Turn right. Immediately move to the left lane to stay on FL 26 as the road splits. Drive 1.8 miles to the entrance, on the left.

Most visitors come to see the living-history farm, open on Saturday and Sunday from September through July. Made up of several original buildings brought in from various locations around the county, including a hand-hewn longleaf pine cabin, board and batten kitchen, and a one-room schoolhouse, the farm is populated with residents in period costume. The volunteers tend to livestock, produce syrup from the sugar cane crop, spin and weave cotton and wool, and do the various chores that were regularly performed on a 1800s north Florida farm. Although a nominal admission fee is charged for the farm tour, the educational center and trails are free. The annual Farm

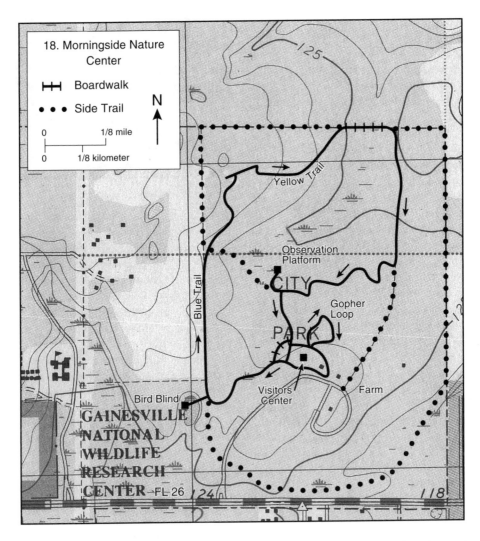

and Forest Festival and Cane Boil attract large crowds.

After you drive in on the entrance road, park in the first parking lot on the left. Walk down the paved path in the direction of the NATURE CENTER sign. Stop at the center, which contains rest rooms and a classroom filled with reference materials, to pick up the trail map and the guide to wildflowers found at Morningside Nature Center—270 varieties. There are almost 5 miles of trail

throughout the preserve, a series of nested loops. This hike follows a 2.6-mile route through the heart of the pine flatwoods and sandhills habitats.

Start your hike in front of the building, following the BIRD BLIND/OBSERVATION DECK sign to the White Trail. White diamond and orange lightning blazes lead you into the dry pine flatwoods along a broad needle-strewn path. You come to a T intersection with a trail to a cypress dome. Turn left. Netted pawpaw displays slender white blossoms on the edge of stand of low blueberry bushes. A sea of saw palmetto sweeps around the snags of old longleaf pines. When you reach the trail junction, continue straight to follow a short spur trail down to the bird blind, a replica Seminole home, a chickee, nestled under the oaks. You can sit on a bench hidden behind the palm fronds and peep through the blind to watch the coming and goings of birds attracted to a variety of feeders and birdbaths. A palm warbler splashes itself in the water, while a bright male cardinal pecks at some seed. Identification cards help you to identify birds on the spot.

When you're done at the bird blind, return to the trail junction and turn left. Just before you get to the next T intersection, watch for a white-diamond–blazed side trail to the left. This short spur leads to the marsh overlook observation deck. Depending on the season, the shallow marsh may be dry. Returning to the main trail, turn left, and make a right at the T intersection to start walking on the Blue Loop. The full Blue Loop runs 3 miles around the perimeter of the park, following the fence line. Oaks and vines obscure the old fence so it is hardly noticeable; on the right, pine flatwoods stretch out as far as you can see. The purple blooms of spiderwort peep out from beneath tall wax myrtles. Settlers in Florida collected the hard wax myrtle berries and boiled them in water, skimming off the wax for candle making. By boiling its leaves, they could create a hot wash that relieved external itching, and the powdered bark of its roots was used as an ingredient in a home remedy called "composition powder," which fended off colds and chills.

Water oak and sweetbay magnolia shade this portion of the trail along the fence line. At 0.6 mile the Yellow Loop joins in from the

Roserush

right. Continue straight. You briefly walk through a dense area of young pines, and then enter a wetter forest where red maple and sweetgum predominate, showing off their colorful leaves in winter. At 0.7 mile turn right to follow the Yellow Loop as it heads into the heart of the wet pine flatwoods. Grapevines form a natural arbor across the beginning of the trail. In spring you'll notice the many bright orange and yellow wild bachelor's buttons rising from the damp earth. With stems so slim they vanish from view, hatpins' white button blooms hover over the footpath like tiny constellations.

When you come to the fork, turn left, following the yellow blazes. Scattered charred snags stand out against the green-on-green of the pine flatwoods. Tiny oyster fungi emerge from cracks in the bark at the base of a longleaf pine. The taller, older longleaf pines are second-generation pines that survived the logger's axe thanks to their misshapen trunks, which bloated as they closed around the deep catface scars created during the turpentine era. Check the taller pines and you'll notice the catfaces, some with strips of metal still embedded in the tree trunks. The forest feels vast and open, the understory a dense blanket of saw palmetto with islands of wiregrass where blueberry, gallberry, and bracken fern take hold. In the distance to the left, a wall

Longleaf pine savanna

of oaks delineates the western edge of the park. At 0.8 mile a spur trail leads over to a broad sinkhole on the left. Pennywort flourishes in its damp bottom. In wetter seasons it serves as a pond, draining rainfall off the flatwoods and down into the aquifer.

After 1.1 miles you reach a T intersection and rejoin the Blue Loop. Turn right and follow the park's edge on the combined Blue and Yellow Loops, reaching a boardwalk through a cypress dome. A bench provides a place to sit and observe the accompanying marsh. Tall clusters of cinnamon fern edge the wetland, which is ringed with young pond cypresses. The bottlebrush-like white blooms of the titi catch your eye. This small Florida tree thrives in the marshes of wet flatwoods, often forming impenetrable thickets.

Once you leave the boardwalk, turkey oaks surround you as the trail rises up into the sandhills. When you reach the trail junction, turn right to follow the Yellow Loop along an old road that heads straight down the boundary of the two ecosystems—sandhills on the left, flatwoods on the right. Tall sand live oaks form a canopy over the trail, raining their crunchy leaves across the footpath. As you transition into a more open area, wiregrass covers the forest floor, reminding you that you're walking through a relict longleaf pine savanna, the very type of forest that William Bartram encountered in 1774 as he made his way north from the village of Cuscowilla: "a vast pine forest and grassy savanna, well-timbered, the ground covered with a charming carpet of various flowering plants." Around you, spring wildflowers delight—slender greenish-ivory blooms of narrow-leaf pawpaw, slim fluffy bottlebrushes of sandhill wireweed, and tall dark cones of blackroot. You pass a jeep trail leading off to the left; continue straight, following the triangular

yellow blazes. Young pines grow in perfect rows in a pine plantation on the left. Watch for the telltale explosions of orange sand across white sand, the sure sign of a gopher tortoise burrow.

When you reach Marker 12 at 1.6 miles, you come to the junction of two trails. An orange lightning-strike blaze leads straight. Follow the yellow blazes to the right. A zebra swallowtail flutters between the blooms of a blackberry thicket. The footpath is a little difficult, cut like a firebreak through a choking understory of grapevines and wax myrtle. Curving to the right past a TRAIL CLOSED sign, you see a blaze painted on a catfaced pine, and beyond it, Marker 8. Keep alert for a side trail to the right. This white-diamond–blazed trail leads to a swamp overlook, ending at a stand of tall longleaf pines and a TUPELO MARSH sign. A short boardwalk leads to the observation platform above the fern-choked marsh, where a small grove of water tupelo thrives, a tree rarely seen southeast of the Suwannee River. Turn around, and as you descend the boardwalk notice how the tall pines all sport catfaces. You can see through the base of one of the pines, cut for turpentine on both sides of its trunk, metal strips still embedded in its bark. Follow the white diamonds back to the main trail. Turn right. Stay to the left at the next fork, following the white diamonds, where the yellow blazes take off to the right to complete the Yellow Loop. Unusually bright orange, a cluster of mustard yellow polypores emerges from rotting pine logs.

As the trail curves around, you reach a fork at 2 miles, behind the education center. Turn right and follow the white blazes around the edge of a replica Timucuan village, passing Marker 5 as you come up to the CYPRESS DOME BOARDWALK sign. Turn right. The boardwalk zigzags through the cypress swamp, where titi trees dangle their bright white blooms. Tall wheat-colored stalks of Florida threeawn thrive along the edge of the wetland. After the boardwalk ends you come to a T intersection. You've completed the loop at 2.2 miles. Turn left to return to the education center. Following the white blazes, walk around the back of the center past the ecosystem diorama and the native plants garden, watching for the GOPHER LOOP TRAIL sign. Turn left to follow the pink-dot blazes for a walk through the sandhills. When you see the fork in the trail, keep left. Wiregrass fills the spaces between the many varieties of oaks. Watch for gopher tortoise burrows and the flash of bright blue as a southeastern five-lined skink skitters past. The trail curves to the right, and you come to a junction with a firebreak. Keep right, walking past a mimosa tree. A greenbrier vine swirls up and around the trunk of a longleaf pine. Roserush rises from the wiregrass, a pale lilac spring wildflower blooming from a 2-foot-tall leafless stem, its strange squared-off petals showing fringed edges. Off to the left, you see the parking lot. The trail curves to the right just before you come up to a left-hand turn. Turn left for a shortcut to the parking lot, or go straight to continue back to the educational center. As the footpath dovetails into the paved trail, turn left to keep walking to the parking lot, completing your 2.6-mile hike.

19

Gum Root Swamp Conservation Area

Total distance (circuit): 2.6 miles

Hiking time: 2 hours

Habitats: Hardwood hammock, oak hammock, sandhill, floodplain forest

Maps: USGS 7½' Orange Heights, St. Johns Water Management District map

As years of drought wore on, lake levels dropped throughout Florida. In Newnan's Lake, just outside Gainesville, the vanishing waters uncovered an astounding archaeological find. In the spring of 2000, students studying at the outdoor education center in Gum Root Swamp Conservation Area walked along the dried-up lakeshore, searching for an old logging camp. They noticed strange patterns on the lake bottom and started to carefully dig, unearthing an ancient canoe. After reporting the find, the class returned with state archaeologists, searching the cracked lake bottom. By the end of the summer, more than one hundred canoes were found, the largest single discovery of aboriginal canoes ever found in North America. In 2001 the lake was designated a National Historic Site.

They shouldn't have been surprised. The Seminoles called this lake Pithlachocco, the place "where boats are made." For thousands of years a large village occupied the north shore of the lake. Artifacts discovered in the area date back to 3000 B.C. After studying the canoes, researchers reburied them in the thick lake mud, preventing these fragile finds from disintegrating in the open air.

The trails at the Gum Root Swamp Conservation Area lead you out to the edge of Newnan's Lake, meandering through both the location of the ancient village and subsequent cypress logging operations. To get there, take I-75 exit 382, Gainesville/Williston at FL 121. Head north to first traffic light and continue straight on FL 331. Crossing US 441 after 2.2 miles, keep to

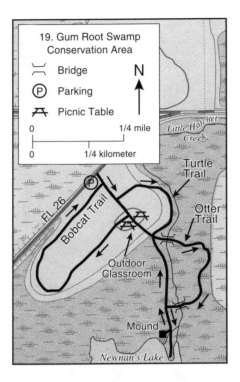

19. Gum Root Swamp
Conservation Area

⌒ Bridge N

Ⓟ Parking

🏕 Picnic Table

0 .... 1/4 mile

0 .... 1/4 kilometer

the right as the road splits at the WALDO ROAD sign, and continue on FL 331 another 3.3 miles to the traffic light at FL 24/26/20 (East University Avenue). Turn right, immediately getting in the left lane to stay on FL 26 as road splits. Pass Morningside Nature Center (Hike 18). Keep left where the road splits again. Soon after you pass the GUM ROOT PARK sign at the blinker at NE 27th Avenue, keep alert for the GUM ROOT SWAMP CONSERVATION AREA sign on the right, 11.6 miles from I-75.

Start your hike at the kiosk. The trail map shown is not accurate; it depicts proposed trail routes and amenities planned for the future. The City of Gainesville and the St. Johns Water Management District coordinate efforts in this park as the city continues to use it as an outdoor education center. As you leave the kiosk, walk around the gate and head down the broad jeep trail to a clearing in the oak hammock. A trail sign on the right marks one end of the Bobcat Trail; save that loop until later. For now, head straight under the spreading live oaks, following the trail as it curves to the left, passing a pitcher pump before coming up within sight of a cluster of picnic tables and a pavilion. When you reach the TURTLE TRAIL sign, turn left. As you walk through the oak hammock, follow the yellow blazes. The trail curves to the left. You emerge at Little Hatchet Creek, its shores lined with cypresses—a floodplain forest. The trail swings sharply to the right and follows the creek. Keep your eye on the yellow blazes since the footpath is indistinct, zigzagging through a maze of cypress knees. The narrow trail works its way up to the south side of the picnic area and pavilion. When you reach the kiosk, you've hiked 0.5 mile. Turn left to follow the Otter Trail. Blazed in red, this trail starts at the bridge and provides a loop out to Newnan's Lake. As you cross the wide bridge, look down into the creek at the many cypress logs. Floated downstream during logging operations, these logs became stuck in the streambed and were never removed.

The Otter Trail weaves between cypress knees, leading uphill into a hardwood hammock of hickory, laurel oak, and ironwood. You walk through open woods, laurel oaks towering overhead, as the trail twists and turns its way back down to the cypress floodplain. Keep alert for red blazes as the footpath is indistinct in places. You glimpse an open expanse off to the right, and the trail curves right to head toward it. As the trail jogs up and over a hummocky area, be cautious of poison ivy. The trail continues across an island of tall loblolly pines, paralleling Newnan's Lake. You can see blue sky through breaks in the forest to your left. A footbridge leads down off the small pine

Little Hatchet Creek during the dry season

island. Winding through another labyrinth of cypress knees, you emerge at a large bridge over Little Hatchet Creek. After you cross the bridge, you come to a T intersection—red blazes lead right and left. Turn left, following the rough and hummocky route toward the lake; the blazes peter out as the route is still under construction. The footpath continues to follow the creek but becomes very rough, carved out between the roots and knees of the cypresses. Beware of holes in the trail. At 1.1 miles take a walk off the main trail to the right, where an earthen mound covered in large cypresses sits on the lake's edge. This is likely part of the ancient village, which vanished around 1000 B.C.

At this point, the trail drops down across a narrow creek channel and meanders back along the main flow of Little Hatchet Creek. Mussel and clam shells peek out of the dry sand bottom. Continue to follow the footpath as it winds its way through the cypress knees to a clearing along the lake, where the trail ends. According to the trailhead kiosk, this is the site of a future observation platform. Once the platform is in place, you may be able to see the historic canoes when the lake is low. The discovery of the pre-Timucua canoes in Newnan's Lake almost tripled the number of aboriginal canoes ever found in Florida. Like most ancient canoes, these are hewn from a tree trunk, the interior carved out with the help of fire. The canoes range from 15 to 31 feet in length, and many of them have partitions separating interior sections of the boat, an unusual feature in canoes this old.

Turn around and retrace your zigzagging path back to the broad bridge. At the base of the bridge turn left, following the red blazes upstream. As you skirt them, notice the bizarre shapes of some of the cypress knees—one looks like an upside-down three-legged stool! When you come back up to the first bridge, you pass the remains of a small wooden-hulled boat at the base of the sand bluff in the creek bed. You've hiked 1.5 miles. Turn left to walk into the picnic area. Used as outdoor classroom, the pavilion shelters a reproduction of one of the Newnan's Lake canoes.

As you pass the picnic table, look for the BOBCAT TRAIL sign next to a couple of pieces of rail, perhaps remnants of one of the old logging railroads that ran into this swamp. Turn left to follow this route, blazed in blue. It starts out under a high canopy of live oaks and then enters upland oak hammock. A warbling vireo calls out from a wax myrtle. Watch for movement through the open understory—there may be several white-tailed deer browsing the swamp lilies on the edge of the floodplain. Saw palmetto fronds fan out from tall trunks as you pass a split oak on the left, fallen over and double branched. At 1.8 miles the trail clambers up onto an old logging tramway, following it until it ends at the edge of the floodplain forest. Turn right and drop off the footpath into the cypress, dodging the knees as you walk. Royal ferns rise out of the damp black soil. You catch glimpses of open water through the trees off to the left.

The trail rises onto an island in the floodplain, with a canopy of spreading live oaks overhead. A pileated woodpecker works its way up a towering loblolly pine. The trail meanders back and forth to the edges of the island as it makes its way down this narrow sliver of land. At 2.1 miles you turn to the right and drop down across the floodplain. The trail rises into sandhills, becoming sandy underfoot. Laurel oaks surround a slash pine plantation. You hear the sound of traffic on FL 26 as the trail curves to the right. Fluffy lumps of deer moss create extensive patches underneath the sand live oaks and gnarled rusty lyonia. This is "The Moss Place," one of the environmental stations for the outdoor classroom. As you rise up into an oak hammock, a soft carpet of pine needles covers the footpath. When you come to the end of the Bobcat Trail, turn left. You've completed the loop. Retrace your route along the broad entrance trail back to the kiosk and parking lot, completing a 2.6-mile hike.

20

Paynes Prairie Preserve State Park

Total distance (3 circuits and 2 round trips): 20.6 or 22.1 miles

Hiking time: 12 hours or 2 days

Habitats: Prairie, freshwater marsh, hardwood hammock, oak hammock, bayhead, floodplain forest

Maps: USGS 7½' Micanopy, park map

While exploring the state of Florida in 1774, naturalist William Bartram reached the edge of the "great Alachua Savanna," a vast prairie he described as "a level green plain, above fifteen miles over, fifty miles in circumference, and scarcely a tree or a bush of any kind to be seen on it." Cattle and horses ranged the plain, their owners living in the nearby Seminole village of Cuscowilla. Bartram spends many pages of his *Travels* recounting the natural wonders of this broad basin. Later named Paynes Prairie, in honor of Seminole Chief Payne, the savanna remains a thriving ecosystem despite centuries of cattle ranching and sporadic flooding. Designated a wildlife sanctuary in 1961, it became a Florida State Park in 1971, with a mission of returning the prairie and its surrounding habitats to their original state, more in tune with the descriptions of William Bartram. Bison and wild horses were reintroduced, and populations of white-tailed deer, wild turkey, marsh rabbit, and fox now thrive. Paynes Prairie Preserve State Park is a herpetologist's delight, home to thousands of alligators, snakes, turtles, lizards, and frogs. If the sound of slithering creatures alarms you, stick to the Wacahoota and Chacala Trails since they don't take you out into the savanna. On all of the trails, expect wildlife sightings.

Spread out across twenty-one thousand acres, the trails at Paynes Prairie Preserve State Park cover a lot of ground. Because of the driving distances between trails and the amount of time you'll spend walking in full sun, you'll want to split up your hiking into two or three days. Use the Pug Puggy campground as your home base, or look for accommodations north of the park along US 441 or I-75 in Gainesville. To drive to the main entrance, take I-75 exit 374. Head east on CR 234 for 1.3 miles past Micanopy, a popular stop for antiques aficionados. At the T intersection with US 441, turn left. Continue 0.6 mile north on US 441 to the park entrance, on the right. When you pay your Florida State Parks entrance fee, ask for a map of the hiking trails. The trailhead for the Chacala Trail is 1 mile along the entrance road. A left turn takes you 0.3 mile down to the campground and then to Lake Wauberg, the starting point for the Lake Trail. It's 2.6 miles up the entrance road to the visitors center parking area, the starting point for the Wacahoota Trail and Jackson's Gap.

DAY ONE: Wacahoota Trail, Cone's Dike, and Bolens Bluff
11.7 miles

WACAHOOTA TRAIL

From the parking lot a narrow paved trail leads into the woods to the visitors center. At the fork, keep left. If the visitors center is open, stop here first for an overview of the history of the prairie, presented in a video and through exhibits. The center's hours vary but are usually 10 AM to 4 PM Monday and Tuesday and 9 AM to 5 PM Wednesday through Sunday. The Wacahoota Trail starts to the left of the visitors center. Follow the paved path downhill through a forest of live oak, southern magnolia, ironwood, and cabbage palm. You can see the open prairie just beyond the treeline and the outline of the tower up ahead. The pavement ends at the tower after 0.2 mile. It rises up several

stories, giving you a treetop view of the vast expanse of Paynes Prairie. The first level of the tower is handicapped-accessible.

At the base of the tower, an unpaved path leads into the forest—the Wacahoota Trail. Follow it through the shady hardwood hammock along the edge of the savanna, past stands of American beautyberry. Where narrower trails take off into the forest, keep to the main trail. An area off to the right served as an outdoor classroom for interpretive talks. The trail curves to the left under spreading live oaks, passing a jumble of limestone boulders as it ascends into an oak hammock with scattered slash pines. Two wild turkeys herd their peeping chicks into a thicket for safety. You pass a reconstruction of a Seminole home, a chickee, in an open grassy area, utilizing the trunks of cabbage palms as upright posts and the fronds as a roof.

The trail curves to left, dropping down into the shade. Passing under a series of grapevine-laden live oak and southern magnolia, it crosses a bridge and emerges alongside the visitors center. Turn right on the paved path and follow it back past the center to the next trail junction, halfway back to the parking lot. You've walked 0.7 mile. To continue on to hike Cone's Dike, turn left at the wrought-iron bench. Turn left again at the JACKSON'S GAP sign in front of the rest rooms, where the trail wanders through the picnic area and into the woods.

CONE'S DIKE

When you reach the T intersection at the fence line, you meet the Jackson's Gap Trail. This trail connects the Chacala Trail at the western edge of the park to the Cone's Dike Trail. Turn left, walking along a broad jeep trail that drops downhill beneath spreading live oak and sweetgum, reaching

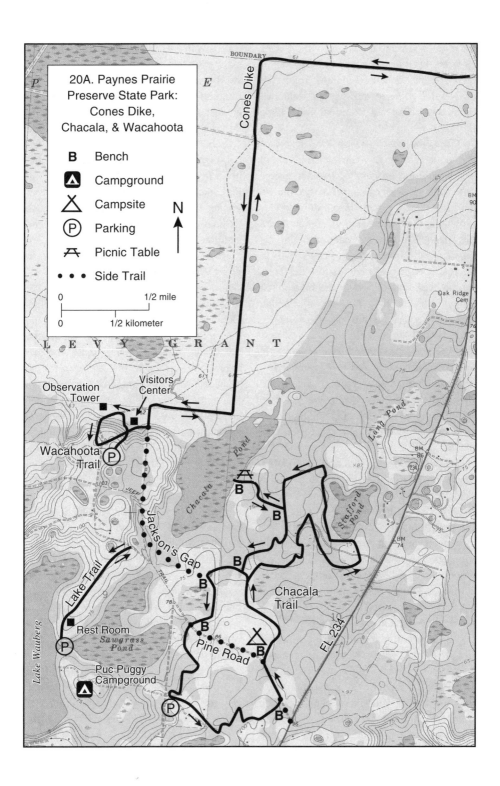

20A. Paynes Prairie
Preserve State Park:
Cones Dike,
Chacala, & Wacahoota

B Bench

🏕 Campground

⛺ Campsite

Ⓟ Parking

🪑 Picnic Table

••• Side Trail

N

0   1/2 mile

0   1/2 kilometer

BOUNDARY

Cones Dike

P

E

L E V Y   G R A N T

Observation
Tower

Visitors
Center

Wacahoota
Trail

Ⓟ

Chacala
Pond

Long Pond

B

B

B

Stafford
Pond

Jackson's Gap

Chacala
Trail

Lake Trail

Lake Wauberg

Rest Room

Sawgrass
Pond

B

B

Pine Road

B

Puc Puggy
Campground

Ⓟ

Ⓟ

B

FL 234

Oak Ridge
Cem

the gated access to the savanna at 0.9 mile. Note the OPEN RANGE sign and its warning—bison, cattle, and wild horses roam the savanna. If you see any, keep a safe distance away. This trail, like most in the park, is shared with bikes.

Once you pass through the baffle into the open savanna, you're in a different world, an open expanse of treeless green. There are no trail markers for the Cone's Dike trail—just follow the dike. Keep alert for reptiles in the nearby slough. A marsh rabbit zigzags across your path. You'll notice the soft sand is torn up in places by wild horses that wallowed across the trail. Look for the hoofprints of horses and bison, their beaten trails leading out into the prairie grasses. At 1 mile the dike turns right. Young cherry and sweetgum trees push out into the drier portions of the savanna. In search of a meal, a red-shouldered hawk launches from a sweetgum, cruising out over the prairie. After 1.5 miles the dike turns left. In the early morning, the trees paralleling this section of the dike provide cool shade.

Paynes Prairie is a rare north Florida example of "Big Sky." It's been a gathering place for humans for a long time. Spanish missionaries visiting the Timucua left their horses here to roam, and both the Seminoles and subsequent white settlers ranged their cattle across the expanse. During the Civil War, Confederate cattle drives would stop here to fatten up the cattle before pushing them north to the Georgia border. Off in the distance, you can see a ridge that marks the far edge of the prairie, topped with a handful of buildings and towers—the city of Gainesville. As the fence line narrows down, a thin border of wax myrtle and young oak separates you from another stretch of prairie, a privately held cattle ranch. Around you, the savanna

pulses with life. The air resounds with constant birdsong. If you listen carefully, you can hear lizards and snakes moving off the footpath ahead of you. A white-tailed deer leads her fawn off the dike, disappearing into the tall grass. A red-winged blackbird cruises in for a landing on top of a dog fennel; their dried, tall husks stretch off to the horizon. A black racer slithers off the path and into the slough. Briefly, a forest of Virginia willow and sea myrtle crowds close to the dike on both sides, growing out of the sloughs. The trail becomes hummocky underfoot. Tall thistles look like bizarre works of art, their stems dangling purple blooms like tentacles.

After 2.4 miles the fence line ends. Cone's Dike continues into the center of the savanna. Scattered Virginia willows and elderberries break up the landscape, and cattails poke up from the slough. Purple passionflower runs rampant over one section of the dike, climbing up the dog fennel, spilling over onto the trail, and showing off its bright purple blooms and fruit like miniature watermelons. You pass an instrumentation station at 2.9 miles and come up to a pond on the left. The trail meets the fence line and curves left past the pond to follow it, along a thicket choked with blackberries and sea myrtle. Crossing a culvert, the trail parallels a wide slough, thick with pennywort and arrowroot. A dense thicket of blackberries on the bank of slough provides a tasty treat in early May. A great blue heron squawks as it wings skyward. Numerous animal trails lead down to the water—but don't follow them. Alligators abound anywhere water pools in this savanna.

The dike curves to the right around the waterway, where cattails wave in a stiff breeze. You see a clear channel in the distance between the shaggy pond cypresses. You've hiked 3.5 miles. A rat snake stretches across the trail, its muscles tensed as it sniffs the air. It spills over the edge of the embankment and down into the canal. A small stand of sugarberry trees provides shade at 4 miles. The dike now parallels a canal on the right, lined with moss-draped pond cypresses. A green-crested night heron stands close to the water. Resist the temptation to walk down to the canal, and keep alert for the splashes of alligators. You can see the marks where alligators have slid down the sand banks. The water has a greenish hue, casting reflections of the plant life around it. Stand and watch for a while, and you'll notice the alligators—many alligators. In times of drought, they congregate in the savanna's few canals and ponds, where standing water still remains. Don't be surprised to count 50 or more along this mile-long stretch of trail.

Marsh grasses shimmer in shades of green in the sweeping bowl between the dike and a peninsula poking out into the prairie. As the dike turns away from the canal, you reach a sign that says RESTRICTED AREA. ACCESS PROHIBITED EXCEPT ACCOMPANIED BY A RANGER. During the winter months, you can sign up for ranger-led backpacking trips through the prairie. This is the end of the Cone's Dike Trail, at 4.7 miles. Turn around. You see the vast sweep of the prairie off to the bluffs on the edge of Gainesville. Follow the dike, retracing your path. You pass the instrumentation station at 6.5 miles, and the treeline at 8 miles. Turn right, following the dike back around to the gate on the prairie's edge at 8.5 miles. Pass through the baffle and walk back up the broad jeep trail to the trail junction with the Chacala Trail. Turn right to return to the parking lot. You'll pass back through the picnic area and rejoin the paved trail. At the T intersection, turn left. When you reach the parking lot, you've completed an 8.8-mile hike.

BOLENS BLUFF

Bolens Bluff lies outside the park's main gate. Drive back down the entrance road, past the ranger station. When you reach US 441, turn right. Head north 3.4 miles. The trailhead parking lot is on the right. Like the state park, it's open 8 AM to sunset. Check the trail map and information on the kiosk after you pass through the baffle to the trail. A broad, sandy path leads into the hardwood hammock under a canopy of sweetgum and oak. The loop starts at the split rail fence, where a START sign points to the right. A pioneer family settled this high ridge above the prairie, which continued as a ranch until 1970. The youth of the trees around you attests to the former farm. Narrow side trails lead off to small depressions and into the forest; keep to the main trail. Young cabbage palms push up through the sandy soil. As the habitat transitions to oak hammock, the live oaks here are one hundred years old and more, their sweeping limbs fuzzy with resurrection fern, shading the trail. Bikes share this trail, so you may run into sections of soft sand. The trail curves to the left, passing through a clearing of bright white sand before reentering the oak hammock. When you come to the second clearing, continue straight. Large live oaks fringe the edge of the open grassy clearing. From the bench you can look down a broad corridor into the savanna. At 0.7 mile is the eastern end of the loop. For a walk out into the savanna to an observation tower, head down the bluff to what was a steamboat landing. In the late 1800s the prairie became a lake—Alachua Lake—just deep enough to support steady steamboat traffic carrying oranges and passengers from the south shore across to the railroad in Gainesville. But a sudden change in geologic fortune ended the easy sailing. In 1892 the lake dropped 8 feet in 10 days, vanishing down the now-unplugged Alachua Sink, the sinkhole that drains the entire prairie into the Floridan Aquifer. Millions of fish lay dying in the sun, and the steamboat *Chacala* became permanently mired in the mud. Alachua Lake was no more.

As you enter the savanna, you're surrounded by the calls of birds. Because this trail is short and free to the public, it's a popular destination for birdwatchers. Mist rises from distant water holes. Scattered groups of Virginia willow provide sporadic shade. As on Cone's Dike, you'll hear the rustling and scurrying of many creatures, including the marsh rabbit, the southern water snake, and the eastern glass lizard. A marsh rice rat scurries across the trail. Looking more like a rounded puff of fur than a traditional rat, this rodent creates its own beaten paths through the marsh.

Although the dike continues out through a gate farther into the savanna, your turnaround point is the observation platform at 1.4 miles. The small amount of elevation it provides allows a sweeping view of the savanna. Off to the left, you can see US 441 cutting across the grassland; the taller buildings of the University of Florida tower on the far bluffs. To the right is the eastern edge of the savanna, lost in the mist. Turn around and follow the dike back to Bolens Bluff. Marching out into the dry edges of the savanna, sweetgum provide the first snatches of shade on the return route. When you reach the top of the bluff at 2.2 miles, turn right to follow the return loop. In the shade of the hardwood hammock, trumpet vines carpet the ground and cascade over tree limbs, dripping with large, orange trumpet-shaped blooms during the spring and summer. The trail keeps near the edge of Bolens Bluff, but the forest obscures any further views of the savanna. Two plum trees flank a small clearing. When you come

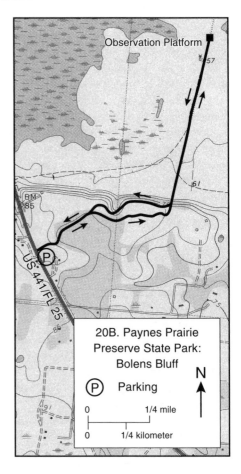

20B. Paynes Prairie Preserve State Park: Bolens Bluff

to the split-rail fence, you've completed the full loop. Continue straight, reaching the parking lot after 2.9 miles.

DAY TWO: Chacala Trail and La Chua Trail
8.9 or 10.4 miles

When you rise in the morning, head to Lake Wauberg for a short walk out to the lake. From the campground, turn left to follow the park road down to the lake. Once you reach the parking area, turn right, and head down to the parking spaces close to the end. A paved trail starts next to a DANGER: NO PETS BEYOND THIS POINT sign. Believe the sign—

The prairie draining into Alachua Sink

don't risk your dog's life. This unusually large parking lot used to accommodate swimmers who came here in summer to enjoy the beach. As the park's alligator population grew, the lake became too dangerous to swim in. The wheelchair-accessible paved trail leads down to a boardwalk along a swampy arm of the lake, a great spot for wildlife observation. You'll always see alligators, often sunning on the shores. Cross the boardwalk to the picnic area and rest rooms. From the back of the picnic area behind the rest rooms, the Lake Trail, a broad jeep road, leads 0.8 mile one-way to the park entrance road. Since it traverses mostly open meadows, hike it only if you want to use it as a connector to reach the visitors center or the Chacala Trail from the campground. From the end of the Lake Trail to the visitors center and Cone's Dike, turn left and walk 0.7 mile to the visitors center parking lot. To connect to the Chacala Trail, turn right and walk 0.9 mile to the Chacala Trail trailhead. Otherwise, turn around and retrace your path back to the picnic area on Lake Wauberg, crossing the boardwalk back to the parking lot to complete your morning stroll.

CHACALA TRAIL

The trailhead for the Chacala Trail starts directly across from the road leading down from the entrance road to the campground and Lake Wauberg. Since this trail is open for horseback riding, you'll see several hitching posts in the parking lot. From the trailhead kiosk head straight past the sign-post, following the CHACALA POND sign. You're walking through a former ranch, reforested in loblolly pine and laurel oak. The trail is marked with white blazes painted on fence posts, but the obvious footpath is broad enough for two hikers abreast. You pass a bench. Along many sections of the trail, you see trees cut and dying, the victims of the southern pine beetle. The trail winds between oak hammock and scrubby flatwoods. Despite being a multiuse trail, the footpath is in pretty good shape.

When you reach the T intersection with Pine Road, turn left, past the bench. It's a rough, sandy jeep road, tough going in places. As you enter the shade of an oak hammock, keep alert for the trail junction on the right at 1 mile. Turn right as indicated by the CHACALA POND sign. Star-shaped blooms of sweetbay magnolia lie in drifts of white across the footpath. Slender hatpins rise above the damp forest floor. A five-lined racerunner scampers across the trail. Although it lies between scrubby flatwoods and bayhead, the footpath is firm, carpeted by pine needles. A dense understory of saw palmetto yields to a sparser understory of wax myrtle under the pines. You reach a bench at a trail junction at 1.5 miles, with a CHACALA POND sign pointing right and a JACKSON'S GAP sign straight ahead. Turn right.

As it winds through the pine flatwoods, the trail curves to the left. The tree canopy lifts, becoming a mixed forest of oak and sweetgum, progressing into a shady oak hammock. At 2.1 miles you see the GROUP CAMP AREA sign. Groups must preregister at the ranger station before using this campsite, the only backpacking campsite in the park. Located 0.2 mile down a side trail, the campsite boasts a pitcher pump, a composting privy, barbecue grills, tent pads, a horse hitching area, picnic tables under a pavilion, and benches around a fire ring.

Passing an old fence line, you continue into a mixed hardwood hammock of hickory, elm, sweetgum, and ironwood. Saw palmettos crowd close to the trail as it meanders back into scrubby flatwoods. You pass between sections of fence discouraging you

Passionflowers

from turning off onto an old overgrown road. Deer moss thrives beneath the rusty lyonia and wax myrtle. Turning left back into a hardwood hammock, the trail curves to the left across a clear-cut. Fence posts with blazes mark the way across. After you cross a jeep trail in the middle of the clearing, follow the blazes back into the woods. The trail curves along the edge of the devastating clear-cut in the shade of the forest. To the right, through breaks in trees, you can see an open grassy area–adjoining ranchland along the prairie. As the trail curves left away from the open area, it enters a hammock filled with grand old live oaks of extreme girth, their spreading limbs covered in resurrection fern. At 3.7 miles you reach a bench. A CHACALA POND sign points to the right. Head down the trail corridor to the right. You pass an old fence blocking and old trail to the left just before you start walking along a fenceline. There's blue water ahead! Passing through a floodplain forest on a causeway, this side trail ends at a picnic bench on Chacala Pond, at 4.1 miles. Marsh grasses and aquatic plants ring the edge of the lake, providing good hiding places for alligators. Although the view is limited, it's a beauty spot, worth the hike down this trail.

Turn around and return to the trail junction with the main trail. Turn right. The trail twists and turns through the oak hammock, which yields to a mixed loblolly and oak forest. You pass a split-rail fence blocking an old trail. Continue straight. Emerging out at another clear-cut, the trail keeps to the edge. At the next T intersection you see a PINE ROAD sign pointing right and a bench on the left. This is where the Jackson's Gap shortcut trail (back at 1.5 miles) comes in. Turn right and reenter a forest of towering slash pines. At 5.3 miles you come to a T intersection in this majestic cathedral of pines. To the right, the JACKSON'S GAP sign directs hikers up the connector trail to the visitors center and Cone's Dike; to the left, the PINE ROAD sign points toward the parking lot. Turn left. You soon emerge into a cleared area, following posts with white blazes, before you enter another forest of pines. Reaching Pine Road at 5.7 miles, cross it. The trail drops into the shade of an oak hammock, winding back out into scrubby flatwoods out on the edge of a cleared area, where forest is slowly regenerating, the understory plants like pawpaw, blueberry, and wax myrtle thriving. Scattered oaks remain to provide shade. Back in the oak hammock, the trail swings left. You return to the trailhead kiosk after 6.2 miles, completing your hike.

LA CHUA TRAIL

To drive to the La Chua Trail at the North Rim Interpretive Center, leave the park entrance and turn right onto US 441 north. Passing Bolen Bluff, you start to cross the prairie. Naturalist Archie Carr called this stretch of highway "the best two miles in all the long road south" from the Smoky Mountains. Built in the 1930s, this was the first of two highways (I-75 lies off to the west) to disrupt the natural rhythm of the prairie. When you reach the middle of the prairie, stop at the WILLIAM BARTRAM TRAIL sign. A short boardwalk leads to a pond, where you're sure to see herons, moorhens, and alligators. Notice the tall white conduits under the highway? Completed in 2000, the Florida Department of Transportation Ecopassage project alleviated the long-standing problem of thousands of reptiles and amphibians dying while attempting to cross US 441 every year. On one trip along this stretch of highway, Archie Carr counted 765 snakes. Now, snakes and lizards, skinks and alligators can slither their way under the highway. You'll often see motorists stop on the broad shoulder of the highway to look at the alligators in the ditch below.

After you cross the prairie, keep alert for the Florida Trail Association office on the right. Soon after, you'll see a sign for the airport. Turn right onto FL 331, 4 miles north of Bolens Bluff. When the road splits, keep to the right. At the traffic light, 2.2 miles later, turn right onto SE Fourth Street. When this road ends after 0.9 mile, keep right to turn onto SE 15th Street (CR 2043). You'll pass Bouleware Springs Park just before coming to a bend in the road. At 1 mile take the right turn off the bend and head straight into the park entrance, Camp Ranch Road. This entrance is only open on weekdays, and the gate is locked at 5 PM. On weekends and holidays, park at Bouleware Springs and walk in on the Gainesville-Hawthorne Rail Trail. If you walk in on the rail trail, your landmark is a modern-style privy. Make a right turn just after it to walk up Camp Ranch Road to the La Chua Trail parking lot.

Sign in at the kiosk at the end of the parking lot and take a quick peek in the interpretive center before heading out on the La Chua Trail. As the trail drops down the bluff into a stand of oaks, you hear the sound of rushing water. Look off to the left for a waterfall dropping into Alachua Sink,

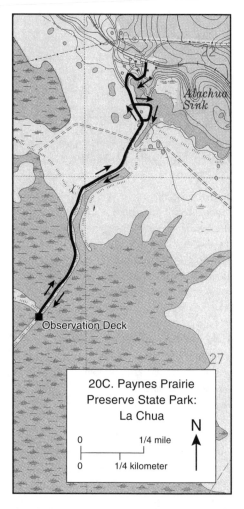

the drain of Paynes Prairie. The water level never rises; the sink is a window straight into the Floridan Aquifer. As the trail rounds the upper edge of the sink, you'll come up to two warning signs: one about wild bison, the other about alligators. From this point forward, the trail passes through the park's prime alligator territory. You will see dozens, if not hundreds, of alligators. Use common sense while walking: Do not approach an alligator, keep close watch on your children, and *don't* walk a dog on this trail.

At 0.2 mile you reach a T intersection

with a jeep road. Turn left, following it out into the savanna. At the ALACHUA SINK sign, turn left. A broad expanse of dark water sits at the base of the bluff. In it, darker forms drift. Look closely. You'll be amazed at the sheer number of alligators before your eyes. Don't scramble down to the water for a better look—stay on the bluff. Even in Bartram's day, this portion of the sink was a gathering place for alligators. "In and about the Great Sink, are to be seen incredible numbers of crocodiles," Bartram wrote, "some of which are of an enormous size . . . if permitted by them, I could walk over any part of the bason and the river upon their heads . . . " These denizens of Paynes Prairie are strictly alligators, however. Florida's crocodiles only thrive along the state's most southerly shores.

The trail curves around, following a channel upstream back to the jeep trail. Turn left and follow the jeep trail across a fenced culvert, continuing along a broad swampy basin. Alligators leave narrow muddy trails through the wetland, and their eyes peer from dark puddles beneath the purple spikes of pickerelweed. Watching a great blue heron stalk a frog between the pennyworts and water hyacinths, you hear the slap of alligator tails against mud. Water pools in a low spot in the marsh, attracting dozens of alligators. With gleaming yellowish-black skin, young alligators cruise the shallows, twisting sideways to snatch small fish. Ponderous and gray, the older alligators—some up to 10 feet long—lie still with mud piled up on their backs to keep them cool. A Florida softshell turtle halts its progress across the trail, its nearly translucent skin glistening. Packed with blood vessels that accept oxygen and expel carbon dioxide when submerged in water, its leathery skin stretches taut across a flat shell.

The turtle's protruding eyes and pronounced snout seem fitting for this alligator-filled environment. Bartram wrote, "They are carnivorous, feeding on any animal they can seize, particularly young ducks, frogs, and fish." No doubt the vast numbers of hatchling alligators add to their meals as well.

As the trail curves to the left to follow the marsh, water hyacinths lie in a soft quilt of lilac and green, obscuring the mud and the creatures below. A red-winged blackbird fusses from its precarious perch atop a waving dog fennel, defending its territory. Two sandhill cranes pick their way across the marsh. At 1.1 miles you reach a right-hand turn as the trail leaves the marsh and parallels a canal toward an observation platform. Several chicken turtles sit at the bottom of the dry canal channel, keeping cool by burying all but the tops of their shells into the muck. The trail ends at 1.4 miles at the observation platform. From the top you can see US 441 slicing across the savanna. On the left, the broad sweep of the savanna goes on to the east. You see several large forms in the distance—American bison, wandering wild and free across the prairie.

Turn around and retrace your path back along the marsh to Alachua Sink, wandering out along the bluff for one last look at the alligators. A few minutes after you pass the back side of the ALACHUA SINK sign, you come to the LA CHUA TRAILHEAD sign. Turn off the jeep trail and follow the narrow path to the right, back past the waterfall splashing down into the aquifer. At the trail kiosk, add some comments to the register about your wildlife sightings. You reach the parking lot after a 2.7-mile hike. If you parked at Bouleware Springs, walk down the paved road to the rail trail and turn left to head back to the parking lot, completing a 4.2-mile hike.

21

Goethe State Forest

Total distance (3 circuits): 14.9 miles

Hiking time: 8 hours

Habitats: Pine flatwoods, scrubby flatwoods, cypress domes, sandhills, pine plantation, bayheads, oak scrub, freshwater marsh, flatwoods ponds

Maps: USGS 7½' Tidewater, Yankeetown, Bronson; park maps

A legend in Levy County, timber baron J. T. Goethe (rhymes with "no fee") once held nearly fifty thousand acres of prime longleaf pine forest stretching north from Dunnellon to Bronson. After he died, the state of Florida acquired Mr. Goethe's land in 1992, establishing Goethe State Forest. Although many of the tracts have been clear-cut and replanted time and again, there are a handful of spots—primarily in the Apex Tract—that have sat untouched for 60 years or more. More than 100 miles of forest roads run through these quiet forests, now a playground for equestrians. Although two of Goethe State Forest's three trail systems are part of the Florida State Forest Trailwalker program, the prettiest of the three—the Apex Trail—is not. In all cases, hikers share the trail with horses and bicycles, making for rough going wherever the soft sand has been churned up. As footpaths go, the Apex Trail has the best treadway. Because of the tough walking conditions, count on no more than a 2-mile-per-hour pace while hiking these trails, and sometimes less. The three trails are best tackled as separate outings to each particular trail system. Backpackers must contact the forestry office for a special-use permit for camping; there are no designated campsites, but plenty of places to pitch a tent. Check with forestry officials regarding hunting season regulations and restrictions, as they vary from tract to tract and year to year.

Three separate trailheads access the three trail systems in Goethe State Forest, all reached via CR 337 in Levy County.

From the south take I-75 exit 341, Belleview. Follow FL 484 for 21 miles west to Dunnellon. Cross US 41 and continue straight; the road becomes CR 40. After 4.2 miles turn right on CR 336. Drive 5.7 miles to the junction with CR 336. Turn right. The Tidewater Trail entrance is on the right.

From the north take I-75 exit 358. Drive west on CR 326 through Marion County's horse farms. After 9.3 miles you cross US 27. Continue on CR 326 into Levy County. At 15.7 miles you come to a stop sign; the highway turns left. Within a few moments you cross railroad tracks and reach US 41. Turn right to follow CR 326. Make the first left and continue along CR 326. You cross FL 121 after 21.9 miles. At 25.3 miles you reach CR 337. Turn right to drive to the most northerly tract, Black Prong, just 1 mile up CR 337 on the left, or turn left on CR 337 to access the Apex or Tidewater (13.2 miles south) trailheads.

TIDEWATER TRAIL

As you drive into the forest to access the Tidewater Trail system, follow the signs to the parking area for the trailhead. It's on the edge of a large field used by equestrian groups for campouts. You have a choice of several nested loops, and any choice qualifies for the Trailwalker program: the 2.5-mile Yellow Trail, the 4.5-mile Blue Loop, the 7.5-mile Red Loop, and the 10.5-mile Purple Trail. This hike follows the Purple Trail and returns on the Red Loop, a 7-mile, three-and-a-half-hour outing with several potential campsites for backpackers.

Pick up a map at the kiosk. Since the trail is blazed in only one direction, a map is essential—you must follow the signs, blazes, and directional arrows carefully. Starting out in an oak hammock, the trail crosses over an old railroad bed used by the logging com-

pany. Follow the blazes—purple dots on white diamonds—to ensure you stay on the correct forest road. At the first fork, keep left. The footpath gets rough quickly, churned up by horses. You're surrounded by a dense forest of longleaf pine—a pine plantation, young pines lined up in neat rows, interspersed with older pines that lift their crowns well above the rest of the canopy. Curving to the left, the trail parallels CR 336, emerging at a T intersection with a jeep track that comes in from the highway. Turn left, away from the highway, at Marker B. The trail briefly becomes a causeway through a seasonally flooded stand of pond cypress. Bamboo grows up from the shallows of the marsh. At 1.4 miles you reach the most important intersection on this trail—the junction of the Purple, Blue, and Yellow Trails. Off to the left, the Yellow Trail is your quickest route back to the parking lot, for a total hike of 2.5 miles. Straight ahead, the Blue Trail provides the remainder of a 5.5-mile hike back to your starting point. Turn right to continue on the Purple Trail.

As you walk through the pine flatwoods, notice the large bayhead off to the left. The dense cluster of loblolly bay, swamp bay, and sweetbay magnolia indicates a permanent area of standing water in the forest. Bracken fern pokes out of the edges of a sea of gallberry. When you reach the wide, very badly churned up section of soft sand, skirt along on the left edge. The forest opens up; you see young longleaf trees in their grass and candle stages. To cope with the frequent lightning-sparked fires that rage across the pine flatwoods, the longleaf pine has a thick, protected fire-resistant stem in the first five years of its life in its grass stage, when it concentrates on forming a strong root system. The pine then suddenly spurts up to 3 feet tall in a single season, into the candle stage.

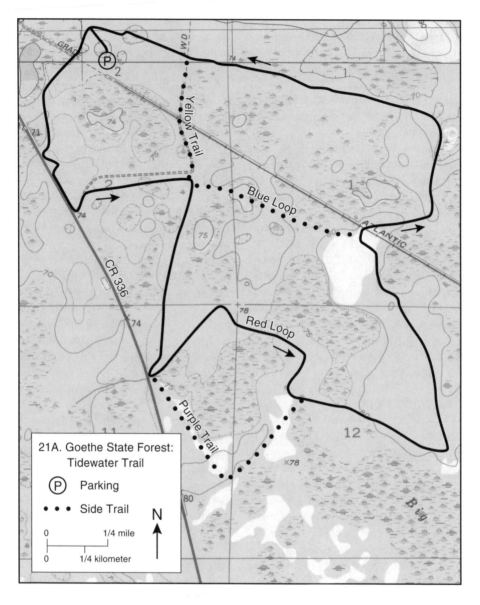

21A. Goethe State Forest:
Tidewater Trail

(P) Parking

• • • Side Trail

N

0   1/4 mile

0   1/4 kilometer

After 2.2 miles the trail is once again near CR 336. Watch for the sign for the Red Loop. Turn left to start the loop. It's a wide grassy track leading down a corridor of pine, away from the highway. Coming to a crossroad of old trails, the red loop swings to the right. A white-banded tree marks the intersection of a jeep trail from the left. Continue straight. As you pass through a bayhead, tannic water drains across the trail. Two yellow sulfurs play tag amid the sweetbay magnolia blooms. At 3 miles you reach a T intersection with gravel underfoot. The trail turns right, following the red diamonds. Curious, a swallow-tailed kite hovers overhead, easy to identify by its forked tail. These black-and-white raptors, a globally threatened species, spend spring in Florida, nesting and raising their young before returning to the South American jungle in late July.

Just past a double red blaze with an arrow, the Red Loop meets the Purple Trail at 3.2 miles. Turn left at the T, back onto a track torn up by horses. A blue-gray gnatcatcher flits by, landing in a Carolina willow. You pass a 4 MILES TO GO sign at 3.4 miles. As you come to stretches of soft sand, try to walk in the tire tracks from the rangers' vehicles. You're once again following purple blazes on white diamonds. At the fork in the trail, turn right. You pass through an oak hammock with a nice layer of pine duff, a perfect place to pitch a tent on an overnight outing—but no reliable water source is available. At the next trail junction the trail makes a hard left, transitioning into a sandhill habitat. You spy deer moss peeking out of the wiregrass and old man's beard on downed branches. An 8-foot-tall stump on the right illustrates the difference between the heartwood of a longleaf pine, thick with crystallized sap, and its outer wood. Known as "lighter pine," the heartwood makes a perfect fire starter. Passing a tiny patch of oak scrub, a bright sandy bald with scattered myrtle oak, Chapman oak, and St. John's-wort, the trail makes a sharp right turn at a double blaze. You've hiked 4.5 miles. When the Blue Loop comes in from the left, continue straight. The trail swings sharply right past a blackberry patch and up a small rise— the same rail line you crossed at the beginning of the hike—before descending into a dense and shady oak hammock. Turning away from the rail line, you skirt the edge of a cypress dome. Startled, a flock of wild turkeys takes to the sky.

At the next fork in the trail, take a hard left. Straight ahead is a pine plantation; the trail turns to parallel a meadow replanted with young longleaf pine. An American kestrel soars overhead moments before a fox squirrel shimmies down a laurel oak and scampers across the trail, its black and tan fur gleaming in the sun. After 6 miles a trail comes in from the meadow, forming a T intersection. Turn left, skirting another bayhead. The drooping ivory blooms of a dog banana, a variety of pawpaw, catch your eye. To treat their kidney problems, the Seminoles once used these flowers to make an herbal tea.

Covered in resurrection fern, gnarled sand live oaks create an unbroken canopy above this section of the forest. It's another great place to pitch a tent, your water resources limited to the ephemeral bog in the last bayhead. Dropping out of the oak hammock and turning to the right, the trail returns to the pine flatwoods. At 7 miles the Yellow Trail comes in from the left. Soon after, the purple blazes lead you out onto Saddle Pen Road. Turn left. The trail follows this limestone road for the next 0.5 mile, bringing you back to the open grassy camping area next to the Tidewater Trail trailhead. Cut across the field to the parking lot. Outfitted with water faucets and a pitcher pump, the campsite caters to equestrians. There are picnic tables and trash cans, but no rest rooms—just a portable toilet located near the hunt check station on Saddle Pen Road. Reaching the parking area, you've completed a 7-mile hike.

APEX TRAIL

The Apex Trail system is 5.5 miles farther north on CR 337, reached through the same entrance as the new Goethe State Forest Visitors Center. Although this is not part of the Trailwalker program, it is by far the best

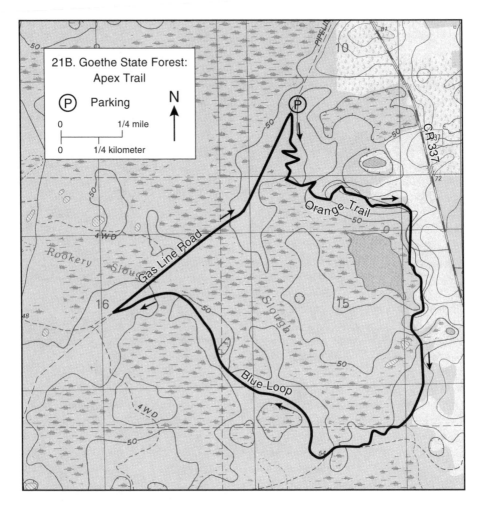

hike in Goethe State Forest, epitomizing what the forest stands for–the preservation of longleaf pine forest. Stop in the visitors center for a set of trail maps. This trail system contains five different loop trails: the 11.7-mile Red Trail, the 11.5-mile Orange Trail, the 6.4-mile Pink Loop, the 6.4-mile Green Loop, and the 4.5-mile Blue Loop. This hike follows the Orange Trail and the Blue Loop for a loop hike of 4.5 miles, a two-hour trip.

If you start your hike at the kiosk, you'll need to hike 1.2 miles on Gas Line Road,

increasing your overall hike to 5.7 miles. Instead, if the road remains open to vehicles, drive in on the hard-packed limestone to the trailhead, marked by a sign on the left that says ORANGE TRAIL, with an orange diamond and Marker B. Park off the road– there is room for two cars. Follow the orange diamonds along the narrow grassy track through the dense pine flatwoods. A ground skink squirms into the wiregrass. One longleaf pine arches over the trail, showing signs of a catface deeply scarred by many years of burns. As the trail turns a

Water lilies on a flatwoods pond

corner it enters a grove of older longleaf pines and young cypresses. These older pines are the salvation of the red-cockaded woodpecker, a species that nests only in living longleaf pines at least a century old. Watch for the telltale sign of a nest: sticky sap dripping down the tree trunk like candle wax. This forest has one of the highest populations of red-cockaded woodpeckers in the peninsula.

At 0.4 mile a needle-strewn area on the left would make a great camping spot—if it's dry, of course. The trail weaves its way through densely packed pines. When you reach the fork, turn left. Stretching away in perfect rows, the young pines in front of you are part of a pine plantation planted on sandhills. A silver-spotted skipper lands on the waxy ivory blooms of a sandhill milkweed. Two white-tailed deer graze between the pines. The trail curves around the pine plantation, coming to a fence line. It turns

right, heading straight up the rows of pines. A bumblebee chases a white sulfur away from the juices of a thistle. Sweeping off to the left are the broad, open pastures of horse farms. You come to an old piece of fence with barbed wire wrapped around it. Just beyond the orange blaze and a sign that says ORANGE TRAIL is a CONNECTOR TRAIL sign to the left. The Connector Trail uses Saddle Pen Road to connect this loop with the Tidewater Trail system, creating a popular weekend route for horsepackers. Continue on the Orange Trail, walking along the edge of an old pasture replanted in longleaf pines. You pass a snag filled with woodpecker holes—the red-cockaded woodpecker isn't the only woodpecker in this forest. Watch for the redheaded woodpecker, a large bird distinctive by its blood-red head and black and white alternating bands across its back.

Reaching the edge of a pine plantation, the trail swings to the right. You see the colorful lady lupine, its spiky purple orchid-like blooms rising up from a circle of thick fuzzy leaves. Keep alert at the next fork, where the trail keeps to the right. Dark red fruits cover the prickly pear cactus, and a blackberry thicket rains fresh berries on the ground. Both attract the gopher tortoise, a resident of the sandhills. Listen for the sounds of leaves rustling high overhead, and you might catch a glimpse of a fox squirrel nibbling on acorns, its tawny coat standing out against the green leaves of a water oak. Rounding a cypress dome, the trail forms a boundary between the natural forest on the right and the disturbed old pastureland on the left. At 1.3 miles you reach an arrow that points left. The trail enters an older forest, following another arrow. Emerging back into a pasture filled with young longleaf pines, you see dozens of sandhill milkweeds, with their distinctive variegated purple-pink leaves. After passing a metal deer stand, you come to a yellow arrow shortly followed by double orange blazes. The trail reaches a T intersection and turns right at 1.8 miles, lined on both sides by a mature pine plantation with an understory of wax myrtle and scattered saw palmetto. The habitat shifts to a healthy pine flatwoods, and the trail becomes grassier as you pass cypress domes and bayheads. A bird swoops down from a longleaf pine—the zebra-striped back of red-cockaded woodpecker in flight.

At 2.2 miles you reach double-diamond blazes of orange and blue as you meet the intersection with the Blue Loop at Marker C. Turn right, heading straight into the pine flatwoods. Scattered clearings mark where infestations of southern pine beetle have been cleared. Just above your head, a highbush blueberry dangles dainty pink bell-shaped blooms. At the fork, stay left. Unfurling from a ball to its 2-foot length, a full-grown pygmy rattler slips off the footpath and into the undergrowth. You hear the crashing of deer as they push through the saw palmetto. As you walk through bayhead drainages, the trail becomes wet in spots. Clusters of cinnamon ferns edge the footpath. The blooms of bog buttons float in the air like starry constellations, three-dimensional representations of the sky suspended above the grass of the trail.

After 3 miles you come to a fork. Keep left. On the right, a cleared area with a carpet of pine needles would make a fine campsite, but you'd have to rely on the unreliable bayheads as a swampy water source. Watch for the catfaced snag on the right. When you reach a yellow arrow and a double blue-diamond blaze, you meet up with a limestone road—the road where your car is parked. You've hiked 3.4 miles. Turn right to walk down Gas Line Road. There is no traffic, just the sound of wind in the pines and birds in the trees. Created by road building, a marshy slough parallels the road. Keep alert for wildlife. Startled at your approach, a little blue heron flies up to a pine branch. A yellow arrow points left—the continuation of the Red Trail. Stay straight. Pause for a moment at the blackwater ponds, covered with water lilies in full bloom. Dozens of frogs form a chorus. Rounding a mile bend, the road parallels another slough, pennywort growing profusely on the edge of the dark water. After you round the next bend, you see your car. The bright spot straight ahead is a pasture in the distance. In the forest to the right, a couple of catfaced snags have rotted through, looking like trees with legs supporting their trunks. You reach the TO APEX TRAILHEAD sign, completing the 4.5-mile hike. If you parked at the kiosk, continue up the limestone road, which curves left along the pasture fenceline, and end at the kiosk after a hike of 5.7 miles.

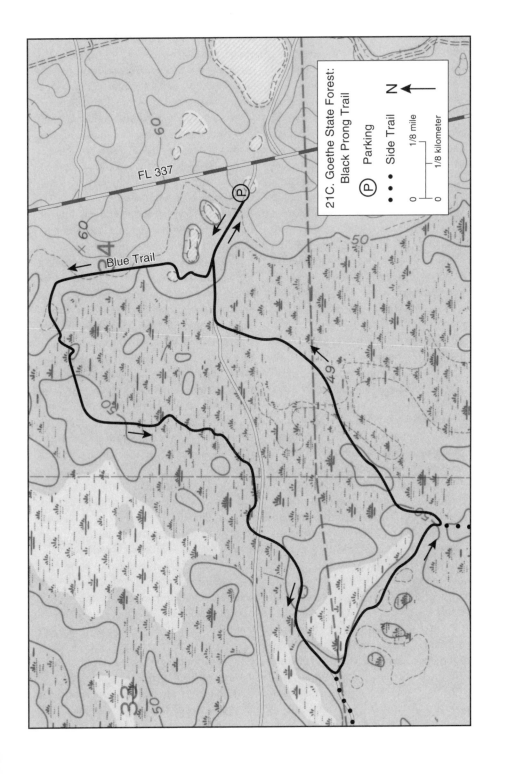

21C. Goethe State Forest:
Black Prong Trail

Ⓟ Parking
•••• Side Trail

0   1/8 mile
0   1/8 kilometer

N ←

FL 337

Blue Trail

60

60

× 60

× 4

50

49

33

50

BLACK PRONG TRAIL

The northernmost trailhead in Goethe State Forest, Black Prong is 7.7 miles north of Apex along CR 337, just 1 mile north of FL 326. Although the Black Prong Trail system is part of the Florida State Forest Trailwalker program, this area appeals more to equestrians than to hikers. A 1981 firestorm ravaged much of the pine forest, and recent habitat restoration efforts left scars from bulldozers and prescribed burns throughout the trail system. There are three marked trails: the 3.5- to 5-mile Blue Trail, the 7-mile Red Trail, and the 10-mile Orange Trail. If you choose to hike here for the Trailwalker patch, go for the shortest route—following the blue blazes on a 3.4-mile loop starting at the Black Prong trailhead, next to a small picnic area.

Following the blue blazes down the limestone road, you enter an oak hammock, reaching the BLUE TRAIL sign at 0.2 mile. Turn right. Although another sign says ROAD CLOSED TO VEHICLES, it's obvious that large trucks have rumbled through here. The area is logged out, leaving only scattered longleaf pines. Numerous firebreaks slice through the bayheads. When you come to a T intersection at 0.5 mile, turn left. Pines crowd close to the road, with a virtual mat of blueberry bushes beneath them. The smell of pine is in the air, rising up from damp needles touched by morning fog. At the fork, stay left. Deer moss grows between the blueberry bushes, and you see the tracks of deer and bobcat intermingled in the soft sand. Look for places where the deer moss has been grazed. Reindeer lichen flourishes in a patch of bright white sand, and cinnamon ferns stand out sharply against the scorched earth. When you reach the fork, turn left. You pass a tall stand of longleaf pine and a grove of scrubby sand live oaks. A charred stump rises from a clump of saw palmetto, showing off a metal strip embedded in a catface. After you pass the double diamond blaze and an arrow, you come to a T intersection with a hard-packed limestone road at 1.3 miles. Turn right, rejoining the route of the Orange and Red Trails. A zebra swallowtail dances between several daisy fleabane. At 1.5 miles a big yellow arrow painted on a brown sign indicates a left turn onto another forest road, across from a cypress dome.

Limestone yields to sand as you enter an oak hammock with stately old live oaks, their spreading limbs covered in resurrection fern. Embedded in a laurel oak's trunk is a sign, EVENSTOCK ROAD, that's been used for target practice. Shaded by the oaks, a flat area on the right at 1.7 miles would make a good, but dry, campsite (there is no drinking water). Follow the road between the posts of a cable gate. On your left is a tangled mass of loblolly bay and grapevine, an impenetrable thicket forming a drainage area. On your right, the forest has burned. There are many strange cuts in the forest, as through a bulldozer went through years ago, pushing excess dirt off the road and into the woods.

You come to a fork at 1.9 miles. The Red and Orange Trails go right; the Blue Trail goes to the left. Turn left. A sign says ECOLOGICAL RESTORATION IN PROGRESS. Straight ahead, the entire area is burned and cut, a terrible scar the on landscape. To restore the natural longleaf pine and wiregrass ecosystem that burned in 1981, the forestry people have cut down the oak hammock that took its place. At the next fork, keep left. An ancient cedar stands in a circle of oaks, with a woodpecker hole bored straight through its thick trunk.

At 2.1 miles you reach the decision point for the length of the hike on the Blue Trail. To the right, the long loop leads through the devastated area, a forest that won't regenerate for a decade or more. Stick with the short look—continue straight, passing tall clumps of beargrass. Watch for gopher tortoises wandering in search of prickly pear fruits. An armadillo scrabbles through the underbrush. You rejoin the long loop of the Blue Trail at the next fork, at 2.3 miles. Turn left, walking under the cool shade of the oak hammock. At the next T intersection the Blue Trail turns right. Look carefully, and you'll see some coontie growing in the shade of the oaks. As the trail comes out into the sun, you pass through a stand of sweetgum. At the T intersection, turn right. You've hiked 2.9 miles. You're back on the hard-packed limestone road, which has little shade. Continue along the road, passing the beginning of the Blue Trail, to complete your hike at the parking area after 3.4 miles.

III

Ocala National Forest

Silver Glen Spring

22

Ravine Gardens State Park

Total distance (circuit): 2.1 miles

Hiking time: 1.5 hours

Habitats: Seepage slopes, bluffs and ravines, freshwater marsh, hardwood hammock

Maps: USGS 7½' Palatka, park map

In the 1930s the Federal Works Project Administration (WPA) and the Civil Works Administration (CWA) joined with other governmental bodies to pull together an ambitious project in post-Depression Palatka—planting a massive garden in and around a natural deep ravine in the middle of the city. More than 250,000 ornamental plants and 95,000 azaleas later, it was described in 1934 as the "Nation's Outstanding CWA Project." Trails led down and around the depths of the ravines, where bubbling artesian springs poured forth clear streams; two massive suspension bridges for foot traffic spanned the ravines. A scenic drive wound around the top of the gardens, giving drivers a chance to glimpse the thousands of azaleas in bloom each March. The city of Palatka turned Ravine Gardens over to the state of Florida in 1970, and it became a state park.

Despite the massive numbers of nonnative plants added to the natural ravine landscape, the forest has had the last laugh. Ornamentals still thrive just behind the visitors center in a set of formal gardens, and azaleas spill over some of the steep slopes. But a natural hardwood forest, lush with ferns fed by the seepage slopes, thrives at one end of the ravine; a freshwater marsh fills another. Tall loblolly pines climb up some of the hills. This hike describes the steepest and most challenging route around the park—following the trails along the walls of the ravines, in some places a scant narrow path along a precipitous drop. Families with young children will find a quick

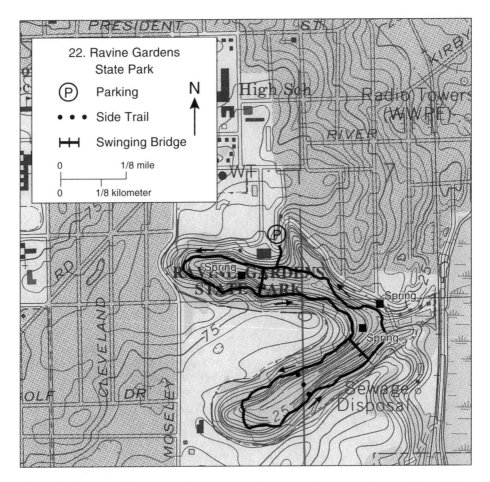

trip to the bottom of the ravine less worrisome, where they can meander along flat trails from one end of the park to the other.

Ravine Gardens State Park sits in the middle of Palatka. All major roads have signs directing you to the park. From the intersection of FL 19 and FL 100 in Palatka, drive 1.4 miles east to Mosley Avenue. Turn right. Watch for the signs. Turn left on Silver Lake Road. From FL 19 you can also take FL 20 east for 1.7 miles to Mosley Avenue. Turn right, following Mosley Avenue 0.5 mile to the traffic light at Silver Lake Road. Turn left. The park entrance is 0.1 mile down Silver Lake Road, on the right. As you enter

the park and pay your Florida State Parks day-use fee, ask for a map of the hiking trails. Drive past the Court of States, the formal gardens to your left, and find a parking place either in front of the visitors center, near the picnic pavilion, or near the garden center, the small building with the William Bartram Trail historical marker in front of it. After exploring the St. Johns River in 1774, botanist William Bartram worked his way west across the state through this region, stopping at "the great Alachua Savanna" (Hike 20) before reaching the village of Talahasochte. Known to the Creeks as "Puc Puggy," the flower hunter, Bartram was the

---

Ravine Gardens State Park

A barred owl peers out from the foliage

first explorer to identify and catalog Florida's vast array of botanical wonders, taking specimens back to his Philadelphia patron for cultivation.

After a stop at the visitors center, start your hike by heading down through the picnic pavilion on the side of the center. A series of staircases takes you down the garden terraces to the start of the trail inside the ravine. Columns of limestone stand guard at the ends of the formal gardens. Wind past the gazebo, past tall specimens of East Palatka holly, an endemic variety of American holly, and continue down the stone stairs to a brick walkway. Descend down a curving set of stairs, past a planting of sago palms and between two pillars. Turn right, walking down one more staircase to the trailhead for the Bamboo Springs Trail.

One of the delights of Ravine Gardens, especially for kids, are the rough and rugged 1930s swinging bridges across the ravine. Start your walk by turning left at the trailhead sign to cross the first bridge, which sways underfoot with your every step. Turn right and climb the stone steps up to the Bamboo Springs Trail. As you walk through the azaleas, the trail drops down broad steps that take it halfway down the side of the ravine. You'll want to experience this hike at least once during late February through mid-March, when the colorful azalea blooms cloak the hills. A channel on the right side of the path funnels water downhill during rainstorms, preventing erosion. A sea of sword ferns sweeps down to the watercourse pouring out of Bamboo Springs. Invasive air potato vines attempt to take over the garden. Brought to Florida from West Africa, these vines spread like kudzu, swarming over trees and shrubs, choking out sunlight. In Africa their edible underground tubers are cultivated as a crop. Some varieties of the plant contain the steroid diosgenin, used in the manufacture of birth-control pills.

As you pass a tall stand of saw palmetto, a bridge leads to the right. Continue straight as the trail curves to the left to loop around a side ravine, where water spills down the slopes to feed banana palms thriving in the moist sand bottom. A massive southern magnolia arches well out over the ravine; two barred owls perch in its branches, curiously regarding you. Despite its nocturnal feeding habitats, the barred owl is the owl most commonly seen sitting in tree branches during the day. Its rounded features can be mistaken for a barn owl from a distance, but you'll identify this owl immediately when you hear its "who cooks for you" call.

After you pass a staircase coming down from the road, continue straight. The trail drops down a staircase past sword ferns and azaleas to Bamboo Springs, a set of piped artesian wells bubbling to create a clear flowing stream pouring downhill under the young bald cypresses. The trail climbs up the ravine slope from here, along a wetland choked with Asian bamboo. A gray squirrel with a thick coat sits on a railing, gnawing on a hickory nut. Passing an overgrown staircase, you ascend to the curve in the trail, following the west end of the ravine. Beyond Marker 12 you feel like you're on a goat track, following the narrow path along the ravine's slope as you get a great view of the wetlands around Bamboo Springs. Climbing up under live oaks and southern magnolia, you're behind and below the visitors center. Turn left at the trail junction, keeping to the ravine slope. Returning to the beginning of the Bamboo Springs Trail at 0.7 mile, turn right, crossing back over the suspension bridge. Turn left at the far end to follow the trail east along the ravine's slope. You come to a fork where a staircase leads to the right. Turn left. Dropping down again, you see young cypresses growing along the creek. The trail climbs uphill again under live oaks that arch out over it. Another staircase comes in from the right. Continue straight. Although side trails lead left to the ravine's bottom, stay with the main path. The trail turns to the right and climbs up a set of rocky stairs.

At 0.9 mile you come to another suspension bridge across the ravine and a staircase leading to the bottom. Beyond it lays the Azalea Trail. Continue straight, walking past the AZALEA TRAIL sign into a dense forest of azalea bushes, rising up to 12 feet high. Months after the fragrant pink blooms fall off, you can still catch the faint sweet aroma rising from the forest floor. The trail climbs up and over a bridge over a side ravine. An ironwood arches over the trail, its branch touching the ground on the far side.

You see a duckweed-choked spring seep pond down the hill. At 1.1 miles a bridge leads to the left across the murky pond. Walk out and survey the pond, and then return to the main trail, which climbs back up the bluff through a corridor of azaleas. Air potatoes and grapevines struggle for control of the ravine, while saw palmettos with long trunks reach out from the trail's edge. At the T intersection, keep left. Stay right at the next fork to continue on the outer perimeter of the ravine. Here, the slopes are covered in grapevine, air potato, and tall lantana. At the 12/11 sign, turn left, down into the ravine. On your right, monstrous southern woods ferns thrive in the dampness of a seepage slope. Each fern's fronds are large enough to be a fern itself. This is the eastern end of the ravine, nearest the St. Johns River. A series of boardwalks carries the trail over seepage springs, where ferns cascade over the slopes—giant sword fern, woods fern, and netted chain growing up to a foot tall. You hear a rustling in the leaves as a Florida box turtle backs up into its den. This threatened species is a subspecies of the eastern box turtle, distinguished by its unique radiant shell pattern and three toes on its hind feet.

As you leave the eastern corner of the ravine, a wooden staircase takes the trail up a heavily eroded slope. A lush hardwood hammock spills down the ravine slopes. The trail sticks to a narrow plateau along the ravine slope and becomes precipitous in places, with sharp drops and no railings. The habitat yields to oak hammock, and you pass a staircase to the right leading to a picnic table and grill. A bench provides a place to rest before you continue. The trail is steeply pitched toward the ravine; walk cautiously. Banana plants peep out of the more common undergrowth below. You come to a set of staircases; one leads down to the suspension bridge that crosses back to the start of the Azalea Trail. Ascend the staircase to your right. As you pass another staircase, this one leading up to the road, continue straight, and you can see the serpentine curve of road dropping down into the ravine. Take the staircase to your left (the fourth you have encountered), which leads down into the ravine, ending at the edge of the road. Turn left to walk through the gardens down to the pond. Cross the bridge over the pond and turn right, following the trail along the water. You smell sulfur in the air—fumes from a sulfur spring, set back in the forest on the far side of the road—as you walk along the next pond. Water lilies drift across the dark water, where a musk turtle floats along the weedy edge. You see a sign, 17, part of an old exercise course. Continue to walk along the water.

At 1.8 miles you come to a clearing.

Keep to the left side of the ravine. As you round the curve you see the original suspension bridge in the distance. Turn right to cross a small bridge over the shallow sandy creek, ascending back into hardwood hammock. At the T intersection, turn left. Loblolly pines tower overhead. The trail curves to the right around a duckweed-choked pond, and roots make the footpath more difficult. You climb up a steep slope to another T intersection with an ADOPT A TRAIL sign. Turn left, walking past wild indigo and Spanish bayonet. The trail curves around a large southern magnolia, dropping down into a corridor of azaleas. A wooden staircase carries the trail up and over a large fallen tree allowed to rot on the ravine slope. You ascend up a steep slope to a trail junction. Turn right. Emerging on the park road, turn left. Walk back to your car, completing your hike after 2.1 miles.

23

St. Johns Loop

Total distance (circuit): 3.6 miles

Hiking time: 1.5 hours

Habitats: Flatwoods, hardwood hammock, floodplain forest

Maps: USGS 7½' Satsuma

In 1845 Robert E. Lee led a U.S. Army Corps of Engineers survey of Florida, returning to headquarters with a potential path across the center of the state. It wasn't until the 1930s, when a private company formed to start digging the canal, that the difficult job—performed by hand—was started. Workers only managed to create a ditch near Belleview, south of Ocala, before the money ran out and the project collapsed. In 1968 the Army Corps of Engineers stepped in. Building the Rodman Dam where the Ocklawaha River flowed into the St. Johns, they altered the natural flow of this cypress-lined river, once a significant steamboat route into central Florida. No longer could manatees swim freely upstream to their wintering grounds; the new Buckman Lock caused the death of more than one of these gentle creatures. Behind the dam, more than nine thousand acres of forest drowned, creating a mecca for anglers looking for largemouth bass.

In 1969 environmentalists took action. Forming the Florida Defenders of the Environment, founder Marjorie Harris Carr (wife of acclaimed Florida naturalist Archie Carr) gathered together like-minded Floridians with a single purpose: stop the canal. If completed, the canal would destroy the Ocklawaha River and flood the pristine Silver River. By 1971 President Richard Nixon agreed to halt construction of the canal, and within five years, Florida legislators officially deauthorized the project. In 1990 the U.S. Congress concurred. Within the next decade, the lands that had

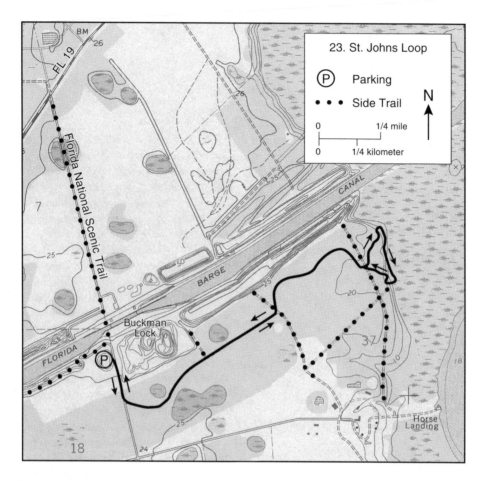

been set aside for the canal passed into public hands, becoming Florida's first Greenway–the Marjorie Harris Carr Cross Florida Greenway.

From its start at Buckman Lock, the St. Johns Loop provides a look at the river forests along this 1960s section of the canal. If Florida environmentalists win their final battle over the fate of the Ocklawaha River, these lands will return to their original precanal state, as the U.S. Forest Service has ordered the state of Florida to remove Rodman Dam by June 30, 2006, rendering Buckman Lock and this segment of canal obsolete. Part of the Cross Florida Greenway,

the St. Johns Loop is on the northern edge of the Ocala National Forest, only 10 miles south of the intersection of FL 20 and FL 19 in Palatka. From I-75 take exit 352, Ocala. Head east on FL 40, passing Silver Springs and the Ocklawaha Visitors Center (Hike 29) before you come to the intersection of FL 40 and FL 314 at Nuby's Corners. Drive north on FL 314 through the Ocala National Forest, passing Lake Eaton (Hike 28) before you reach FL 19 at Salt Springs. Continue north on FL 19 for 12.8 miles. The turnoff is just after the entrance to Caravelle Ranch. Turn onto Boys Ranch Road under the large sign, and continue 1.9 miles to the St. Johns

Loop trailhead sign. Turn left and follow the rough paved road back another 0.4 mile to the parking area at Buckman Lock.

From the parking lot and picnic area, head back down the paved road for 0.2 mile until you reach a green sign with a hiker on it, on the left. The St. Johns Loop trail begins here. Despite its name, the trail doesn't reach the shores of the St. Johns River—instead, it loops along the edge of the river's extensive floodplain forest. This interpretive trail starts off down a broad forest road through a wet pine flatwoods shaded by tall slash pine and sweetbay magnolia, with a dense understory of gallberry and cabbage palm covered in grapevine. Although the trail is only open to hikers, don't be surprised to come across signs of horses that have passed through. The damp environment invites netted chain, royal fern, and cinnamon fern to thrive, as well as the ubiquitous poison ivy. Don't stray off the trail or you'll end up in poison ivy. Honeysuckle climbs up the thick trunks of slash pines, infusing the forest with its fragrance.

As the forest opens up at 0.7 mile, you see a large live oak on the left. You cross a forest road. The preserve is crisscrossed with many jeep trails, so keep careful watch for interpretive signs and hiker-symbol signs to lead you down the correct route. Notice the charring on the trunks of the saw palmettos and pines—quite apropos for the adjacent ROLE OF FIRE interpretive sign. Fire is an important component of healthy pine flatwoods as it clears out the small oaks that would otherwise take over the habitat and transform it into Florida's climax forest, the oak hammock. The trail rises, and the habitat changes slightly to a dry pine flatwoods, where an unbroken expanse of saw palmetto engulfs the bases of scattered slash pine, longleaf pine, and sand live oak. A six-lined racerunner emerges from an abandoned gopher tortoise burrow. You cross a firebreak and continue straight, noticing many candle-stage longleaf pines popping through the saw palmetto understory.

After 1 mile the trail comes to a T at the base of a large live oak. Turn left, and then immediately right, following the route designated by the hiker sign. Parched saw palmettos line the trail, their fronds turning a soft golden orange. Yellow-eyed grass emerges from the footpath. Soft puffs of old man's beard coat fallen trees. Startled, a wild turkey crashes through the underbrush, skimming the underside of a live oak as it takes to the sky. As you enter an oak hammock, you see a longleaf pine and a turkey oak leaning on each other for support, their trunks fused together. Spreading sand live oak provides plenty of shade. At 1.4 miles you come to a junction where the trail you're on continues, but the hiker sign indicates that your route turns right. Briefly paralleling a jeep trail through soft white sand, the trail crosses it, continuing into the shade of an old oak hammock with a tall canopy of gnarled sand live oaks. Sphagnum moss carpets the ground. Keep to the open path on the right side of the hammock. You're walking through an old homestead. Off to the far left are several artifacts: a steel cable, a piece of a roof, a grill. The trail becomes a narrow footpath into the dense forest, passing more interpretive signs. As it rounds a bend to the right, the trail continues downhill and reaches another hiker sign. Turn left. You're walking along the floodplain forest of the St. Johns River, where bald cypresses grow tightly together. With careful concentration, you can make out a ribbon of blue beyond the trees. Look up, and you'll see the brilliant purple blooms of cardinal wild pine, flourishing in this humid swamp—along with

Candle-stage longleaf pine peeping above saw palmetto on the St. Johns Loop

thick clouds of mosquitoes. Step up your pace as you walk along the cypresses. Just upriver from this point is Horse Landing, now a part of the privately owned Rodeheaver Boys Ranch. In 1864 the 2nd Florida Cavalry Company H, headed up by Capt. John J. Dickison, joined with the Milton Light Artillery to fire on the *Columbine*, a Union gunboat that was steaming up to the landing. Snapping the gunboat's rudder chain, they disabled the vessel, which struck a sandbar. As the Confederates kept their fire on the ship, the captain and crew surrendered. Of the 148 soldiers on the *Columbine*, only 66 survived; many drowned attempting to escape to the far shore. The battle marked the only time in military history when a cavalry company sunk a ship. Civil War buffs reenact the Battle of Horse Landing every November, the weekend before Thanksgiving, at the adjacent Rodeheaver Boys Ranch.

The trail continues as a narrow footpath skirting the edge of the swamp, crossing plow lines from the former plantation. Trumpet vines crawl up sweetgum trees, dangling their bell-shaped flowers overhead. When you come to the next trail marker, keep right. Cinnamon fern, bracken fern, and netted chain cover the steep slope leading down to the floodplain forest. The trail rises up into an oak hammock and reaches a T intersection. Turn right and walk into the deep green hardwood forest. The footpath becomes difficult due to the spacing of the plow lines—a lot of constant ups and downs. Emerging in a clearing, the trail continues to undulate over plow lines

until it comes out under the oak hammock with its debris pile of artifacts. After 1.8 miles you've completed the loop. Continue straight to retrace your path back to the trailhead. Turning left out of the oak hammock, cross the sand road into the scrubby flatwoods. Take care when you pass the next hiker sign facing away from you to make a left at the T. After walking through the shady hammock and open flatwoods, you return to the large oak tree that marks the intersection of three forest roads. Walk up to the tree and turn right on the broad main trail at 2.4 miles. This trail leads back out to the paved road. Turn right to continue down to the parking lot at Buckman Lock, ending your hike after 3.6 miles.

For a look at the Cross Florida Barge Canal, wander down the section of the Florida National Scenic Trail that heads along the canal. Crossing the canal here at Buckman Lock, the Florida National Scenic Trail continues south into the heart of the Ocala National Forest. Alternatively, you can scramble up the equestrian trail on the far side of the entrance road to walk along the spoil piles created by the dirt removed to make the canal, providing you a view along the canal. If you want a better look at Buckman Lock—it's fenced off on this side—drive back out to FL 19 and head north 2.9 miles, across the Cross Florida Barge Canal bridge, and turn right down Buckman Lock Road. Park near the visitors center or the rest rooms and walk over to the observation deck for a sweeping view. Although it was built to serve major commercial traffic, the lock now only provides boaters on the St. Johns River access to Rodman Dam.

24

Salt Springs Loop Trail

Total distance (circuit): 1.9 miles

Hiking time: 1 hour

Habitats: Sand pine scrub, oak scrub, oak hammock, bayhead, floodplain forest, freshwater marsh, hardwood hammock

Maps: USGS 7½' Salt Springs

Trapped within the limestone for millennia, ancient seawater mixes with the Floridan Aquifer to form an unusual set of saline springs, pushing 52 million gallons of water a day down Salt Springs Run. Laced with sodium, potassium, silica, and magnesium salts, Salt Springs has attracted visitors since the early 1900s, when people came to "take the waters" for their supposed curative powers. Today's visitors are outdoors enthusiasts enjoying the constant 74-degree swimming hole at Salt Springs Recreation Area, one of several developed campgrounds in the Ocala National Forest.

A little more than a mile south of the springs, Salt Springs Run empties into Lake George, the largest of the St. Johns River's chain of lakes. The Salt Springs Loop provides hikers free access to a scenic view over Salt Springs Run, a quiet place to sit and watch the healing waters slip by.

To find the Salt Springs Loop Trail, take I-75 exit 352, Ocala. Drive east on FL 40, passing Silver Springs and the Ocklawaha Visitors Center (Hike 29) before you come to the intersection of FL 40 and FL 314 at Nuby's Corners. Continue north on FL 314 through the Ocala National Forest, passing Lake Eaton (Hike 28) before you reach FL 19 at Salt Springs. Turn right. A signpost marks the trailhead on the left along FL 19, just 0.5 mile south. If you are coming from I-95, take exit 268, Ormond Beach, and head west on FL 40 through Barberville and Astor, turning north when you reach the blinker at FL 19. Drive 15 miles on FL 19, passing the Yearling Trail (Hike 26) and

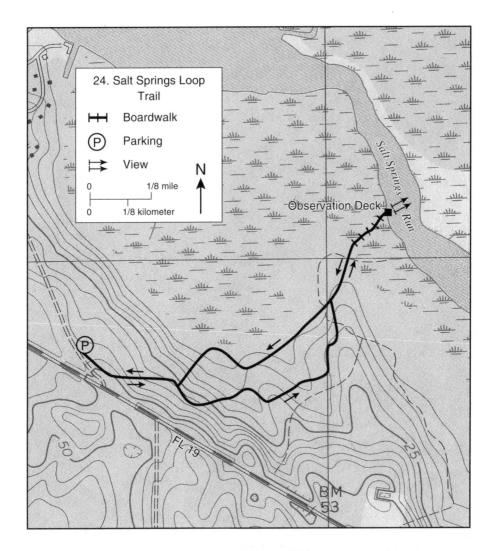

24. Salt Springs Loop Trail

⊢⊣ Boardwalk

Ⓟ Parking

⇨ View

N

0 ⊢⊣ 1/8 mile

0 ⊢⊣ 1/8 kilometer

Salt Springs Run

Observation Deck

Ⓟ

FL 19

50

25

BM ×53

Silver Glen Springs (Hike 25). It's a little difficult to see the turnoff from this direction, so keep alert after you see the small brown National Forest sign alerting you to an upcoming trailhead.

Although there is no camping along this short trail, two National Forest campgrounds are nearby. Choose a rustic site at Shanty Pond by following the signs just south of the trailhead along FL 19, or head for the popular developed recreation area at Salt Springs, 1.3 miles north on FL 19. The Salt Springs Visitors Center, with maps and information about all of the campgrounds and trails within the Ocala National Forest, lies just 0.2 mile north of the Salt Springs Recreation Area, in a shopping center on the left.

Starting from the trailhead parking lot, walk up past the SALT SPRINGS TRAIL AND OBSERVATION PLATFORM sign. Curving away from the hum of traffic on FL 19, the trail

Salt Springs Run

cuts a broad path through an oak scrub, where Chapman and myrtle oaks crowd around young sand pines. You head downhill into this forest in miniature, a perfect habitat for the Florida scrub-jay, where the oaks are no more than 12 feet tall. Keep alert for scrub-jays scrabbling through the underbrush, turning over oak leaves they placed to mark their caches of acorns.

As you come to the Salt Springs Loop Trail kiosk, a fat brown anole skitters away. The map on the kiosk shows the loop and its two connectors, which lead to the parking area and to the observation platform on Salt Springs Run. Pink and white blotches of lichen decorate the trunks of the sand live oaks around you; resurrection fern attempts to establish a foothold in the crooks of trees. A southeastern five-lined skink flashes its brilliant blue tail as it hides itself under the fallen ivory blooms of a narrowleaf pawpaw. As you proceed down the slope, you pass a bench.

At 0.2 mile you reach the trail junction at the top of the loop. Continue straight. A split-rail fence blocks off the crossing of an old jeep trail. The footpath continues forward through a narrow corridor afforded by the scrub oaks. Look closely at the tiny gardens of lichens that the oaks host—turquoise stringers of old man's beard, tiny star-shaped lichens, and lichens with spiky cones. As the trail continues downhill, you pass by a snag decorated in cracked cap polypore, a dark fungus with black undersides. Passing under a Florida dogwood that displays showy blooms in early March, you see cardinal wild pine flourishing in its branches, its purple-tipped flowers opening in April. Below, steps of oyster fungi envelope a rotting log. Although the scrub is desertlike, this is a moist pocket within it, with epiphytes in the trees and fungi coating every dead surface. You step out into the full sun into an area where larger snags stand, some still covered in resurrection fern. Flanked by two dogwoods, a southern magnolia stands ready to burst into bloom, its dinner plate–size blossoms partially open. The trail reenters the shade of the oak scrub and continues downhill. Take a moment to examine the resurrection ferns at eye level on the sand live oaks. Looking at the underside of each frond, you see golden spores, the fern's method of reproduction. The trail rises slightly, and you begin to see young sand pines amid the oaks. As you catch a glimpse of sky between the trees, the canopy lifts. You walk under gnarled sand live oaks draped in Spanish moss, with younger myrtle and Chapman oak below. Rusty lyonia grows tall, mingling with the oaks. A zebra swallowtail looks for the delicate white blooms of a deerberry. As the trail continues to drop down, it meanders through clumps of saw palmetto. Slash pines break through the understory.

Emerging at a T intersection after 0.7 mile, you come to a large sign that indicates the direction and distance to the observation platform and the parking lot. Turn right, walking down a broad path between loblolly pines. The trail drops down into a bayhead and crosses over a bridge before descending into an oak hammock with spreading live oaks. After passing a bench, the trail curves gently to the right, carpeted by pine needles. You reach a boardwalk through a floodplain forest; cinnamon and royal ferns thrive under the shade of sweetgum and cypress.

After 1 mile the trail ends at an observation platform on Salt Springs Run, where there is a panoramic view of the water as it flows out into Lake George. An immature bald eagle soars overhead on its way to the lake, resplendent in its stippled white and brown feathers. Moorhens squawk as an al-

Sensitive brier

sand and small particles of shells are thrown up with the waters." Describing "Alph, the sacred river" as gushing forth from a "mighty fountain . . . 'mid dancing rocks," Coleridge echoes Bartram, his fantasy river "five miles meandering with a mazy motion."

Turn around and head back on the board-walk, retracing your path through the hammock and up to the bottom of the loop. When you return to the big sign, continue straight on the broad trail. As you ascend into the scrub, notice how the temperature rises, a significant difference from the edge of Salt Springs Run. Aging sand pines lean over the trail. A white sulfur flutters around the yellowish-green blooms of a saw palmetto, the blooms at the end of spikes that stick out and flop over into the trail. After the blooms drop off, berries emerge, ripening in September. While the Timucua once used the berries as a food source, herbal remedies from saw palmetto berries are used today to treat bladder and prostate problems.

Following the ecotone between oak hammock and scrub, the trail continues uphill, curving in front of a split-rail fence at 1.5 miles. Passing another bench, you see a saw palmetto raising its fronds well up into the air on long, slender trunks. As you walk, you're accompanied by the constant crunch of oak and magnolia leaves underfoot. Like little balls of slender pink fibers, the blooms of a sensitive brier cascade over a split-rail fence section. The trail curves to the left, and then ascends sharply up into oak scrub, reaching a T intersection at 1.7 miles. You've completed the loop. Turn right. It's a slow long rise up through the oak scrub to return to the trailhead. Reaching the map kiosk, the trail jogs left and heads uphill, ending at the parking area after 1.9 miles.

ligator drifts past. The water is clear; look down and see the aquatic grasses waving, the bass and bluegill floating past. Duck potato blooms in the shallows, and white morning glories pop through the poison ivy on the water's edge. Wind ripples the water. A canoe glides by, the canoeists intent on watching the water. Inspired by the vivid descriptions of Florida published in 1792 by naturalist William Bartram, Samuel Taylor Coleridge set his epic poem *Kubla Khan* in this fascinating scene. When Bartram visited Salt Springs in 1774, he described it as an "amazing crystal fountain . . . which meanders six miles through green meadows, pouring its limpid waters into the great Lake George," where within the spring, "white

25

Silver Glen Springs

Total distance (round trip): 3.1 miles

Hiking time: 1.5 hours

Habitats: Pine flatwoods, oak hammock, hydric hammock, bayhead, floodplain forest, oak scrub

Maps: USGS 7½' Juniper Springs

With a rambling walk along the broadest portion of the St. Johns River, the trails at Silver Glen Springs provide unexpected insights into the natural beauty of the waters that shape the edge of the Ocala National Forest. This popular recreation area attracts families who canoe the run and swim in the first-magnitude springs, which quickly flow off to Lake George. Open from 8 AM to 8 PM, the Silver Glen Springs Recreation Area costs $3 per person to enter (ages six and up). It's well worth the admission fee for a hike along the St. George Trail, with its sweeping views of Lake George. As a bonus, you get to enjoy the short Spring Boils Trail, which leads to historic bubbling springs that feed Silver Glen Run. Since the park has a reputation as a party spot on summer weekends and is overrun with boaters anchoring near the spring, it's best to visit on a weekday to enjoy serenity as you stroll the trails.

Silver Glen Springs is set on the eastern edge of the Ocala National Forest. From the west take I-75 exit 352, Ocala. Drive east on FL 40, passing Silver Springs and the Ocklawaha Visitors Center (Hike 29) before you enter the Ocala National Forest. You'll pass Juniper Springs (Hike 27) a few miles before you reach the blinker at FL 19. If you are coming in from the east or south, take I-95 exit 268, Ormond Beach, and head west on FL 40 through Barberville and Astor to the blinker at FL 19. At this intersection, turn north on FL 19 and drive 6.2 miles to the Silver Glen Springs Recreation Area, just across from the Yearling Trail (Hike 26).

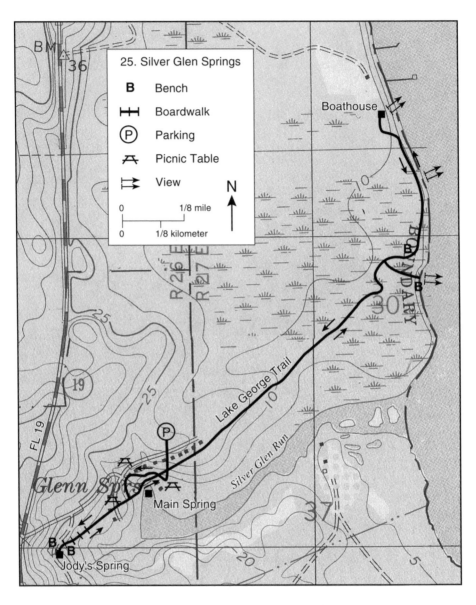

Start your hike by walking by the general store (which rents canoes and tubes for use in the run) and heading down to Silver Glen Spring. The picnic grove sits in a beautiful live oak and cedar hammock surrounding the main spring. When you reach the fence line along the spring, follow it around to the right. Stairs provide access for swimming. Looking down into the main spring, you'll marvel at the crystal-clear water with its slight aquamarine tint. The spring boil rages with tremendous power as it pushes the surface of the water upward above its deep sinkhole-shaped vent, blowing iridescent fossil snail shells upward like confetti and pouring 72 million gallons a day downstream into Lake George. As you walk along the fence, you come to a second spring, the Natural Well, roped off to keep swimmers out. Thick eelgrass emerges from this spring vent, attracting swirling schools of mullet and striped bass, seagoing fish that have taken up permanent residence in these warm waters. Continue along the fence, rounding the Natural Well, passing another staircase that leads down into the spring.

At 0.2 mile you come to the SPRING BOILS TRAIL sign, accompanied by a bear-warning sign from USFS. The state's largest population of Florida black bears roams the Ocala National Forest, and food left out on the picnic tables can tempt bears down toward the spring. If you see a bear, don't panic—consider yourself fortunate as bear sightings are rare. No one has ever been harmed by a Florida black bear, the smallest subspecies of the black bear. The trail leads into the leafy shade of hickory and sweetgum trees. Cabbage palms reach for the forest canopy. Crossing a small bridge over a side stream, you see the purple blooms of spiderwort poking out of the grasses in the understory. Winding along the ecotone between oak hammock and hydric hammock, the trail passes under an enormous hickory with an unusual bulge in its trunk. A red buckeye displays bright red blooms all winter. Railroad ties hold in the hard-packed sand that makes up the footpath, preventing it from washing away into the hydric hammock. Netted chain grows in damp spots. The trail becomes a boardwalk, heading downhill toward a clear spring run. Use caution as the boardwalk may be slippery.

You reach a small platform with a great view of the sand boils. This is Jody's Spring, where in the opening to Marjorie Kinnan Rawlings's novel *The Yearling*, Jody seeks the cool serenity of the spring. Constantly erupting, the tiny spring boils push bubbles of sand up from the bottom of the stream. Walk up to the next platform, where the trail ends at the beginning of the run. One hyperactive boil pushes up mocha-colored sand over the white-sand bottom of the glassy stream. Small fish dart through the shallows. Turn around and walk back down the trail. As you pass under the hickory tree, notice that the bulge is a massive cavity on this side of the tree, large enough to serve as home for a family of raccoons. Follow the fence line back around the springs and continue forward to the line of old live oaks. Look closely, and you'll notice that they're growing atop massive shell mounds—middens from the Timucua, who lived along the St. Johns River for more than three thousand years.

Turn left and walk up the pathway, along the edge of the middens. You reach the trailhead for the Lake George Trail on the right, behind the general store. You've walked 0.8 mile. Turn right and follow the broad footpath under a stand of unusually old and gnarled cedars. Each tree splits into multiple trunks and is covered in a thick coating of resurrection fern. Since this trail ends near an old boathouse, it's possible that the cedars were planted on purpose to line the old road. Off to the right, a hardwood hammock fills a bowl along the edge of Silver Glen Run; you can see water sparkling through the gaps in the trees. As you cross a service road, an arrow urges you forward. The trail winds under enormous live oaks, their limbs a garden of resurrection fern. As you pass by a bench, the forest closes in, a dense hardwood hammock of sweetgum, hickory, and cedar. Immense loblolly pines, up to 8 feet in circumference and 100 feet tall, rise like pillars from drifts of pine needles. Spanish moss cloaks hickory limbs.

Lake George

At 1.1 miles a trail joins in from the left, and you continue straight, past a TRAIL sign that points the way. You duck under a bower of grapevines draped between sweetbay magnolias in a bayhead. Netted chain and woods fern thrive around the culverts that drain the bayheads and wet flatwoods. You walk through a cathedral of oaks, its floor a sweeping swath of saw palmettos. Passing another bench, the trail drops down into the cool shade of more sweetbay magnolias, and then rises up into the familiar environment of the Big Scrub—edged by rusty lyonia and sand pine, broken up by groves of gnarled sand live oak. After 1.5 miles you reach an OVERLOOK sign. Turn right, walking under the canopy of oaks. You glimpse open sky at the end of the corridor. This side trail ends at a clearing along Lake George, where a bench commands a sweeping view of Florida's second-largest lake. It's not just a lake, but also a river—this is the St. Johns, flowing through the widest point of its chain of lakes on the way to the Atlantic Ocean. Mats of hydrilla float past cattails in the shallows. Laden with Spanish moss, live oaks arch over the water, a smooth mirror reflecting their forms. Saw palmettos grow right up to the water's edge.

After taking the time to enjoy the view, turn around and return to the T intersection. Turn right. You pass a botanical sculpture, a hickory arch in the forest. The trail curves to the right through a patch of bamboo; the aroma of the open water fills the air. Within moments, you're walking along Lake George, 1.7 miles into your hike. Benches provide another opportunity to sit and revel in the view, framed by moss-draped cypresses. Following the lakeshore, the trail stays up on a moderate bluff along the water. Citrus trees scent the forest with an alluring aroma. You hear the putt-putt-putt of an outboard motor as a boat comes into view. Finding a suitable hole, the anglers stop and set up their gear, casting for largemouth bass in one of Florida's premier fishing spots. A brisk breeze blows off the watery expanse—it's nearly 5 miles to the far shore. From an observation point on a high bluff, take in the sweeping vista. Lines of clouds are reflected in the perfect mirror of the still water. Scan the surface carefully, and you'll be able to pick out the loglike forms of enormous alligators resting in the shallows. Moorhens cruise into a cove, squawking. A red-tailed hawk swoops out of a cedar, grabbing a mullet firmly in its talons.

As you continue down the trail, it curves away from the lake briefly into the shade of a forest. When you reach the split-rail fence, look out to the northeast, and you can see the remains of an old boathouse. A marsh extends off to the right, busy with the chatter of wading birds. The trail ends here, at 2 miles. Turn around and return the way you came, savoring the walk back along the lake. When you pass the LAKE GEORGE sign, the trail turns away from the lake. At 2.4 miles you pass the spur trail to the left. Continue straight. At 2.7 miles you reach a fork. Keep left to return to the parking area. Crossing the service road, you emerge at the trailhead, just behind the general store. Turn right to return to the parking area, completing 3.1 miles of hiking. Grab your swimsuit and towel and head downhill to the spring to cool off after your hike.

26

The Yearling Trail

Total distance (circuit): 5.5 miles

Hiking time: 2.5 hours

Habitats: Sand pine scrub, oak scrub, sandhills, oak hammock, sinkhole

Maps: USGS 7½' Juniper Springs, park map

When Marjorie Kinnan Rawlings wrote her Pulitzer Prize–winning novel *The Yearling* in 1938, it provided America's first heart-wrenching look at post–Civil War Florida, where settlers struggled to scrape a living out of tangled forests of saw palmetto and pine. Her characters were based in reality. In the harsh Big Scrub, homesteader Reuben Long settled Pat's Island, near Silver Glen Springs. In 1933 Rawlings spent a week with Reuben Long's son Calvin's family. Calvin Long told Rawlings stories of his childhood in the scrub and about his brother's attempt to raise a young deer as a pet–stories on which she based the tale told in *The Yearling*.

In Florida's scrub, an island is a place where a slight amount of elevation over the surrounding scrub allows a different habitat to take root–in the case of Pat's Island, sandhills covered with longleaf pine. Long's descendents continued to raise cattle in the scrub until the federal government bought their land as part of the new Ocala National Forest.

Honoring both the novelist and the Long family, the Yearling Trail is a new approach to Pat's Island–historically accessed by hikers via the Florida National Scenic Trail. Dedicated in 2001, the Yearling Trail opens up this historic site to the general public by providing easy access from a new trailhead and parking area on FL 19, just across from Silver Glen Springs (Hike 25). From the blinker at the intersection of FL 40 and FL 19, turn north on FL 19 and drive 6.2 miles

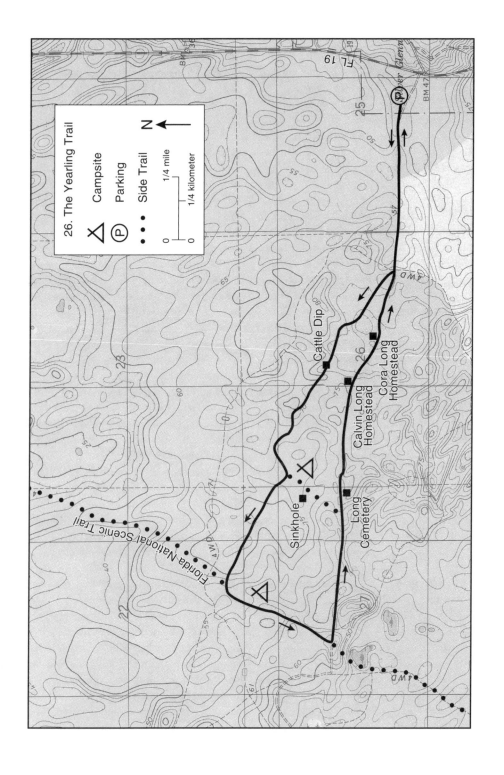

26. The Yearling Trail

△ Campsite
Ⓟ Parking
•••• Side Trail

0 ⎯ 1/4 mile
0 ⎯ 1/4 kilometer

N ←

Cattle Dip

Cora Long Homestead

Calvin Long Homestead

Long Cemetery

Sinkhole

Florida National Scenic Trail

to the trailhead, which is marked by a large sign on the left.

As you start your hike on the Yearling Trail, notice the scrub surrounding you. The tall sand pines succumbed to a raging wildfire, a crucial component of healthy scrub forests. Saw palmetto and scrub oak carpet the open hills. Scrub oaks 3 to 5 feet tall, myrtle oaks, Chapman oaks, and sand live oaks provide a perfect habitat for the Florida scrub-jay. Scattered throughout the miniature forest is the waxy-leaved Florida silk bay, an aromatic tree related to the bay whose leaves are used for flavoring Italian cooking. Stop at the kiosk to review the map. The Yearling Trail provides two easy loops. Your route follows the outer loop, which uses a small segment of the Florida National Scenic Trail as a connector. Blazed in yellow, the Yearling Trail is clearly marked at each trail intersection and has numbered posts corresponding to points of historic interest on the map. Soon after the kiosk, you reach an intersection with an old wagon road. Continue straight. The road is paved with fossil shells. After 0.5 mile a road veers off to the right; a post with a yellow arrow indicates you should continue straight.

Where tall sand pines have fallen across the trail, it becomes an obstacle course. Eastern towhees scamper through the underbrush, saw palmettos hang heavy with dark berries, and old man's beard trails in seafoam streamers from dead pine branches. After you enter the forest, you come to a trail junction—the beginning of the loop, at 0.8 mile. A signpost with double yellow blazes says JODY'S TRACE (named after the young boy of the novel). Turn right and follow the trail into a dense stand of longleaf pine, descending down a long, low slope. The aroma of damp pine needles fills the air. Silk bay and scrub oak grow under the longleaf, the merging of the ecosystems—the taller oaks are sand live oaks competing for the canopy. Numerous small but deep holes parallel the trail; be cautious of stepping off the footpath. A solution hole lies off to the left, a broad sinkhole with pines growing out of its bottom. Beargrass, a delicate variety of yucca once used for basket weaving, rises out of the drifts of pine needles. The distinctive black and brown fur of a fox squirrel catches your eye. The squirrel sits in a turkey oak, surveying the forest. Growing up to 2 feet tall, the fox squirrel is a creature of the sandhills and the largest of Florida's squirrels.

As you approach the edge of the island, the longleaf forest yields to sand pines. Wiregrass creates a taupe fog across the forest floor. Scrub oaks cluster together, creating short groves. Walk this trail in late February, and you'll catch the migration of the American robin, during which time thousands of birds settle down into the scrub, searching for seeds and insects. The trail slopes down and around another broad solution hole, passing tall clumps of prickly pear cactus. At 1.4 miles you come to a fence and Marker 2, the location of Reuben Long's son Calvin's old cattle dip, a concrete trough set into the ground. Cows were led into the dip and immersed into a solution of pine tar, sodium carbonate, and arsenic trioxide to eliminate ticks, a preventive measure against tick fever. The federal government mandated this treatment from 1906 until 1961 for all cattle shipped out of Florida. High levels of arsenic contaminate the ground surrounding cattle dips such as these.

Just past the cattle dip, watch for an unusual double-trunked longleaf pine, where one trunk wraps around the other in a tangled embrace. Orange mounds indicate the presence of pocket gophers, a reclusive rodent that spends its life underground, building tunnels and feeding on roots. The trail

Long Cemetery

winds past coontie, perhaps planted by the settlers, who soaked and dried the roots to make a starchy flour for arrowroot bread. At Marker 3, the site of an old homestead, the ground is covered in blooming lichens. Step off to the right to see the remains of the foundation. As you walk down this section of trail, you'll notice both saw and scrub palmettos. Saw palmettos have serrated edges on their stems, which come to an abrupt end where the frond starts. On the scrub palmetto, the stem is smooth and extends up into the frond, ending in a point. Loose threads dangle from the scrub palmetto, and scrub-jays pluck these to line their nests.

The trail veers left, away from the homestead's old road, as you rise up into an oak hammock. At 2 miles you come to a junction with a cross trail—the short loop. A camping spot sits off to the left. Turn right to continue on the outer loop. You immediately come up to the edge of one of the most notable features of Pat's Island, a gigantic sinkhole. A seep spring, where water dripped off bare limestone walls in the bottom of the sinkhole into catch basins, provided a trickle of water for the settlers, who would otherwise rely on their cisterns or take the long, dry walk down to Silver Glen Springs. As Rawlings wrote, "The water level lay so deep that wells were priceless." Dogwoods flourish along the steep slopes of the sinkhole, as do hickories. A row of benches provides a place for visitors to sit and relax on the lip of this giant bowl full of hardwood forest. Where the trail forks at Marker 5, stay to the left, and walk past Marker 6. Resurrection ferns cover the trunks of towering sand live oaks—an unusual pairing since the ferns need dampness, and these oaks prefer a dry environment. But in this humid microclimate at the edge of the sinkhole, the ferns survive.

At 2.5 miles you reach the orange-blazed Ocala Trail, a segment of the Florida National Scenic Trail. Turn left to continue to make the loop. A pink mottling of red blanket lichen crawls up the gnarled trunks of sand live oaks. You pass a dry campsite off to the left as the trail winds along the edge of Pat's Island. Looking off to the right, you can see the difference in the habitat, the line where the sandhills end and the scrub begins. Dating back to the era of these old homesteads, a large old dogwood rises behind Marker 7. Keep alert through a section of charred trees where you can easily lose the blazes; keep to the left in the charred zone as the thick carpet of pine needles obscures the treadway. The trail veers to the left through a corridor of myrtle oaks and Chapman oaks as it rises up a hill into an oak hammock.

At 3.2 miles you reach the intersection with the yellow-blazed trail. Turn left to stay on the Yearling Trail. Marker 8 is on the left, in front of what little remains of Reuben Long's homestead—a cistern, used to cache rainwater. The trail descends down from the homestead site into an oak hammock, passing a short stretch of rosemary scrub. Just around the rosemary on the right you might find a deer scrape. Look closely for the "scrape" in the sand, where a buck rolled around to make an impression and snapped twigs in the oaks above. The scrape marks a spot through which many deer pass, leaving messages of their presence to each other by rolling in the sand and urinating on the spot—and leaving hunters a clue as to where the deer pass.

The Long Cemetery sits off to the right at Marker 9. Reuben Long is buried here, as are many of his children, their tombstones fading with age. As you walk out of the cemetery, continue straight. The trail junction sign marks the incoming cross trail from the sinkhole. Turn right at the sign onto the Old Granville Road, a faded wagon track through stands of longleaf pine with tall thin trunks. A bed of deer's tongue fills one clearing, exploding in purple blossoms every fall. At 4.1 miles Marker 10 marks the spot of the homestead of Calvin Long, who lived on Pat's Island from 1878 to 1935. Two cabbage palms stand sentinel over what little is left to mark human presence: a shard of pottery, a piece of glass. When the movie version of *The Yearling* was filmed in 1946, this location was used as the setting of the homestead.

The opening in the forest at Marker 11 is the site of Calvin Long's daughter Cora Long's homestead. Cabbage palms flank the open area. A zebra swallowtail settles on one of the many large yellow blooms of a tall prickly pear cactus. Across the road, the forest looks like it's perched on a ledge of sand. You continue through the dense forest of longleaf pine, passing a red cedar. Mistletoe grows in the tops of bare trees. Walking down the wagon road, you meet the back side of a sign—and the end of the loop. You've hiked 4.7 miles. Continue straight, retracing your route along the broad path through the sand pines to return to the parking lot after 5.5 miles.

27

Juniper Run Nature Trail

Total distance (round trip): 1.4 miles

Hiking time: 1 hour

Habitats: Floodplain forest, hardwood hammock

Maps: USGS 7½' Juniper Springs

Surrounded by the dryness of the Big Scrub, the world's largest scrub forest, Juniper Springs is a playground of hydrological wonders, the center of a junglelike oasis of riotous growth. From the depths of the Floridan Aquifer, crystalline waters emerge from dozens of fern-shrouded springs, flowing together to form glassy Juniper Run. At Juniper Springs you'll find every sort of Florida spring imaginable: a massive outpouring from a cavern at the headspring, tiny bubblers along the bottom of the run, constant seeps along the loamy slopes, eerie flat boils like video screens, and giant boils thrusting perpetual clouds of sand skyward. To present this symphony of hydrology to you, a 1.4-mile nature trail winds between Juniper Springs and Fern Hammock Springs.

From I-75 take exit 352, Ocala, and head east on FL 40 into the Ocala National Forest. After 31 miles the entrance to Juniper Springs Recreation Area is on the left. From I-95 take exit 268, Ormond Beach, and head west on FL 40 through Barberville and Astor. After you pass the blinker at FL 19, keep alert for the park entrance on the right. As you drive into Juniper Springs, you cross the Florida National Scenic Trail. Since admission to the recreation area costs $3 per person, combine your hike with other outdoor recreation such as swimming, picnicking, camping, or canoeing. The large developed campground dates back to the 1930s, and the canoe run is one of Florida's most pristine paddling destinations.

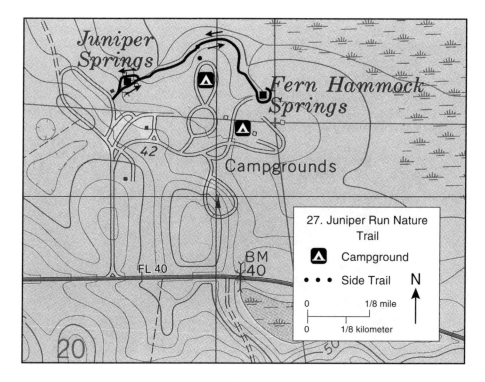

27. Juniper Run Nature Trail

⚠ Campground

• • • Side Trail

N

| 0 | 1/8 mile |
| 0 | 1/8 kilometer |

After you park, walk up to the entry kiosk with its map of the canoe trails. Start your hike along the paved stone path. Off to the left, palm warblers flit between sand live oaks growing out of a sinkhole. Walk up to the concession area, through a breezeway flanked by rest rooms and a store, where you can rent canoes for the four-hour journey down Juniper Run. Continue straight ahead to the spring, keeping to the right side of the basin to start the trail. Even from a distance, you can see tapegrass waving in dense thickets at the bottom of the spring, the water as transparent as glass. An old mill sits at the outflow of the basin, shaded by a dogwood dripping with white blooms. Steps lead down into the cool clear water, which is a constant 72 degrees. Follow the paved path around the spring. Take the left fork to walk over and look down in the main spring, from the ledge where

divers plunge into the spring vent. If you see a flicker of movement in the depths, follow it carefully—it may be an American eel. Born out in the Atlantic Ocean, in the grassy Sargasso Sea, these creatures follow inbred instincts to swim up Florida's rivers, seeking out the springs in which their ancestors once lived. The eels live out most of their lives in these crystalline waters, returning to the sea only to mate and die.

Once you return to the trail junction, turn left. The pavement ends at the Old Mill House exhibit. Step inside for a quick look at the history of the Juniper Springs Recreation Area. One of a handful of Civilian Conservation Corps projects sprinkled across Florida, the walled-in Juniper Springs swimming hole was created in the early 1930s. The original 15-unit campground relied on electricity generated from the waterwheel inside this mill. Dedicated in

Juniper Springs headspring

1936, the nature trail is part of the legacy left by the CCC. As you continue past the mill, turn left at the kiosk at the NATURE TRAIL sign. Clusters of needle palms thrive at the base of the waterwheel. These cold-tolerant relatives of the saw palmetto prefer damp environments with exposed limestone. Sword ferns spill down the slope to the clear spring run, and royal ferns rise tall above the water. Lazing in a tree branch, a small blond-colored squirrel catches your attention—an aberration in the gray squirrel gene pool, perpetuated for generations along Juniper Run.

The trail approaches a stone bridge that leads to the picnic area. Turn right to follow the trail along Juniper Run. As you walk along, you see canoeists prepping their gear as they push off from the canoe launch on the other side of the stream. Look down, and you'll notice tiny spring boils below the

JUNIPER CREEK NATURE TRAIL sign. These small bubblers throw up perpetual fountains of sand. By keeping the streambed in suspension, they create a tiny pool of quicksand. Crossing a bridge over a slender drainage into the run, you follow the interpretive trail. Cabbage palms arch overhead, and coontie grows in the shade. Keep left at the fork. Needle palms grow lushly on both sides of the footpath. Dense patches of marsh and sword fern crowd along the waterway. As you pass an overlook, the trail jogs to the right. Notice the humidity? No matter the time of year, this forest remains damp and luxuriant, a microclimate fed by the bubbling springs. As the trail turns away from the run, it winds through saw palmettos cloaked in grapevines. Crossing a bridge, the trail swings back along the edge of the water-course. Standing out like the color of a red crayon, blotches of red blanket lichen flourish on a sand live oak. You reach a trail junction with a sign indicating this as the halfway point. The trail that leads right ends at the campground; your route continues straight. But first, take a moment to sit on a bench and enjoy the crystalline stream, watching the fish drift by. Signs warn against wading as the fragile bottom of the run—and the veinlike channels that feed the tiny springs themselves—can be destroyed with a single footstep.

Continuing down the trail, you see a live oak and cabbage palm locked in a tight embrace, their shallow root systems snaking across the footpath, creating numerous small holes suitable for southern toads and cotton mice. Black polypore fungus grows in shelves across a fallen black gum. As you swing back toward Juniper Run, young loblolly bay trees fill the forest with their slender trunks. You cross over a bridge spanning a tiny dark spring, black and oily, looking like a petroleum seep. A downy woodpecker picks at the bark of a tall white bay tree. Spanish bayonet peeps out of the understory.

At 0.5 mile you reach Fern Hammock Run, which flows to your left, toward Juniper Run. Fallen cabbage palms choke the streambed. Like giant feather dusters, royal ferns emerge from the tops of rotting pilings for an old bridge across the run. The water displays a hint of turquoise; eelgrass waves in thick patches. Arriving at the edge of Fern Hammock Springs, you reach a T intersection. Although the sign says NATURE TRAIL CONCLUSION, RETURN TO SWIMMING AREA BY RETRACING THE TRAIL, turn left to explore this glistening pool. A broad bridge crosses the waterway. On the left you see a giant boil in aquamarine and turquoise, where a snapping turtle rises from the depths. Keep walking and watch the water. In the cove, the spring boils look like postmodern video screens, hypnotic gray images flickering across a milky turquoise base, splashes of wet paint across the floor of the spring.

Follow the trail around the spring to the left, past a log-and-stone CCC picnic pavilion. Shoelace fern dangles from the trunk of a cabbage palm. The trail ends at a concrete bench. Sit and watch the boils, as well as the dance of the bluegills and musk turtles through the aquamarine hues of the springs. Notice the tiny white eggs of apple snails, the clusters clinging to limbs hanging out over the water—a smorgasbord for a limpkin seeking an afternoon snack. A slider and several Florida red-belly turtles sun themselves on a cabbage-palm log. Turn around and retrace your path, turning right to cross the broad bridge. As you walk over the bridge, look straight down over the left side to see the most furious spring boil within Fern Hammock Springs, which rages across the bottom of the pool like a dust storm on the Sahara Desert.

At the trail junction, turn right to follow the nature trail back to Juniper Springs. Sparkling as the sun hits them, fossilized snail shells in the bottom of Fern Hammock Run gleam with a pearly iridescence. After you pass the canoe launch, you arrive at the stone bridge in front of the old mill. Cross over the bridge. Back on the stone sidewalk, you meander along the edge of the picnic area and around the shallow end of the spring, fenced off to keep children in the shallows. Take in one last view of the shimmering waters before you depart, walking through the concession area back to the parking lot to complete your 1.4-mile walk.

28

Lake Eaton Trails

Total distance (2 circuits): 4.1 miles

Hiking time: 2.5 hours

Habitats: Sand pine scrub, oak scrub, hardwood hammock, oak hammock, floodplain forest

Maps: USGS 7½' Lake Kerr, park map

In the heart of the Ocala National Forest is the Big Scrub: more than five hundred thousand acres protecting the world's largest scrub forest, a desertlike natural habitat with its own unique flora and fauna. While many of the National Forest's hiking trails lead to bubbling springs and shimmering streams, the trails at Lake Eaton are different. Two trails radiate from the parking lot: the 2.3-mile Lake Eaton Loop Trail, which leads to scenic views along the shoreline of marshy Lake Eaton, and the 1.8-mile Lake Eaton Sinkhole Trail, which takes you on a journey into the depths of a giant sinkhole, containing a mature hardwood forest.

To drive to Lake Eaton, take I-75 exit 352, Ocala. Head east on FL 40 for 13.4 miles, passing through Silver Springs, driving past the Ocklawaha Visitors Center (Hike 29) and over the Ocklawaha River before coming to a stoplight at FL 314. Turn left. Drive north 9 miles to Forest Road 86, on your right just a little past the intersection with FL 314A. Look for it just north of the HUNTERS' EDUCATION CENTER sign. Turn right on FR 86, a dirt road, and follow it 1.1 miles to FR 79. Turn right; the trailhead parking is on the left after 0.3 mile. Both trails start from the parking area.

LAKE EATON LOOP TRAIL

Heading west out of the parking lot, follow the LAKE EATON TRAIL sign to cross FR 79 to the Lake Eaton Trail. After 0.1 mile you reach the beginning of the loop, marked by a kiosk with a trail map. Turn right. Fragile-looking sand pines tower up to 50

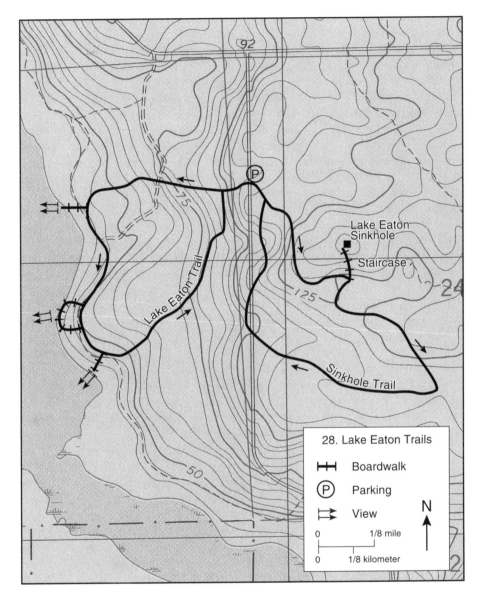

28. Lake Eaton Trails

⊢⊣ Boardwalk

Ⓟ Parking

⇢ View

N

0   1/8 mile

0   1/8 kilometer

feet tall in this dense sand pine scrub. Long seafoam stringers of old man's beard dangle from the crooked branch of a sand live oak, twisting in the wind. Rusty lyonia shades the trail. This forest has two distinct canopies: the tall sand pines brushing the sky, and the scrub oaks, especially Chapman and myrtle oaks, growing up to 10 feet tall.

After you pass a bench with Florida rosemary growing behind it, the trail crosses a jeep road. The terrain has a noticeable downhill slope. A former side trail comes in from the right, but an arrow urges you to continue forward. The habitat shifts to an oak scrub, dense with saw palmetto. Loblolly pines shower their needles on the footpath, creating a thick carpet of pine duff. Soon after you start to see the lake off to the right, just beyond the trees, you come to a boardwalk on the right leading out to the lake at 0.8 mile. Stroll out through the floodplain forest and enjoy the view. Royal ferns emerge from the stump of an old cabbage palm, while southern magnolia showers its sweet fragrant petals on the edge of the pond cypress swamp. Standing on a broad deck along the water's edge, you have a sweeping view of Lake Eaton. Yellow lotuses drift across the shallow dark water, their leaves riffled by the breeze. A slash pine forms an arch over the water off to the right. You can see other decks and a boat ramp on the far side of the lake, the home of the Hunters' Education Center—a service of the Florida Fish and Wildlife Conservation Commission, where the public can take courses on fishing, hunting, orienteering, and a handful of other outdoors skills. Off to the left, the developed area is the Lake Eaton Campground, the closest campground to these trails, just a little way down FR 79.

As you walk back to the main trail, a sign accurately indicates the distance back to the parking area. Turn right. When you reach an intersection with a service trail from the left, you've walked a mile. Continue straight, following the trail as it parallels the lake and enjoying the scenic views. At the next side trail, turn right. Your walk through the floodplain forest takes you to a boardwalk out along the lake, which has opportunities for bird-watching. Listen closely, and you can hear the chorus of bullfrogs in the swamp. Leaving the edge of the lake, the boardwalk loops around to return to the main trail. Enjoying the humid forest, cardinal wild pine

thrives on the cypresses. With a slight gain in elevation, you enter a hardwood hammock surrounded by hickory, blackjack oak, and cherry trees. When you reach the main trail, turn right.

At 1.3 miles you reach the last side trail to the water. Turn right and walk down to the observation platform along the marsh that formed in a cove of Lake Eaton. A heron screeches on the far shore, its head barely poking above the arrowroot. A cardinal roosts in the feathery branches of a young pond cypress. Be cautious of the poison ivy around you. Turn around and retrace your path. Turn right at the fork, and you arrive back on the main trail. Turn right to continue through an oak hammock. After the trail makes a sharp left at a fenced-off road, an arrow points you down the trail, which rises up into a young sand pine scrub. Looking like Christmas trees, the sand pines are no more than 20 feet tall. The trail twists and winds in the shade, following a corridor of scrub oaks. Some of Florida's most rare plants—scrub milkwort, scrub buckwheat, and scrub morning glory—grow here on the ancient dunes that form the scrub. An osprey swoops low, letting out a creel. Look up: A large osprey nest sits in a tall pine off to the right. The osprey is a large black and white raptor, up to 2 feet tall and with a 6-foot wingspan. If you want to see the osprey tending their young, bringing back fish from the lake to feed the family, hike down here between December and April. Ospreys mate for life and return to the same nest every season.

The habitat transitions from the young sand pine scrub into older sand pines, tall thin pencil-sticks of trees with a low canopy of oak scrub growing beneath them. At 2 miles you reach a bench and cross an obscured forest road with a patch of Florida rosemary growing on the right. The aroma

Lake Eaton

from these dome-shaped shrubs smells much like sagebrush. Rosemary scrubs form as patches within the sand pine scrub, where clusters of rosemary thrive in otherwise bald patches of sand. In a process called allelopathy, each bush releases a natural herbicide into the sand to inhibit the growth of its seedlings and other plants—thus the neat spacing between the plants. When a fire races through the scrub the chemical dissipates, allowing at least one seedling to take root to replace its parent before the process begins again.

After 2.2 miles the trail reaches the end of the loop at the kiosk. Turn right and continue uphill to the parking lot, completing this 2.3-mile loop.

LAKE EATON SINKHOLE TRAIL

The Lake Eaton Sinkhole Trail starts out of the northeast corner of the parking lot. From the trailhead sign follow the footpath to the kiosk that marks the beginning of the loop. Turn left. The trail winds through the sand pine scrub, with its low canopy of myrtle, Chapman, and sand live oaks. Foamy deer moss thrives under the scrub oaks, nestled in among the oak leaves. A brown anole skitters up a blueberry bush. At 0.5 mile the trail starts to descend, approaching the sinkhole. Looking through the trees, you can see the vast gap in the forest ahead. As you reach the rim of the sinkhole, the trail becomes a boardwalk. A kiosk explains how sinkholes form.

The boardwalk gives you a great perspective on this enormous sinkhole. Comparable in size to the Devil's Millhopper (Hike 16), it's an open bowl 462 feet around and 122 feet deep. Looking straight across, you can see young sand pines rising off the far rim. By disturbing the scrub landscape as it did, the sinkhole created a cooler, damper environment where mixed hardwoods could flourish. As you walk down the steep staircase into the sinkhole, notice the dogwood in bloom. Cabbage palms rise up from the steep slopes, while southern magnolias and hickories thrive in the very bottom. Because the scrub is so dry, you see no trickles of water down the slopes as you do at the Devil's Millhopper. But during a rainstorm, plenty of water feeds this microcosm of forest. From the bottom landing it's a long climb back up the stairs.

When you return to the top of the staircase, turn left. A few footsteps after the stairs end, a 0.5-mile shortcut trail to your right heads back to the parking lot—a bailout point for exhausted hikers. To stay on the main trail, continue straight. You pass a bench under the sand pines. As the trail rises, it enters a more open scrub—lots of small sand pine, silk bay, and rusty lyonia, a perfect environment for the Florida scrub-jay. An eastern towhee perches on top of a silk bay, its brown, black, and white coloration reminiscent of a small robin. Pocket gopher mounds erupt from the footpath,

each a deep orange hue. These small rodents are rarely seen as they spend most of their lives underground and alone, digging networks of tunnels up to 500 feet long.

At 1 mile you reach a T with no distinct marking as to where the trail goes next. Turn right. After the trail makes the turn, the habitat changes to sand pine scrub with low oak understory, which provides some decent shade. Keep alert to movement around the Florida rosemary bushes, and you may catch a glimpse of a rare Florida sand skink sunning itself. The only sand-swimming lizard in North America, this endangered skink burrows into the scrub, using swimming motions to propel itself just under the surface of the sand. Its atrophied limbs and a transparent lid over its eyes help it to move freely through the sand.

Passing another bench at 1.5 miles, the trail continues to rise through sand pine scrub until it meets the shortcut trail coming in from the right. Just ahead is the kiosk at the beginning of the loop. Turn left to return to the parking lot, completing the 1.8-mile trail.

29

Silver River Connector Trail

Total distance (round trip): 3.6 miles

Hiking time: 1 hour, 15 minutes

Habitats: Cabbage palm flatwoods, oak hammock, freshwater marsh, floodplain forest

Maps: USGS 7½' Ocala East, park map

Back in the days when steamboats plied the Ocklawaha River and logging crews worked their way through the riverside forests, a fellow named R. M. Harper noticed that something was a little different where the Silver River flowed into the Ocklawaha. He discovered that rambling out of the cypress-lined floodplains was a unique habitat: a damp mixed forest of oaks, cabbage palms, and loblolly pines. Calling this unusual pine flatwoods a "loblolly pine/cabbage palm bottom," he remarked on the many species that seemed to be at the southern limits of their range. The year was 1915, and loggers were busy chopping down the woods, the southernmost largest tract of loblolly pine left in Florida.

Jump ahead more than 70 years. As the state of Florida, through its various agencies, acquired more and more land around the Silver River, it opened Silver River State Park on the south shore. A few years later the U.S. Forest Service established the new Ocklawaha Visitors Center, the western gateway to the Ocala National Forest. Within the same decade the Marjorie Harris Carr Cross Florida Greenway became reality, protecting lands along the rivers that were once slated to be flooded as part of the Cross-Florida Barge Canal, an environmental nightmare of a project that was shut down in the 1970s. Working across these lands, the short but pleasant Silver River Connector Trail links the Ocklawaha Visitors Center with the Ray Wayside Park, home of the Ocala Boat Basin along the Silver River,

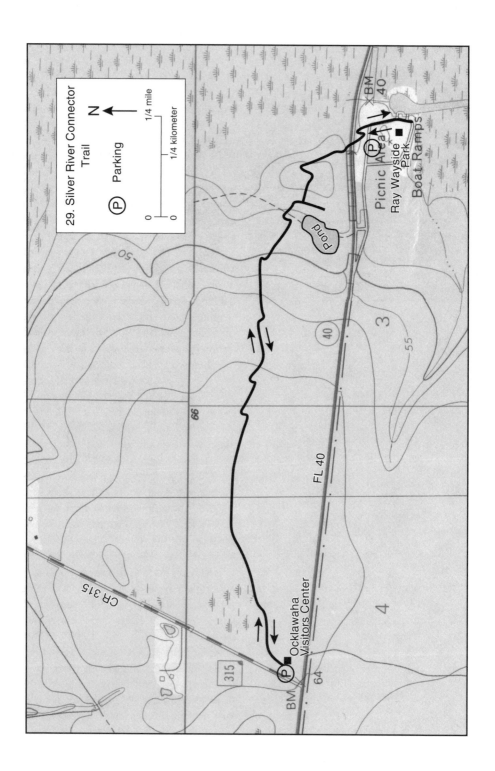

29. Silver River Connector
Trail

P Parking

N

0 ⌐ 1/4 mile
0 ⌐ 1/4 kilometer

a popular put-in for canoeists and kayakers headed up the pristine run.

To find the Ocklawaha Visitors Center, take I-75 exit 352, Ocala, and head east on FL 40 for 10.9 miles, passing through Silver Springs before you reach CR 315. Turn left. Make an immediate right into the parking lot. Before you start your hike, explore the visitors center, which contains rest rooms, maps and information on other trails in the Ocala National Forest (Hikes 23–28), and a bookstore. Be sure to register before you start out on the hike. You must return here before 5 PM so that your car isn't locked behind a gate.

To start the hike, retrace your route back along the entrance road to the kiosk on the right. Follow the trail along the split-rail fence. A lone sign mentions R. M. Harper's discovery and the many species found at their southernmost limits in this forest, such as cedar elm, bluff oak, and box elder. Most of the pines you see are third-growth forest. After the southern pine beetle invaded this area in 1997, the majority of the second-growth loblolly pines were chopped down to try and prevent the spread of this insidious insect across the Ocala National Forest.

The trail curves along the fence to a second kiosk. Pause for a moment for information on habitats and an overview of the Marjorie Harris Carr Cross Florida Greenway, a major wildlife and recreation corridor that stretches from the Gulf of Mexico at Yankeetown to the city of Palatka along the St. Johns River. Continue forward into the forest, passing a stump of a bluejack oak coated with shelf mushrooms. Shumard and water oaks crowd in on the well-defined footpath, and you hear the constant hum of traffic on FL 40. Segments of split-rail fence steer you away from making turns down old forest roads. Scrabbling around in the underbrush, a marsh rabbit appears, pausing

in the trail before it bolts to safety. You walk along young stands of loblolly pine and pass under goldfoot ferns dangling from the tops of cabbage palms. Coated in thick green moss, one cabbage palm shows off a strange fluted base, reminiscent of a vase.

You come to the first trail marker at 0.4 mile, a footprint in orange on a cypress post. Continue straight. Water collects in grassy low spots in the trail. In the winter, sweetgum rain crimson leaves across the footpath. A tall swamp chestnut oak hugs a loblolly pine, and foamy deer moss grows beneath the bracken ferns. Young cabbage palms emerge from the forest floor, full fronds bursting from thick trunks, looking like trees buried up to their necks. Pine needles rain down on the canopy of low oaks, dangling from branches like tinsel on a Christmas tree. You see torn-up ground—the sign of feral hogs rooting through the forest.

After 0.8 mile the trail reaches a fence. Turn left to follow a narrow path into the forest. Straight ahead of you, a cabbage palm emerges through the crook of a water oak's branches. The ground beneath your feet is squishy, thick with moss and black earth. Fences guide the narrow path into the increasingly damp forest. Crossing over an old ditch dug by hand through the forest, the trail rises slightly into a sandy area. A live oak arches across the trail, its limbs carpeted with a thick, healthy growth of resurrection fern, its base nearly 6 feet around. When you reach the next footprint trail marker, just across from a section of fence, you've walked 1 mile.

Dodging more wet spots in the footpath, you pass an old deer stand. The trail emerges into a clearing ringed by large live oaks and then veers to the right, back into denser forest. High on the branches of one live oak are the bright purple-red blooms of cardinal wild pine. As you pass another fence, saw palmetto crowds the trail. The understory changes significantly, choked up with gallberry and rusty lyonia, willow oak and grapevine. At 1.3 miles you climb over a small rise. Off to the right, a marshy pond sits behind the pines. A chorus of bullfrogs rises from the reeds. Yellow lotuses drift across the open water. Grapevines dangle low from a pine tree over the trail, reminiscent of a Tarzan movie. In the 1930s film producers used these junglelike floodplain forests of the Silver River as a stage for Olympic gold medalist Johnny Weissmuller, playing Tarzan to Maureen O'Sullivan's Jane. Descendents of the rhesus macaques used in the Tarzan movies still roam wild through these forests, surprising canoeists and delighting tourists.

The trail curves to the right to parallel a hand-dug canal filled with healthy duckweed and pennywort, elephant-ear lining its edges. As the trail curves around the pond, take a moment to step off the trail onto the mounds of earth to survey the pond. With a handful of sky-blue feathers peeking out from its white coat, an immature blue heron picks through the shallows, attempting to spear a frog. Back on the trail, the road noise increases, as does the thick growths of epiphytes on the trees: ball moss, wild pine, and Spanish moss. Netted chain and woods fern thrive in the damp dark soil as you enter the floodplain forest, twisting and winding down toward the river. A towering live oak stands dead ahead, vines dangling from its high branches. The trail curves around it, and you brush against the immense fronds of a cabbage palm. Straight ahead, you see the piers of the Cross Florida Barge Canal bridge. Built in the 1970s to cross the planned canal, it now carries FL 40 over the floodplain forest. Coming up and over a rise, you emerge

under the bridge at pier 6. Continue under the bridge to find the jeep road that leads down to a gate, the entrance to Ray Wayside Park. When you see the footprint marker, you've hiked 1.6 miles. Walk around the gate and cross the road.

A limestone monument just outside the park's entrance pays homage to Walter Ray, an area pioneer who died in 1938. Dedicated in 1952, this park is pretty small—a few picnic tables, a playground, a place for people to fish. The main attraction is the boat ramp. You can see the Silver River straight ahead through the pavilion, but the glimpse comes at a price: Marion County charges pedestrians $1 to enter the park. The view isn't fantastic as the boat basin was built to launch craft into the Silver River and is not on the river itself. If you pay the fee at the self-pay station and wander over to the picnic table at water's edge, you can catch a glimpse of the Silver River down at the end of the channel. Rest rooms sit next to the boat launch, and there's a separate hand-launch site for putting in canoes and kayaks. If you wander inside the park, walk down to the hand launch. Sit along the water's edge for a spell and watch herons looking for a meal, poking through clumps of golden club. A sign next to you says SILVER RIVER STATE PARK, marking the boundary of the park, which encompasses both sides of the river here at the river's mouth.

After walking 1.8 miles you must turn around and retrace your route back to the visitors center unless you have a second car here in the parking lot. As you exit the park, turn left. Walk up the road until you see the yellow gate hidden in the trees on the right. Continue straight across under pier 5 to find the trail on the other side, just to the left of the piers. Walking through the floodplain forest, you emerge at the pond.

Turn right. At each of the various turns, pay attention to special trail markings, such as the split-rail fences and footprint markers. When the trail makes a sharp right turn back onto a broad jeep trail, you've walked 2.8 miles. Passing both kiosks, continue on to the parking area outside the visitors center, completing your round-trip hike of 3.6 miles.

30

Dunns Creek
Conservation Area

Total distance (circuit): 3 miles

Hiking time: 1.5 hours

Habitats: Floodplain forest, pine flatwoods, bayheads, freshwater marsh

Maps: USGS 7½' San Mateo, St. Johns Water Management District map

Draining Crescent Lake, Dunns Creek winds through deep, dark cypress swamps as it flows to the St. Johns River. Canoeists avoid it—too many alligators. As John Muir explored this area in 1867 on his thousand-mile walk to the Gulf of Mexico, he noted the character of these swamp-fed tributaries, "in deep places as black as ink, perfectly opaque, and glossy on the surface as if varnished. It is often difficult to ascertain which way they are flowing or creeping, so slowly and so widely do they circulate . . . "

Using the forest roads and trails of Dunns Creek Conservation Area, you can explore the fringes of Dunns Creek, where a primitive campsite sits along the edge of the cypress swamp. Although the trails are shared with horses and bicycles, they remain in healthy shape. Wildflowers abound in the wet flatwoods and shaded hammocks surrounding the swamp. Except in the dead of winter, this is prime mosquito habitat. As a Wildlife Management Area, these lands are closed to hiking during hunting season. Check the calendar for this area on the Florida Fish and Wildlife Conservation Commission web site http://www.florida-conservation.org before heading out here to hike.

If you're traveling southbound on I-95, take exit 298. Follow US 1 south for 14 miles to FL 100 in Bunnell. Northbound on I-95, take exit 284, Flagler Beach/Bunnell. Follow FL 100 west for 4.8 miles, crossing US 1 in Bunnell. Continue west on FL 100 for 21.5 miles, most of the way to San Mateo. Keep alert for a sign that says TRAM

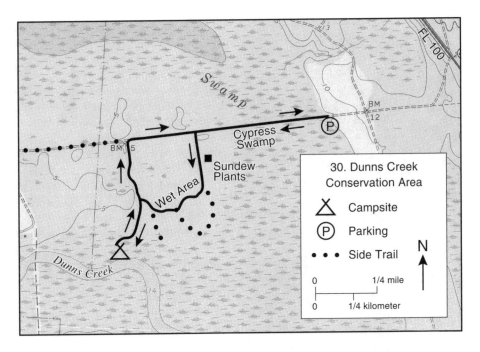

ROAD, on the left. From US 17 drive 2.7 miles east on FL 100, passing Pinecrest Road before you reach Tram Road on the right. Tucked in the underbrush is the DUNNS CREEK CONSERVATION AREA sign. Use caution driving down Tram Road as it's a narrow one-lane jeep track through the forest. After 0.5 mile it emerges at an open area on a curve. Turn left and park near the kiosk, where you can pick up a map before heading out on the trail.

Although several routes snake through this conservation area, this hike follows a loop out to the primitive campsite, maximizing your exposure to unusual plants and wildflowers. Wet flatwoods mean wet hiking, so expect to slosh through some puddles. Exit the parking lot onto Tram Road, turning left at the DOE BAY ROAD sign. Walk down the grassy expanse to the gate, slipping around the gate on the left. As you enter the floodplain forest, the trail becomes a causeway surrounded by tall bald cypress, sweetgum, and red maple.

A red-shouldered hawk cries out from a tree-top—you've invaded its territory. Netted chain and cinnamon fern grow lush and full along the sides of the road. Tannic water laps at both sides of the causeway. Look carefully at the cypresses—the high-water mark is several feet up their trunks, well above the surface of the trail. Don't attempt this hike if this causeway is flooded since the terrain continues to slope down toward Dunns Creek. Small black fish dart through the dark water; ferns emerge from tiny islands and rotting stumps. Epiphytes thrive in the humid air—look up to see wild pine, ball moss, and Spanish moss clinging to the trees. Pignut hickory trees rain their giant edible nuts on the footpath, which becomes hard-packed loose limestone. A ladder brake fern is reflected in the dark water. You walk past the stump of a giant cypress, more than 10 feet in circumference. Like most of Florida's cypress forests, these woods were logged a century or more ago. Prized for its natural resistance to rot, the

Sundews

narrow trail behind the sign that says CLOSED TO MOTORIZED VEHICLES AND BOATS. Gallberry and saw palmetto form the understory under the pines, and both slash and longleaf pine intermingle through the wet flatwoods. Look down at the thousands of glistening red blobs, huge glossy masses spilling across the footpath—an unparalleled garden of carnivorous sundew plants. Step carefully. These dime-size plants trap insects on their leaves; their red hue comes from thousands of tiny hairs coated with a sticky fluid. When an insect lands on a leaf, the hairs fold in, holding the insect down. Each leaf acts like both a trap and a stomach—glands in the hairs drown the insect in sticky fluid before pouring out digestive juices to consume it, providing the plant with sustenance in these nitrogen-poor soils. In spring, tiny reddish-pink flowers cover each sundew plant.

When you reach a trail crossroad at 1 mile, continue straight. The trail that leads to the left runs parallel to the trail you are on and eventually rejoins it, but because it skirts so close to the edge of the floodplain forest, it floods, with water flowing deeply across the footpath in places. Your trail blazes on into wet flatwoods, where the trees show scars of a forest fire. The marl footpath can be mucky and sticky in places, especially after a rain. Be careful of slipping and sliding. Armadillos don't mind the mud—you'll see signs of their rooting everywhere. Listen carefully for rustling under the saw palmettos, a sure sign that there's an armadillo nearby.

As the terrain rises a little you see more gallberry, and the footpath fills with sundews and scattered white violets. The trail curves to the right, paralleling the distant creek. After crossing a firebreak, the terrain rises out of the muck, past trumpet-shaped wild petunia and tall, thin hatpin rising from

wood of the cypress tree was considered ideal material for housing and packing crates. Lumber companies built tramways for narrow-gauge railroads to run deep into Florida's cypress swamps, where loggers chopped down trees aged a thousand years and more—all the better for the number of board feet they would yield—leaving to our imaginations the grandeur and glory of these original stands of virgin cypress.

The trail leaves the cypress swamp and emerges into the sun, passing a small open marsh. As the trail rises the pines take over, intermingled with damp-loving loblolly bay and sweetbay magnolia. Water collects in ditches on both sides of the trail. At 0.7 mile you come to a clearing with PARKING AREA signs on both sides, opened to hunters during hunting season. Turn left and follow the a central stalk like pins out of a pincushion. A red-bellied woodpecker works its way up a hickory trunk, its bright red head gleaming in the sun. Bursts of star rush, shaped like tiny poinsettias, show off their white centers. Jagged yellow petals surround the plump center of bauldina, a member of the daisy family. Look for Florida elephant's-foot, its tiny tubular flowers emerging from the tops of long, hairy stems.

At 1.3 miles you reach a fork in the trail. Keep left. Within a few moments you emerge at a T intersection with a grassy jeep track. Turn left. At 1.5 miles the road ends in an open hammock under towering live oaks, the location of the Dunns Creek campsite. Pitch your tent anywhere under the trees in this nice flat area along the edge of the floodplain forest. Look through the cypresses, and you can catch a glimpse of a ribbon of water in the distance to the left—Dunns Creek, still a good 0.25 mile away. Overgrown with duckweed, a narrow canal slices through the floodplain forest, linking the edge of the hammock with the creek. Loggers probably created the canal to float logs out to the creek and down to the St. Johns River. The floodplain forest is dark and shady, filled with the humming of insects and the croaking of tree frogs. Cypress knees poke through the dark, rich mud. Bright red blooms similar to a coral bean top the red buckeye, a poisonous member of the horse chestnut family. Although it's often found as a shrub, the red buckeyes on the edge of the campsite rise up to tree level. Its colorful blooms appear between January and April.

Turn around and retrace your steps up the forest road, passing the T intersection you came in on. Continue straight along the grassy lane. You pass a side trail on the left, and the road curves to the right through the pine flatwoods. At 2 miles you reach Tram Road. Turn right. Similarly broad and grassy, the trail makes a beeline through the pine flatwoods. Walking through more wet flatwoods, you come across puffball mushrooms popping out into the footpath. Continue straight at the next crossroads, where a flock of wild turkeys strut down the side trail. After 2.2 miles you return to the beginning of the loop at the PARKING AREA signs. Continue straight, walking down the causeway through the cypress swamp. Walk around the gate and up to the trailhead parking area, completing your 3-mile hike.

31

Welaka State Forest

Total distance (circuit): 7.4 miles

Hiking time: 4 hours

Habitats: Scrubby flatwoods, pine flatwoods, oak hammock, floodplain forest, bayheads, sandhills

Maps: USGS 7½' Welaka, park map

Judging from its name, you would never dream of Mud Spring's beauty. Yet as you emerge from the forest Mud Spring surprises you, a glassy pool overflowing with crystalline waters, a window into an underwater garden where striped bass and sheepshead shimmer as they dart between waving tapegrass, strands of strapleaf sagittaria, and curving streamers of coontail. Containing two trails within the Florida State Forests Trailwalker program, Welaka State Forest provides shaded campsites along the St. Johns River; the pristine Mud Spring; and long walks through hammocks and flatwoods. Linking together the Mud Spring Trail and the Johns Landing Trail, you can enjoy a circuit hike of 7.4 miles.

From I-95 exit 268, Ormond Beach, head west on FL 40 to its intersection with US 17 in Barberville. Drive north 19.1 miles on US 17. When you reach CR 308 in Crescent Lake, turn left. Continue 8.4 miles west. CR 308 comes to a T intersection with CR 309. Turn right and drive 3.3 miles to the Mud Spring entrance of Welaka State Forest, 1.2 miles past the fire tower on the left. En route you pass the road leading to the Fort Gates Ferry, Florida's oldest continuously operating ferry, started in 1856. It crosses the St. Johns over to Salt Springs across Little Lake George.

After you park, pay the $2-per-person Florida State Forest entrance fee at the Mud Spring Trail kiosk before starting off on the trail. Follow the mint green blazes into the pine flatwoods. When you reach the trail junction, turn right. Little plank bridges carry

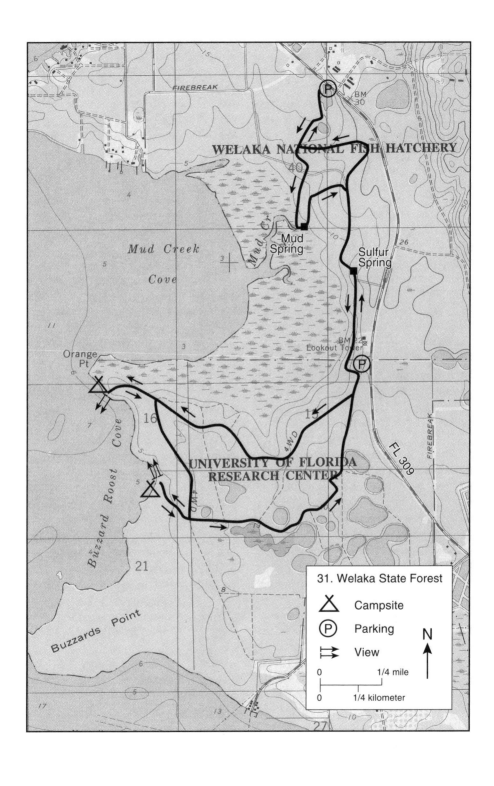

FIREBREAK

WELAKA NATIONAL FISH HATCHERY

40

Mud
Spring

Sulfur
Spring

26

Mud Creek
Cove

BM
22
Lookout Tower

Orange
Pt

16

15

4WD

UNIVERSITY OF FLORIDA
RESEARCH CENTER

FL 309

FIREBREAK

Buzzard Roost Cove

21

Buzzards Point

31. Welaka State Forest

Campsite

Parking

View

N

0   1/4 mile

0   1/4 kilometer

you over the drainages of bayheads scattered throughout the longleaf and pond pines. Tall and gnarled sand live oaks stand in small groves. Overhead, a red-tailed hawk screams in fury as two red-winged blackbirds dive-bomb the larger bird, protecting their nest.

At 0.3 mile you meet the junction of the return loop. Continue straight, past the SPRING sign. Blueberries and bracken ferns crowd the understory. After you cross a bridge you come to a trail junction. Bear left. At the next intersection a sign says EAGLE NEST ROW. Continue straight across, following the mint green blazes into a mixed hardwood forest full of oak and southern magnolia. Dropping down past towering saw palmettos, the trail crosses two short boardwalks through a floodplain forest of hickory, red maple, and cabbage palm. At 0.7 mile you emerge in a clearing with a picnic pavilion off to the left; Mud Spring lies directly ahead. Turn right. No larger than a swimming pool, this breathtaking spring pumps out as much as 1.4 million gallons of water each day, flowing under the trail through a culvert into the short Mud Spring Run, which reaches the St. Johns River in 0.5 mile. Arrowhead thrives along the outflow. Take a few minutes to walk around Mud Spring and peer into its depths, a true aquatic garden. The delicate light green fibers of puffy southern naiad quiver in the constant rush of water; fuzzy coral-like strands of coontail wave to and fro. A largemouth bass flashes through the depths, vanishing into the spring vent. Glinting sunlight creates radiant patterns across the water's surface as a cottonmouth moccasin swims to the far shore.

Walk away from the spring and head uphill around the left side of the picnic area, passing the BOBCAT CROSSING sign as you enter the pine flatwoods. The broad trail continues along a forest road into a pine plantation. At 1 mile you reach an intersection with Eagle Nest Row. Turn right, continuing downhill through the pine plantation. Walk straight through the next crossroad. The trail descends into the shade, where loblolly bay and sweetbay magnolia infiltrate a forest of slash pine. Caught in the open, a wild turkey launches toward the sky. The trail drops down through a small cypress swamp, where water seeps under the thick rock that makes up the footpath. You see a sign, SULFUR SPRING. Take the short detour to the left to visit the spring. Sulfuric water pours out of a small spring vent, leaving a fine greenish-yellow coating of sulfur on branches and leaves fallen into the water. Pygmy killifish, with a single yellow stripe down their sides and aquamarine dots on their tails, shimmer in the shallows. Behind the vent, the water is stagnant.

Returning to the main trail, turn left. As it rises uphill, you pass a bench in the shade of some large live oaks. Continuing uphill, the trail rises toward a pine plantation. A scrubby ridge on the left is covered in deer moss and reindeer lichen, tiny sand live oak and myrtle oak. Passing a road coming in from the left, you can see traffic on CR 309. At 1.7 miles you're behind the fire tower at a bench; a trail comes in from the fire tower parking lot and crosses the main trail. Turn right and follow this short interpretive loop into a cypress and red maple swamp, where a boardwalk and platform afford a good view of the murky forest. The loop pops out at the Johns Landing Trail kiosk, the beginning of the second of the Trailwalker trails in this state forest. Turn right.

Marked by orange blazes, the Johns Landing Trail leads to two scenic campsites on the St. Johns River. Follow the orange blazes down around the fire tower parking area and south to the open pine flatwoods.

The view from Orange Point campsite

Turn right off Eagle Nest Row onto Indian Pond Run; off to your left is a gate blocking the road that leads to the fire tower. The trail parallels CR 309 briefly before swinging right at a fork for Longleaf Lane and a sign for Orange Point. You walk along the edge of a small burned zone in the pine flatwoods. After you pass the next LONGLEAF LANE sign, water seeps across the trail from a swampy bayhead. Crossing a firebreak, you continue straight, coming to a trail junction with an ORANGE POINT sign. Continue straight. The trail becomes narrow, winding through a swampy oak hammock, the forest dense with cabbage palms. At 3.4 miles you reach Orange Point, the first campsite on the St. Johns River. Camping is by permit; contact the state forest office in advance. Even if you aren't here to camp, sit on the bench and savor the view. Tucked away in a hammock on a bluff, the tent sites surrounding the fire ring command incredible panoramas of cabbage palms and shimmering water, one of the loveliest campsite views in Florida. On the far side of the river, the Ocala National Forest provides an unbroken wall of wilderness. The bluffs are old Timucuan middens, spilling snail shells out into the sunshine and into the river. Just south of the state forest lies Mount Royal, a ceremonial mound visited in 1774 by William Bartram as he paddled up the St. Johns. Looking out across the unsullied river, you get a feel for what Florida still looked like in Bartram's day.

Turn around and walk back down from Orange Point to the last trail junction. Turn right on Deer Run. The trail is a grass-covered dike above the wet flatwoods, paralleled by a ditch. A dense oak hammock sits off to the right, stretching out to the river. Yellow-star grass shows off its six-pointed blooms. Clusters of bluestar glow light blue around their yellow centers. After you pass an unmarked side trail to the right, the dike becomes a shell mound. For more than a century, before their archaeological significance was realized, Timucuan middens were used to pave roads. When you reach the JOHNS LANDING sign at 4.2 miles, turn right, walking through the pine flatwoods right up to the river's edge. This campsite isn't as beautiful as the one at Orange Point, but it has more room for tents—a good place for group camping. From the bench you get a sweeping view across the St. Johns. Don't be surprised to see anglers hanging out along the forest's edge, looking for a perfect bass hole.

Return back along the trail to the HAMMOCK HIDEAWAY sign and head straight across the trail intersection. You're walking through wet slash pine flatwoods sprinkled with bayheads; ditches on each side of the trail collect the tannic water as it drains toward the low spots. Bog buttons thrive in the wet areas. Frequent firebreaks cross the trail. When the path broadens, you pass a grove of sand live oak, and the trail rises up into a dry oak hammock with lots of crunchy leaves in the footpath. At 5 miles you reach a bench. Several trails cross the main trail; stick with the orange blazes. When you reach the INDIAN POND RUN sign, turn left to parallel CR 309 to complete the flatwoods loop. The trail winds around a large flatwoods pond on the right, its surface covered with water lilies. You finish the Johns Landing loop when you pass the LONGLEAF LANE sign at 5.7 miles. Continue straight, following the orange blazes back up to Eagles Nest Row. Turn left and retrace your route back behind the fire tower and past Sulfur Spring, reaching Bobcat Crossing at 6.6 miles. Turn right to follow the lime green blazes; the trail makes an immediate left into the forest, wandering through an oak hammock with scattered longleaf pines, a climax forest overtaking sandhills. The trail descends through the forest to a T intersection, where you complete the Mud Springs Loop after 7.1 miles. Turn right at the PARKING sign and follow the mint green blazes out of the forest. You reach the Mud Spring Trail kiosk, completing a 7.4-mile hike.

Blackrock Beach on the Talbot Islands

32

Ralph E. Simmons Memorial State Forest

Total distance (circuit): 7.1 or 9.3 miles

Hiking time: 4 or 5 hours

Habitats: Sandhill, floodplain forest, hardwood hammock, seepage slopes, pine plantation

Maps: USGS 7½' Boulogne, St. Johns Water Management District map

Running up and along the St. Marys River, which forms the border between Georgia and Florida, the trail system through Ralph E. Simmons Memorial State Forest provides the Florida peninsula's northernmost hike. Backpackers can enjoy their choice of two riverside campsites with views of Georgia across the placid water. But wildflowers provide the best reason to hike this state forest—these woodlands are a delight for amateur botanists. You'll need an excellent identification guide to figure out many of the species you see here, since this forest provides a refuge for rare and globally endangered species such as Bartram's ixia, hartwrightia, purple baldwina, toothache grass, and hooded pitcher plants.

Driving north around Jacksonville, take I-295 exit 11B, US 1. Head north 12 miles on US 1 to Callahan, where US 301 joins your route. Driving southbound on I-95 into Florida, take exit 373, Yulee. Follow A1A northbound for 12 miles to the traffic light in Callahan and turn right on US 1/301. From Callahan it's 18.2 miles north on US 1/301 past Hilliard to Boulogne, just south of the state line, where you turn right on Lake Hampton Road. After 1.6 miles you pass the southern entrance to Simmons State Forest. Continue another mile to Penny Haddock Road, turning left at the RALPH E. SIMMONS STATE FOREST sign. Drive 0.8 mile to the next sign and turn left to the main recreational entrance, with a small parking area and trailhead kiosk.

Pause at the kiosk to study the map of the forest. These trails are multiuse, shared

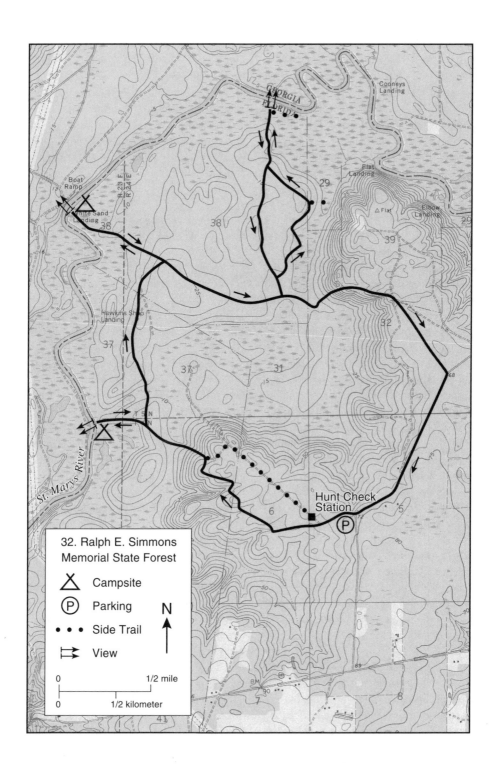

GEORGIA
FLORIDA

Cooneys
Landing

Boat
Ramp

Flat
Landing

29

△ Flat

Elbow
Landing

20

White Sand
Landing

38

R 23 E
R 24 E

38

39

32

68

Hawkins Shop
Landing

37

37

31

St. Marys River

T 5 N

6

Hunt Check
Station

5

P

32. Ralph E. Simmons Memorial State Forest

△ Campsite

Ⓟ Parking

••• Side Trail

⊢⇉ View

N
↑

0 ——————— 1/2 mile

0 ——————— 1/2 kilometer

with horses and bicycles, but are lightly used and in good shape. Between the lack of blazes and signage in this forest and the number of extra roads that aren't shown on this map, it's easy to get lost. Be sure you have both map and compass in hand before starting out on Forest Road 1, just beyond the gate. The hike starts in the gently rolling sandhills of the St. Marys River basin, shaded by towering loblolly and longleaf pines. Watch for morning glories peeking from the wiregrass. At 0.2 mile you reach a fork in the road at a hunt check station with a portable toilet. This forest is off-limits to hikers during the hunting season. Check the Florida Fish and Wildlife Commission web site at www.floridaconservation.org for specific dates. Keep to the left at the fork to walk a broad, mowed grassy swath through the sandhill. Scattered loblolly bay and titi trees indicate the presence of water on a seepage slope. Look carefully in the underbrush for small groups of hooded pitcher plants. As the trail rises, oaks dominate the landscape. Unusually gnarled water oaks show off scalloped leaves in fluffy bunches. Turkey oaks and white oaks compete for the biggest leaves, and bluejack oaks flaunt their slender leaves. But beneath the oaks, the wildflowers flourish. Watch for the long cones of blackroot and the delicate bell-shaped petals of beard tongue. It's hard to miss the electric-blue blooms of the erect dayflower scattered throughout the wiregrass. Although the flower's shape looks like it belongs in the pea family, it's a type of spiderwort. Bright yellow stamens add a splash of contrast to the bloom.

Tucked away under tufts of wiregrass, gopher tortoise burrows are evidence of one common resident of the sandhill. Although an endangered species, the gopher tortoise continues to make a strong comeback, thanks to refuges such as this

and steep penalties for the consumption of tortoises. Once a staple food in north Florida, the gopher tortoise was referred to as "Hoover's chicken"—for the unmet campaign promise of a chicken in every pot—and consumed as soup. You'll see two of the tortoises' favorite meals as you hike: prickly pear cactus, with its succulent fruits, and gopher apple, the short, shiny-leaved plants growing in clusters along the trail's edge.

A patch of ground thick with reindeer lichen looks almost out of place under the oaks. Curving to the right past a borrow pit, the trail meets up with FR 1 at a T intersection at 1.1 miles. Turn left, walking along the edge of a lush, dark hardwood hammock with stands of bamboo and patches of woods ferns. Blackberries grow large and juicy along the left side of the road, maturing in June. Underfoot, the road becomes scattered slag, minimizing the road's erosion by the constant trickle of water from seepage slopes. Pipewort rises from the trail's edge like a cluster of white-headed pins stuck in a voodoo doll. Growing up to 3 feet tall, each stem supports a single white button like a mushroom cap. Watch for star-rush, a four-leaved grass with white streaks radiating from the center, and the brilliant magenta globes of the smooth-leaved sensitive brier. These vinelike plants snake across the trail, showing off its presence by its fuzzy blooms.

Dropping down through a forest of young loblolly pines, fragrant with morning dew, you come to a trail that leads off to the left. Skip this trail—it connects the northerly trail system with the trail system accessed from Lake Hampton Road—and continue up to the NO MOTORIZED VEHICLES sign and camping symbol at 1.5 miles. Even if you're not backpacking, you'll want to walk down for your first glimpse of the St. Marys River.

St. Marys River at White Sand Landing

Mats of buttonweed weave through the grasses underfoot, showing off delicate white four-petal flowers. Dropping down from the sandhill, you enter a hammock of mixed hardwoods, the trail shaded by sweetgum, American holly, and water oak. At 1.7 miles you reach the campsite, a clearing on a bluff above the river. Benches encircle a fire ring, and a short trail to the left leads down to the water's edge, a tiny cove under tree limbs. Although the view is limited, a nice cool breeze comes off the water. Relax for a moment at the benches. If you're camping, be sure to call the forest office in advance for a permit. Campsites are first come, first served.

As you return back up the trail, notice the unusual live oak on the left. After the tree fell over, several branches sprouted vertically as thick as trees. The trunk then rotted away, leaving the section with the branches suspended nearly a foot above the ground, perpendicular to where the trunk is rooted in the earth. When you reach FR 1 at a T intersection, turn left to walk down through a pine plantation of young loblolly pines. Where a culvert carries a small stream under the road, a hardwood hammock lines the scant trickle of water. As the road rises back up into sandhills, wax myrtle acts as the dominant understory under tall loblolly pines.

After 3 miles you reach a T intersection, a broad space that serves as a parking area for hunters, with FR 2. Turn left to walk down to a truly scenic spot on the St. Marys River. After you step over a cable gate, the trail continues through the loblolly pines. Watch for highbush blueberries dripping with luscious fruits in late June. When you come to an intersection with a trail heading to the right, ignore the painted arrow and continue straight. You pass a w sign as the trail curves to the right, crossing over a ditch. Red maples with slender leaves and red stems provide shade as the habitat transitions to hardwood hammock, where the star-shaped leaves of sweetgums rain in crimson and purple on the footpath each winter. At a faint fork in the road, keep to the left. An armadillo crashes through dead saw palmetto fronds as bald cypresses flank the trail, which becomes the high ground in the river's floodplain forest. At 3.6 miles the trail ends at White Sand Landing, where a campsite (no benches, no fire ring) sits on a bluff. Below, a shimmering white beach awaits, providing a sweeping view of the tea-colored water lapping at young cypresses on the Georgia shore.

Turn around to head back to the trail junction of FR 1 and 2. As you leave, look carefully for greenfly orchids mingled with the resurrection fern up on the high limbs of the oaks. When these inconspicuous orchids bloom in summer, they display yellowish-green petals with a pouting lower lip of magenta on white. Once you reach the trail junction, head straight. The PARKING AREA sign should be on your right as you pass it. Wildflowers cluster in a small seepage on the right. Like pink prayer flags, the blooms of tall meadow beauty wave from atop long stems. Passing a trail to the left, the road rises through more sandhill, shaded by loblolly pines, and then curves to the left past a large white diamond sign on the right and a cable gate. The scattered yellow blooms under the pines are yellow aster, blossoming atop tall, thick bouquetlike stems. A red chokeberry bursts with deep crimson fruits that resemble crabapples.

At 4.9 miles you come to a trail that leads off to the left. This is your decision point regarding the length of this hike. If you'd like a little more adventure, another glimpse of the St. Marys River, and the opportunity to wander on narrow pathways

A pygmy rattlesnake lies coiled among pine needles

through silent forests, turn left for a 2.2-mile loop hike. Otherwise, continue straight on FR 2, shortening your total mileage to 7.1 miles.

If you turn left for the longer hike, immediately keep alert for a fork in the trail in front of an old oak tree. Take the right fork, the trail less traveled, into the dark shade of a dense pine forest, where the pines rain their needles down like tinsel on the oaks and high bush blueberries. Skirting two cabbage palms, the trail wanders past large patches of narrow-leaf pawpaw. Notice the short gnarled trees with tiny leaves and slender black thorns. These are one-flowered hawthorn, a member of the rose family. Blooms give way to reddish and yellow-green fruits by summer. When you reach the T intersection at 5.4 miles, turn left. Watch for the black flash of a fox squirrel's tail as it clambers a pine trunk.

At the next T intersection, at 5.8 miles, turn right. This broader path leads over to the bluffs of the St. Marys River, dropping

through a mucky trickling stream under bald cypresses en route. Although the trail seems to go upstream along the river, it is not maintained beyond your first glimpse of the river through the saw palmetto. You can beat a path through the underbrush for a clearer view. Turn around and retrace your steps to the last T intersection. Passing the trail you came in on, continue straight. A massive armadillo pauses while digging, clicking its long claws together as it sits up, disturbed by your footfalls. Tread carefully on this grassy path, watching for the curled-up form of a pygmy rattler. Although tiny, these venomous snakes can strike quickly.

After 7.1 miles you pass the beginning of the loop, the fork leading away from the oak tree. Continue straight, and within a few footfalls you're back to FR 2. Turn left. The road makes a sharp left turn at a sign that says BENCH MARK, transitioning from sandhills into hardwood hammock. Slag carpets the road here, and walking on the stones can be a bit rough. Along the ditches on the sides of the

---

road you'll see button snakeroot, a member of the carrot family, with distinctive bristly cone-shaped flowers atop thick stems. The yellow blossoms atop slender stems are broad-scale yellow-eyed-grass, one of the tallest varieties of yellow-eyed-grass, rising more than 3 feet tall. The road meanders past two borrow pits. In the second one, on the right, several loblolly pines stand upon slender columns of sand, roots dangling, ready to topple in a strong wind. As you rise back up into the sandhills, the road becomes sandy underfoot. A swallow-tailed kite makes lazy circles overhead.

The landscape ahead of you opens up: a section of sandhill with charred oaks, the result of logging and burning. At 7.9 miles you come to a T intersection where FR 2 turns right. Turn right and follow the broad grassy path down to the distant gate. Again, you're immersed in the flora of the sandhill. Ivory blossoms top the waxy-leaved sandhill milk-weed. A breeze ruffles the leaves of shiny blueberry bushes, displaying the silvery-blue underside of each leaf. Slash pines provide the high but sparse canopy. You reach the gate at 8.4 miles. Walk through the pass-through and turn right to walk down Penny Haddock Road to return to your car. Even here, along the dusty road, wildflowers abound. A zebra swallowtail zooms in on a colorful orange spray of butterfly weed. The tall, pale lilac wildflower is roserush, its distinctive square petals sporting fringed edges. When you see the state forest sign, turn right to return to the parking lot after 9.3 miles of hiking, completing your hike.

33

Cary Nature Trail

Total distance (circuit): 1.4 miles

Hiking time: 45 minutes

Habitats: Pine flatwoods, bayhead, cypress dome, seepage slope

Maps: USGS 7½' Bryceville, park map

Bzzz . . . bzzz . . . bzzz. You hear the flies before you see them. Creeping ever closer, you find a stand of hooded pitcher plants waving on a sheltered seepage slope, their carrion-smelling flowers attracting a new crop of black flies. Drawn by the bright red veins and white spots on the pitcher-shaped leaf, the fly climbs in. Oops! Tiny downward-pointing hairs force the fly downward into the trap. Glands at the bottom digest the hapless insect.

At Cary State Forest you have the opportunity for a highly accessible, close-up look at these carnivorous plants in the wild. The 1.4-mile Cary Nature Trail is a great short jaunt for kids and persons of limited mobility—it's well graded, good for a stroller, and is wheelchair-accessible with assistance. Families may wish to take advantage of the "primitive" campsite: It's tents only ($5 per night per tent), but showers and rest rooms are provided. Contact the forest office in advance for a State Forest Use Permit before staking your tent. An outdoor teaching pavilion, the S. Bryan Jennings Environmental Education Center, is available for public use (scout groups encouraged) by preregistration with the forest office.

From I-10 exit 343, Baldwin/Starke, head north on US 301. The highway makes two sharp turns through the town of Baldwin before becoming open road again. After you pass CR 119 and the Bryceville fire station, you see a WELCOME TO CARY STATE FOREST sign on the right. Keep alert for the first turnoff to the right at the DIVISION OF

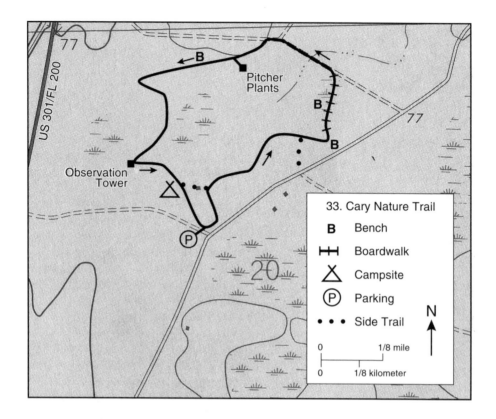

33. Cary Nature Trail

B	Bench
⊢⊣	Boardwalk
⟨Λ⟩	Campsite
Ⓟ	Parking
• • •	Side Trail

N

0   1/8 mile

0   1/8 kilometer

FORESTRY sign, 9 miles north of I-10. Follow the limestone-paved Pavilion Road for 0.4 mile to the trail kiosk and grassy parking area at its intersection with Fire Tower Road. After you park, pay your $2 state forest usage fee and pick up a trail map at the kiosk. The Cary Nature Trail is also a Florida State Forests Trailwalker trail, so grab a postcard to send in after the hike.

The trail starts just across Pavilion Road at the TEACHING PAVILION AND NATURE TRAIL sign, following the powder blue blazes into the pine flatwoods. Around you, the longleaf pine flatwoods are recovering from a fire. Although the bark of the tall pines is charred, gallberry, woods fern, and saw palmetto fill the understory with greenery. The footpath is delineated by logs on either side

of a grassy path. You quickly approach a clearing. The environmental center sits to the right, with picnic tables and benches scattered around it; on the left is the bathhouse and rest rooms for the camping area. Cross the jeep track and walk under the power lines to reach the NATURE TRAIL sign. Follow the path into the forest. A shrubby St. Peter's-wort shows off its yellow blooms in spring, a puff of delicate stamens emerging from the center of each four-petaled flower. Pale meadow beauty peeps between reedy grasses with strawflower tufts, and longleaf pines shower their needles on the footpath. The trail is broad enough for three people to walk abreast. Looking off through the woods to the right, you can see the roof of a picnic pavilion. The habitat shifts, becoming damper, as loblolly bay and red maple fill the forest. Star-shaped marsh pinks display their pale pink blossoms, and orange wild bachelor's button pokes up from the grassy forest floor. A brown anole skitters up the deeply textured bark of a longleaf pine. Lichens in shades of white peeling paint to seafoam to khaki carpet the zigzagging limbs of a possum haw.

You arrive in a clearing with a bench as the trail comes up to a boardwalk with the ADAM'S WILDERNESS TRAIL sign. The boardwalk carries the trail through a cypress dome. A white-tailed deer crashes through the dense underbrush. A tall stand of longleaf pines stands out in sharp relief against the blue sky, sunshine filling each needle with an inner glow. Pond cypresses form the core of the cypress dome, a cool, damp place where hundreds of cypress knees jut from the forest floor. Coated in a thick wrap of moss, one clump of cypress knees looks like a natural sculpture. A shaded bench gives you a place to sit and contemplate the cypress swamp. Look up, and you'll see a nest built with pine needles, nearly 2 feet wide, dripping out of the crook of a tupelo tree.

At 0.5 mile the boardwalk ends at a T intersection with a jeep trail. Turn left at the NATURE TRAIL sign and follow the blue blazes down the road. The broad, open jeep track is in full sun, edged by pine flatwoods. It crosses a swampy area where the swamp drains under the road. This is your first opportunity to see hooded pitcher plants up close. These carnivorous plants grow out of the seepage slope on the right side of the road. In spring, the pitcher plants show off their thick, rubbery blooms of red, green, or yellow, each emitting a carrion-like odor that attracts insects.

When you come to the intersection of Hog Track Road and Moccasin Slough at 0.7 mile, the NATURE TRAIL sign guides you to turn left. Follow this grassy strip through the forest, watching along the drainage areas on both sides for more hooded pitcher plants. They prefer the shade, thriving in spots where the sphagnum moss is especially thick and seepage is constant, even in dry seasons. It's odd to see deer moss juxtaposed with pitcher plants since they generally prefer different soils, but along this road, they grow together. The tiny seeds of low panicum create a mauve fog above the grass. Keep alert—the trail has been rerouted. It quickly turns to the left and enters the woods just before you encounter the next NATURE TRAIL sign. Crossing a short boardwalk over the drainage ditch, you reenter the pine flatwoods. Gallberry flaunts its plump, black astringent berries, once boiled down to serve as ink by early settlers, who called it inkberry. Stands of tall, thin longleaf pine look like pencils in comparison to the mature trees behind them. Young cypresses form a dome under the pines. A downy woodpecker drums a tune against a snag.

Watch for the side trail to the left. Wander down it into the shade of a cypress dome, where a beautiful natural garden of pitcher plants flourishes along the boggy edge of the marsh. The hooded pitcher plant is a threatened species, although it is Florida's most common variety of pitcher plant. Its red-veined and white-spotted trumpetlike leaves grow nearly a foot high, curving inward to create the "pitcher" that traps the flying insects and ants that venture inside.

When you return to the main trail, turn left. The footpath becomes spongy, the pine duff thick underfoot. A Gulf fritillary clings to a tarflower in full bloom. At the 1-mile mark you reach a bench. In the distance you can see an observation tower rising over the forest understory. A small toad pauses in its

Trails from the observation tower at Cary State Forest

traverse of the trail. With a white stripe down its black and gray mottled back, it's *bufous quercus,* the oak toad, a common inhabitant of the pine flatwoods. The oak toad breeds in the small grassy puddles and pools that appear in the flatwoods after a heavy rain. Listen for its peeps—it sounds like a baby chicken.

When you reach a T intersection at 1.1 miles, the observation tower is off to your right. Walk over and climb up. It's a steep ascent, and the railings are old and splintery, so take care how you place your hands. At the top you face a grassy clearing carved out of the forest to attract deer. Turn around for a panoramic view of the pine flatwoods, with the trail leading off into the distance. Be especially careful descending the steep stairs. Returning to the T, it looks like a fork from this direction. Keep to the right, following the blue blazes. You'll pass a trail coming in from the right, and then walk down a corridor of slender pines into the camping area and past the bathhouse, across the jeep road and under the power lines. Keep alert as the trail makes a right turn into the forest. Walking back through a different part of the charred forest, you emerge on Pavilion Road, at the upper end of the parking area. The activity around the horse trailers is a bunch of equestrians unloading their horses for an outing on the Red Root Trail, an 8-mile horse trail that winds through the Cary State Forest. Turn to the left and walk back to your car, completing this 1.4-mile hike.

34

Fort Clinch State Park

Total distance (3 circuits, 1 round trip): 11.6 miles

Hiking time: 6.5 hours

Habitats: Maritime hammock, salt marsh, freshwater marsh, coastal strand

Maps: USGS 7½' Fernandina Beach, park map

A long, slender peninsula reaches out to form Florida's most northeasterly tip, reaching out toward Cumberland Island, Georgia. Upon it, guarding the mouth of the St Marys River, is a massive brick fortress dating back to 1842 that was built to defend Florida's crucial deepwater port of Fernandina. During the Civil War, Confederate soldiers occupied this position at the northern terminus of the Florida Railroad, which carried goods across the state to the port at the Cedar Keys (Hike 10). Standing guard, George Dorman of the First Florida Battalion heard General Trapier's surprising order to evacuate. "We received orders to spike the guns and evacuate the place. I suppose they found out that the Yankees were going to land . . . "

As the Confederate soldiers left Fernandina on March 3, 1862, the Union gunboat *Ottawa* steamed into port, capturing one of Florida's most valuable cities without a struggle. "We *captured* Port Royal," said Union Commodore Du Pont, "but Fernandina and Fort Clinch have been *given* to us." The Confederate Army's retreat from Fort Clinch became a festering wound for Florida governor John Milton, who felt that the Confederacy was more than willing to sacrifice his state to the Union. Several weeks later, he wrote to Jefferson Davis: "I was not only surprised but mortified at the conduct of our troops at Fernandiana, and that conduct has sealed forever the fate of poor Florida!"

The Union Army retained control of Fort Clinch for the remainder of the war, adding

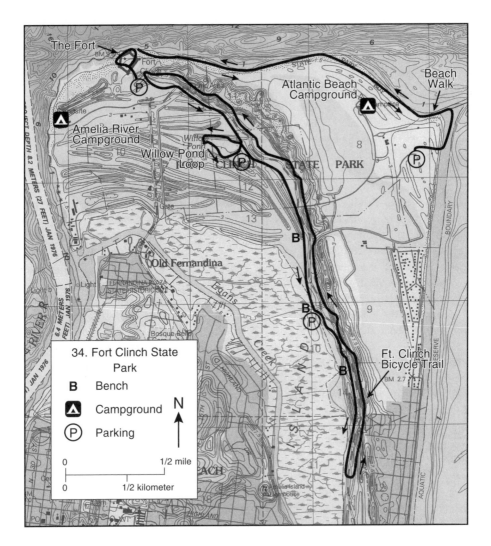

34. Fort Clinch State Park

B Bench

A Campground

P Parking

N

0   1/2 mile

0   1/2 kilometer

additional fortifications until 1867. Fort Clinch was garrisoned again during the Spanish-American War, and then sold by the U.S. Government in 1926. During the Great Depression, the developers who planned to build along the peninsula couldn't pay their taxes, so the state of Florida bought the land in 1935 for $10,000 with the "fort thrown in." Workers from the Civilian Conservation Corps toiled from 1937 to 1942 to restore the fort. Opened to the public in 1938, Fort Clinch State Park offers an array of seaside activities. Besides hiking, biking, picnicking, and fishing, you can tour the fort or enjoy the salt breezes through either of its two campgrounds on an overnight stay.

To get to Fort Clinch, take I-95 exit 373, Callahan/Fernandina Beach. Head south on FL A1A, crossing the causeway. Continue into Fernandina, and you come to a traffic light at Atlantic Avenue after 15 miles. Turn right, still following FL A1A. Continue another 1.5 miles to the park entrance, on the left. When you pay your entrance fee, ask the ranger for trail maps and a guidebook to the Willow Pond Nature Trail. As you drive in on the entrance road, you pass some spectacularly large dunes on the right. A canopy of maritime hammock shades the road as well as the park's hiking trails. Keep alert for trail crossings. At 1.4 miles past the ranger station, you see a small parking lot on the left at Egan Marsh. This is one of several parking areas with trailhead access. At 2 miles you pass the turnoff to the right for the Atlantic Beach Campground, with its beach access for your beach hike. At 2.4 miles you see the Willow Pond parking area on the left. Park here, and use this trailhead to access both the Willow Pond Nature Trail and the Fort Clinch Bicycle Trail.

WILLOW POND NATURE TRAIL

Facing the large gray WILLOW POND sign with the trail map, you find a confusing array of choices. Four trails lead away from the parking lot: the two ends of the loops for the Willow Pond Nature Trail and the Fort Clinch Bicycle Trail, respectively. Start your hike to Willow Pond by taking the trail directly to the left of the WILLOW POND sign. If you arrive on a Saturday, hook up with the guided walk held at 10:30 AM.

As the trail drops down it approaches Willow Pond, a body of fresh water on this peninsula surrounded by saltwater, home to a small colony of alligators. On the right is a nice view down the length of the pond (actually part of a series of ponds, depending on the water level), where the green duckweed lays across the pond surface like a linoleum floor in a 1940s diner. A spur trail to the left takes you down to a bench with a nice view of the main body of Willow Pond, fringed in willows. When you see the

CAUTION: ALLIGATOR CROSSING sign, it's not a joke! Notice the roughed-up ground where the alligators drag themselves from one pond to the other. As you walk along the pond, you hear a weird noise: *gwunk-gwunk, gwunk-gwunk.* Watch the duckweed carefully. It's the call of a baby alligator, scarcely a foot long, pushing along the surface of the duckweed in search of its mother. Don't wait for her to show up. Continue straight, walking between the two ponds. You reach a trail junction with a bench. Unless the water is high, continue straight, between the cedars, and head down along the edge of another large segment of pond, not much more than a duckweed-covered mudflat. When you reach the fork, the high-water trail comes in from the right. Turn left. Paralleling another pond, the trail continues down a row of sugarberry trees, distinctive with their knobby bark. Also known as sugar hackberry, their sweet fall berries provide wintering birds with a good food source.

Crossing a bridge over a slow-moving stream at 0.3 mile, the trail rises up under the low branches of large American holly trees, circling around a deep hollow filled with forest. Woods ferns grow in the damp bottom, while red bay and live oak rise from the hollow, their branches covered in resurrection fern. You come to a trail junction with the Willow Trail at a bench. Turn left, walking along the low side of the tall relict dunes covered in red bay and saw palmetto. Downhill to the right, you see a pond choked with duckweed, with a spur trail leading to it. Continuing on the main trail, you round a bend and come to a trail junction. Turn left, emerging after 0.6 mile at the parking area.

FORT CLINCH BICYCLE TRAIL

Don't let the name put you off. Built by the local Spoked Flight Bicycle Club, this

Maritime hammock along the Fort Clinch Bicycle Trail

popular single-track trail winds through 6.1 miles of the park's maritime hammock and provides a strenuous but enjoyable hike. Be sure to pack adequate water for the trek. Although the route is shaded the entire way, the hills will give you a serious workout. Be courteous to bikers and step off the trail when you hear them coming.

Start your hike from the Willow Pond parking lot at the large FT. CLINCH BICYCLE TRAIL sign to the *left* of the WILLOW POND sign. As you walk under the spreading red bay trees and live oaks, you catch a glimpse of duckweed-covered Willow Pond off to the right. The trail climbs up and over relict dunes, as it will for the next 6 miles—a continual up-and-down with few breaks. Dipping out onto the entrance road to skirt a dried-up creek, it returns back into the dark and shady forest. You drop down through a low drainage filled with Hercules-club, and then climb up and over a hill. At 0.5 mile you cross a jeep road used by the rangers. Continue straight, winding through the hammock to where you see your first glimpse of the salt marsh. From that far shore John Muir took in his first Florida landscape, when he landed in Fernandina in October 1867. Muir expected Florida's floral embrace, but "such was not the gate by which I entered the promised land." Instead, he saw these salt marshes before you, "belonging more to the sea than to the land . . . sunk to the shoulders in sedges and rushes."

After meandering through a grove of spindly yaupon holly, you emerge at a spot at 1 mile where you can walk out to the edge of the salt marsh and take in a sweeping view. The squat industrial plant on the horizon is St. Marys Paper. Off to the left, you see the Amelia Island Lighthouse, which originally stood on Cumberland Island. It was taken down and rebuilt in Fernandina in 1838, making it the oldest

structure standing on the island. It is the only remaining lighthouse from Florida's period as a U.S. Territory, and its light can be still be seen 19 miles out to sea.

As you wind along the edge of the salt marsh, you walk behind tall sea myrtle, which show off their fluffy blooms in fall, and then back into a forest of slender yaupon holly. When you reach the point where Egan Creek flows under the park entrance, you see a WARNING: ALLIGATORS sign—the creek is fresh water. Take a short side trip on the narrow spur trail along the creek. Fiddler crabs scatter as you step down through a low spot, and an ibis skims across the salt flats. The spur ends on a cedar-topped promontory with nice views of the marshes and Egan Creek. When you return to the main trail, turn right. The well-defined footpath continues to wind through maritime hammock, past gnarled and knobby southern magnolias, making you step over the trunks of fallen trees. Vegetation crowds closely. After climbing each steep slope, you'll enjoy nice views over the marsh from the top. At 1.5 miles the trail swings out to the edge of the entrance road to an old parking area and bench before reentering the forest under an archway of red bay. When you see the STEEP DIP AHEAD sign, take it seriously. The incline down the far side of the dune is so steep that you might want to slide down the leaf-covered trail on your backside. There's nothing to assist you down the slope, and the leaves are slippery, so stay to the right-hand side. You walk beneath immense southern magnolias, their bark covered with patches of green moss. At the STOP sign, the trail crosses the entrance road to begin its return trip along the ocean side. Be cautious of poison ivy along this stretch. The trail twists and turns past American beautyberry, saw palmetto, and red mulberry. The sand is soft around some of the sharper curves. The trail continues under an enormous red bay tree, its branches forming a canopy across a curve. Stand still for a moment, and you can hear the roar of the waves just beyond the forest as well as smell the sharp, inviting tang of the sea—nature's symphony, playing to all the senses.

After 2.6 miles, passing behind some rangers' residences, you emerge on the entrance road at a STOP sign. Turn right and walk along the edge of the road to skirt the tall dunes that spill down to your feet. Keep alert for where the trail reenters the forest and turn right to follow it up the steep and twisting path. You return to the road at another STOP sign. Turn right and walk along the road briefly to go around another dune. You reenter the forest across from the old parking area on the left side of the road, ducking under the low red bay limbs. The sheer size of the dunes forces the trail closer toward the road. When it turns away it enters a narrow valley between tall dunes, shaded by box elder. Hercules'-club rises from a bowl filled with saw palmetto. Crouching low under a bower of wax myrtle, you walk between beds of woods ferns as the trail winds back toward the road, emerging at a STOP sign at Egan Creek. Continue over the bridge, and the trail drops down into a forest of yaupon and sugarberry. You briefly follow Egan Creek, a sluggish freshwater stream, before the trail swings out toward the road. The calming aroma of cedar and bay leaf fills your lungs as you drop down to cross the road to the Atlantic Beach campground at 3.8 miles. Tall slash pines rain their needles on the footpath. At another STOP sign the trail turns right onto the road to skirt another large dune, continuing back under red bay dappled by resurrection fern before it dips down through an intermittent creek. Watch for deer and grazing gopher tortoises in the grassy clearings

off to the left. You reach a STEEP DIP AHEAD sign, but this dip is milder—the one beyond it is rougher and has no warning sign.

Coming to a fork at 4.3 miles, you have a chance to bail out on the hike. If you take the left fork, you'll emerge across from the Willow Pond Parking Area, where your car is parked. If you want to complete the full 6.1-mile loop, continue along the right fork to follow the trail up to the north end of the island. You pass a small brick structure topped in resurrection fern in an area where the saw palmettos grow tall and thick, their trunks lifting well off the ground. The sound of the ocean waves draws closer, creating a strange counterpoint to pine needles underfoot and woods ferns along the edge of the trail. At the next STEEP DIP AHEAD sign, be cautious of roots that can trip you up on your way down. At a STOP sign the trail turns right onto the entrance road to skirt a drainage. Watch for it to turn right back into the forest. You come to another STEEP DIP AHEAD sign before a drop into a dry drainage. After meandering through a hammock with lots of cabbage palms and cedars, the trail emerges on the entrance road at 5.1 miles. Turn right, in the direction of the sign with the picnic and playground symbols. Cross the road and turn left into the parking lot for Fort Clinch. The fort and rest rooms are on the far side of the lot—the start of the Fort Clinch Walking Tour (described below). Keep alert for the trailhead sign on your left, where the trail climbs up a steep hill into the forest. The sweet scent of pine fills the air as you walk through a grove of loblolly pine.

At 5.4 miles you cross the road to the Amelia River Campground, continuing into the maritime forest on the other side. At the fork a sign says STEEP DIP to the right, OPTION to the left. Turn left to emerge on the entrance road. Turn right to skirt around the

Fort Clinch

deep ditch before you and return to the forest. Both trails rejoin; turn left. At the next STEEP DIP AHEAD sign the trail drops down through a hollow between two sand ridges. On the upslope there's a fence to prevent bikers from catapulting over the ridge. The trail curves left, continuing its undulating path over the hills. A side trail to the left leads to a bench on the entrance road. Continue straight. The trail does another drop through a deep drainage, which you can circumvent by walking around it on the road. A shrill cacophony of cicadas rises and falls. As the trail climbs up through a patch of saw palmetto, you can see your car ahead. You emerge at the Willow Pond parking area after 6.1 miles.

FORT CLINCH WALKING TOUR

From the Willow Pond parking area, continue your drive north on the entrance road.

At 2.9 miles the turnoff to the left leads to the Amelia River Campground. Continue straight to the parking lot at Fort Clinch, at the end of the road at 3.1 miles. From the parking lot, walk up to the museum and bookstore and pay your $2 admission before entering the grounds of the fortress.

Savor the strong sea breeze as you walk across the open area leading up to the moat and imagine a step back in time to 1864. As you cross the drawbridge and enter the fort, the smell of wood smoke fills the tunnel. Civil War–era reenactors roam the fort, leading groups on tours or just going about their duties. You may tour the fort on your own or hook up with a group if you see one. On certain weekends during the year, the fort is fully garrisoned by either Confederate or Union regiments.

As you emerge out of the tunnel, notice the building right in front of you, the storehouse and dispensary. The brown brick structures around you are the original portions of the fort; the remainder was added from 1864 through 1867 by Union regiments and the Army Corps of Engineers. Following the Third System design of fortress building, Fort Clinch has a two-wall fortification: one masonry, one earthen. Batteries stand on the masonry walls. Third System fortresses such as Fort Clinch were designed as a coordinated system of coastal defenses in the aftermath of the War of 1812.

Walk counterclockwise around the buildings and peek into the open interiors to see how the garrison lived. As you walk around the enlisted men's barracks, notice the grand pillars on the back of the building. Continue past the well and turn left into the long brick tunnel to access the southwest bastion of the fort. Within this tunnel and bastion you'll see the unique architectural details that make Fort Clinch a national treasure, including some keen masonry tricks for roof support: flying buttresses, vaulted archways, and hexagonal archway systems, with bricks facing downward in the ceilings in some of the tunnels. Notice the gothic pentagonal ceiling inside the bastion, which eliminates the need for a central pillar.

Climb up the extremely narrow, winding granite staircase to emerge atop the bastion, where you take in a sweeping view of the fort and Cumberland Sound. As you leave the bastion, turn left, walking out on a wooden staircase to access the earthen ramparts. The guns are mounted on granite blocks atop a tabby (oyster shell and mortar) wall that tops the earthen impoundment. As you walk along the wall, listen to the slap of waves against the jetty and feel the sting of salt air in your face. A ring-necked gull swoops low over the fishermen

busy at the river's mouth. Beyond the Spanish bayonets, a staircase leads down to a dark chamber, another bastion at the very mouth of the river. Descend and investigate, exploring the gothic architecture that looks out on the river and the beach. As you leave, turn left to walk along the inside of the exterior scarp. You feel blasts of cold sea air as you pass each gun hole.

When you reach the staircase, turn right and climb back up to the top of the ramparts for a great view down the sweep of the beach along the Atlantic Ocean. Walk down the broad ramp to the inner courtyard. Turn right and check out the quarters tucked into the inside wall: the powder room, the laundry, and the medical quarters. Cross the open green back to the last building flanking the entrance, the guard room. When you leave the fort, continue back to the museum and take a look at the exhibits that explain the history of Fort Clinch. After an hour or so of exploring, you've completed a 0.6-mile walk.

ATLANTIC BEACH HIKE

From Fort Clinch drive 1.1 miles up the entrance road to the turnoff for the Atlantic Beach Campground. Turn right. After 0.4 mile turn right—the campground lies straight ahead. Drive another 0.2 mile through the dunes to the parking lot.

Start your hike by walking up the boardwalk over the dunes, past the changing area and rest rooms. Sea oats grow densely where you descend to the beach. Turn left. Be sure to time your hike so you are there as low tide is going out, and returning as the tide is coming in, to ensure hard-packed sand underfoot for a comfortable walk. A long jetty and fishing pier dominate the horizon. The bronze beach sand shimmers as sunlight plays across beds of broken coquina shells. Rivulets of tidewater flow off toward the waves, forming pools riffled by the wind. Sea oats line the dunes above you; look carefully for the spreading tendrils of beach morning glories, their white blooms standing at attention in the breeze. After rounding the peninsula, you pass underneath the fishing pier at 0.6 mile. Great mats of greenish-brown seaweed lie strewn across the shoreline, looking spongelike from a distance. As you approach the boardwalk to the Atlantic Beach Campground, you see a jetty stretching off into the distance, merging with the horizon. Starting at Cumberland Island, it protects the shipping channel into the St. Marys River, which pours out into the Atlantic Ocean in front of you. A shrimp boat steams into the channel, nets lifted high, returning with the day's catch.

Beyond this boardwalk, waves have sliced off the fronts of the dunes. Coming up to a promontory where pelicans, terns, and gulls gather, you get a clear view of Fort Clinch, its squat masonry structure hugging the St. Marys River. Around the curve, the dunes roll down to the high-tide line, dense with vegetation. Incoming waves become calmer due to the distant jetty. At 1.5 miles you pass a coastal light out on a wooden platform. The dunes increase in size, virtual windswept mountains up to 40 feet high. On the sand beneath your feet, a moon jellyfish lays stranded in the sun, baking like a giant fried egg. As you approach the fort, the near dunes are sliced off by storm waves, a shelf providing a perfect perch for chattering herring gulls. You see a green channel marker and a jetty dead ahead, reaching out from one flank of the fort to the river's mouth. Off to the left is a path up and over the dune line, leading to the parking area at Fort Clinch. Continue up the beach, reaching the granite jetty at 2.2 miles. Sit and rest on the rocks and watch the fishing boats before making your return trip down the beach.

On the way back, notice how the trees sweep up close and low to the dunes, as if a giant comb had been run through them. Pay special attention to the birds fluttering amid the dune vegetation. Painted buntings spend their summers here, nesting near the sea. A northern waterthrush clings precariously to a waving bloom of a century plant. After you pass under the pier, you'll curve back along the beach past the sunbathers. Watch for the cut through the dunes on the right, leading you back up to the boardwalk and out to the parking lot. When you return to your car, you've completed a 4.3-mile hike.

35

Talbot Islands

Total distance (5 round trips, 2 circuits): 11.1 miles

Hiking time: 6 hours

Habitats: Maritime hammock, coastal strand, coastal scrub, freshwater marsh, saltwater marsh, oak hammock, hardwood hammock

Maps: USGS 7½' Mayport; park maps

With miles of untrammeled beaches, shimmering salt marshes, and dark maritime forests, two quiet barrier islands lie just north of where the St. Johns River completes its 310-mile journey to the sea. Divided up into two adjoining state parks, Big Talbot Island and Little Talbot Island, these islands provide an immersion into an undeveloped Florida shoreline, a rare and glorious experience. The pirate Blackbeard landed on these shores, leaving behind rumors of buried treasure. But if you're after a true treasure, bring a camera—Florida's most colorful bird, the painted bunting, nests here in the spring. Together, both parks provide numerous hiking opportunities scattered along 7 miles of coastal highway.

If you're headed southbound on I-95, take exit 373, Callahan/Fernandina Beach. Head south on FL A1A for 11.6 miles. Just after you cross the Intracoastal Waterway, turn right on Amelia Island Parkway. After 3.3 miles you reach a stop sign and blinker at FL A1A. Turn right. FL A1A turns left within 0.7 mile. After you reach the second roundabout inside Amelia Island Plantation after 1.9 miles, continue along FL A1A another 4.4 miles to the entrance to Big Talbot Island State Park, on the left side of the road. From I-95 northbound, take exit 358A, FL 105 (Heckscher Drive). Follow it east, crossing under FL 9A. After you drive another 9.2 miles on FL 105, watch for FL A1A, which merges in from the Mayport Ferry. Continue on FL A1A north for another 2.3 miles to the Fort George River Walk, the southernmost hike described in this narrative.

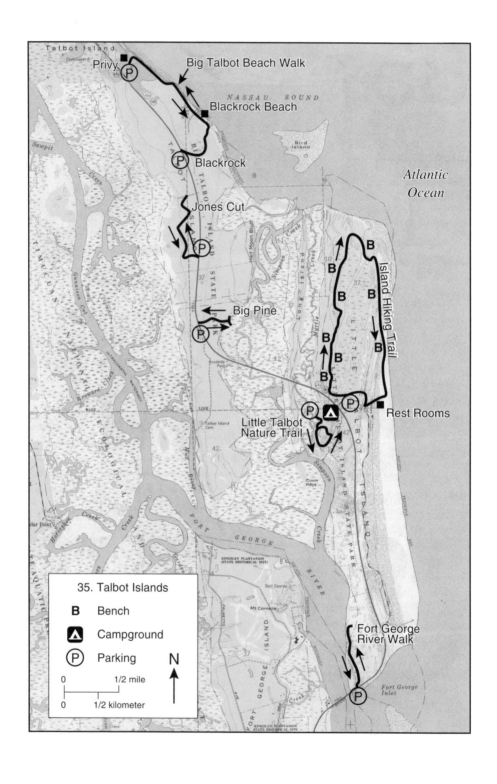

Talbot Island

Privy

Big Talbot Beach Walk

NASSAU SOUND

Blackrock Beach

Blackrock

Atlantic Ocean

Jones Cut

Bird Island

Big Pine

B B
B
B B
B B
B B
B B
B B
B

Island Hiking Trail

Rest Rooms

Little Talbot Nature Trail

Fort George River Walk

35. Talbot Islands

B Bench

▲ Campground

Ⓟ Parking

N

0 ————— 1/2 mile

0 ————— 1/2 kilometer

Although you must pay a fee to enter either Big Talbot Island State Park (at the Bluffs Picnic Area) or Little Talbot Island State Park, all trails with trailheads starting on FL A1A are free to the public, open sunrise to sunset.

BIG TALBOT ISLAND BEACH WALK

Although both parks are on the same stretch of highway and overseen by the same ranger station, Big Talbot Island State Park has its own separate self-pay station for the Bluffs Picnic Area and its beach access. A gate controls access to the area, which is open 8 AM to sunset. In addition to the picnic area and composting toilet, this spot offers beach access down below the high bluffs to some of the island's most beautiful scenery. Park your car and head down the staircase to the beach. This is a 1-mile, low tide–only hike—high tide laps at the base of the bluffs—so be sure to check your tidal chart before heading out.

At the bottom of the staircase, turn right. Amelia Island lies across the channel, and dazzling white sandbars break up the blue water. Dunes top some of the sandbars, which provide some protection to this stretch of beach, slowing down fierce waves before they reach this sensitive shore. You can see breakers off in the distance, beyond the sandbars. As you walk up the beach, notice the unusual limestonelike formations underfoot. These black "rocks" aren't rocks at all—they're compressed sand and decaying vegetation, shaped by water to mimic rocks. Step hard on the edge of one, and it crumbles. Sliced off by high waves during storms, the bluffs drop live oaks down on the beach. Sun-bleached skeletons of trees remain, creating shade for fiddler crabs and highways for sea lice.

After 0.5 mile of walking on the tawny sand, you reach a promontory of black rock pounded by waves. Big chunks of the faux stone lie scattered about and piled up, reminiscent of the black lava beaches of Santorini, Greece. Be cautious if you climb up on the rocks; they are both slippery and prone to crumbling under your feet. On the far side of a wave-washed chasm, the beach stretches off into the distance, creating another cove. Turn around and walk back up the beach to the boardwalk, completing your 1-mile beach walk.

BLACKROCK TRAIL

The most popular of the Talbot Island trails, the 1-mile Blackrock Trail leads to one of the prettiest beaches in Florida, enabling you to enjoy another mile or more of beach walking. From the BIG TALBOT ISLAND STATE PARK sign, drive 1 mile south on A1A to the roadside pulloff and cable gate, on the left. The trail is a broad path, a beautiful wide corridor through the maritime hammock, with sand live oaks providing shade. Saw palmettos frosted with greenbrier flank the trail, and slash pines rain their needles on the footpath. Sculpted and gnarled by sea breezes, a coastal scrub forest of myrtle oak, sand live oak, and rusty lyonia creates an overhead canopy as the trail curves to the left, and then to the right. You spot a streak of brilliant blue—the head of a painted bunting in flight. With a deep orange chest and yellow and green feathers along its back, the male painted bunting shows off the most colorful plumage of any Florida bird. The female is also showy, cloaked in bright greens. Painted buntings migrate to the northeastern coast of Florida in late spring, raising three or more hatchlings in a tiny cup of a nest. In late summer the family wings south, migrating to Mexico and Central America.

As you walk along, an eastern towhee picks at ants in the footpath. The trail curves left into a stand of extremely tall, windswept live oaks. Rounding another curve, you come to a fork in the trail. Keep right. The wind picks up, riffling your hair in the salt breeze as you emerge to face the surf at Blackrock Beach after 0.5 mile. Ephemeral as each crashing wave, the shoreline changes every day—sometimes the high tide reaches the bluffs, and sometimes scattered clusters of rock lie strewn across the golden sand. If you pick your way around the peninsula on the right, you reach a quiet beach where waves carve caverns into the dense sand mixed with vegetable matter, forming the black earth posing as rock. With the fronds of saw palmettos dangling over the voids, it resembles a Hawaiian seascape.

At the end of the trail, turn left to continue your exploration, walking between the remnants of an eerie forest of wave-washed oaks, giant driftwood sprawled across the sands. Osprey nest in the tall snags of the oceanfront forest, and at times you can see a dozen or more of them scouting the water for fish or preening atop the trees. Walk across the ledges of black rock, skirting potholes and tidal pools teeming with aquatic life. Under the incessant sun, the ledges gleam with streaks of coppery green and brown across a black base. After 1 mile you reach the promontory en route to the Bluffs Picnic Area. With a second car, you could carefully scramble over these rocks and continue to hike up the beach. For now, enjoy the view. Returning back up to Blackrock Beach, watch for the cut for the trail. Use the Blackrock Trail to return to your car, completing your 2-mile walk.

JONES CUT TRAIL

Continue south on FL A1A another 0.9 mile past the Blackrock Trail. Keep alert for the trailhead on the right, a slight opening in the trees marked by a small JONES CUT sign. You must park along the shoulder of the road. To start this 1.5-mile hike, step over the cable gate. Walk past a sign that prohibits the removal of artifacts. The trail is a broad old forest road through a mature maritime hammock with tall red bay trees, southern magnolias, and live oaks. Spindly yaupon holly grows in the shade of a knobby-barked sugarberry tree. As the trail curves right under a large southern magnolia, it comes to a T intersection with another faint trail. Turn right. You pass a stand of slash pines on the left, which tower well over the surrounding bluejack and laurel oaks. The trail narrows, the corridor defined by saw palmetto. Dog-hobble grows out of the footpath. Covered in resurrection fern, the limbs of massive live oaks knit a canopy overhead.

As the trail continues up a slight rise, you enter an oak hammock. The trail becomes indistinct as you come up to Jones Cut, a broad ditch through the forest. Woods ferns grow from its moist bottom, and pickerel-weed shows off its purple blooms. The trail becomes narrower and narrower as it parallels the ditch until it finally fades away without any warning at 0.7 mile, leaving you to face a wall of forest. Turn around and retrace your path. After you emerge from the corridor of saw palmetto, watch for a stand of six tall cabbage palms on the right. After the trail drops through a small drainage, watch for a stand of pines on the right. Keep alert on the left for the return trail, where the morning sun glints off the pine trunks in front of you. Turn left onto the return trail and walk back out of the maritime hammock, completing your hike after 1.5 miles.

BIG PINE TRAIL

Continue south on FL A1A for another 0.6 mile past Jones Cut to a pulloff on the left for the Big Pine Trail, a 0.8-mile trek out to the edge of the salt marsh. The trail starts off by winding through the maritime hammock, with tall live oaks and laurel oaks shading the footpath. As you follow the curve of the trail around a large deadfall, it takes you into a slash pine forest. Be cautious of poison ivy—it abounds along this trail, often creeping into the footpath. Another fallen tree, a large red bay, seems to still be alive, its carpet of resurrection fern lush and green after a recent rain. Enormous live oaks shelter a patch of netted chain in a low damp spot. A persistent salt breeze sweeps through the forest; you can see a border of blue beyond the trees.

Ivy covers the forest floor, threatening to bury the narrow, unkempt footpath as you draw closer to the salt marshes. Resplendent in its golden skin, a broadhead skink suns on a rotted log, inches away from a massive white jelly tooth mushroom. You come to a trail junction at 0.3 mile. Turn right and follow the spur trail downhill, down the steep sandy bluff to the very edge of the salt marsh. A mat of dead black needlerush provides a platform to step out and take in the sweeping view of the salt marsh, where the swift current of a saline creek races by. Gnarled cedar and red bay overhang the bluff, casting shadows on the needlerush. A large patch of sea oxeye thrives in the shade of a bay tree.

Climb back up the bluff and return to the main trail. Turn right. Surrounded by a dense hedge of saw palmetto, the trail comes to its end at an open spot on the bluff, without a clear view of the water. You've walked 0.4 mile. Turn around and retrace your path back out to the road, completing an 0.8-mile hike.

ISLAND HIKING TRAIL

Continuing south on FL A1A, drive 1.6 miles to the entrance to Little Talbot Island State Park, on the left. If you have not already paid your Florida State Parks en-

Beach morning glory

trance fee at Big Talbot Island State Park, you must do so here. At 3.8 miles, the Island Hiking Trail is the longest of the hiking trails in the Talbot Islands. Ask for a map at the ranger station, and be sure to mention that you're hiking the trail—you must register for this hike and sign out when you're done. Just past the ranger station, turn left and park in the small parking lot.

Start your hike by walking back up the entrance road, past the ranger station, until you reach the trailhead on the right. Follow the bark-chip path down past a large sign with a map of the trail. You pass the first of many benches as you start down the mowed corridor, surrounded by a coastal scrub. Cabbage palms rise from the undulating dunes, and grapevines and greenbrier cover the sand. Reindeer lichen flourishes in the deep sandy bowls. Stay on the footpath as the dune zone is delicate. The trees around you, including yaupon and wax myrtle, red cedar and red bay, are gnarled and windswept. As you descend into a dark maritime hammock, sand live oaks shade the trail. Slash pines rise out of a depression on the left. Stringers of old man's beard wave from the twisted branches of a crabapple tree. A tiny southern toad hops out on the footpath, its brown, mottled skin creating a perfect camouflage against fallen oak leaves.

Pausing at a bench, you hear the roar of

Ghost crab

the waves, although you're looking down into deep bowls filled with forest. The trail gets shadier after 0.7 mile, passing under a tall canopy of slash pine with a lower canopy of live oak and red bay. An unusually slender Spanish bayonet grows along a curve just beyond a shaded bench. An American beautyberry shows off its delicate springtime blooms. At 1 mile an arrow confirms your route. The trail becomes a causeway through a forest of pines; scattered cabbage palms lift their fronds through the limbs of taller oaks. American holly fills the hollows. Look for the cedar waxwing, attracted to the maritime hammock by the berries of the southern red cedars. A scarlet tanager perches in a high branch of a live oak.

Paralleling a low spot on the right filled with a pine forest, the trail swings to right and crosses the low spot on a causeway, rising up past a directional arrow at 1.5 miles. The sound of the waves increases.

You walk through a stretch of open dunes with spectacular hills rising up on the right and pass another bench. Put those sunglasses on now—you'll need them to follow the footpath, which shimmers in the heavy glare of the sun off the bright soft sand. Virginia willow grows up to the edge of the trail. More dunes rise up to the right, large bowls rippled by the wind. Reindeer moss clusters in the low spots. Look for the scrape marks of gopher tortoises crossing the trail as you weave in and out of the open dunes and small pockets of pine forest. A white sulfur alights on a swaying maroon blossom of a tall Spanish larkspur. You head up and over the dunes, following only the suggestion of a trail, the footpath continually wiped clean by the prevailing ocean breezes. Tall sea oats cap the dunes.

At 2 miles you reach a bench overlooking the sea. A sign at the shoreline says HIKING TRAIL RETURN, with an arrow pointing to the right. Turn right and walk down the beach. The dunes show erosion up to 10 feet high, the near vegetation dead in the aftermath of a heavy storm. Enjoy the silence and the shelling—this is a remote location, more than a mile from the nearest beach access. If you take your shoes off to walk the sand, be cautious of the many moon jellyfish strewn across the shore. A ghost crab emerges from its hole, intent on dragging a dried-out jellyfish inside for its dinner. A row of pelicans streams by overhead as you walk by Marker H. Look straight ahead and slightly left into the waves, and you can see the buildings of Mayport. As Mayport is home to the Mayport Naval Station, you may see a destroyer emerging from the mouth of the St. Johns River. Look up on the dunes and notice the vines spreading across them, topped with numerous glowing white blooms—beach morning glories. You pass Marker G at 2.7 miles. Here the dunes are more stable, held in place by thick patches of sea oats. The red-tipped gray sticks and sign near the dune line mark a sea turtle nest. Every summer, endangered loggerhead turtles return to this beach, depositing 50 or more eggs in a nest scooped out in the sand above the high-tide line. With a few weeks, the hatchlings emerge and make a mad dash for the safety of the sea.

After you pass Marker F at 3.2 miles, keep alert for the boardwalk. Climb up and over the dunes on the boardwalk into the main beach parking area, where you pass the rest rooms and picnic area. Walk down through the parking lot and turn right on the park road, keeping to the mowed edge. After you pass the ranger headquarters, you arrive back at your car, completing your 3.8-mile hike. Stop in at the ranger station to sign out and to ask for the combination to the campground gate so you can visit the Little Talbot Nature Trail.

LITTLE TALBOT NATURE TRAIL

In your car, leave the Little Talbot ranger station and cross FL A1A to the campground entrance. Using the combination the ranger gave you, unlock the gate and drive in. Lock it behind you before you head down the campground road. Make the first left and follow the twisting one-lane road until it ends at the canoe launch. Park here and walk back up the campground road, past site 37. The 0.8-mile Little Talbot Nature Trail starts directly across from site 39, at a trailhead sign with a box full of maps. Follow the white blazes down a well-defined footpath, which winds through cedar, yaupon, and large slash pine. You emerge out onto the edge of the marsh, with fiddler crabs scuttling out of your way. An osprey wings by, a mullet firmly gripped in its talons. At the trail junction continue straight toward the next white blaze. A short spur trail leads over to the edge of the marsh, where you can watch hundreds of fiddler crabs scrambling into the dark juncus at the sight of your shadow. These salt-loving rushes are a member of the lily family and bloom with tiny flowers like miniature lilies.

Turning away from the marsh, the trail rises into a stand of cedars before it swings back out to afford another broad view of marsh. Curving left, it follows the edge of a patch of sea oxeye. In front of you is a forest of extremely gnarled live oaks, thickly draped in Spanish moss and resurrection fern. During high tide the marsh may invade the footpath. The trail curves away from the marsh into a dense forest of yaupon, red bay, and cedar, continuing into a stand of slash pines. A faint trail leads left up a tall dune; continue straight. At 0.6 mile you emerge into a short stretch of blinding white sand. An arrow confirms your route as you drop down into a thicket of young cabbage palm under live oak and wax myrtle. The trail continues to lose elevation as you once again see the sweep of the marsh. Merging back to your starting point, the trail completes the loop. Turn right to exit, and then go left onto the campground road to return to the canoe-launch parking area, finishing your 0.8-mile hike.

FORT GEORGE RIVER WALK

Your last opportunity to hike on the Talbot Islands comes just before the bridge over the Fort George River, 2.7 miles past the Little Talbot Island State Park entrance. It's another hike to save for low tide. Pull off into the parking area on the right. Your 1.2-mile walk starts at the BICYCLES AND PEDESTRIANS ONLY sign. Follow the well-worn path across the dunes and around a small cove of turquoise water, popular with anglers. A ring-billed gull wheels overhead, calling out with a mournful cry. Windswept and gnarled, a stand of cedars dangles waxy white berries over the channel.

Follow the faint track along the water's edge, winding through the vegetation. Erosion leaves the pink fleshy roots of sea purslane exposed to the sun. Pelicans perch on sandbars in the channel, watching the mullet jump. As you step over a mucky, marshy spot where the tide filters in, fiddler crabs dive into their holes under the black needlerush. Mounds of greenbrier top the rolling dunes. If you are unsure of the footpath, keep close to the water. A lone cluster of sea oats holds one dune in place.

The trail becomes a faint two-wheel track dipping in and out of the rushes. As it swings back out to a small beach, you face a hillside of beach morning glories in full bloom. A sweet aroma like honeysuckle rises from the dunes. Disturbed from its feeding, a white heron wings away. After 0.6 mile the soft, wet beach ends at a sand bluff topped with greenbrier. Turn around and retrace your path along the river, completing a 1.2-mile hike when you reach the parking lot.

36

Fort George Island

Total distance (2 circuits): 4.2 miles

Hiking time: 2.5 hours

Habitats: Salt marsh, freshwater marsh, hardwood hammock, oak hammock, disturbed areas

Maps: USGS 7½' Mayport

Containing the site of numerous periods of human habitation and the highest hill on the southeastern Atlantic coast, Fort George Island delights visitors who have a keen interest in exploring Florida's history. Although much of the island is a Florida State Park under the care of the rangers at nearby Little Talbot Island (Hike 35), a small, historically significant corner is managed by the National Park Service as a far-flung part of the Timucuan Ecological and Historical Preserve (Hike 37). This hike introduces you to both parts of the island, with room for further exploration by car, on bicycle, or on foot.

From I-95 southbound take exit 362A, following FL 9A southbound 8 miles. Exit at FL 105 (Heckscher Drive) and head east. From I-95 northbound take exit 358A, FL 105 (Heckscher Drive). Follow it east, crossing under FL 9A. After you drive another 9.2 miles on FL 105, watch for FL A1A, which merges in from the Mayport Ferry. Drive 0.6 mile past the ferry to Fort George Road, on the left. Turn left and follow Fort George Road, a narrow, winding road flanked by salt marshes. After 0.5 mile you pass a tabby ruin dating back to the mid-1800s before coming to a fork in the road. Keep right. You are entering Fort George Island Cultural State Park, a rustic park with numerous inholdings. Markers along the road correspond to the Saturiwa Trail driving-tour booklet, which is available at the ranger station at Little Talbot Island. Continue 1.5 miles along the road and park on the right at the Ribault Clubhouse.

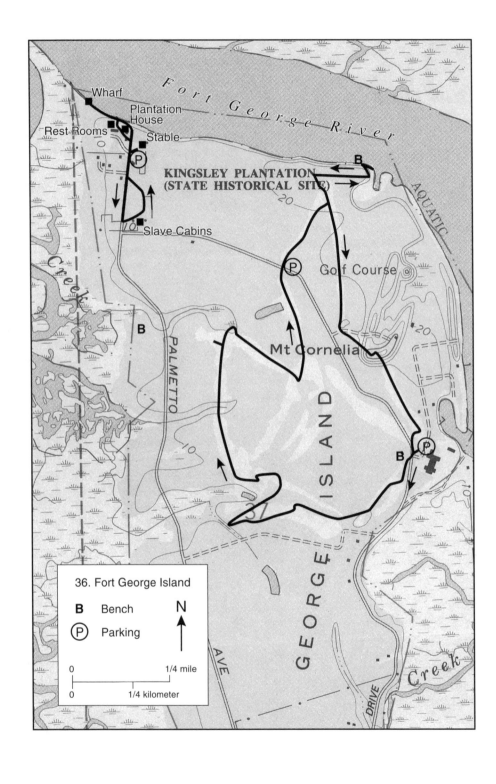

Wharf

Plantation House

Rest Rooms

Stable

P

KINGSLEY PLANTATION (STATE HISTORICAL SITE)

B

Slave Cabins

Fort George River

20

P

Golf Course

AQUATIC

20

B

PALMETTO

Mt Cornelia

GEORGE ISLAND

B

P

37

Creek

AVE

DRIVE

Creek

36. Fort George Island

B   Bench

N

P   Parking

0   1/4 mile

0   1/4 kilometer

Opened in 1928, the Ribault Club attracted the affluent country-club set with its yacht basin, lawn-bowling courses, and golf course. The clubhouse was built on top of the ruins of the posh Fort George Hotel (1875–89), which had been constructed on top of a prehistoric shell midden.

FORT GEORGE TRAIL

Directly across the entrance road is a bicycle symbol. Start your hike by crossing the park road and walking past the bench to the first set of interpretive markers. They explain about the Fort George Golf Course, which closed in 1991. The original 9-hole course expanded to 18 holes in the 1960s. This long stretch of disturbed vegetation ahead of you is the first of the course's fairways. A succession of plants has slowly started to reclaim the fairways. After heading down the fairway, flanked by spiderwort and Hercules'-club, the trail enters the shade of an oak hammock. Off to the left is a private residence; the ribbon of white beyond it is a view of the salt marshes. Surrounded by one of the healthiest stretches of salt marsh in Florida, Fort George Island sits at the confluence of the Fort George and St. Johns Rivers. Prior to the arrival of Europeans on Florida's shores, the island provided a sheltered home to the Timucua and their predecessors, who gathered oysters, planted corn, and built large villages here. Keep a close watch for scattered oyster shells along the trail, which indicate the location of one of the many massive middens on the island.

Emerging out into the bright sand, the trail follows the curve of another fairway, dancing in and out of the shade. Two great horned owls launch from the upper branches of a massive live oak, scanning the rough weeds in search of field mice. A river cooter squats in the trail, intent on completing her clutch of eggs. Although this island is ringed by salt water, it boasts one freshwater pond–Blue's Pond–with a healthy population of turtles and alligators. A five-lined race runner zips across the footpath. You'll commonly see these heat-loving skinks basking in open, sandy stretches of the trail. Along the open fairway, watch for the burrows of young gopher tortoises and the disturbed ground caused by armadillos rooting for grubs. As the trail transitions into an oak hammock, you catch your first glimpse of Blue's Pond at 1.2 miles.

The trail turns right to cross a causeway over the marshy end of the pond, filled with clusters of tall sand cordgrass. A wall of wax myrtle prevents a clear view of the open water to the right, but you can hear the warble of alligators just beyond the trees. The pond is named for retired Navy Admiral Victor Blue, who arrived on the island in the 1920s with the intent of forming a private Army-Navy Club. Admiral Blue planted the adjoining slash pine plantation, along with several other stretches of pines on this side of the island, in order to create forests where there once were vast plantation fields from an earlier era. Prior to the Civil War, the island was dominated by large plantations that grew cotton and sugar cane. When you complete this loop, you'll visit Kingsley Plantation, one of Florida's few remaining examples of plantation culture.

Passing through the pine plantation, the trail enters a mixed hardwood hammock with a tall canopy overhead, where hickory and sweetgum dominate. Grapevine and greenbrier spill across the forest floor. The live oak hammock into which you continue is one of many; these massive trees were planted in the 1800s to divide the plantation fields. Resurrection fern cascades down the limbs of an oak arching over the trail. After you round a curve to the right

Fort George Trail

past a stand of winged sumac, the trail meets a T intersection at the PERCHES ON THE FAIRWAY sign, at 1.7 miles. Curious as to how the fairways become revegetated, students from the University of North Florida study plant succession by combing through bird droppings for seed pods. Turn left at the sign. When you reach the next trail junction along the fairway, turn left. You walk past a tumble-down cottage, the remains of one of the old golf course buildings, and cross another fairway with bird perches before sticking to the shade of the live oaks along the edge of the open ground.

After 2 miles the trail emerges under a gnarled old southern magnolia at the park entrance. Cross the road and turn left, walking down to the small parking lot to its trailhead. Meandering along the edge of another fairway, you reach a fork. Hikers can turn left and strike out across the open fairway to the distant tree line. When you reach the T intersection, turn left to enter the hardwood hammock, following the direction indicated by the arrow. This is a spur trail out to Point Isabella, which is thought to have served as a wharf during the plantation era. At the next T intersection, turn right. Keep alert for a side trail to the left. Follow it over to the very edge of the sand bluffs along the Fort George River for a sweeping view of the river and the salt marshes stretching beyond to Little Talbot Island. A fence discourages visitors from climbing down the very steep, soft sand slope. When you return to the main trail, turn left. Where the trail divides in three, take any path—they rejoin at the top of a large staircase. Carefully walk down the staircase to the edge of a channel, the former anchorage for yachts visiting the Ribault Club. Rusted chains drape over the concrete retaining wall, where a yellow-crowned night heron strides purposefully along, watching for fish in the channel.

Since the spur trail ends here, you'll have to head back up the stairs and retrace your path back out to the last fairway, reaching the trail junction at 2.6 miles. Continue straight past the trail you came in on and past the bicycle trail merging in from the right. As you walk up the fairway, notice the enormous white blooms on the southern magnolias on the forest's edge. Deer browse the short grasses close to where the live oak hammock begins. As you walk under the live oaks, look up and study the branches closely for a glimpse of a greenfly orchid, which show off their delicate yellowish-green blooms in summer. Look even more closely at the forest floor, and you might be rewarded with the sight of a cluster of coral-root orchids rising from the thick carpet of oak leaves. Virtually camouflaged by their color combination against the leaves, these tall, slender orchids are summer bloomers as well, displaying brownish-yellow blossoms with striped pink lips.

As you emerge onto the next fairway, notice the large number of gopher tortoise burrows. You pass a trail coming in from the left as you rise to the top of Mount Cornelia. At 65 feet above sea level, this is thought to be the highest hill on the entire southeastern Atlantic coast. Dug into the hill on the right is a virtual gopher tortoise condominium: More than a dozen holes of varying sizes head into a slope that the tortoises apparently found extremely easy to dig into. The trail makes a steep, precipitous drop down the far side of Mount Cornelia through the shade of a dark hardwood hammock and over a layer of old concrete pavement. Meandering across the fairway through blooms of purple spiderwort, the trail passes a crabapple tree and a cherry tree before it ends at the Ribault Clubhouse parking area, completing a 3.4-mile loop.

Kingsley Plantation

KINGSLEY PLANTATION

To enjoy a short stroll around the historic Kingsley Plantation, continue your drive along the park road, passing an area of private homes before the road turns to dirt. When it comes to a T intersection, turn right into the entrance road to Kingsley Plantation, driving between the ruins of slave cabins. Managed by the National Park Service, the site is open 9 AM to 5 PM daily. After you park in the small parking area, walk in the front gate past the kiosk, taking in the view of the plantation house and the Fort George River. The plantation was established in 1791 by John McQueen, who sought his fortune under a policy of the Spanish government of Florida that invited Americans to homestead on land grants throughout east Florida. By 1799 McQueen instructed his more than three hundred slaves to cut timber and plant Sea Island cotton. But bad debts forced McQueen to sell out to Georgia planter John McIntosh in 1804, who became wealthy off the production of this Fort George plantation. Zephaniah Kingsley, a slave trader, took ownership of this plantation in 1812 after McIntosh participated in a localized rebellion meant to wrest control of Spanish Florida into American hands.

The barn on the right is made from brick and tabby, a concoction of oyster shells (dug up from the ancient middens) and mortar, the lime-heavy mixture a precursor to modern-day cement. In front of you lies the plantation house, with an interpretive center and bookstore. Turn left to follow a footpath down past the rest rooms to a new observation deck and pier on the river. On sunny afternoons you'll see kayakers plying their way up the channel. As you continue along the waterfront, make a stop at the plantation house. Zephaniah Kingsley lived here with his wife, Anna Madgigine Jai, a slave he had bought in Senegal and later freed, and their children. Anna oversaw the plantation, with its population of nearly 70 slaves. Perhaps because of Anna, Kingsley believed in the task system of organizing his slave labor. Unlike the usual "gangs" of slaves in the South who worked all day on a specific part of the plantation, the task system allowed slaves to complete a set number of daily tasks, leaving them personal time to hunt, fish, and farm for their own families.

Returning to the parking lot, you've walked 0.5 mile. Continue down the bark-chip trail that parallels the entrance road down to the slave cabins. Keep to the right at the fork, and you'll soon end up at the reconstructed slave cabin. Although small, each cabin housed a family of slaves. Turn left and walk up the row, noticing the fireplaces in each tiny living room. In 1821, when Florida became a U.S. Territory, Zephaniah Kingsley served on the Legislative Council. He strove to establish liberal policies to free slaves and ensure the rights and privileges of free blacks in Florida. Unfortunately, his colleagues turned a deaf ear. Disgusted by this "spirit of intolerant prejudice," Kingsley moved Anna and his sons to Haiti in 1837, establishing a new plantation with some of his slaves from Fort George Island. This plantation eventually passed into the hands of his relatives. Walk back along the row of cabins to the parking lot, completing your 0.8-mile tour of the plantation.

As you leave Kingsley Plantation, head straight down the park road to complete the driving loop. Notice the tall cabbage palms lining both sides of the road along a stretch once called "The Avenue of Palms." Although they are nearly obscured by towering live oaks, the palms are more than two hundred years old. Hidden in the nearby forest is the Spanish mission site of San Juan del Puerto, built in 1587. It stood for nearly a century and provided the Jesuit priests a home while they ministered to the Timucuan villages on the island.

Although no camping is permitted within either Kingsley Plantation or Fort George Island Cultural State Park, nearby Huguenot Memorial Park offers developed riverside camping at bargain-basement prices—less than $8 per space. A city of Jacksonville park with beach access, Huguenot Memorial Park is located on the south end of Fort George Island, 0.9 mile north of Fort George Road on A1A, at the blinker. The park commemorates the landing of Florida's first French Huguenot settlers in 1562, who escaped religious persecution in France.

37

Timucuan Ecological and Historical Preserve

Total distance (2 circuits): 5.5 miles

Hiking time: 3 hours, 15 minutes

Habitats: Hardwood hammock, maritime hammock, salt marsh, freshwater marsh, coastal scrub, pine flatwoods

Maps: USGS 7½' Mayport, park map

A patchwork of public lands on both sides of the St. Johns River, the Timucuan Ecological and Historical Preserve encompasses several sites of cultural and ecological interest. The Kingsley Plantation at Fort George Island (Hike 36) displays one of the state's rare historical treasures, a cotton and sugar cane plantation dating back to 1799. Across the St. Johns River, several pieces of the preserve harbor other rare treasures: the landing site of the French who claimed Florida for France in 1562; the site of Fort Caroline, the first French settlement in the New World; and the massive shell middens of a Timucuan village along the St. Johns River.

From I-95 southbound take exit 362A, following FL 9A southbound 11 miles. From I-95 northbound take exit 358A, FL 105 (Heckscher Drive), to access FL 9A, driving southbound into Jacksonville. After you cross the St. Johns River, take the first exit—FL 113, Southside Connector. From downtown Jacksonville take the Southside Connector 11 miles to this same junction. At the first traffic light, turn left on Merrill Road. This road quickly merges onto Fort Caroline Road. After 4.3 miles through the suburbs, Fort Caroline Road makes a left. Continue straight on Mt. Pleasant Road for another 1.2 miles to the THEODORE ROOSEVELT AREA sign on the left. Turn left through the second gate. This is an automatic gate, and its hours are posted—usually matching sunrise and sunset for that day. A one-lane dirt road leads 0.1 mile down to the parking area, where you'll find rest rooms, picnic

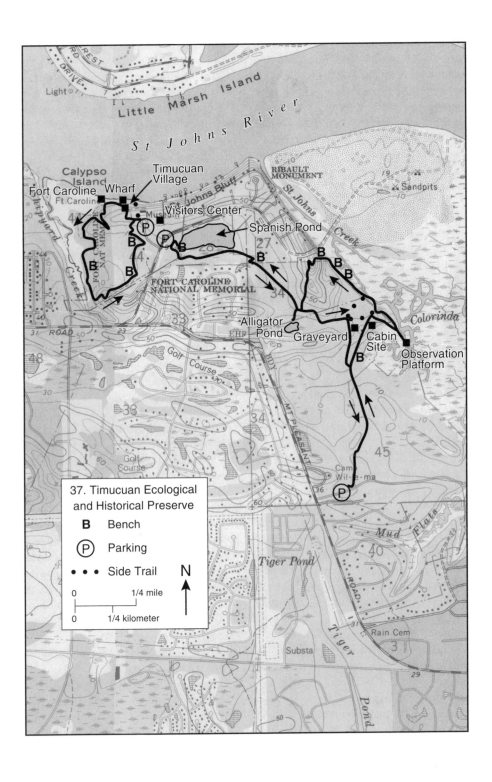

Light

Little Marsh Island

St Johns River

Calypso Island
Timucuan Village
Fort Caroline
Wharf
Ft Caroline
Mus.
Visitors Center
Spanish Pond
RIBAULT MONUMENT
Sandpits
St Johns Creek

B
B
B
B
B
B
B
B
Colorinda
Alligator Pond
Graveyard
Cabin Site
Observation Platform
B

FORT CAROLINE NATIONAL MEMORIAL

Golf Course

Golf Course

Cam Wil-e-ma

37. Timucuan Ecological and Historical Preserve

B Bench

P Parking

••• Side Trail

N

| 0 | | 1/4 mile |
| 0 | 1/4 kilometer | |

Mud Flats

Tiger Pond

Substa

Rain Cem

Tiger Pond

tables, and a trail kiosk with maps. The trail system within the Theodore Roosevelt Area stretches most of the way to Fort Caroline, so it's possible to link this hike with the Fort Caroline hike rather than driving between the two. Before you start hiking the 4.2-mile loop (not including the Fort Caroline loop), make sure you have adequate time to complete the hike and exit the park before the gate closes.

THEODORE ROOSEVELT AREA

In Willie Browne's eyes, Theodore Roosevelt was a hero. When Willie Browne was just 19 years old, he heard Roosevelt speak of his concerns about our vanishing wilderness, stating, "it is time for the country to take account of its natural resources and inquire how long they are likely to last." Willie Browne grew up in this forest, his family homestead. Materially poor but land rich, he lived without modern conveniences in a small cabin in these woods until his death in 1970. He willed the land to The Nature Conservancy to create a preserve in perpetuity.

In our eyes, Willie Browne is a hero. It's a rare man who turns down wealth in order to preserve his values and pass his heritage on to the next generation, but that's what Willie Browne did. "I could have sold the land. I could have bought fancy clothes. I could have traveled the world . . . but I like the woods." Honoring his gift, the Willie Browne Trail is the most popular of the trails in Timucuan Preserve. Shared with bicycles, it provides a 1.5-mile loop, a well-groomed walkway with mileage markers at every 0.25 mile, and many benches. Starting along this wide trail, you walk through a hardwood hammock shaded by pignut hickory, live oak, and tall bluejack oak. Towering slash pines carpet the trail with their needles, and red bay clings to the slopes of Hammock Creek. At 0.5 mile you encounter a kiosk labeled WILLIE BROWNE LOOP. This marks the start of the loop portion of your hike—and for most of the trek, you'll be leaving the comfort of the Willie Browne Trail for a wilder walk on the rest of the trail system. Turn right. Off through the trees, a bright line delineates the sweep of the salt marsh. Tree frogs fill the forest with their songs: *gul-gat, gul-gat, gul-gat; kwik-kwik-kwik; gwak-gwak-gwak.*

As you pass a bench, a spur trail leads off to the right, down to the salt marsh. You see black needlerush peeking out under the oaks. Up ahead, there's a fork in the trail. Keep to the right, following the broader path. Live oaks and red bays make up the tall canopy of this maritime hammock, where young cabbage palms struggle up from the forest floor. Another spur trail leads to an old building. Continue up to the trail junction, where a flurry of interpretive markers surrounds the remains of Willie Browne's cabin. Take the time to read them; you'll be touched by the generosity of this man who cared enough about his land to live a simple life, leaving the forest untouched for all to enjoy.

This is where you leave the easy trail for a bit of adventure. Continue straight toward the TIMUCUAN TRAIL sign, and then veer right, following the Round Marsh Trail. This spur trail heads downhill into the marsh under red mulberry trees. Fiddler crabs scuttle out of your way as you walk into the marsh, through a low spot bordered by sea oxeye. You're atop an ancient Timucuan midden, evident from the large number of shells spilling out from beneath tree roots. Salt air fills your lungs.

When you reach the junction of the Round Marsh and the Timucuan Trails, take a moment to step out to the salt marsh. Walk up to the edge of the tidal creek flowing

Round Marsh

swiftly past, edged with sea oxeye and glasswort, and you can clearly see how it is a midden: The roots of trees spill out across the oyster shells. Across the creek, large cranes unload container ships at Jacksonville's port. Continue straight as the slim finger of midden becomes slimmer. On the far edge of the salt marsh, seven ibises sit in a snag. Gnarled cedar and yaupon cling to the shell bed, some with thick stringers of old man's beard that look like green Spanish moss. Stunted prickly pear cacti struggle to survive amid the oyster shells. At 0.9 mile the trail ends at an observation platform, with its panoramic view of Round Marsh and the St. Johns River.

Return back down the midden to the last bench and turn right to follow the Timucuan Trail. This narrow, rugged trail twists and winds over massive shell mounds. As you dip through spots dug out to remove shells

for building and road material, and you see the bright white oyster shells spilling out from beneath the lush hammock, just think—this is a centuries-old landfill. Will our landfills of today host such vibrant forests in the future? As the trail swings out to a narrow ridge, it provides a sweeping view of the St. Johns estuary. It climbs and climbs until it reaches a junction with a trail coming in from the left. A few paces off to the left, you see the yellow-and-white marble gravestone that marks the final resting place of Sgt. John Nathan Spearing, a solider from the Confederate States Army. Continue along the edge of the salt marsh, following the Timucuan Trail as it becomes increasingly more difficult, with steeper grades and rough roots underfoot. Poison ivy and Virginia creeper intermingle as a ground cover but generally stay off the footpath. You pass several benches—which appear at opportune moments to let you take a breather after each strenuous climb—and another incoming branch of the Timucuan Trail from the left. Where the trail seems to fork at a faint junction, keep to the left. At 1.5 miles you reach a T intersection at a TIMUCUAN TRAIL sign. Turn right. Climbing another steep section, you're relieved to come to another bench. Stop and enjoy the salt breeze before you complete the climb. You descend through a coastal scrub on the far side of the hill. Florida rosemary and myrtle oak crowd close. A canopy of sand live oak and rusty lyonia shades the trail. At the next unmarked T intersection, make a left, heading downhill as the trail winds through the scrub. Soon after the habitat abruptly changes to hardwood hammock, you reach the T intersection with the Spanish Pond Trail, at 1.7 miles. Turn right.

This part of the hike is an out-and-back walk to Spanish Pond, which lies close to Fort Caroline. In 1565 a contingent of five hundred Spanish soldiers marched north from St. Augustine to attack the new French settlement. They rested along the shores of the pond during a downpour. The next morning, they attacked and captured the French fortress. As you pass the 0.5 MILE marker for this trail, oak scrub yields to hardwood hammock. At 2.1 miles you reach a bench at a break in a fence—joining together two separate sections of Timucuan Preserve. The trail becomes broader, meandering under sparkleberry and past Hercules'-club. As saw palmettos press close to create a corridor, you pass a blocked-off road to the right and start across a boardwalk over a marshy part of Spanish Pond. Watch for the tall blooms of rabbit tobacco, as well as the blackberry bushes that yield succulent blackberries in June.

The trail continues through pine flatwoods, with dense masses of greenbrier and grapevine growing up over the saw palmetto understory. You cross a second boardwalk edged by young slash pines. As you pass a bench, the trail becomes hard-packed limestone. At 2.5 miles you reach a platform—which looks out over the view of Spanish Pond—with a bench. The boardwalks to the right and straight ahead lead to a parking area directly across from the entrance to Fort Caroline National Memorial. Unless you've parked a second car here or want to extend your hike by visiting Fort Caroline and its nature trail on foot, turn around and head back along the Spanish Pond Trail.

After you walk across the second boardwalk, keep alert for a fork in the trail, where you need to keep to the right. Moments later, you cross through the park boundary fence. When you reach the junction with the Timucuan Trail at 3.2 miles, keep going straight. At the T intersection, where there is an ALLIGATOR POND sign, turn right to explore a short spur trail down to the edge of this freshwater pond. Although the trail ends in a clearing with a bench, unofficial paths wind around both sides of the pond. If you follow them, be cautious—an alligator nest lies just a few feet from shore! Mother alligators furiously guard their nests and their hatchlings, rebuffing intruders who might cause harm to their young.

When you return to the junction with the Spanish Pond Trail, continue straight. You come up to a kiosk regarding the Spanish Pond Trail. The trail turns left, and the footpath broadens as you walk through hardwood hammock. Highbush blueberries line both sides of the trail as you walk beneath flowering dogwoods. You reach a junction of several named trails. The horseshoe curve in front of you is the Willie Browne Trail; the immediate left, the Timucuan Trail. Turn right, past the bench, to return to the Willie Browne Trail. Just a little way up the hill is the Browne family cemetery, where Willie is buried next to his parents and brother, the folks who cared for this land for so long. At 3.7 miles you reach the end of the Willie Browne Loop. Continue straight across Hammock Creek and walk down the broad corridor and back to the parking lot. On your way out, take a moment to look at the pictures and quotes from Willie Browne on the kiosk. You've completed a 4.2-mile hike.

RIBAULT MONUMENT

Leave the Theodore Roosevelt Area, turn right, and drive 1.2 miles up to the intersection with Fort Caroline Road. Turn right. Follow this road 0.3 mile to the Fort Caroline and Spanish Pond entrances and continue another 0.5 mile to the sign for the Ribault Monument, on the left. The area is open 9 AM to 5 PM. Although there's no hike here, the historic site is worth a look. On May 1, 1562, three years before the founding of the Spanish colony at St. Augustine, French Huguenots landed at this bluff and claimed Florida for France. Jean Ribault named the river The River of May to commemorate the date of his landing. The column that stands tall on the edge of the St. Johns River is based on the one placed here by the French, copied from one of the many drawings of Jacques Le Moyne, the colony's resident artist. According to his illustrations, the Timucua who lived along to the river came to the tall pillar and left offerings of worship.

In 1564 French Huguenots built Fort Caroline for their protection as they established Florida's first European colony, with more than two hundred soldiers, artisans, and their families settling on St. Johns Bluff. Turn around and drive back down to the Fort Caroline entrance to explore this oft-forgotten chapter of Florida history.

FORT CAROLINE

Managed by the National Park Service, this historic site is open daily 9 AM to 5 PM. Stop in the visitors center to gain an understanding of Timucuan history and the French colony before wandering into the forest along the Hammock Nature Trail, which starts off to the right of the building next to a kiosk with a map. When you come to the first fork, stay right, following the FORT sign. Tall live oaks, draped in Spanish moss, shade the trail. The trail swings around, presenting a view of the St. Johns River. At the trail junction, the fork to the right leads back to the visitors center. Continue left, passing an interpretive exhibit of a Timucuan village with a hut, a garden, and a midden. As one of the members of the settlement, French artist Jacques Le Moyne recorded a wealth of information about the now-vanished Timucuan culture through his detailed sketches. The Timucua lived in dome-shaped, palm-thatched huts such as these; grew crops such as maize, pumpkins, beans, and arrowroot; gathered wild nuts and berries; and hunted the many fish and mammals along the river, including the manatee. During the summer months, you can see manatees out in the river from the pier off to the right.

As you come up a rise, you reach a trail junction. Ahead of you is the replica of Fort Caroline, its original location lost to the shifting river sands over the centuries. Pass the start of the nature trail and continue on to the replica fort, based on the paintings of Le Moyne. It's a small earthen fort, edged on its sides by wooden walls. You can clamber up the battlements and peer over the sides. A water-filled moat protects two sides; the river curves around the remainder of the fort. In 1565 the founder of St. Augustine, Pedro Menendez de Aviles, marched here with five hundred of his troops to roust the French from Florida, after Jean Ribault attempted to attack the Spanish colony at St. Augustine. Taking the fort by surprise, they murdered 140 settlers, sparing most of the women and children. Nearly 50 settlers, including Le Moyne, escaped by boat and returned to France.

As you leave the fort, turn right to walk down the nature trail. Thoughtful and informative interpretive markers explain the context of the forest as the meeting place of the Timucuan and French cultures. You see a lot of witch hazel, which is not commonly found in Florida but is present in the maritime hammocks of the northeastern coast. The Timucua used a compress of the bark and roots of witch hazel to treat insect bites—undoubtedly a remedy appreciated by the French. They also used the oil from wax myrtle leaves as an insect repellent. Passing a bench on the right, the trail swings left and uphill under a canopy of oaks, passing Marker 5. Peeking through the trees on the right, you can see patches of salt marsh scattered through the forest. Topping a small hill, the trail drops down past another bench and crosses a salt marsh on a bridge at 0.5 mile. As you head back uphill, twisted rusty lyonia rise up to 20 feet tall.

At the gate, a NATURE TRAIL sign points left and uphill, past a bench on the right. A walking stick pauses on a witch hazel leaf. The habitat transitions into a pine forest, with a saw palmetto thicket underneath tall slash pines. As you wind around a corner, you come to a NATURE TRAIL sign with an arrow pointing left. You reach a bench at 1 mile. Turn left. The trail drops down into a low spot, swinging right past a bed of netted chain and a bench surrounded by lush cinnamon fern. You reach a T intersection with a jeep intersection, with NATURE TRAIL and VISITORS CENTER signs pointing left. Turn left. When you come to the next set of signs, turn right to head back toward the parking lot. At 1.2 miles you reach a T intersection with the main trail. Turn right and walk past the kiosk to the front of the visitors center, completing your hike at the parking lot after 1.3 miles.

38

Kathryn Abbey Hanna Park

Total distance (circuit): 2.7 miles

Hiking time: 1.5 hours

Habitats: Maritime hammock, hardwood hammock, freshwater marsh

Maps: USGS 7½' Jacksonville Beach, park map

There's no doubt that Jacksonville is Florida's biggest city in terms of land mass—it encompasses all of Duval County. And of *all* of the Jacksonville City Parks, the Kathryn Abbey Hanna Park at Mayport provides the most outdoor-recreation choices for everyone: beautiful Atlantic Coast beaches, developed and primitive camping, saltwater and freshwater fishing, and separate trails for mountain bikers and hikers.

From downtown Jacksonville take Atlantic Boulevard (FL 10) 12 miles east to FL A1A north. Drive 3.5 miles north on Mayport Road, continuing straight on FL 101 when FL A1A turns left. At Wonderwood Drive, turn right to enter the park. Coming from the Mayport Ferry (FL A1A south), drive 2.5 miles to Wonderwood Drive; turn left and follow it 1 mile into the park. When you stop at the entrance to pay your $1-per-person daily admission fee, ask for a map of the trail system. Follow the entrance road until it ends; a sign to the left points to PARKING AREAS 10–11 for beach access. Park here, by the sign that says TRAIL G.

Start your hike by following the orange blaze that leads into the woods on the *left*—the blaze on the right is your return route. You immediately plunge into the cool shade of a maritime hammock, which parallels one of the many old ditches that crisscross the park. Pignut hickory and red mulberry trees shade the footpath. To distinguish the hiking trail from the biking trail (since they often draw close together), the park has stenciled the letter *H* on many of the trees along the trail. It can be a little confusing to follow the

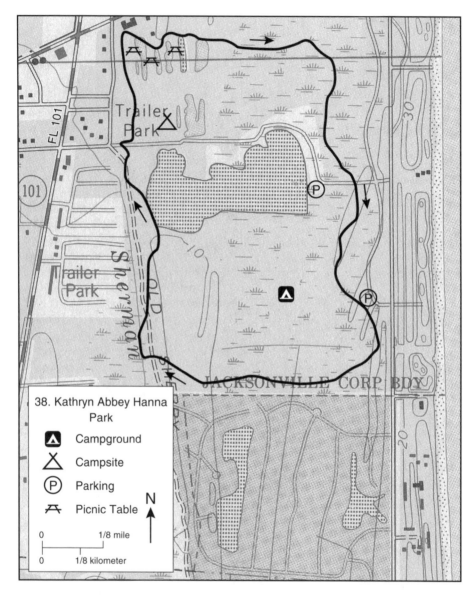

38. Kathryn Abbey Hanna Park

▲ Campground
△ Campsite
Ⓟ Parking
🛆 Picnic Table

N ↑

0   1/8 mile
0   1/8 kilometer

correct footpath because of the multiplicity of trails, so be sure to watch for that H at every decision point.

Keep right at the first fork, where the biking trail parallels on your left. At the next fork the trail heads downhill to the right. Crossing a bridge over a duckweed-choked ditch, the trail drops into a low area. Cabbage palms tower overhead, while netted chain and bracken fern thrive in the damp, cool soil. After you cross a couple of bridges, the trail pulls in parallel to the bicycle trail again. Spiny Hercules'-club towers over the trail. Also called wild lime, it's easy to identify by its thorny trunk and compound, fernlike clusters of leaves. In the spring watch for tiny clusters of greenish-white flowers, which attract bumblebees to this oddly shaped tree.

After you walk across a bridge made of cabbage palm logs, the trail rises up under a spreading red bay tree, thick with green tufts of resurrection fern. At the T intersection, turn left. You come to a junction with the bicycle trail. The hiking trail turns abruptly right. Watch for the H blaze as you walk down a corridor between saw palmettos. A little den in the base of a fallen cabbage palm provides shelter for an opossum family. At the next T intersection, turn left. Small, gnarled yaupon hollies crowd the trail. A common component of the maritime forest, the berries of the yaupon provided the Timucua with their beloved "black drink," a caffeine-rich purgative that warriors drank before going into battle. The yaupon's Latin name, *Ilex vomitoria*, attests to its effectiveness.

At 0.7 mile you emerge at a junction with several bicycle trails in front of the park's boundary fence. Turn right, following the fence line until you see a double-blazed tree and an H—turn right again, following the footpath into dense forest. At the T intersection you can see water shimmering just beyond the trees. A BUNKY'S EXPRESS sign points right—one of the bike trails. Turn left to walk along the lake. Pause on the bluff for a cool breeze and the view across the water, where you'll see great blue herons and snowy egrets plumbing the shallows for their meals. The developed campground is visible on the far shore.

Shaded by tall live oaks and red bays, the trail continues to wind around the lake. Watch for oyster shells in the trail—evidence of ancient Timucuan shell mounds scattered through these woods. Keep left at the fork. When the trail reaches an old road,

don't continue straight—turn right, walking toward the lake. An osprey soars overhead, a bass dangling from its talons. Watch on the left for the next H blaze leading into the woods. Be cautious of the thick mats of poison ivy on both sides of the footpath as you meander through the maritime hammock. A cardinal streaks past, its red feathers standing out against the deep, dark greens of the forest. When you reach the trail intersection at 1.3 miles, continue straight.

Winding through yaupon and southern red cedar, the trail turns left to parallel a swampy slough. Keep alert for alligators—despite the suburban sprawl on the edges of the park, wildlife thrives. At the T intersection, turn right. Vegetation crowds in closely. When you reach a junction of trails at a fence, turn right to follow the orange blazes. The next T intersection is at 1.5 miles. This is a great spot to take a break at the picnic table on the little island off to your right, just over the bridge. But the trail continues left from the T, emerging through a set of concrete posts into a developed area. Cross over the bridge and continue out into the Hanna Park Fish Management Area, along a set of stocked freshwater ponds ready for anglers to cast into. Continuing straight across the dirt road that leads to the primitive camping area, you reach two trailhead arches—one for the biking trail, one for the hiking trail. Although this is an official-looking trailhead with a map, no parking is provided. If you're staying in this campground, however, you'll want to start your hike from here.

Walk through the hiking-trail archway into the forest, meandering along a little drainage filled with woods ferns. Half hidden by a fallen leaf, a southern toad trills. The trail swings up to the right, shaded by tall live oaks. Watch your footing through this section as the trail goes in and out of

A glimpse of the lake from the hiking trail.

small drainages and up and over clusters of roots. The gigantic fronds of young cabbage palms fill in the understory. As the soil becomes wetter underfoot, the mix of trees changes to a low-lying hardwood hammock. Red maple and sweetgum add to the colors of the forest, and a post oak rises well above the footpath. Lush beds of netted chain fill damp hollows as you walk along a beautiful corridor of trees, a ridge above the wetness of the forest. After drawing parallel to the bike trail, you can see open sky beyond the forest and another lake, this one at the park's main picnic area across from Parking Area 8 (for the beach). At 2.4 miles you cross the entrance road to the picnic area, reentering the forest under another trailhead archway to walk along a duck-weed-covered slough.

Where the trail crosses the paved road into the developed camping area, a concession stand sits off to the right—the Happy Spot, a great stop for ice cream or a cold drink. Continue under the trailhead archway on the far side of the road. Spanish moss hangs like draperies from a spreading live oak, shading the trail as it curves left at an overlook on a bluff along a stream. Old southern magnolias tower overhead, carpeting the footpath with their gigantic crunchy leaves. A yaupon tree arches over the trail,

its slender trunk strangely twisted as though a snake were wrapped around it. You suddenly emerge from the shady forest out to your car, completing the 2.7-mile hike.

After your hike, take the time to visit the beach and cool off in the waves. Boardwalks lead from the parking areas through gnarled forests of sand live oak and over tall, windswept dunes topped with cabbage palms and sea oats. The strands of white sand attract sunbathers from all over the region. This is a busy weekend recreation destination for the Jacksonville metro area—book well ahead if you plan to use the campground on a weekend. The developed campground is extremely popular, while the primitive campground (tents only) appeals to beginners and families trying out their tents.

Kathryn Abbey Hanna Park is open 8 AM to 6 PM November through March and 8 AM to 8 PM April through October. Plan your day (or weekend) around multiple activities: enjoy a hike and the beach, have a picnic, fish in the ponds, bring a canoe to explore the lakes, or take a bike to explore the 11 miles of biking trails. Because of the popularity of the trail, the narrowness of the single-track trail, and the extremely limited visibility along the route, hiking the bike trail is *not* recommended.

39

Jennings State Forest

Total distance (2 circuits): 6.7 miles

Hiking time: 4 hours

Habitats: Sandhill, seepage slope, bayhead, floodplain forest, hardwood hammock, freshwater marsh

Maps: USGS 7½' Fiftone, St. Johns Water Management District map, park map

Not far from downtown Jacksonville, the secluded sandhills of Jennings State Forest provide a home for herds of deer, flocks of wild turkey, and the rambling Florida black bear. Four hiking trails wander through its undulating terrain; two of them are part of the Florida State Forests Trailwalker program. On the 1.8-mile Fire and Water Nature Trail, creative interpretive information teaches you about the roles of fire and water in maintaining the sandhill and bayhead environments. The 4.9-mile North Fork Black Creek Trail appeals to backpackers, who make camp at the primitive campsite in the forest along Black Creek. Two shorter trails form briefer loops along the North Fork Black Creek Trail.

To reach Jennings State Forest from Jacksonville, take I-295 exit 4. Follow FL 21 south through suburban Orange Park for 7.9 miles. Turn right on CR 220A at the JENNINGS STATE FOREST sign. Drive 4.1 miles to Live Oak Lane. Turn right at the sign. The pavement ends, and you pass the Old Jennings Recreation Area parking lot after 0.5 mile. Continue another 0.5 mile to the kiosk for the Fire and Water Nature Trail; park along the left edge of the road.

FIRE AND WATER NATURE TRAIL

Pick up an interpretive brochure at the kiosk before you start out on the Fire and Water Nature Trail, following the lime-green blazes down a broad forest road. Be alert for snakes as pygmy rattlers enjoy sunning along this section of the trail. Where you pass Marker 1, sandhills rise up on the left,

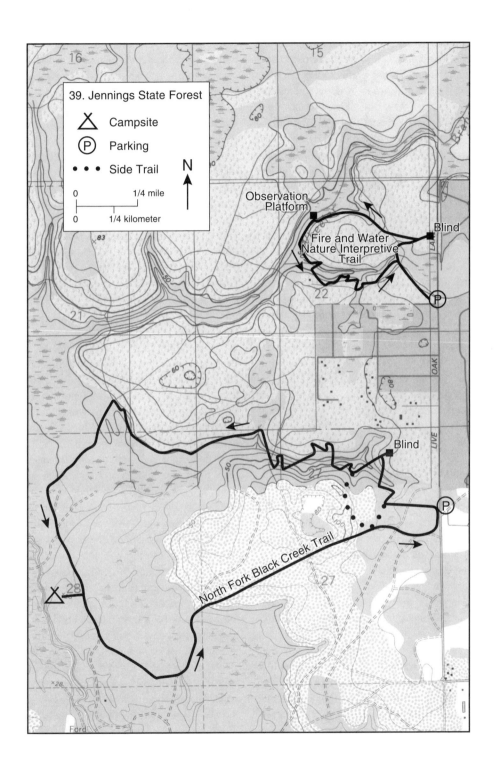

39. Jennings State Forest

△ Campsite

Ⓟ Parking

• • • Side Trail

N

0   1/4 mile

0   1/4 kilometer

Observation Platform

Blind

Fire and Water Nature Interpretive Trail

Blind

North Fork Black Creek Trail

and a bayhead (also called a baygall) drops down to the right, indicating the damp spot in the terrain. Bright white blooms decorate the loblolly bay trees in early summer. At the WILDLIFE VIEWING BLIND sign, turn right. This is the beginning of the interpretive loop. Walk down to the blind by taking the next right and following the powder blue blazes. After a couple of jogs through the sandhill, the blazes end at the blind—a quiet spot where you can sit on a bench and peer out through the openings to watch for quail and brown-headed nuthatch, summer tanager and Bachman sparrow.

Return back up the spur trail to the main trail and turn right. Keep alert as the blazes soon leave the forest road and traverse the sandhill, leading you on an extremely narrow track through the wiregrass, under the longleaf pines. Watch for colorful wildflowers: delicate whitish-blue blooms of bluestar, tall purple stalks of blazing star, and the daisylike blossoms of roserush, with its oddly squared-off petals. As it passes Marker 4 at 0.4 mile, the trail swings to the left to go around the bayhead. Look carefully before you turn, and you'll catch a glimpse of hooded pitcher plants to the right of the marker, thriving in the dampness of the seepage slope. The trail rejoins a forest road again, which winds along the edge of a ravine above a tannic blackwater stream. A shady hardwood hammock spills down the slope, creating a slope forest. Pause at the observation deck at Station 5 for a glimpse of the winding stream. To see it, walk to the edge of the deck and look straight down.

After the forest road rises up a long slope, it reaches a sign that points you to the right, down a narrow steep track into the slope forest. Crossing the blackwater stream, you climb up the slope to a T intersection with a forest road, the site of Marker

7 at 1.2 miles. Turn left. You're back in the sandhill. In a short while, blazes lead the trail parallel to a seepage stream off to the left, where a profusion of carnivorous plants grow: delicate butterworts and bright red sundews. If the trail along the stream is too overgrown, stick to the forest road. Make a left at the T intersection. When you see the WILDLIFE VIEWING BLIND sign at 1.6 miles, you've completed the loop. Continue straight to return to the trailhead. After you complete the 1.8-mile hike, drive back down Live Oak Lane to the spacious parking area at the OLD JENNINGS RECREATION AREA sign. This is the start of the North Fork Black Creek Trail, as well as two shorter loops that introduce you to segments of the sandhill environment.

NORTH FORK BLACK CREEK TRAIL

Starting from the trailhead at the Old Jennings Recreation Area, this 4.9-mile trail provides an up-close look at sandhill habitat, with the opportunity to backpack out to a primitive campsite along the North Fork of Black Creek. After you pass through the gate, turn right and walk to the Trailwalker sign. Start your hike by turning right to follow the firebreak along the fence line. This section—as well as many other points in the trail—is shared with the Evans Horse Trail, making for rough footing through the soft sand. As you turn the corner to follow the fence, a well-defined footpath parallels the firebreak on the left. Stick to that, and watch for the orange double blaze that indicates a left-hand turn off the firebreak and into the sandhills. At the next trail junction, continue straight. You'll pass a turnoff for the Bird Blind Loop, which leads to a wildlife viewing blind that is just visible down in a clump of oaks. If you have time, stop and hide behind the blind, where you might see a wild turkey or a deer wander by.

Beard tongue

When a horse trail rejoins the hiking trail, the going gets rough as you hike along the edge of a sandhill area that experienced a recent burn. At the next trail junction, a sign points to the right for the Longleaf Pine Loop—an orange-blazed shortcut route if you wish to return to the trailhead. The horse trail continues straight. Turn right to follow the North Fork Black Creek Trail downhill on a narrow track that plunges into a hardwood forest surrounding a sinuous, clear sand-bottomed stream. Immediately turn right after crossing the bridge and follow the trail along the mucky stream slope until it turns uphill. Imprinted in the dark mud is the paw print of a Florida black bear. Sighted frequently in this area, the endangered Florida black bear is the smallest subspecies of the black bear family, with grown males weighing no more than 350 pounds. At least 1,500 of these bears roam Florida's forests.

At the top of the hill, the trail rejoins a forest road. Turn left. Pay close attention to the shrubs on the left side of the road—in May, these blueberry bushes are loaded with succulent fruit, attracting birds and bears. Highbush blueberries grow scattered along the right side of the road. After 1 mile you reach a junction with another forest road, deeply rutted by four-wheel-drive vehicles. Cross over it and step over the cable gate to continue walking down the road you're on, which marks the ecotone between hardwood hammock and sandhill. A red admiral alights on a patch of deep orange butterfly weed. Narrow-leaf pawpaw scatters its fading petals across the wiregrass.

When you reach the T intersection at 1.5 miles, turn left and drop down across the stream drainage, rising back up into sandhills. Again, you're walking along the edge of the hardwood hammock that surrounds the stream. The horse trail joins in from the left and continues up until you reach a bench at a messy intersection of trails and torn-up forest roads. Signs with symbols for camping, hiking, and horseback riding point in various directions. Turn left and drop through another drainage, where rocks have been laid down to keep the road from getting muddy. A stand of cattails surrounds a small freshwater marsh, where a leopard frog croaks a cheery tune. The hardwood hammock closes in, creating welcome shady stretches.

At 2.4 miles the trail becomes a causeway through a floodplain forest of slim cypresses. When another road comes in from the right, continue straight. You soon meet up with a tributary of the North Fork of Black Creek. Dark, tannic water flows silently across the road, blocking your route. Look off into the forest on the right for your crossing, a series of boards that bridge the stream. After 2.8 miles blue blazes lead off to the right to the campsite. Wander down the 0.1-mile side trail to set up camp. It's an open area ringed with tall oaks and has an established fire ring and several sand-filled platforms for pitching tents. A faint trail leads farther into the woods and down to the creek itself, the campsite's water source. A ground skink plays peek-a-boo within the nooks and crannies of a rotting stump.

Walk back to the main trail and turn right, rising up away from the lowlands and back into the sandhills. Scattered loblolly pines drop their cones on the trail. At the fork, be careful: A double blaze seems to indicate a right turn, but you should keep to the left. At 3.5 miles you reach a T with another forest road. Turn left. When you emerge at the top of the hill at a firebreak, turn right. These sandhills have been logged and burned, leaving only scattered trees across the soft, open sand. The footpath becomes extremely difficult, deeply churned up by horses. Wherever possible, stay to the right of the trail, zigzagging between the bushes to avoid the softer sand. The lack of blazing makes this section especially tricky since many roads snake off in all directions. Stay with the most obvious path, the one that's churned up. After 4 miles you come to a confusing intersection of forest roads. Continue straight. Cross the next road junction, and the horse trail joins in from the left. The footpath improves as it rises up to meet an unexpected junction of orange blazes: The incoming Longleaf Pine Loop comes in from the left. Continue straight. You'll soon see the picnic table at Old Jennings Recreation Area and your car just beyond in the parking area. After 4.9 miles you've completed the most difficult hike in Jennings State Forest.

40

Black Creek Ravines Conservation Area

Total distance (circuit): 7.8 miles

Hiking time: 4 hours

Habitats: Sandhill, clayhill, seepage slope, river bluffs and ravines, hardwood hammock, oak hammock, oak scrub, freshwater marsh

Maps: USGS 7½' Middleburg, St. Johns Water Management District map

Steep ravines, seepage slopes, and panoramic river views characterize the Black Creek Ravines Conservation Area, a popular destination in the Jacksonville area for hikers and horseback riders. Sitting just south of Middleburg, the preserve rests on a curve in Black Creek, a blackwater stream broader than many of Florida's rivers. Backpackers can enjoy a restful night at a secluded primitive campsite on a high river bluff; day hikers will delight in picking blackberries and tracking the many gopher tortoises that call these sandhills home. Although the 965-acre tract is bisected by high-tension power lines, the open area beneath the wires contains seepage slopes with an incredible diversity of rare and unusual wildflowers, from bearded grass-pink to the hooded pitcher plant.

To get to the Black Creek Ravines Conservation Area from Jacksonville, take I-295 exit 4. Follow FL 21 for 13.3 miles south to Middleburg. Turn left on CR 218 toward Penney Farms. Drive 2 miles to Green Road, watching for the BLACK CREEK RAVINES sign. Turn left. Follow Green Road for 0.9 mile, past the end of the pavement, to the parking area on the right.

Start your hike at the kiosk, where you can pick up a trail map. Note that the trail system contains three interconnecting loops blazed in white, yellow, and red. Although horses share the trail system—making for difficult footing in some of the soft sandy areas—no bicycles are allowed. Walk through the gap in the fence and follow the narrow

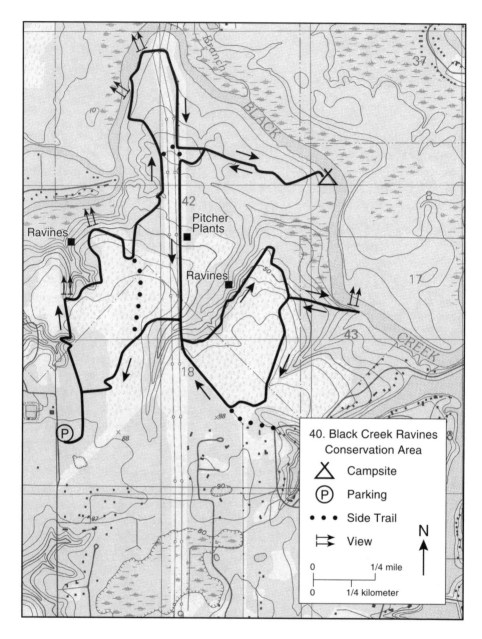

**40. Black Creek Ravines
Conservation Area**

✕ Campsite

Ⓟ Parking

• • • Side Trail

➤ View

N

0   1/4 mile

0   1/4 kilometer

trail through the sandhills as indicated by the arrow marker and white diamond blazes. A healthy growth of wiregrass covers the forest floor. Passing under gnarled sand live oaks, the trail makes a sweep to the left be- tween clumps of foamy deer moss. When you reach the first intersection with a jeep trail, white diamonds lead straight and to the left. Turn left. At the fork, the white trail keeps to the right as it enters the shady oak hammock. Once used as pastureland, the cleared sandhills are now a forest of laurel oaks.

As you walk along, notice the many gopher tortoise burrows. These burrows can run 40 feet long and up to 10 feet deep, with just enough space for the tortoise to squeeze in. Each adult tortoise creates as many as nine different burrows across its territory, places of refuge when danger approaches. The gopher tortoise is a benevolent landlord—when the owner isn't in residence, other creatures move into its cool, damp home. More than 360 different species of animals will move into a gopher's burrow, including snakes, mice, opossums, quail, armadillos, burrowing owls, toads, and lizards. For this reason the gopher tortoise is a cornerstone species of the sandhill, the tortoise population a good indicator of the health of the habitat. And by all indications, this is an extremely healthy sandhill habitat. Don't be surprised to see a half dozen gopher tortoises during the duration of your hike.

At the next fork, both the blazes and an arrow indicate a left turn onto an old woods road, the sand churned up by horses. A spiky devil's-walkingstick towers overhead. At Marker 2 you see a hitching post at 0.4 mile. Take the short spur trail down to where it ends at a fence above the edge of the ravine. Since the trails are generally routed away from the sensitive environments of the ravines, the overlooks are your best vantage points for looking down into them. It's a bowl filled with forest, the basin a moist environment fed by a seepage slope. At the second overlook the slope drops off steeply behind the fence. Wood and royal ferns carpet the base of the ravine, benefiting from the cool, damp microclimate.

Keep to the right at the next fork. Off to the left, through the trees, you can see an open area beyond a distant fence—the Ravines Golf Course. Follow the trail as it curves to the right, away from the golf course. Highbush blueberries tower up to 10 feet tall, loaded with delicious fruits in mid-June. Keep left at the fork, where coral beans show off their gaudy red blooms. Beargrass peeks out between the tufts of wiregrass under the pines. Disturbed from its meal of gopher apple, a gopher tortoise looks up. Its broad gray shell indicates it's an adult. Thought to live more than 40 years, these tenacious creatures grow slowly, reaching adulthood when their shell is 9 inches long or longer. The sandhills of Black Creek Ravines provide everything they need. From gopher apples to pawpaws, and from prickly pear fruits to blackberries, it's a smorgasbord for these quiet giants. Their endangered status in Florida comes primarily from loss of habitat to development and decades of trapping for food.

Heading downhill through a dense oak hammock, the trail takes the right fork at the next junction. A stand of deer's tongue lets off a faintly vanilla aroma. Also known as vanilla plant, its leaves were once picked and dried to add flavoring to tobacco. At the T intersection, turn left. You immediately see yellow blazes—the beginning of the yellow loop, at 1.3 miles. Turn left to follow the yellow blazes into the shade of an oak hammock. The trail drops down into a moister area, with titi, sweetgum, and loblolly bay. A thick carpet of needles cushions your footfalls. In wetter times, a temporary streambed carves its way down the trail, cutting deeply into the sand.

After 1.6 miles you emerge into the glaring sun under the power lines. The trail turns left to parallel the forest, quickly curving back into the shade. You pass a spot with an opening out to the power line, a

Black Creek

cross trail for the southern end of the yellow loop. Continue straight. As the trail loses elevation, the hardwood forest becomes more varied, with ironwood, mulberry, Allegheny chinquapin, and southern magnolia. Pignut hickories pepper the trail with their immense nuts. After the trail curves to the right and drops downhill rapidly, you catch your first glimpse of Black Creek off to the left, a ribbon of open space beyond the trees.

Watch for the small spur trail at 2.2 miles. Duck under the trees to scramble out to the edge of the bluff for a sweeping view of the broad expanse of water. Water hyacinths bob along the shoreline. Wave to the anglers tucked in close to shore, keeping their boats in the shade. A little farther down the trail, a live oak arches out over a small inlet. You can sit and dangle your feet over the water. As the trail turns away from the creek, it emerges under the power lines, turning right to follow the power lines uphill. Off to the left is a marsh choked with young Virginia willows. Royal fern and pickerelweed compete for space with the water hyacinth. On the drier slopes of deep red clay, pink meadow beauty raises its colorful blossoms to the sun. A wizened little loblolly pine struggles to mature in the thick, rootbinding clay that forms the tree into a natural bonsai. Sundial lupine shows off bright purple flowers each spring. Its fuzzy seed pods are poisonous, but Florida's ancient tribes made a tea from its leaves, used to control nausea and internal hemorrhaging.

At the trail junction, turn left at the camping symbol to follow the yellow-blazed spur trail back to the primitive campsite. You enter the shade of an oak hammock with laurel oaks and scattered southern magnolias. Rounding a curve to the left, you pass a trail to the right. At the fork another campsite symbol encourages you to take the right fork. At the T intersection, take a left: A campsite symbol points the way. Coming up to Marker 5, you can see Black Creek off to the left, down at the base of the bluff. The trail ends at a picnic table and fire ring tucked in the forest, high above the creek on the bluff. A steep side trail leads down to the water. After 3.5 miles you can pitch your tent in the clearing and enjoy the solitude of the river bluffs.

Retrace your steps along the spur trail and keep to the right as you pass the back side of the first campsite sign. Where the trail curves right, turn left on a narrow trail that leads away from a fencepost. It's a shortcut back to the main route but should not be used if the terrain has been especially wet thus far. Passing through a bayhead, it climbs up through a field of sundew, a tiny carnivorous plant with sticky red stems, and emerges under the power line, coming to a T with the jeep road. Turn left. In late May you can stuff yourself silly with the profusion of plump blackberries that grow along the sides of the trail. The sweetest berries come from bushes growing in damp spots. As you approach the section of trail where horses have churned up the soft sand, look to the left. There's an amazing abundance of hooded pitcher plants growing in the low spots, dense thickets of their spotted leaves shimmering in the breeze. Although the power line may seem a boring, difficult walk, enjoy the diversity of wildflowers. Admire the delicate bearded grass-pink, an orchid that enjoys the company of the hooded pitcher plant. Look closely for hairy wicky, tiny clusters of pink flowers with dark pink stripes inside. Watch for Bartram's ixia, an endangered lilac-colored iris that blooms from April through June. Naturalist William Bartram discovered and sketched this flower during his travels through north Florida in the 1770s. No matter the time of

Swamp azalea

year, there's always something blooming on these seepage slopes.

To keep out of the worst of the soft sand, stay to the left or right of the jeep road. At 4.7 miles you meet up with the red-blazed loop. Pass the trail to the right, cross the drainage, and keep climbing the slope. At the top of the hill, take a left on the red loop, walking down the transition zone between sandhill and hardwood hammock. Watch for swamp azaleas, which display their slender, fragrant white blooms in May and June. The forest on the left drops off into a ravine. When you reach the T intersection at 5.6 miles, turn left to follow the red-blazed spur trail down to the preserve's best scenic view. You pass several sassafras trees, a species more common to the Appalachians than Florida, but in north Florida the sassafras thrives. Related to the aromatic red bay tree, the crushed bark of sassafras trees smells like root beer, a product once made from its roots.

When you reach Marker 7, at 5.9 miles, you come to a small clearing. It's the site of Green Camp, once a hunting and fishing camp for the former owners of this land. Nothing remains but the clearing–and the incredible view of a broad curve in Black Creek. Pause on a log and enjoy the breeze, or follow the trail down either fork to where it ends at the water's edge. You can step down into the waters of the creek, tannic but reflective, to cool down on a hot day. Be mindful of alligators and snakes if you decide to take a swim. No camping is allowed at this spot, but it makes a wonderful midday break. Returning back up the hill, enjoy one last look at Black Creek before retracing the red blazes back to the last trail junction. Turn left. Since horses have churned up the footpath, stay to the left or right. Wildflowers add splashes of color to the sandhills. On white colic-root, blossoms like small white balls radiate from a central stem. A yellow bloom with daisylike petals tops off Florida's native dandelion, called greeneyes. Bright orange blooms characterize butterfly weed.

After 6.6 miles you come to a junction with a spur trail coming in from the right. It's the preserve's access for a residential area along Lake Asbury Drive, but no parking is available at that trailhead. Continue to follow the trail as it curves to the right. When you reach the power line, turn right to follow the red blazes, enjoying yet another carpet of wildflowers. Pass the beginning of the red loop and continue down the steep seepage slope. Hatpins flourish in the dampness, and a stand of hooded pitcher plants sits off to the right. After you cross the drainage, turn left. You walk past several small persimmon trees as you enter the slight shade of the sandhill, with turkey and bluejack oaks overhead. Scattered sand pines grow amid the forest. When you meet the white loop at Marker 6 after 7.2 miles, continue straight to follow the white-blazed trail down a narrow footpath. Watch your feet—gopher tortoises have dug burrows in this trail. A post oak shades the trail with thick draperies of Spanish moss over its limbs. You curve past a low-lying stand of loblolly pine as the trail weaves through a dense oak hammock. Emerging at a jeep trail, you've completed the loop. Continue straight to return to the parking lot, finishing your 7.8-mile hike.

Atlantic Coast

Salt marshes on the Tolomato River in Guana River State Park

41

John P. Hall Sr. Nature Preserve

Total distance (circuit): 7 miles

Hiking time: 3.5 hours

Habitats: Pine flatwoods, bayheads, floodplain forest, freshwater marsh

Maps: USGS 7½' Green Cove Springs, St. Johns Water Management District map

Although an extensive network of old forest roads crisscrosses the Bayard Point Conservation Area, providing access for hikers, bikers, and equestrians, only one section of this 9,898-acre preserve truly caters to hikers: the John P. Hall Sr. Nature Preserve. Hunting is not permitted in this area, and a hiking-only blue-blazed trail leads to a forested campsite. You can continue on from that point onto trails shared with horses and hike out to a beautiful campsite on the St. Johns River, well worth an overnight stay.

From I-95 take exit 318 and follow the twists and turns of FL 16 west for 16.4 miles as it makes its way to the St. Johns River. After you cross the river, keep alert for the trailhead parking area on the left. From US 17 the preserve lies only 2.3 miles east along FL 16, just south of downtown Green Cove Springs. Park at the trailhead with the JOHN P. HALL SR. NATURE PRESERVE sign. Before starting off on your 7-mile hike (or overnight backpacking trip; no permit is required for camping, but sites are first come, first served), stop at the kiosk and grab a copy of the map. It's a good rough guide to the preserve, but it doesn't clearly show the hike route.

After you pass through the gate, immediately turn left on the blue-blazed hiking trail. The trail edges along the parking corral, turning right and into the pine flatwoods. Bracken ferns grow in the shade of saw palmettos under the slash pines. Traversing a series of bog bridges over a low bog underneath loblolly bay trees, the trail then

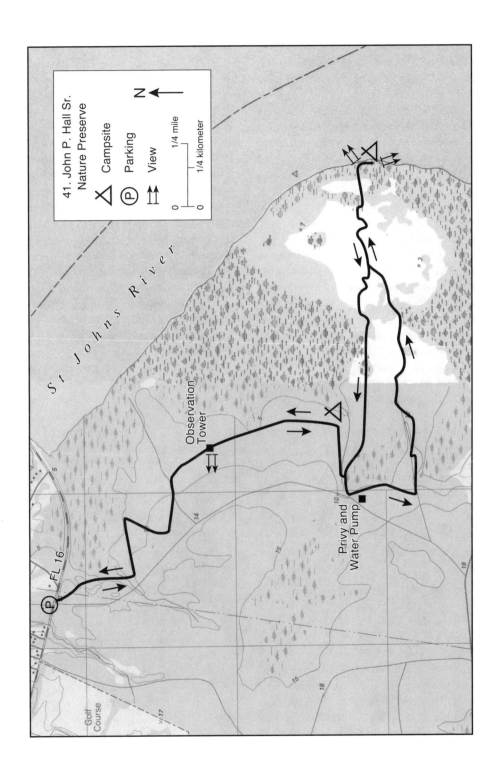

41. John P. Hall Sr.
Nature Preserve

△ Campsite
Ⓟ Parking
⇈ View

N

0   1/4 mile
0   1/4 kilometer

St Johns River

Observation
Tower

Privy and
Water Pump

FL 16

Ⓟ

Golf
Course

crosses one of the preserve's many horse trails and continues straight. It's a needle-strewn footpath winding through laurel and live oaks, stands of pine, and tall cinnamon ferns. A white-tailed deer races off through the open understory. As damp spots appear in the trail, it becomes rougher, going up and over gatorbacks—the colloquial term for annoying saw palmetto trunks—that cross the trail. A live oak arches overhead, dripping with resurrection fern. Sparkleberry dangles its juicy fruits above its red peeling bark. After crossing over a small ditch, the trail rises up into drier flatwoods with a thick carpet of saw palmetto under the pines. At 0.3 mile the trail makes a sharp right at a burned catfaced stump with a mostly intact turpentine cup hanging from it. Booming just after the Civil War, turpentine processing was once the state's second largest industry, after logging. Workers led miserable lives in the turpentine camps, trapped by their debts to the company store. Slicing into pine trees with an axe, they would form a series of V-shaped notches that encouraged the sap to run downwards into the clay collecting cup. The cups would be gathered and poured into a central vat, the sap boiled down into turpentine. Although Florida's last turpentine camp closed in 1949, small family operations continued. The pines in this forest were tapped for turpentine up until the 1960s.

As the trail turns to the left, you walk down a corridor of deerberry underneath the tall pines. A tangle of grapevines lifts over the saw palmettos. On a bend, highbush blueberries tempt you with their dark blue fruits in late spring. Scattered bluejack oaks and southern magnolias grow between the pines. The trail merges onto one of the preserve's roads at 0.7 mile, your blue blazes straight ahead briefly joined by the white diamonds of the horse trail.

Walking along a cleared area on the right of the jeep trail, you see an observation platform towering over the forest. You reach the platform after 1 mile. Climb up to survey the open ground, where deer browse around the edges. Look off into the pine flatwoods on the other side and listen closely for woodpecker activity—from here it's easier to spot the bright red heads of woodpeckers bobbing against tree trunks.

Just a dozen feet beyond the platform, the blue-blazed trail leaves the horse trail by turning left, becoming a narrow track through the dense pine flatwoods. It pops back out at an intersection of jeep trails. Follow the blue blazes forward onto a jeep trail. The horse trail merges back in from the left. Continue straight, with both white diamonds and blue blazes leading the way. You pass a jeep trail coming in from the right. Blueberries abound along this stretch of trail, attracting Carolina wrens and brown-headed nuthatches. Birdsong fills the forest. The trail rounds a curve with large blue blazes painted on a tree. Expect damp spots on sections of the trail as water seeps from the adjoining bayheads into the low spots. At 1.5 miles you come to a fork where the trails part ways—the horse trail heads to the right, and the blue blazes lead to the left. As you walk, notice the delicate variety of low panicum grass with seeds forming misty mauve balls. From your hiker's-eye view, they look like tiny constellations sparkling above the trail.

Keep alert for the next fork, which comes up quickly. The blue blazes lead you off the jeep trail and into the forest on a narrow path. You emerge at the first campsite, a clearing in a hardwood hammock, at 1.6 miles. Several logs provide natural benches around a fire ring. If you camp here, your nearest water source is downhill at the tree line, where murky water stands still in a cypress

View from Bayard Point Campsite

swamp just to the east of the campsite.

The trail continues through the campsite and skirts along the floodplain forest that accompanies the stream, where sweetgum and red maple show off their colorful leaves in winter. To the right, pine flatwoods stretch off to the horizon. Dropping down into the shady forest along the stream, the trail follows the edge of the still water settled around the bases of large bald cypresses. A southern magnolia towers overhead, trailing a long grapevine. Sensing danger, a black racer curled up at the base of a slash pine unfurls and moves into the shadows. Across the stream channel you can see a clear-cut area, part of the forest removed due to an invasion of the southern pine beetle.

You come to a junction at 1.8 miles: red blazes lead to the right, blue and red blazes to the left. Turn left, crossing the cypress-lined stream on a bridge. Turn right and fol-

low the stream southward on its opposite bank; if you pause for a moment, you can see its slow flow. After the trail skirts the clear-cut, it drops into the cool shade of an oak hammock, passing under a sprawling live oak covered in resurrection fern. You cross a small bridge and emerge at a T intersection with the COUGAR TRAIL sign. Red diamonds lead to the right and left. Turn right to walk up to the outdoor education center, with its kiosk and picnic area, latrine and pitcher pump. The blue blazes end at the kiosk, which contains information on two short trails, created by local students, that lead out of this site: the Cougar Trail (a 0.4-mile loop, of which you've just walked half) and the Legacy Trail (a 0.6-mile linear trail, which leads into a very swampy part of the flatwoods).

To continue your hike, you'll be walking on trails shared with horses. Follow the white diamonds away from the kiosk and to the south, down a narrow corridor through the mixed pine forest. Despite the pine-needle carpet, the horses do rough up the footpath. Passing through an unmarked trail junction, you see a profusion of wildflowers in a damp area in the trail—fat yellow bachelor's button, delicate bog button, and blue butterwort, a carnivorous species that traps insects in its sticky flowers. Glistening like globs of raspberry jelly, carnivorous sundew plants also crowd the damp spot. A plantation of young pines rises to the right. The young pines close in all around as the trail comes to a T intersection with a grassy track. Turn left, out into the sunshine. Although there's no shade along this part of the hike, the walking is easy. Pine forests line both sides of the track. The white blazes leave the grassy track at 2.3 miles, headed south—don't follow them. Stay on this established road. A swampy slough sits off to one side on a curve. You pass another clear-cut area, and a white diamond with a W on it—the first of many, all indicating the location of test wells for the water management district. A brief respite of shade comes when the road ducks into a forest of oak and sweetgum. It emerges out into an open area of broad meadows punctuated with younger pines and edged by older pines and stands of flat-topped goldenrod gleaming yellow in the sun.

At 3.2 miles you reach a junction with the red diamond—blazed trail, which comes in from the left. The grassy track continues straight. Turn off the track to follow the red blazes to the right. The trail narrows as the forest closes in, a mix of slash pine and loblolly bay. Rising up into a shady live oak hammock, you catch a glimpse of blue in the distance—the St. Johns River. After 3.6 miles you've reached the scenic Bayard Point Campsite on the St. Johns River. It's a cleared area on a low bluff, with picnic

tables and a fire ring. Beds of waving blue flag irises thrive under the tall bald cypresses. Walking past the campsite sign, there are numerous small clearings where you can pitch a tent in a beauty spot with a cool river breeze, the air heavy with the tang of water and fish. The irises march into the floodplain forest, filling the dark understory with their colorful blossoms. Over in a shallow section of the river, surrounded by cattails, an alligator thrashes, its tail smacking hard against the water as it attempts to drown its prey, a heron.

Leave the campsite and retrace your path along the red diamond trail. When you come to the point where the red diamonds diverge from the jeep trail, swinging right and across the grassy road into the woods, follow them. This is also a horse trail, and it will be a little torn up in places. As the trail winds through the pine forest into denser woods, you must work your way around puddles—the trail is the low spot in the pine flatwoods. At the bayhead look for the large old pines with their catfaces from turpentining, some of them with the metal collectors still embedded in the tree. When you reach the fork, keep to the right. At 4.8 miles the trail comes to a T intersection along the edge of a large clear-cut. Turn right, in the direction indicated by the double blaze. Walking across the clear-cut, you see signs of life, gallberry and wax myrtle stirring to regain a foothold, sweetgum taking root in small openings, saw palmetto lifting charred fronds to the sun, centers of green pushing out the dead, crisp edges. After 5.1 miles you complete the loop by coming back to the trail junction at the COUGAR TRAIL sign; the outdoor classroom lies straight ahead. Turn right, following the red blazes.

To return to the parking lot, you must retrace the first 1.9 miles of trail. After you cross the stream, turn right at the junction of the red and blue blazes. It's easy to lose the blue blazes along this section of the trail; just remember to keep the stream to your right until you find the campsite in the forest. Be careful to follow the blue blazes out of the campsite. When you reach the T intersection with the jeep trail, turn right. Follow the blue blazes carefully, crossing an unmarked road before you enter a narrow trail into the forest. The trail pops out next to the observation tower; turn right. You've hiked 6 miles. At the next jeep trail continue straight across, into the woods. Passing the stump with the turpentine cup, you're in the home stretch. After you cross the bog bridges, the trail turns to the right to parallel the parking lot, emptying you out on a jeep road just outside the gate. Returning to the parking lot, you've completed a 7-mile hike.

42

Stokes Landing Conservation Area

Total distance (circuit): 2.7 miles

Hiking time: 1 hour, 15 minutes

Habitats: Pine flatwoods, salt marshes, oak hammock, upland hardwood hammock, coastal savanna, freshwater marsh

Maps: USGS 7½' South Ponte Vedra Beach, St. Johns Water Management District map

Tucked away behind a suburban St. Augustine neighborhood, Stokes Landing Conservation Area is a hidden gem of the St. Johns Water Management District, providing an outdoor classroom for local schools and beautiful panoramic views of the salt marshes along the Tolomato River for hikers.

If you're headed northbound on I-95, take exit 318 and follow FL 16 east for 5.3 miles to US 1 (Ponce de Leon Boulevard). Turn left, driving north on US 1 for 6 miles, passing the St. Augustine Airport. Keep alert for a restaurant on the right with a London double-decker bus parked next to it; your turnoff is just before the restaurant. Southbound travelers on I-95 can take exit 329, heading east on CR 210 for 3.4 miles. When you reach US 1, turn right and drive 8.1 miles south until you see the double-decker bus—and Venetian Boulevard—on the left. Follow Venetian Boulevard for 0.3 mile to Old Dixie Drive. Turn right. Turn left at the next street, Lakeshore Drive. It becomes a dirt road through a residential community as you drive another 0.7 mile to the Stokes Landing Conservation Area parking area, on the right.

A kiosk with the park map sits in one corner of the parking area. Pick up a map and interpretive guide, and start your hike by walking through the "Access Point" baffle. A narrow trail, blazed with white diamonds, leads away from the picnic table and into a thicket of saw palmetto that fringes a small salt marsh in the pine flatwoods. Cabbage palms and loblolly pines show charring from

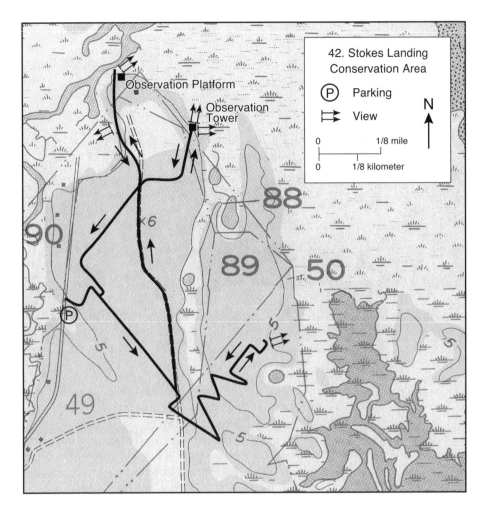

forest fire. This trail provides a gateway to a network of preexisting forest roads that local Boy Scout Troop 787 utilized to create signposted and blazed hiking paths through this 274-acre preserve.

When you reach the T intersection, you're presented with a sign with an enormous number of choices: Raccoon Run Loop and Marsh Point to the right, Interpretive Trail, Stokes Creek Landing, and Observation Deck to the left. This 2.7-mile circuit will visit all of the points of interest, so start your hike by turning right.

Follow the yellow diamond blazes into a hardwood hammock of hickory, sweetgum, red bay, live oak, and scattered southern red cedar. As the trail curves left, the forest understory becomes denser, thick with wax myrtle, saw palmetto, highbush blueberry, and younger trees.

At the next T intersection the sign indicates Raccoon Run Loop to the left and Marsh Point to the right. Turn right, passing under a large red mulberry tree. Some of its leaves look like mittens, just like a sassafras tree. Signs continue to direct you to Marsh

The Tolomato River estuary

Point. At the second sign, make a 90-degree left onto another forest road into the pine flatwoods, a forest of scattered loblolly pines that merges into a coastal savanna along the salty Intracoastal Waterway. At times of high tide, these flatwoods easily soak up with water, making for a squishy hike. The trail is rough and hummocky, a little difficult in places. Dark woods ferns poke up from the shade of blackberry thickets. At the fork, stay left on the broad trail. When you reach a double blaze, a jeep trail takes off to the left. Don't follow it—stay on the main path. Within a few moments you come to Marsh Point, the edge of a vast salt marsh along the Tolomato River. A broad expanse of black needlerush stretches out to the river. A few footsteps later the trail ends, surrounded by a natural hedge of saw palmetto. You've walked 0.7 mile. Turn around and retrace your steps back to the last MARSH POINT sign.

When you reach the T intersection, turn right at a double yellow blaze. Follow the forest road back to the RACCOON RUN LOOP sign and continue straight. Now that you're back in the shade of a dense hardwood hammock, notice the clamor of gray squirrels looking for hickory nuts feed on. The trail curves to the right, past a W sign that indicates a Water Management District testing well. Live oaks and red bay trees arch over the footpath, providing deep shade. Lantana crowds the trail, with two different types of bright bi-color blooms—yellow and pink, and yellow and orange. Young cabbage palms fill the forest understory with their huge fronds. A barred owl swoops down out of a live oak.

Curving to the left, the trail emerges at a junction after 1.3 miles. A sign to the right says OBSERVATION DECK. Turn right. A little opening in the forest shows off a patchwork of plants crowding a freshwater marsh—arrowroot with yellow blooms, sand cord grass, and climbing hempweed, which shows off its tiny white blossoms year-round. You walk under a canopy of spreading live oaks draped in Spanish moss. The broken remnants of oyster shells and clams in the footpath remind you that the Timucua once lived here, enjoying the constant salty breeze. Star rush and purple spiderwort flank the trail as it splits to go around an island of trees, and then curves to the right to Marker 9, the observation tower. Climb up, and you'll be rewarded with an incredible panorama of the salt marshes and the Tolomato River. Sit, relax, and enjoy the view. Off to the right is a sweeping expanse of salt marsh. Notice the lazy winding channels, the product of slow erosion by the tides. On the salt flats, a great blue heron picks its way across the mud, searching for snails. Look straight across the river for a gleam of white to pick out Shell Point at Guana River State Park (Hike 43). To the left, a couple of residences poke out of the forest along the marsh. A line of ibises soars low, nearly grazing the black needlerush. At the base of the tower, a short path allows you to walk out onto the mud flats and watch the fiddler crabs scurry away. A zebra swallowtail flits between the sea oxeye, a variety of daisy adapted to the rigors of the salt marsh.

Retrace your steps back to the trail junction and turn right. White blazes lead you into the shade of red mulberry, live oak, and southern red cedar laden with white berries. The forest opens up into scattered loblolly pines along a salt marsh, which intrudes into the footpath. At the bottom of one salty puddle, two fiddler crabs lock claws in an impromptu skirmish. Curving back into the cool shade of the hammock, you see a ribbon of blue sky straight ahead through the trees. The trail ends at 2 miles, at a covered pavilion with picnic tables. One is set directly on the edge of the salt marsh, a great place to watch the marine life, fiddler crabs, and wading birds. Take some time to enjoy this perspective of the marsh, where thousands of tiny crabs part as you step out onto the salt flats.

Turn around and follow the trail back to the trail junction with the OBSERVATION DECK sign pointing left. Turn right, walking under the canopy of live oaks. A clumpy shrub, bedstraw St. John's-wort, spills over with orange-yellow blooms. At the fork, turn left. The oak hammock yields to a mix of pines and oaks. When you reach the PARKING LOT sign pointing to the right, you've completed the loop. Turn right and follow the narrow trail through the saw palmettos back to the parking area, completing your hike after 2.7 miles.

43

Guana River State Park

Total distance (circuit): 9 miles

Hiking time: 5 hours

Habitats: Salt marsh, maritime hammock, oak hammock, pine flatwoods, scrubby flatwoods, coastal scrub, upland hardwood hammock

Maps: USGS 7½' South Ponte Vedra Beach, park map

Imagine watching a family of dolphins round up fish in the surf or taking a walk through an aromatic forest of red bay trees, the salt breeze riffling the leaves. Imagine standing on a platform above a marshy lake, following the antics of little blue herons and fussy coots, or spending a quiet moment's contemplation on a bench at the edge of a salt marsh, watching the tide pour across the oyster flats. With a network of trails circling a peninsula between the Guana and Tolomato Rivers, Guana River State Park offers north Florida's most enjoyable day-hiking experience.

From I-95 take exit 318 and follow FL 16 east for 5.7 miles into St. Augustine, crossing US 1. The road ends at a stop sign on San Marco Avenue (business US 1). Turn right and drive 0.6 mile to the stoplight at May Street. Turn left on FL A1A north, driving 9.5 miles through South Ponte Vedra Beach. The entrance to Guana River State Park is on the left. After you pass through the self-pay Florida State Parks fee station, there are rest rooms off to the right. Parking is on a long dam that separates the saltwater Guana River (on the left) from the lagoon of Guana Lake (on the right). It's a favorite spot for anglers and crabbers. Drive down to the far end of the parking area.

To access the trail system, pass through the gate and hike down the rest of the dike until you reach the cool shade of the maritime hammock. Just under the trees, after 0.2 mile, you'll see a large kiosk with maps and park brochures. Six trails within the park boundary allow you a variety of lengths of

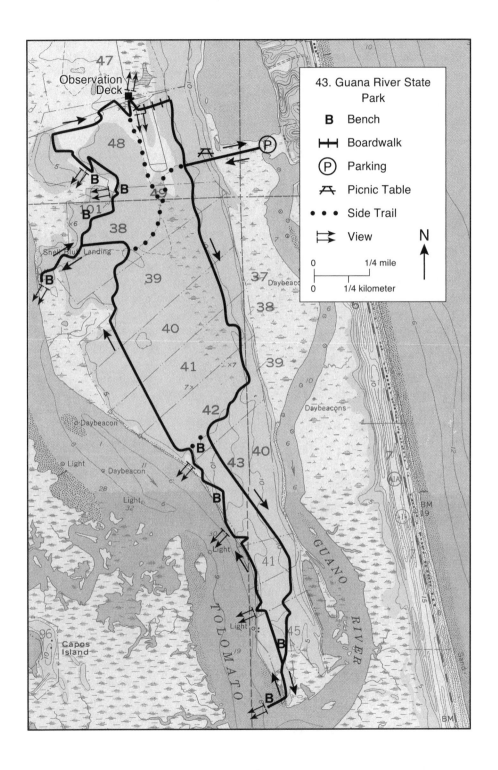

43. Guana River State Park

B Bench

⊢•⊣ Boardwalk

Ⓟ Parking

⊼ Picnic Table

• • • Side Trail

⇉ View

N

| 0 | 1/4 mile |
| 0 | 1/4 kilometer |

Observation Deck

Shell Bluff Landing

Daybeacon

Daybeacon

Light

Light

Daybeacons

GUANO RIVER

TOLOMATO

Light

Light

Capos Island

BM

hikes and are open to biking. A seventh trail leads into the adjoining Guana River Wildlife Management Area, where hikers and bikers may use the jeep roads. On the narrow stretches of trail, make a point of stepping off the trail as bikers catch up to you in order to limit their erosion of the footpath.

This hike follows a 9-mile circuit around the perimeter of the trail system. After you've signed in at the trail register, continue down the jeep road to Marker 1, which is topped with a map. Markers designate each trail junction, making it easy to follow the trail if you pay attention to the color of the loop you're on. There are no blazes on the trails. Turn left to hike the Purple Trail, which narrows down and meanders through the maritime hammock. A canopy of live oak, red bay, and laurel oak provides shade, interspersed with small stands of towering loblolly pines. The constant breeze carries the inviting aroma of the red bay tree. Its fragrant leaves are closely related to the bay leaves used in Italian cooking.

After 1 mile you catch your first glimpse of the Guana River, a ribbon of blue beyond the trees. A tall slash pine rises next to the trail, its tightly closed oval cones providing a clue to its identification. A laurel oak, studded with giant galls, has a base like a beautiful burled bowl. A southern red cedar arches over the trail. The trail turns away from the water, passing under a canopy of large moss-draped live oaks before it reaches the junction of the Purple Trail and the Red Trail just beyond a bench at Marker 2, at 1.8 miles. Behind it, a fence surrounds a large mound. Oyster shells spilling out of the sides of the bulge provide a clue to its origins: a Timucuan shell mound, over which the forest has grown. Turn left and follow the Red Trail, passing by the shell mound. A thick stand of bamboo rises from within a clump of saw palmetto. Off to the right, you

catch a bright glimpse of the salt marshes in the distance, sunlight glancing off the river. A ground skink swims across a mat of leafy debris at the base of a southern magnolia. Crossing over an old drainage ditch, the trail draws closer to the water. The sand live oaks overhead are gnarled and twisted, swept to the right, shaped by the prevailing sea breezes. The vines of hairy indigo thrive on thick mats of pine needles clumped along the sides of the footpath. Dropping down, the trail passes through an open grassy area dotted with cedars, a place that might have been an old road leading away from a wharf on the north end of the peninsula. Gray squirrels noisily scamper up the spreading branches of large live oaks.

At 3.1 miles you reach a T intersection at Marker 11, with its adjoining bench. Turn left to follow a short spur trail out to the very tip of the peninsula, ducking under cedars with oddly twisted branches. Fiddler crabs scuttle out of your way, away from their holes in the damp sand of the trail. You see the sweep of the Tolomato River to your right. The trail ends in a small loop near a bench along the river. Sit and savor the salt breeze. Mounds of oyster shells delineate the edge of the beach. Return to Marker 11 and take the left fork. Notice the loblolly pine and laurel oak joined at the hip. On the left is a gnarled cedar; it's a mass of large knots but very much alive. The scattered metal debris may be the remains of an old shanty; several families once homesteaded this land. Based on archaeological finds, human occupation here dates back nearly five thousand years. It is thought that one of the original Spanish missions in the New World, La Natividad de Nuestra Senora de Tolomato, sat near the Timucuan village that once thrived on this peninsula. In Spanish, the word *guana* means palm.

The trail soon narrows to a single track,

shaded by extremely tall, old pignut hickory trees and bounded by dense thickets of yaupon holly, one of the mainstays of the Timucuan diet. Its berries were boiled into a black drink they called *casina,* which had a hefty kick of caffeine—their answer to coffee. Consumed in excess, it would cause vomiting. At 3.7 miles the trail passes a survey marker and swings out on the low sand bluffs along the Tolomato River. Deeply undercut in places by erosion, the bluffs support a coastal scrub dominated by sand pines. As a boat passes, it throws waves up and under the bluffs. You see a gopher tortoise burrow with an unusual twist—instead of the usual spray of orange sand around the hole, the tortoise has kicked out piles of seashells, having dug into a riverside shell mound. The trail heads back into the shade, passing a tall double-trunked pine before it reaches a bench. It's a short walk behind the bench down to a small sand beach. The pungent tang of sea purslane piques your curiosity. With light green mounds of intertwined plants and tiny white blooms, it grows thickly on the river beaches. Also known as sea pickle, its leaves have been used to treat scurvy and kidney disorders.

Where the trail returns to the edge of the river, the river's shores are covered with sea purslane and bitter panicum, a salt-loving grass. Cedars line the shore. Spanish bayonets thrive in the shade of the woods. Turning away from the river, you round an indentation formed by a salt marsh and approach Marker 9, at 4.7 miles. A bench and sign mark the intersection with the Purple Trail, which came in to this point from the shell mound. Keep to the left to join the Purple Trail, following the outer perimeter of the peninsula. As you leave the trail junction, fiddler crabs dash across the footpath, which can flood slightly during high tide. Turning right, the trail quickly veers away

from the river and back into maritime hammock, passing a murky tidal basin pond. The forest hums with the sharp sounds of cicadas. The canopy lifts higher and higher as you enter a forest of massive live oak decked out in trumpet vines, grapevines, and resurrection ferns. Scattered solution holes punctuate the forest floor. You see blue sky to the left as you approach a long sweep of salt marsh. The sweet fragrance of southern magnolia blossoms wafts down to a bench below. When you come to a junction with Marker 2 and an FVA sign at 5.8 miles, turn left to follow the Yellow Trail down to Shell Bluff. The forest shifts to an upland hardwood hammock with sweetgum, water oak, American holly, and hickory. Pass Marker 6, the junction with the Blue Trail, and continue straight. Within a few minutes you see the open water of the river. A stand of cedars and pines sits off to the right. The trail ends at Shell Bluff, a popular spot for bird-watching and fishing, or just kicking back under the trees to enjoy the breeze and the sweeping view. Across the river, beyond the distant salt marshes, lies Stokes Landing Conservation Area (Hike 42). A family of dolphins swims in a tight circle, trapping a school of fish. As the fish leap out of the water, the dolphins feast.

Turn around and return down the Yellow Trail to Marker 6, turning left on the Blue Trail. At 6.6 miles you see a marker with a butterfly pointing to a trail on the left. Follow the short spur down to where it ends, at a marshy freshwater pond where a boardwalk leads out over the water. If flowers are in bloom along the pond's edges, you're apt to see dozens of butterflies. Returning to the main trail, turn left. Within 0.25 mile you come across another side trail to the left. Cut through a thicket of saw palmetto, the trail ends at a bench with a beautiful view of the salt marsh. Return to the main trail and

Maritime hammock along the Tolomato River

turn left. As the trail curves around the salt marsh, it comes to Marker 5, the intersection with the Orange Trail, at 7 miles. Stay straight. Don't miss the next spur trail, which takes off to the left, winding down through sparkleberry and wax myrtle into a thicket of saw palmetto. A bleacherlike bench provides a stunning panorama of the salt marsh—from the tide spilling over oyster beds up close to the sweep of the Tolomato River in the distance.

Return to the main trail and turn left. The trail curves along the edge of a salt marsh, where feral hogs wallow in muddy holes. A coastal pine flatwoods sweeps off to the right. As you meander away from the salt marsh, star rush lines both sides of the trail. A canopy of live oaks shades the footpath. After 7.5 miles you reach Marker 4. Straight ahead, the Gray Trail leads into the adjoining Guana River Wildlife Management Area. Turn right to follow the Orange Trail, which winds through a thicket of saw palmetto under gnarled sand live oaks. You emerge into a scrubby flatwoods with scattered slash and pond pines. Watch for a short spur trail leading off to the left. It ends at a bench along a winding canal, next to a large mound covered in trees—likely the spoil pile from the dredging. Take a moment to rest and watch for turtles swimming by. Return to the main trail and turn left. The trail meanders along the rim of the flatwoods, skirting the edge of the fence line before curving into the oak forest. You pass through a stand of tall pond pine, their bark charred from a recent fire. Pond pines prefer damp environments and are distinguished from similar-looking slash pines by their odd habit of sprouting needles out of the trunk.

After 8 miles you reach Marker 3: the junction of the Orange, Blue, and Gray Trails. Turn left to take a short but worthwhile side trip on the Gray Trail, out to an observation deck inside the Guana River Wildlife Management Area. Pass through the park gate and walk up past the BIG SAVANNA POND INTERPRETIVE COMPLEX AND OBSERVATION BLIND sign to the boardwalk. Follow it to its end for a scenic view across Big Savanna Pond. Fed by freshwater springs, this shallow marsh attracts hundreds of waterfowl, from coots and teals to limpkins and little green herons. A flock of ibises picks its way across a mud flat. Look up to the tops of the trees on the far shore, and you'll see snowy egrets and great blue herons tending to their nests. A constant symphony of bird calls rise up out of the tall marsh grasses.

Return back the way you came, through the gate and back to the trail junction at Marker 3. Turn left on the Orange Trail and cross the bridge that spans an inlet of Savanna Pond. Under the bridge, a leopard frog crouches by a muddy pool filled with minnows. After a short stretch of oak hammock, you cross a second long bridge. As you return to the live oak hammock, the trail winds through head-high saw palmettos. It emerges at a spot that looks like a parking area, coming to a T intersection with a forest road at the junction of the Gray and Orange Trails. Turn right. It's a brief walk down the sandy road to Marker 1, where you complete the perimeter loop after 8.7 miles of hiking. The road curves past Marker 1 and heads back out through the maritime hammock. When you pass by the kiosk, be sure to sign out at the register on your way out. Continuing out of the forest and along the open stretch on Guana Dam, you end your hike at the parking lot after 9 miles.

Most visitors to Guana River State Park have no idea the hiking trails exist. They're here for the long sweep of golden-orange beaches, accessed by several entrances north on FL A1A. Although the beaches are too steeply sloped and the sand too soft for a nice long beach hike, you may want to spend an afternoon sunning and swimming, cooling down after your hike. Leave the dam area parking, head out to FL A1A, and turn left. Drive 3.4 miles north to the first beach parking area, South Beach Use Area. At 4.3 miles you reach the Midway Beach Use Area (typically the quietest). The park ends after 6.6 miles at the North End Beach Use Area, a busy place on weekends because of its easy proximity to Jacksonville. If you enjoy fishing or paddling, near the South Beach Use Area you'll find a launch point for low-power motorboats (10 horsepower maximum), kayaks, and canoes to explore Guana Lake, a saline lagoon trapped behind the Guana Dam.

44

Anastasia State Park

Total distance (1 circuit, 2 round trips): 10.8 miles

Hiking time: 5 hours

Habitats: Maritime hammock, coastal strand

Maps: USGS 7½' St. Augustine, park map

The beach—a place of shifting sands, roaring waves, constant change, and rebirth and renewal. On Anastasia Island, this sweep of shoreline that shelters St. Augustine has seen a parade of history pass before it, from the Timucua in their canoes and the Spanish explorers who claimed these shores in 1565, who established what is now the nation's oldest continuously occupied European settlement at St. Augustine, to the pirate ships of Sir Francis Drake and the high-society visitors to Henry Flagler's hotels. Storms sweep through, rearranging the channels, creating sandbars, and uncovering hidden tidal pools and stands of coquina.

At Anastasia State Park, the beach attracts sunbathers, swimmers, and surfers. Bicyclists race down the sand flats at low tide; anglers try their luck for snook. Now off-limits to automobiles, this 4.5-mile stretch of white sand and dunes provides north Florida's best beach walk, calling to quiet souls who want to contemplate the surf as they walk down the ever-shifting peninsula.

From I-95 take exit 318 and follow FL 16 east for 5.7 miles into St. Augustine, crossing US 1. The road ends at a stop sign on San Marco Avenue (business US 1). Turn right and drive past May Street, which brings in FL A1A south. Continue 1.9 miles into the old city of St. Augustine, passing the city gates and the grand Castillo de San Marcos. Get into the left lane and follow FL A1A across the Bridge of Lions. Drive another 1.9 miles to the park entrance, on the left just beyond the St. Augustine Alligator Farm.

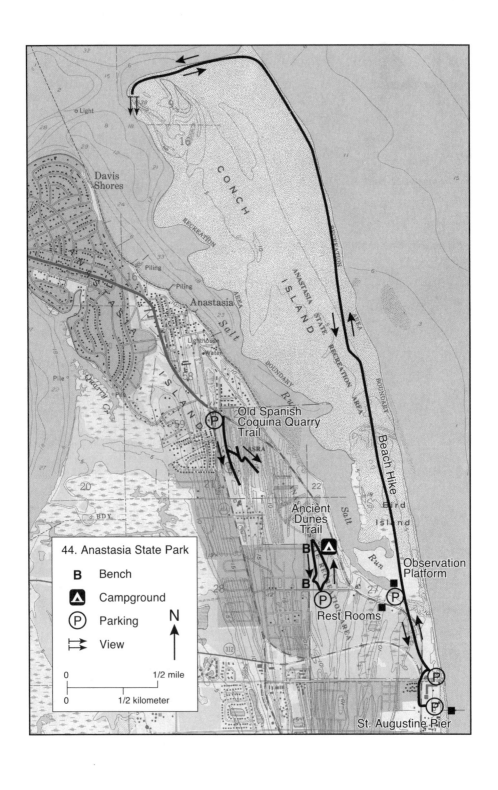

44. Anastasia State Park

B   Bench

△   Campground

Ⓟ   Parking

⇉   View

N

| 0 | | 1/2 mile |
| 0 | | 1/2 kilometer |

Davis Shores

Anastasia

Old Spanish Coquina Quarry Trail

Ancient Dunes Trail

Observation Platform

Rest Rooms

St. Augustine Pier

Beach Hike

OLD SPANISH COQUINA QUARRY TRAIL

Immediately inside the park entrance on the right is an OLD SPANISH COQUINA QUARRY sign. Park here and start this 1.2-mile hike by walking through the gate. Pick up a history brochure. The trail rises up into ancient dunes covered in maritime hammock, the short sand live oak and red bay sculpted by sea breezes, red cedar twisted by the wind. You quickly emerge into a large open quarry. In 1671 the Spanish settlers of St. Augustine selected this site to dig out and cut slabs of coquina, a limestone made up of quartz grains and tiny fragments of seashells and held together by calcium carbonate. Buried in damp sand, coquina is soft and pliable, but as soon as it's exposed to the air, it hardens. The Spanish used this stone to build their fortress, the Castillo de San Marcos, as well as many of the homes and shops in the city. The coquina walls of the Castillo had one particularly interesting property—rather than cracking under bombardment, they simply absorbed the cannonballs.

This is the first of several quarries you'll see along the hike. As you drop down into it, beneath the eroded coquina sand you can see slab marks where tools cut into the limestone outcrops. Meadow pink flourishes in the moist basin. The trail sticks to the left side of the quarry and clambers back out under the far side. After you pass under the low boughs of gnarled cedars, you walk along a series of quarry pits on both sides. A scarlet tanager roosts in the high branches of a tall cedar. As you catch it sunning in the trail, a six-lined race runner scurries away, looking for shelter in the drifts of oak leaves. At 0.2 mile the trail passes through the park-boundary fence and enters the grounds of the adjoining St. Augustine Amphitheatre. Known for its presentation of the official state play, *The Cross and the Sword,* the amphitheater provides an outdoor stage set in the largest of the Spanish coquina quarries.

At the fork, keep right, crossing a paved road. The stand of bamboo along the jeep track hides your view of one of the larger coquina quarries, now a water-filled pond. The trail leads up to its edge. Continue along the quarry to a set of stairs up to the left, leading onto an embankment. Turn left at the top of the stairs, walking over a footbridge over an old pond, which looks like part of a defunct botanical garden. The embankment drops back down to the paved road. Cross it and retrace your steps to the trail junction. Turn right. This path once served as an exercise course, but the stations have rotted away. It's now just a meander through the maritime hammock that's popular with local bikers. You walk past saw palmettos with a silvery-blue sheen, a sign of their saline environment, and under sand live oak and red bay. The trail curves up to the left and loops back down past some abandoned chin-up bars. Passing through a large clump of saw palmetto, you see the paved road off to the right. The trees limbs hang low, so you often have to duck. Sprays of royal fern emerge from a clearing beneath spreading sand live oak. The trail winds between a dense corridor of saw palmettos—the ones on the left are deep green, with tall stems; the ones on the right are silvery blue. As you climb up past a rotting sit-up station, the trail curves to the right. Gnarled rusty lyonia reaches out over the trail. Spindly yaupon holly grows in the shade of larger American holly, both of which have had their historic uses. The yaupon's leaves are high in caffeine, leading the Timucua to use the leaves to boil their ceremonial drink, *casina.* During the early European colonization, the hard wood of the

American holly was carved into false teeth.

As you drop down another hill, the limbs of a red bay graze your head. The trail twists and turns, reaching the back of an abandoned building at 0.7 mile. To your left is another water-filled quarry. Use this as your turn-around point since the trail soon ends at a fence. Retrace your steps back up to the trail junction and turn right, passing through the break in the fence back into the park. Continue straight, dropping down into the quarry and following the footpath along the left. You can see chunks of cut coquina left in place on the north side of the wall. Head across the quarry and rise back out, returning to the parking lot after a 1.2-mile hike.

Continue down the park entrance road and stop at the ranger station to pay your Florida State Parks entrance fee. Drive past the picnic areas and the lagoon—a great place for bird-watching during the winter months—and turn right where you see a NA-TURE TRAIL sign, driving back into the campground. After you pass the camp store, continue straight. The road ends at a NO DRIVING BEYOND THIS POINT sign, with several parking spaces on the right for the trailhead of the Ancient Dunes Trail.

ANCIENT DUNES TRAIL

Start your hike at the trail sign and turn right to follow this 0.7-mile interpretive loop through a maritime hammock. Thickets of yaupon fill the understory, easily identified by the tiny scallops along the margins of their small but shiny green leaves. The female yaupon sport bright red berries. You wander out of the dense hammock into an open area where slash pines cover the footpath in a carpet of pine needles. The sea breeze wafts through the forest. The trail becomes strenuous, clambering up and over the ancient dunes and wandering along the edge

Snowy egret

of a deep bowl filled with saw palmetto before it drops down into it. You rise up to a T intersection with a sign pointing out the various campsite groupings at this end of the campground. Turn left. The trail skirts around and under a large sand live oak. Turn around and look at it, and you'll notice a deep hollow in the tree. Bees buzz around the opening. The glowing form of witches' butter brightens the interior, the brainlike fungus as orange as a jack-o'-lantern.

Numerous side trails lead off to the right to campsites as you continue down the main trail. It curves left through a stand of aromatic red bay. You walk under the massive blooms of southern magnolias, their fragrance drifting down to delight your senses. A native of Asia, the southern magnolia was named for a 17th-century French botanist, Pierre Magnol. They flourish in damp spots within the maritime hammock. After you pass a bench, the trail drops down a steep slope, curving left. At 0.5 mile a staircase leads down the next dune. A slash pine towers overhead as you rise back up out of the dune bowl. American beautyberry shows off its delicate pink blooms with yellow stamens in spring and summer and its deep purple berries during fall and winter. After you climb up another steep dune, take a moment to rest on the bench before climbing down the next staircase. After 0.7 mile the trail completes the loop, ending back at the parking area.

BEACH HIKE

It depends greatly on the season as to where you start your beach hike, and the variance in tides will determine the difficulty of the hike. If you're staying in the park campground, use the main beach access at the end of the entrance road so you're not constrained by the 8 AM to sunset park hours. But if you're staying outside the park and want to enjoy either a sunrise or sunset walk (more enjoyable than walking in the direct midday sun), drive past the park entrance south on FL A1A. Turn left at the light and continue 2 miles to a county parking lot on the edge of the state park, on the left. If that parking lot is full, drive another block to the public parking at the St. Augustine Beach pier and walk back along the sidewalk to this side entrance to Anastasia State Park. Be sure to take adequate water for this shadeless walk.

Start at the park entrance at the county parking lot and walk out onto the beach. It's a popular destination for families on the weekends, so expect to see quite a crowd out sunning at this end of the beach. Jutting out of the sand, boulders of coquina create dangerous riptides in the water, so swimming is prohibited at this end of the park. Off on your left, dunes collect around the gnarled, spindly frames of sand live oaks. Don't be surprised to see chunks of concrete sticking out of the beach. This section of beach used to be the route of FL A1A until persistent storms in the 1970s washed the road out to sea. After 0.4 mile you come to the causeway that leads down from the beach parking area within Anastasia State Park. Rest rooms lie on the far side of the parking lot. An observation deck provides a sweeping view of the seascape.

The crowd thins out as you continue down the beach into the realm of the surfboarding set. At 1.1 miles the moonscape of topped-off sand dunes end, yielding to healthy patches of sea oats on the dunes. The dunes increase in size as you progress, dropping down occasionally to give you a glimpse of the distinctive black and white St. Augustine Lighthouse. Built in 1871, this lighthouse replaced an earlier one dating back to 1824, which tumbled into the sea under the constant battering of waves along the shore. The Frensel lens of the current St. Augustine Lighthouse has guided ships to Matanzas Inlet since 1874.

Due to the constantly changing nature of the shore, you never know what to expect along this beach walk. You may see mussel-fringed tidal pools, busy with ghost crabs, or a beach renourishment project in full swing, sucking up sand through pipes stuck into the sea, pouring it out like wet cement. Well beyond the crowds after 2 miles, you enjoy the constant cool breeze. Bicyclists race by, taking advantage of the hard-packed sand at low tide. It's a perfect surface for walking, too. You see orange, white, and purple coquina shells from the tiny *Donax variabilis* clam scattered in profusion across the sand. The currents be-

---

Anastasia State Park

come dangerously strong as you reach Cape Francis, where brown pelicans, laughing gulls, and royal terns hang out in large flocks at the tip of Matanzas Inlet. You see buildings rising from South Ponte Vedra Beach and sailboats slipping in and out of the choppy inlet. Keep walking around the point.

As you reach the end of the stone jetty after 3.8 miles, the sand becomes softer underfoot, shielded from the waves. The tide creeps behind the rocks to create a tidal lagoon lush with samphire, sea purslane, and glasswort. A ghost crab drags a dying fish up to its hole. Follow the slender track through the soft sand, created by the park ranger's ATV trips along the edge of the dunes. Prickly pear cactus rises from the bright white sand, where sand-dune spurge covers the dunes. Look for colorful anemones on the dune slopes. The track curves upward and rises to become a road on the dunes, looking out over a desertlike plain. You directly face the 208-foot-tall cross that marks the landing site of Pedro Menendez de Aviles in 1565, where he claimed Florida for Spain. At this site the Spanish built their first mission in the New World, the Mission de Nombre de Dios.

At 4.4 miles you reach the end of the peninsula at a turnaround loop, facing the residential section of Anastasia Island. To your right are St. Augustine and the Bridge of Lions, the towers of Flagler College (the former Ponce de Leon Hotel) rising well above the rest of the city. The squat Castillo de San Marcos sits at the mouth of the Matanzas River. To the left you see Anastasia Inlet and the St. Augustine Lighthouse. Turn around and retrace your path back to your starting point, completing an 8.9-mile beach hike.

45

Moses Creek Conservation Area

Total distance (round trip): 12.9 miles

Hiking time: 6.5 hours or overnight

Habitats: Pine flatwoods, hardwood hammock, sand pine scrub, oak scrub, floodplain forest, freshwater marsh, saltwater marsh, bayheads

Maps: USGS 7½' St. Augustine Beach, St. Johns Water Management District map

Encompassing more than two thousand acres, the Moses Creek Conservation Area provides an excellent venue for backpackers who want to explore the salt marshes of the Matanzas River. There are several different ways you can hike this preserve. You can enjoy a small portion of it as a 3-mile round-trip day hike out to scenic panoramas along Moses Creek, or you can take a long day hike or overnight backpacking trip to enjoy the far-flung end of the preserve at Murat Point. The campsites are first come, first served, requiring a permit only if your group numbers six or more. Although there is a pitcher pump near Murat Point, it may not work when you need it. Carry adequate water.

From I-95 exit 305, follow FL 206 east for 2.2 miles to Dupont Center. Cross US 1 at the traffic light and continue 1 mile, past the western trailhead parking area on the left, at the low MOSES CREEK CONSERVATION AREA sign. Continue another 1.2 miles to the eastern trailhead parking area on the left. Although the western trailhead gives you quicker access to the campsite, shaving 1.4 miles off the hike, the eastern trailhead provides a superior hiking experience. Both sets of trails are shared with horses and bicycles.

Pick up a trail map at the kiosk in the eastern parking area and follow the White Trail into the slash pine flatwoods along a broad forest road winding through the pine forest. The dry understory quickly transitions to a wet one with wax myrtle and loblolly bay. Choked with arrowroot, a slough parallels on

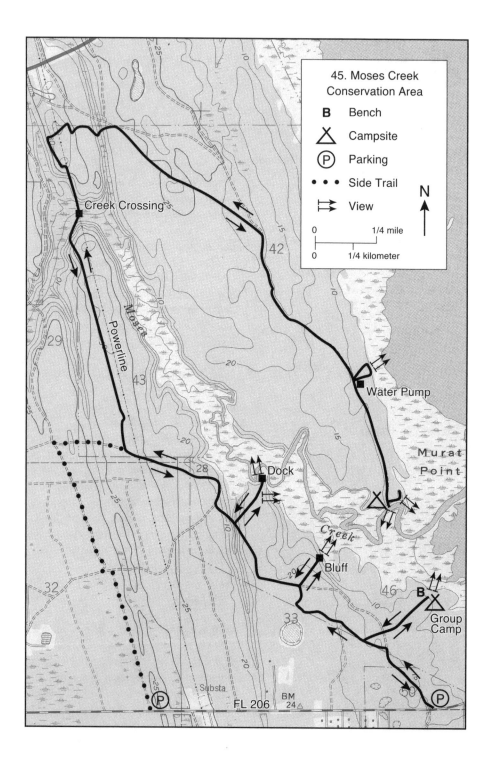

45. Moses Creek
Conservation Area

B   Bench

△   Campsite

Ⓟ   Parking

•••   Side Trail

⇥   View

N

| 0 | 1/4 mile |
| 0 | 1/4 kilometer |

Creek Crossing

42

Powerline

Moses

43

29

Water Pump

Murat
Point

20

28

Dock

15

Creek

Bluff

46

B

Group
Camp

32

33

Substa

FL 206

BM
24△

Ⓟ

Ⓟ

the right. After 0.4 mile you reach Marker 2 at the spur trail to the group campsite. Even if you aren't camping here, the side trail is worth the walk for its sweeping view of Moses Creek and the Matanzas River salt marshes. The trail twists and turns, lined with saw palmetto, and enters a cool and shady oak hammock. Dropping through a dry drainage, the trail rises back up into the hammock as you pass by a snag filled with woodpecker holes. A thick understory of shiny lyonia surrounds you as the trail snakes toward a broad expanse on the left. You see the GROUP CAMPING AREA sign and a storage rack for kayaks and canoes. The campsite includes a fire ring and picnic tables, as well as numerous benches positioned under a spreading live oak as an outdoor classroom. A picnic bench sits on the edge of the salt marsh. Head down through the campsite to the edge of the marsh. Like a watercolor painting, the salt marshes of the Matanzas River sweep away from your feet and off to the distant shores of Crescent Beach.

Heading back up the spur trail, you reach the main trail. Turn right and pass around the gate. The trail rises up into a sand pine scrub with soft white sand underfoot as it passes a trail off to the left. As you walk along a section of trail covered with mulch, you pass an environmental education center, used as a classroom for the St. Johns County students who developed trails and campsites throughout the preserve. The trail skirts a fence and turns right, providing an unobstructed view down a corridor of sand pines. At 1.1 miles you reach an intersection where the main trail turns left and a spur trail continues straight. Walk straight down the spur trail for a scenic view of Moses Creek from the top of a tall sand bluff. Draining bayheads and freshwater marshes well above the tide line, Moses

Creek winds its way into the salt marshes, becoming a tidal creek subject to the ebb and flow of the Atlantic Ocean.

Return back up the spur trail and turn right on the main trail. The trail makes another right, rising up out of the sand pine scrub into a hardwood hammock, where southern magnolia and live oak shade the footpath amid a dense understory of saw palmetto. After 2 miles you reach Marker 3, the junction of the White and Yellow Trails. Turn right for another scenic overlook on Moses Creek. If you're fishing or kayaking, this is your access point as well. The trail rises up out of the hardwood hammock into another sand pine forest, where the older sand pines are leaning over and falling due to their advanced age. Chapman and myrtle oaks fill the understory. As the trail drops down, you can see a sweep of wheat-colored grasses across the salt marsh, framed by the gnarled limbs of sand live oaks. At the fork at Marker 4, turn right and walk down to the floating dock on the salt marsh, where you can take in an unobstructed view across the meanders of Moses Creek. Look for an osprey nest off the left that was built most of the way up the trunk of a large slash pine. In the distance, you can see the parade of seaside homes on the barrier island of Crescent Beach. After taking a few minutes to enjoy the view, continue along the trail as it loops up and around to the high sand bluff that overlooks the backwaters of the marsh stretching across to Murat Point. Look down, and you can see the tidal bore pressing against the outflow of the creek. The White Trail ends here. Turn around and return to the trail junction. Your hiking plans determine your choice of route. If you're headed for the campsites at Murat Point or to the western trailhead, turn right. Otherwise, turn left to return to your car at the eastern trailhead, retracing your path

Fishing on Moses Creek

(minus the mile of spur trails already visited) for a day hike of 3 miles.

If you're hiking to distant Murat Point, follow the Yellow Trail down a slope from the oak hammock into a floodplain forest that drains into Moses Creek. Step across the tannic-colored drainage and continue uphill. At the top of the hill, a trail takes off to the left. Continue straight and follow the yellow blazes into a mature oak scrub under moss-draped sand live oaks. It's a breeding ground for skinks—you see dozens of the colorful six-lined racerunners scampering about. Walking past a feathery wall of young sand pines, you ascend through the scrub. The footpath becomes soft sand—difficult walking. You come to a double blaze in front of a wide desertlike bowl of sand under a set of high-tension lines. Walk straight across the blinding white sand. After 3.2 miles you reach the junction with the Red Trail at Marker 6. Turn right to follow the trail beneath the power line.

Although following a power line isn't very scenic, this section of the trail has its small delights. Since it runs through sand pine scrub, it's open and sunny except in early morning and late afternoon, when towering trees on either side offer some shade. Look down at the massive clusters of reindeer lichen with their beautiful red blooms. Horses badly churn up the center of the trail, so you have to stay to the right or left. Scattered St. John's-wort grows amid the low brush, along with scrub oak, silk bay, and Florida rosemary. Flag pawpaw displays its ivory blooms each spring. You spy a lone coontie hiding in the shade of the adjoining strip of oaks. Side trails lead over to the high-tension lines that go through the property. As the trail rises uphill it transitions into an oak hammock with large live oaks, coming to a sand bluff along the floodplain forest of Moses Creek. The trail turns right to cross under the high-tension lines, and then turns left and drops steeply downhill for a two-step wade across the marshy creek, which narrows and speeds up as it falls down the bluff. Be careful: The limestone pebbles under the rushing water can be slippery. Red maple and pond cypress line the shores of the creek, which is the closest guaranteed freshwater source to the campsite at Murat Point, 2.4 miles away. You climb back uphill under a high-tension tower with a large osprey nest on top, stringers of Spanish moss dangling from the nest.

As the trail climbs the northern bluff, passing a jeep trail from the right, it becomes deep with sand. Watch for a red arrow on a pole. The trail turns left away from the high-tension lines to return to its northerly route along the smaller power line. When you reach the northern boundary of the preserve, turn right to follow the trail back out to the high-tension line. The trail jogs to the left, approaching a northern gate into the park for the nearby residential community, and turns right to follow the fence. When the trail drops down through a bayhead drainage, you're surrounded by the fragrant damp needles of longleaf pine amid the cinnamon ferns. At the top of the rise the trail turns to the right, away from a yellow gate in the fence, at 4.8 miles.

From this point on, the trek out to Murat Point is a pleasant walk in the woods—worth the hassle of the walk along the power line. Follow the red diamonds into a mixed sand pine and oak forest with a low canopy, a beauty spot under the arched sand live oaks and rusty lyonia. Oak leaves and pine needles carpet the footpath, which is nicely compacted underfoot despite its use by equestrians. You come to an intersection with red diamond blazes. Take the left fork. As you walk along, notice how the pinecones on the old sand pines actually petrify against the branches, clinging there until a wildfire springs them open to scatter their seeds. Lyre-leaved sage grows near the pines, its many bell-shaped blooms dangling off the tall central stem. Providing leaves for a tea that the Timucua used for coughs and colds, this herb has also been used in folk remedies to treat warts and cancer.

You enter an oak scrub, the sand live oaks twisted and gnarled overhead, covered in crispy coats of old man's beard and red blanket lichen. At 5.5 miles a sand road comes in from the left; the Red Trail joins it, heading to the right into a young sand pine forest, an ideal habitat for sighting a Florida scrub-jay. Yellow wild bachelor's button pops up along the roadside while gallberry shows off its pink bell blooms. You catch a whiff of vanilla from a stand of tall deer's tongue. The trail continues on a base of limestone pebbles around a small island of longleaf pine before it enters a densely canopied maritime hammock of grand old live oak, laurel oak, and red bay. Streamers of Spanish moss hang from the high branches. You smell the scents of cedars and salt as the trail draws closer to the salt marsh, just beyond the trees to your left. A green-blazed trail leads off to the right; continue straight. Coming to Marker 7 after 6.3 miles, you find a pitcher pump in a clearing under a high oak canopy. Walk through the clearing to an overlook out onto the tidal flats along the Matanzas River. Windswept cedars create a wall on the edge of the salt marsh; ibises pick through the shallows.

Return to the main trail and turn left. Sunlight filters through the live oaks and cedars, creating patterns across the hazy tall grass that covers the forest floor. The trail twists through a stand of laurel oak, and you see a bright spot up ahead—Murat Point. You reach Marker 8 at 6.9 miles, at a T intersection above a lazy oxbow in Moses Creek. Turn right to walk up the bluff to the campsite. Sitting high above the creek, it commands a great view of the salt marsh and provides numerous benches and chairs so you to relax and take in the scene. A small beach lies at the bottom of the steep bluff, and two picnic tables flank the fire ring. As you leave the campsite, notice the Spanish bayonets, a relative of the yucca and member of the lily family. Most of them vanished from this region due to a blight that affected the barrier islands, but these tall specimens look very healthy.

Return to Marker 8 and continue straight on the main trail. At 7 miles it ends at a kiosk; a set of stairs lead down to a small beach where kayaks and canoes can land. However, beyond the kiosk an unofficial trail continues along the edge of the bluffs. Carefully work your way across on the narrow ledge to reach the salt flats around the corner. Fiddler crabs retreat into the glasswort and saltwort with a chorus of clacking from their tiny crab claws. It's a great place to wander, explore the nature of the salt flats, and loop your way back behind the coastal hammock.

To return to the trailhead, retrace your route along the Red Trail, following the red diamonds. Pay careful attention at the fork in the sand pine forest: The jeep trail you are on swings to the right, and your trail turns left into shadier forest. After 9 miles you'll see the bright yellow gate off to the right, and the trail turns left to follow the fence back to the power line. Follow your path back across Moses Creek and keep to the power line up to the end of the Red Trail,

at 10.7 miles. Your return route from here depends on where you left your car. The eastern trailhead is 1.5 miles to the left; the western trailhead is 2.2 miles to the right. Turn left and follow the yellow blazes for 0.6 mile back to their intersection with the White Trail. Continue along the white-blazed corridor, emerging at the eastern trailhead parking area after 12.9 miles.

WESTERN TRAILHEAD (ALTERNATIVE ROUTE)

If your destination is the campsite at Murat Point, you may prefer to take the shorter, less scenic approach to the Red Trail. Start from the western trailhead. Follow the yellow diamonds away from the kiosk and into the young slash pine flatwoods, walking along the edge of a firebreak. After 0.6 mile you reach a trail intersection. A double-diamond blaze seems to indicate a turn, but the Yellow Trail continues straight through the intersection. The habitat yields to sand pine scrub, with lots of deer moss and reindeer lichen. Keep to the right side of the firebreak as the rest of it is too churned up for a comfortable walk. Crossing another firebreak, you enter wet flatwoods with pond pine, slash pine, and loblolly bay.

At 1.1 miles you reach an intersection blazed with double yellow diamonds. Turn right. The footpath becomes very sandy underfoot, and as you progress uphill, sand pines cast shadows across the trail. Climbing a small rise, you then drop into a drainage for a bayhead. Step across the flowing water. The trail rises back into the scrub, where the sunshine makes the leaves of the sand live oaks glow. After 1.5 miles you reach the intersection of the Yellow and Red Trails at Marker 6. Turn left to continue the route to Murat Point.

46

Princess Place Preserve

Total distance (3 circuits): 4.1 miles

Hiking time: 3 hours

Habitats: Sandhill, hardwood hammock, oak scrub, sand pine scrub, salt marsh, freshwater marsh

Maps: USGS 7½' Matanzas Inlet, park map

Located at the confluence of Pellicer Creek and the Matanzas River, Princess Place Preserve protects the oldest homestead in Flagler County, Cherokee Grove. It began as a land grant in 1791 from the King of Spain that was quickly planted in orange groves. In 1886 it passed into the hands of Henry Cutting, a New Englander, who immediately constructed an Adirondack-style hunting lodge on the shores of the Matanzas River using local materials–pink coquina, cedar trunks, and cabbage palm trunks. He also built Florida's first in-ground pool, fed by an artesian spring. Cherokee Grove became a popular stop for New England socialites. Several years after Henry died, his widow, Angela, married an exiled Russian prince. Together, they lived in Cherokee Grove, entertaining royalty in a royal setting, which lead to the name Princess Place. Remaining in private hands until 1993, the homestead then became a Flagler County Park. In addition to a tour of the classic home and grounds, Princess Place Preserve offers several hiking loops and many miles of horse trails that lead into the adjacent Pellicer Creek Conservation Area. All trails are shared with equestrians and bikers, so keep alert while hiking. This hike covers three separate loops within the bounds of the Princess Place Preserve, which is open 9 AM to 5 PM Wednesday through Sunday, closed Mondays and Tuesdays.

From exit 298 on I-95 at US 1, head south 1.7 miles to Old Kings Road, on your left just after you cross Pellicer Creek. Turn left. Drive slowly along the dirt road, which

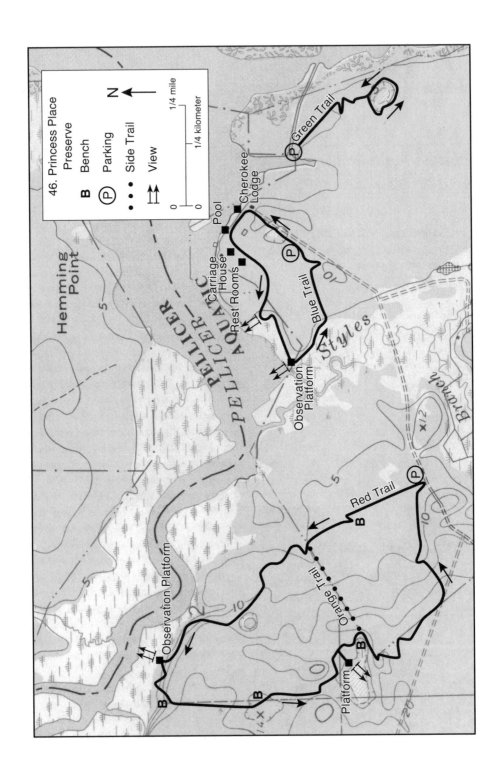

46. Princess Place Preserve

B — Bench
Ⓟ — Parking
•••• — Side Trail
⇈ — View

N

0 · · · 1/4 kilometer
0 · · · 1/4 mile

Hemming Point

PELLICER — PELLICUATIC

Styles

Branch

Cherokee Lodge
Pool
Carriage House
Rest Rooms
Observation Platform
Blue Trail

Green Trail

Observation Platform
B
B

Red Trail
B

Orange Trail
B

Platform
B

briefly exhibits some pavement as you cross a bridge over I-95. You pass the PELLICER CREEK CONSERVATION AREA sign. After 1.5 miles, turn left at the sign for Princess Place Preserve. Drive 1.3 miles on Princess Place Road to the park gate. Continue another 0.3 mile to the Red/Orange Trail parking area on the left to start your first hike.

RED/ORANGE TRAIL

Start at the parking area and take a look at the kiosk for the Red/Orange Trail, which shows the map of the stacked loops. You'll be following the 2.2-mile outer loop, the Red Trail. It's not obvious where the trail starts since the only trail markings are white diamonds indicating a horse trail off to the left. Once you walk through the gap in the fence, continue straight ahead to where you see white diamonds in the distance, at the tree line at the edge of the clearing. You will come up to a white post with an orange arrow. These arrow-topped posts provide trail markers throughout Princess Place Preserve, but most of the arrows are either broken or faded. Watch for the white posts to give you clues as to turns in the trail. A sand road leads off to the left. Keep to the right, following the white diamonds.

After 0.1 mile you pass another white pole. The trail is a broad grassy strip that separates stretches of hardwood hammock. You see broad meadows off to the left, interspersed with trees. The grassy footpath sweeps left around a corner, along the edge of the sandhills. As you round the next corner, you see a freshwater marsh on the right, thick with pennywort. A red-tailed hawk swoops past, dangling a long black racer from its talons. Passing a bench with an interpretive marker, you reach the junction with the interior Orange Trail at 0.7 mile. Turn right at the bench to continue on the Red Trail. As you turn the corner you

immediately see Pellicer Creek, part of an extensive protected aquatic preserve, an important spawning ground for saltwater species such as mullet and blue crab. Across the channel is Faver-Dykes State Park, popular with canoeists and anglers, with a campground along the salt marshes.

The trail curves to the left to parallel Pellicer Creek, providing open views across the broad expanse of marsh. You smell the tang of the salt marsh while noticing the charred saw palmettos, victims of a recent burn. At 0.9 mile the trail reaches an observation deck with a bench, a great place to sit and watch the wading birds out in the salt marshes. Continuing past the observation deck, you see more nice views of the creek. Wild coonties sprout in the shade of the forest. After 1 mile the trail makes an abrupt left turn near a bench to follow a barbed-wire fence. On the other side of the fence the land has been replanted in longleaf pine. You're walking in a cleared space along the edge of an oak scrub, with sand live oaks raining their crunchy leaves down on the saw palmettos below. A couple of white posts confirm your route. The trail passes a bench on the right and curves to the left, entering a climax sandhill habitat. Large sand live oaks compete for space with longleaf pines. Peering through the trees to the right, you see open water—a large freshwater marsh, unusually close to the saline creek. An industrious river cooter kicks her back legs to continue scooping out a hole in the soft sand of the footpath, where she plans to leave her clutch of eggs. As the trail curves along the marsh, you can see an observation deck over on its edge, at 1.5 miles. Walk down between the pines to the deck, where you can sit on a bench and take in a sweeping view of the marsh. A redwinged blackbird clings to a cattail while a white heron stalks the far shore. A dike and

Florida's first in-ground swimming pool

a fence line break up the middle of the marsh, separating the wetlands from open water. Several blue teals settle down and drift across the pond. A little blue heron fusses from atop its fencepost.

Return to the main trail and turn right. You immediately come to the junction with the Orange Trail. Continue straight, passing a firebreak as the trail curves around the marsh, thick in maidencane and sand cordgrass. The tall clusters of sand cordgrass look similar to black needlerush, but these freshwater counterparts provide wintering birds with a necessary part of their diets. Canadian geese eat the stalks of grass, while seaside sparrows survive on its seeds. As you pass another bench, the trail curves away from the pond and continues up a broad pathway with little shade. You pass through a break in a fence, continuing into an old corral at 1.9 miles. Make the first left onto a shaded road under the sand pines.

Dropping down through an oak hammock, the trail emerges into a large clearing—the group campsite, catering mainly to equestrian groups. You see scattered fire rings and picnic benches. Follow the jeep track through the open meadow until you return to the open area adjoining the parking for this trailhead. Walk straight back across to the trail kiosk, completing the 2.2-mile loop.

Continue your drive down the entrance road, passing the FISHING/PICNIC AREA sign on the left. Driving on a narrow one-lane track between the salt marshes, you reach a one-way loop. Keep right and drive along the loop until you see the PARKING AREA sign. Turn left and park in front of the environmental-education center.

CHEROKEE LODGE AND THE BLUE TRAIL

Walk down the park road toward Pellicer Creek to visit the centerpiece of Princess

Place Preserve, Cherokee Lodge. Built in 1887, this lodge is the only period example of Adirondack Camp–style architecture in Florida. Although the interior is not open to the public, you can enjoy a stroll around the expansive porches, peering in through the original water-glass windows to see the built-in cabinets and cupboards, the fine interior wood in extraordinarily good shape. Its walls are coquina blocks, quarried from the beaches on the other side of the Matanzas River. Logs of cedar and cabbage palm support the low-slung roof. Sit and relax a while on one of the rocking chairs, looking out over the river, listening to the mullet jump, and enjoying the constant salt breeze.

On the far side of the house is Florida's first in-ground swimming pool, dating back to the 1890s. A bathhouse sits at one end, with a diving board stretching out over the water. Steps lead down into the depths, covered with a thin film of algae. The artesian well constantly pours water into the upper end of the pool; the water flows out the far end, creating a splashing creek down to the Matanzas River. Walk past the pool toward the next set of buildings, and you'll see the carriage house. Illuminated by a slender shaft of sunlight, an 1890s carriage rests just inside the open door.

Head up the park road past the rest rooms to the kiosk for the Blue Trail. This loop meanders through a hardwood hammock to provide another perspective on Pellicer Creek. As you walk away from the kiosk, past an AUTHORIZED VEHICLES ONLY sign, follow the jeep road that forms this portion of the interpretive trail. Around you, tall oaks reclaim the meadow that was once the plantation's citrus grove. Sprouting out above a knot on a bluejack oak, you see a mass of dark fungus with black undersides—cracked cap polypore. At 0.6 mile you see

your first view of Pellicer Creek along this trail. The trail turns to the left to follow the creek upstream, providing glimpses of water through the trees. When you emerge in an open area, continue straight out to the observation deck along the salt marsh. Here, Stiles and Pellicer Creeks meet in a brackish estuary, where tides push the salt water in through thickets of black needlerush and smooth cordgrass. His head barely visible above the marsh grasses, a kayaker threads his way through the maze of needlerush. Across Stiles Creek you can see the picnic and fishing area where the park's 1.4-mile Yellow Trail used to start at a kiosk. Since the area was closed after a prescribed burn, the kiosk no longer marks the trailhead. The trail may reopen at some point in the future.

Walk back to the tree line and turn right to follow the trail. Nestled in the crook of a tall snag, an osprey nest sits high enough to have a commanding view of the salt marsh. At 0.8 mile a trail breaks through the fence on the right. Keep left, following the main trail as it turns away from the marsh and heads back into the hardwood hammock. A corn snake slips across the trail and dives into the safety of a saw palmetto thicket. When you emerge through a fence line, turn left. Follow the white poles across the park road to the back side of the environmental center, ending your 1.1-mile walk at the parking area.

Leave the parking area and turn left. Make an immediate right at the next road, which leads into the park's campground. Turn left at the HIKING TRAILHEAD sign and follow this one-lane road down past the canoe put-in to a parking area in front of the Green Trail kiosk.

GREEN TRAIL

Start your 0.8-mile hike on the Green Trail by following the white post up the road. Just across from the broad bridge, the trail turns right, facing an AUTHORIZED VEHICLES ONLY sign. A high canopy of live oaks shades the broad corridor. Saw palmettos rustle in the constant salt breeze blowing off the Matanzas River. Numerous interpretive markers provide plant identifications, including the uncommon evergreen wild olive, also known as devilwood. Found in a variety of habitats, it flourishes best near the sea. In autumn it produces dark blue olive-size fruits that remain attached through the winter.

Follow the white posts—most of them missing their green arrows—up to where the trail reaches a T intersection at a pond after 0.3 mile. Giant leather ferns rise from the water's edge. Passing a bench, you turn right to follow the sound of trickling water to its source. You notice a mild smell of rotten eggs as you draw close to the water; the pond is fed by an artesian well piped up into the air, its constant geyser raining down like

a fountain. Off to the right, a trail leads to the campground. Continue straight, following the main trail as it curves around the pond, passing another bench. Star rush rises from the grassy path. Along your right is a hardwood hammock shaded by moss-draped live oaks, and another bench. Notice the pond's outlet, flowing between a dense thicket of saw palmetto. Occasional strong outflows, perhaps from heavy rains, caused the high sandbanks to erode.

Passing a bench, you complete the loop. Turn right between the two white posts and walk back down into the hardwood hammock. Keep alert for some white posts off to the left that lead you on a small circuit past several interpretive markers along a marsh and in front of a large slash pine. Return to the main trail and turn left. When you see the bridge ahead of you, turn left to walk back over to the parking lot, completing the 0.8-mile hike.

47

Washington Oaks Gardens State Park

Total distance (2 circuits, 2 round trips): 4.2 miles

Hiking time: 3 hours

Habitats: Maritime hammock, coastal strand, coastal scrub, saltwater marsh, mangrove swamp

Maps: USGS 7½' Matanzas Inlet, park maps

With trails meandering under groves of ancient live oaks and through seaside gardens of stone, Washington Oaks Gardens State Park provides a variety of pleasant short hikes perfect for hikers of all ages. It's a great place to bring the kids and spend the morning or afternoon strolling along its gentle winding trails through the maritime hammock and a series of formal gardens.

From I-95 exit 289, Palm Coast, take the Palm Coast Parkway east for 3.2 miles, pausing to pay a $1 toll on the Hammock Dunes Bridge. At the end of the bridge, turn left on Camino Del Mar, and then right onto FL A1A. The park entrance is 4.1 miles north on FL A1A, on the left. Alternatively, avoid the toll bridge by taking I-95 exit 284, Flagler Beach/Bunnell. Drive 3.5 miles east on FL 100 into Flagler Beach. Turn north on FL A1A and drive 12.1 miles to the park entrance.

When you reach the park, stop and pay your Florida State Parks entrance fee at the ranger station. Just after you turn left onto the park's main road—old FL A1A, shaded by a thick canopy of grand live oaks—watch for a small sign on the right for the parking lot of the Bella Vista Trail. Depending on how much time you plan to spend at the park, you may want to park here to hike the Bella Vista Trail first. You can also park down at the main entrance for the gardens, since you can slip out of the northeastern corner of the garden to reach the Bella Vista trailhead.

Start at the main parking area, cross the road, and walk up the broad path to the

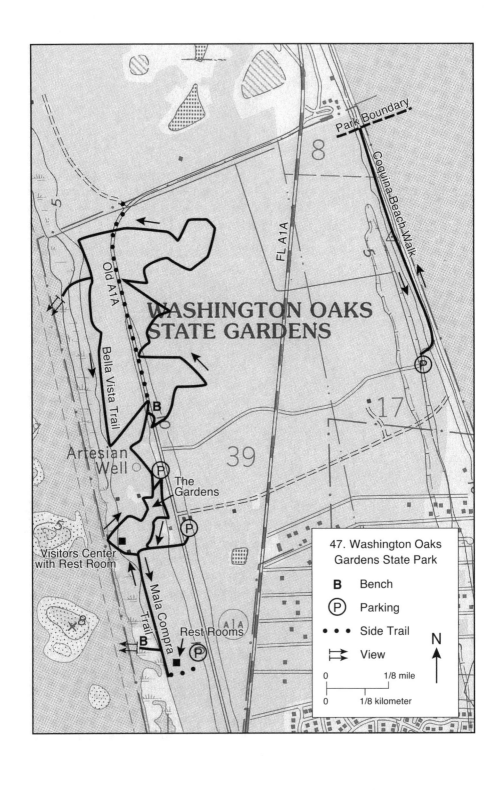

WASHINGTON OAKS
STATE GARDENS

Park Boundary

8

5

Coquina Beach Walk

FL A1A

17

39

Old A1A

Bella Vista Trail

B

Artesian
Well

P

The
Gardens

P

Visitors Center
with Rest Room

5

Mala Compra
Trail

8

B

Rest Rooms

A1A

P

47. Washington Oaks
Gardens State Park

B   Bench

P   Parking

• • •   Side Trail

View

N

0   1/8 mile

0   1/8 kilometer

visitors center, taking in the panorama of the Matanzas River. One of the original Spanish land grants, this was the site of the Bella Vista Plantation, the homestead of Gen. Joseph Hernandez. Citrus groves lined the river's shores. In 1936 Owen D. Young, the chairman of the board of General Electric, purchased the property. He and his wife expanded on the groves, adding a series of formal gardens between their riverside home (now the visitors center) and the highway (now the entrance road). After Young's death in 1964, his wife donated the property to the state to become a state park. After you examine the exhibits in the visitors center, walk over the to the MALA COMPRA TRAIL sign to start your first hike.

MALA COMPRA TRAIL

Starting out through a maritime hammock of red bay, live oak, red mulberry, and cabbage palm, the Mala Compra Trail leads you on a brief but interesting journey down the Matanzas River. The purple blooms of spiderwort peer out of the shadows under the red cedars as you pass the first of many interpretive signs. The scents of cedar and citrus intermingle with salt in the breeze. Resurrection ferns drip from the boughs of live oaks. Snags gleam with a bright sheen, polished by the salty winds.

At 0.3 mile you see a fishing-symbol sign. Turn right and follow the spur trail. It leads past a bench and over a bridge on a murky tidal creek to a small island in the Matanzas River. A picnic table and grill sit off to the right. Continue along the worn path past glasswort and samphire out to a small beach on the river. Hundreds of fiddler crabs scuttle into their holes on your approach. Black mangroves flank a bench on the water's edge, where waves will swamp your feet if a powerboat goes by. This region marks the northern extent of the black mangrove on the Atlantic coast. Each mangrove is surrounded by a network of short breathing roots protruding from the sand, like a little forest of slender cypress knees. Fiddler crabs use the mangrove roots as hiding places as they work their way down the beach.

Turn around and walk back along the spur trail. In its brown phase, a chameleon dashes across the wooden bridge and then jumps on a mangrove leaf, changing to green before your eyes. Two blue crabs work their way across the silted bottom of the tidal creek. When you return to the main trail, turn right to continue along the broad path. A cluster of cabbage palms sits off to the right, their fronds shimmering in the breeze. You pass the gnarled, windswept limbs of a dead slash pine, a perfect perch for an osprey scouring the creek. Watch for coontie growing wild in the shade along the creek's edge. After 0.4 mile the trail ends at a picnic area with rest rooms, set back in the maritime hammock, the tables shaded by spreading live oaks. Turn around and retrace the trail back to the visitors center, completing a 0.7-mile walk.

THE GARDENS

When you reach the visitors center, walk behind it, past the rest rooms, and down the staircase to follow the seawall upriver. There are several shady spots to sit and watch for manatees, which frequent these waters during the spring and summer months. Keep an eye on the waves, and you might spot bottlenosed dolphins. Fishermen work their way through the coves, and oystermen check over the distant oyster beds. You may even see canoeists and kayakers landing on the small islands. The name Matanzas, Spanish for "slaughter," comes from the murder of two ships full of shipwrecked French sailors, led by Jean Ribault, who claimed Florida for France in 1562. Sailing from Fort Caroline (Hike 37) in August 1565, they planned to attack the new settlement at St. Augustine, but shifting sandbars made it impossible for them to enter the river. Caught in a hurricane, they were blown down the coast and shipwrecked in this area. Received by the Spanish under a flag of truce, Ribault and nearly two hundred of his men were slaughtered along these shores. Only the artists, musicians, and professed Catholics were spared.

The trail turns to the right, up a series of broad steps into the hammock to enter the formal gardens that were part of the estate of the Young family. As you approach the arbor, a small deck sits off to the left for relaxing. Stop and look at the old cistern, built by George Lawrence Washington (a relative of the president), the plantation's second owner in the 1840s. It was used to collect rainwater for cooking and cleaning. Enter the gardens through the arbor into the formal rose garden. More stunning than the color of the roses in full bloom is the fragrance they waft across the sea air. As you leave the garden, close the gate behind you. Walk forward to the brick platform and admire the flowers along the placid pools. Make a left turn to start a circuit of the formal gardens. Giant leather ferns droop to meet the clear stream. You walk over many small bridges, surrounded by the sounds of flowing water from fountains. Listen to the birdsong. A cardinal teeters on a low branch, a torn leaf in its beak, building a nest. After you cross a bridge with burbling water emerging out of a rock pile on the right, continue straight ahead into the live oak hammock with its many plantings. After 0.2 mile you reach a sign pointing to the Bella Vista Trail, off to left.

BELLA VISTA TRAIL

After you walk from the gardens across the trailhead parking area, start your 1.8-mile hike on the Bella Vista trail at the trailhead kiosk with its map. At the first trail junction, turn right to follow the white blazes of the Timucuan Loop. It meanders through the maritime hammock, under live oak and southern magnolia, cabbage palm and cherry laurel. Wild coffee peeks out of the shade of the underbrush–*psychotria nervosa* at the northern extent of its range, with its distinctive glossy green leaves sporting dark crimson coffee beans each fall. Oyster fungus cascades over fallen logs. Cross the pavement of Old A1A under an arching red bay and return to the shade of the hammock. Watch for a flock of wild turkey, which roams the forest in the early mornings. The cool salt breeze riffles through a mockernut hickory, and goldfoot fern cascades from a tall cabbage palm. Live oaks create the high canopy overhead, and coontie pokes up through drifts of leaves on the forest floor. The Timucua used the roots of coontie in "sufkee stew," a mainstay of their diet; European settlers dried and ground its poisonous raw roots to make starch for arrowroot bread.

As the trail rises slightly, saw palmettos fill the understory, and you enter an oak scrub: a collection of spindly bluejack oaks and gnarled sand live oaks no more than 15 feet tall. Looking off to the right, you can see blue sky beyond the trees. Only FL A1A divides this forest from the coastal dunes. The trail veers to the left, entering an older, taller hammock of American holly and red bay. The forest becomes denser and darker at 0.5 mile as you pass an immense slash pine with a 6-foot circumference. A tall mound of duff encircles the tree, created from years of accumulation of pine needles at its base.

Natural coquina bridge

Young saw palmettos poke out of the forest floor in single- and double-leaf blades that look like mutant blades of grass. The trail continues back into the oak scrub, where the saw palmetto takes on a silvery blue hue from the salt in the air. The prevailing sea breeze sculpts the branches of the live oaks.

You enter an open, windswept scrub, the habitat of the Florida scrub-jay. The last scrub-jays were sighted here in 1990, and it's suspected that red-tailed hawks caused their demise. Lyonia and saw palmetto makes up dense thicket up to 7 feet high. You see a power line ahead, just beyond the northern edge of park. The trail turns left, returning to the shaded maritime hammock. At 1.1 miles you cross Old A1A again, entering the forest between two tall stone pillars that once served as a gateway to the plantation. You can see the sky through the trees on the right as the trail curves left to parallel the Matanzas River. At 1.2 miles a short spur trail on the right leads out to the edge of the river, ending in a salt marsh full of black needlerush. Passing boats send waves into a sandbar covered with black mangroves.

Return to the main path and turn right to walk under the arched limbs of red bay trees. Creating giant fungal shelves, white cheese polypores protrude from the dense wood of a fallen red bay. The trail makes a sharp left into a grassy corridor flanked with small trees, passing a sugar hackberry with its mottled, warty gray bark. Beds of sword ferns thrive in the shade of the live oaks. You reach the end of the loop at 1.7 miles. Continue straight ahead to the trailhead, completing the Bella Vista Trail after 1.8 miles.

THE GARDENS

Upon your return from the Bella Vista Trail, turn left. Continue along the meandering pathways through the live oak hammock, past benches set in scenic spots for quiet contemplation. When you reach a live oak with a massive staghorn fern dangling from its limbs, turn right to continue along the path, past camellias in full fragrant bloom. A burbling sound rises from an artesian well, drilled in the early 1890s by George Lawrence Washington. Using hollow cypress logs, he routed water from this well to irrigate his citrus groves. The stringy white substance on the bottom of the pond is bacteria living off the natural sulfur from the well, which fills the air with a faint rotten-egg odor. After you return back around the loop to the brick platform, turn left to exit the gardens. At the T intersection with the entrance trail, turn left. Returning to the parking area, you complete the 0.5-mile garden walk.

COQUINA BEACH

Driving out of the park entrance gate, carefully cross A1A and continue straight ahead to the beach parking area for an experience no other Florida beach can offer. Clamber up and over the strand on the boardwalk and look to the north to take in the sweep of the coastal dunes and of the orange-tinged beach with its massive boulders. The boulders are coquina, a limestone formed by the compression of coquina shell fragments such as those that form the sand of this beach.

Leave the boardwalk and turn left. Stroll slowly along this rare rocky shoreline, savoring the unusual views. This is an outcrop of the Anastasia formation, a ridge of limestone that runs along the coast from St. Augustine to Palm Beach. Climb up and peer into the many potholes in the rocks, some creating tidal pools ringed with seaweed, some dry and filled with trapped seashells. Stop and marvel at the ever-changing landscape of towers and bridges in miniature, knobs and rims creating strange patterns across the boulders. Watch the waves break over shelves of limestone, combing through stringers of seaweed. When you reach the signs that indicate the park boundary, you've walked 0.5 mile. Turn around and walk back up the beach, completing your 1-mile stroll at the parking lot.

48

Graham Swamp Conservation Area

Total distance (circuit): 1 mile

Hiking time: 45 minutes

Habitats: Flatwoods pond, Freshwater marsh, floodplain forest, hardwood hammock, bayhead, sand pine scrub

Maps: USGS 7½' Beverly Beach, St. Johns Water Management District map

Scarcely 2 miles from the Atlantic Ocean, water lilies drift across a placid blackwater pond, an aquatic garden nurturing coontail and southern naiad in its depths. Flowing off into a dense cypress swamp, the sparkling waters become the basis of a creek—Bulow Creek, which flows south to the Tomoka River. With 3,042 acres protected as water management lands, the Graham Swamp is a rare place, a freshwater floodplain close enough to the sea to create a barrier to saltwater intrusion. Compared to the protected land, the trail is short—but most of the land is a cypress swamp, dark and wet, inaccessible except by map, compass, and extreme tenacity.

Just down the road from busy Palm Coast, the Graham Swamp Conservation Area sits just off one of the original roads through the region, the Old Kings Road. From I-95 exit 289, Palm Coast, take the Palm Coast Parkway east to the first traffic light. Turn right and follow Old Kings Road south for 1.4 miles to the parking area and trailhead on the left. Although this trail is short, it provides a primitive campsite, ideal for families or for folks taking a "test run" on backpacking. No permit is needed unless your group exceeds six people, but the site (which accommodates four tents) is first come, first served. Be a good citizen and bring along a trash bag to scoop up litter when you see it—far too many visitors to this trail drop their garbage in the forest.

Grab a map from the trail kiosk and start your hike through the entry point to the right of the kiosk. Blazed in red, the trail starts

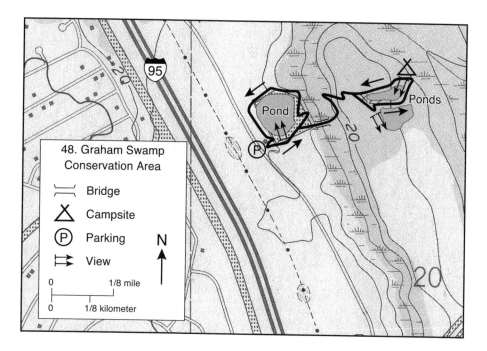

along the southern edge of a large black-water pond. Beautiful sand bluffs on the far shore host a forest of sand pines. Cool coastal breezes push yellow water lilies across the dark water. You descend from sand pines into a dark hammock of sweetgum and loblolly bay, meeting a trail junction at 0.1 mile. Turn right. The trail straight ahead takes you back around the lake, and you'll use it on the return trip.

After dropping through a floodplain forest of bald cypress, the trail rises up onto a small ridge under the shade of southern magnolias, paralleling a shallow tannic creek from which cypress knees protrude. The squishy dark soil underfoot reminds you that this is a floodplain forest, and this trail floods now and again. Crossing over a bridge, the trail rises up into an oak hammock. Elder statesmen of the forest, the live oaks spread their branches out in a seamless canopy. Southern magnolias show off their dinner plate–size blooms. The saw palmettos

have a silvery green tinge, characteristic of these plants when they grow close to the sea. All around you, you see coontie–also known as Florida arrowroot, a native cycad that was once a staple in the diets of the Timucua and Seminoles. Although the raw stem of the plant is poisonous, it was processed–crushed into a powder, washed and strained, and set out to dry to become a starch–and made into bread. If you look in the baby-food section of a grocery store, you can find arrowroot biscuits–made from the pulverized root of the coontie. It's marketed as a digestion aid for babies who are just learning to eat solid food.

After emerging from the hammock, the trail winds through a stretch of sand pine forest. At 0.3 miles you reach a T intersection at another large pond. Turn right. A coot floats among the cattails while a swallow-tailed kite swoops overhead. Nesting in bald cypresses, swallow-tailed kites return to Florida each spring in order to breed and

Flatwoods pond

raise their young. Building a nest from Spanish moss in the tallest cypress in a stand, they lay two eggs and care for their young through July, when the birds migrate to South America. The swallow-tailed kite is a social bird, foraging in flocks and roosting at night in groups of one hundred or more.

As the dike works its way around the pond, you come to another pond off to the right. Stay with the established trail and continue around the pond. A blue heron takes off with a squawk as you approach, causing a small alligator to give up its sunny spot and splash into the water. On the east side of the pond, at 0.4 mile, you reach the campsite. There's not much to it—a couple of logs on the ground make good seats around the fire ring—but since the campsite is set under an opening in the oak canopy, it's a nice place to pitch a tent and look out on the pond. From here, with map and compass and a willingness to get your feet wet, it's possible to explore the backcountry of this conservation area, winding your way along the cypress-lined channels that drain down into Bulow Creek.

To exit the campsite, follow the red blaze out of its north side. The trail is slightly indistinct but leads to the left, paralleling the walk around the dike—but in the shade of the forest. A creek parallels to the left. Coral bean displays its brilliant red blooms, and more coontie is scattered under the trees. As you emerge from the shade, turn right and continue along the pond, back to the T intersection marked by a strongly leaning sand pine with a red blaze. Turn right to retrace this section of trail. When you get to a spot where it looks like the trail goes straight and to the right, turn right—confirming your turn with a red blaze on your right on a cabbage palm. Crossing the creek, you notice bamboo in the floodplain and thick clumps of sphagnum moss clustered around a side pool. A large barred owl wings past, alighting in the top of a young bald cypress to scan the forest floor for signs of prey.

Dropping back off the ridge into the cypresses and loblolly bay, you come to a T intersection at 0.7 mile. Turn right to loop around the far side of the big pond. The saw palmettos crowd closely around this narrow path, which is distinct but not well maintained. Pause at an opening on the edge of the lake, looking down into the dark, clear water to see the aquatic plants that thrive beneath the surface. You hear the chirp of a leopard frog. Watch a few moments as the breeze riffles the lake surface. It's interesting how the water lilies are pushed along by the wind—first gently, looking like they're popping up due to a fish swimming under them, and then more strongly, making the leaves crumple and curl like lettuce leaves in a salad.

A few more minutes down the trail, and you come to a water obstacle—the outflow of the pond. You have two options. Carefully jump across it, or scrabble through the underbrush to the right to walk through a soggy spot. Royal and cinnamon ferns line a shaded opening onto the lake as you wander along a bayhead. The pinecones floating in the water—tightly closed, long, and tapered—are those of the sand pine, which does not open its cones willingly. It usually takes the heat of a forest fire to make sand pine cones burst open and fling their seeds to the winds. As you rise up a steep slope, you curve up into the sand pine forest. Here the trail is broader, easy to follow as you walk along the sandy bluffs above the pond. Reaching a stand of myrtle oaks, the trail veers away from the lake into a shady sand pine scrub, headed toward the entry gate. You return to the kiosk, completing the 1-mile loop.

49

Haw Creek Preserve

Total distance (round trip): 1.6 miles

Hiking time: 1 hour

Habitats: Floodplain forest, oak hammock, hydric hammock

Maps: USGS 7½' St. Johns Park

With its beautiful boardwalk along an unspoiled, slow-moving blackwater creek, little-known Haw Creek Preserve provides a delightful venue for watching wildlife. Comprising slightly more than 1,000 acres, this Flagler County Park protects 2 miles of Haw Creek, which drains swamplands to the east into Crescent Lake.

If you're traveling southbound on I-95, take exit 298. Follow US 1 south for 14 miles to FL 100 in Bunnell. From I-95 northbound take exit 284, Flagler Beach/Bunnell. Follow FL 100 west for 4.8 miles, crossing US 1 in Bunnell. Continue west on FL 100 for another 7.5 miles to FL 305. Turn left. Drive south on FL 305 for 4.1 miles until you reach CR 2006. Turn right. After 1 mile turn left on CR 2007, a dirt road, at the large Russell Landing sign. Drive 2.2 miles, passing the Pellicer Community Center. The road enters Haw Creek Preserve and ends at a parking area along RUSSELL LANDING, a small park with picnic tables and grills, rest rooms, and a boat ramp.

The boardwalk starts down near the boat ramp—look for the trailhead sign. Lifting you up over the floodplain forest of Haw Creek, the trail meanders between cabbage palm and sweetgum, hickory and cypress. A large brown anole clambers up a laurel oak, showing off taupe diamonds and a white stripe down its back. Cardinal wild pine grows in profusion along the trunks of pond cypress. Cypress knees march off into the underbrush. At the first turnoff, turn right. You arrive at a platform along the creek, where a bench provides a peaceful

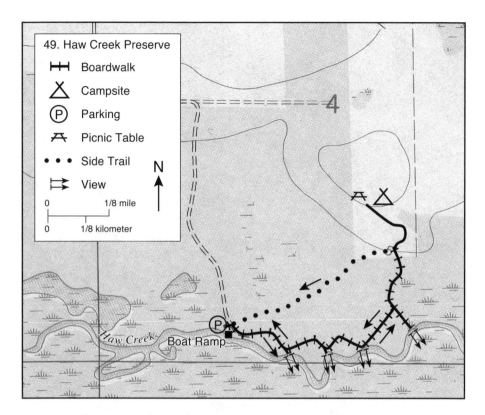

place to sit and look over the placid dark water. The stands of cypress on the far side are blanketed in wild pine. Beware the vine-like growth of poison ivy on a sweetgum on the platform's edge, mimicking a hickory branch. Sweetgum drop their black balls into the water. A pileated woodpecker hammers away at a mockernut hickory, the sound of its big beak echoing down the creek. On the far shore you see a small alligator slide down between the cypress knees and into the water.

Return to the main boardwalk and turn right. Dappled shadows of cabbage palm fronds lie across the trunks of live oaks. With fernlike leaves, a trumpet vine climbs high up a sweetgum, its bright orange bell-shaped flowers swaying in the breeze. Light green goldfoot ferns and long, dark green

streamers of shoelace fern dangle below the fronds of a cabbage palm as you come up to the next turnoff. Butterfly orchids droop over the crook of a live oak. Turn right and walk down to the platform. A green anole races along the brown wood. Above you, a red-tailed hawk lets out its territorial cry. You come to an overlook of a bend in Haw Creek, where young pond cypresses crowd along the curve. Pennywort and elephant ears grow directly below. Look out over the cove to the left, and you can see largemouth bass jumping for flies, leaving trails of bubbles as they sink to the bottom. Sunlight illuminates the leaves of a gnarled bluejack oak, covered in red blanket lichen, creating dappling reflections in the creek below. Off to the right, what you thought was a log starts drifting against the current—the form of an

Haw Creek

alligator nearly 10 feet long. It slowly makes its way into the shallows, settling against the muddy bank.

Head back to the main boardwalk and turn right, watching a green anole leap from leaf to leaf on a saw palmetto frond. The boardwalk crosses over a channel that shows signs of occasionally flooding down into the creek. Scattered deerberry grows throughout the floodplain. Turn right at the next boardwalk for another look at Haw Creek from a broad overlook. A swallow-tailed kite swoops and dives overhead, showing off its distinctive forked tail. These magnificent birds migrate to Florida in February and March from South America. Mated for life, the kites work together to build a nest of Spanish moss and tiny twigs in the tallest cypress they can find, in the same neighborhood of their previous year's nest. Sitting on two eggs for nearly a month, the female accepts food brought from her mate. Both parents raise the chicks on a diet of frogs, snakes, lizards, bats, and small birds.

Back on the main boardwalk, turn right to continue along the trail through a corridor of cabbage palms. Caught working hard on extracting insects from a snag, a downy woodpecker flies off at your approach. Bluejack oaks arch over the trail, providing a canopy for the younger cabbage palms, many festooned with streamers of shoelace fern. At the next side trail, turn right and walk down to the platform, the last one along the creek. An oak branch covered in lichens looks like it's been painted pink and cream. Pond cypresses model their feathery, light green spring growth. Looking out over the broad expanse of water, you see tiny islands upstream, covered in pennywort and elephant ears, providing hiding places for hooded mergansers and limpkins. Cattails crowd the shore.

Ripples radiate outward as a Florida softshell turtle pokes its pointy snout out of the water, breaking up the reflections of clouds that drift across the dark surface. Return to the main trail and turn right.

At 0.6 mile the boardwalk starts to turn left, away from the creek, carrying you under the shadows of live oaks. Standing out in a sunny spot, a cabbage palm shows off its cascade of olive-colored shoelace ferns. A dense bed of blue flag irises flanks the boardwalk, sporting dark purple blooms in the shade on the left and lighter purple blooms in the sun. As the boardwalk ends, it drops you out into a large open field where small chunks of coquina lie scattered about. A swallow-tailed kite performs aerial acrobatics over the open grass—either showing off its sheer joy of flight or chasing dragonflies across the sky—an enchanting ballet in midair.

On the far right side of the field, you see a gray building with a tin roof. Walk over to it and check out the group campsite, available to backpackers by permit from the county parks office. Tucked away in the shade of southern red cedar and longleaf pine, the campsite has a fire ring and a stack of firewood ready for use. A picnic table sits under the gray building, and a water pump provides fresh water. The campsite marks the end of the trail, at 0.8 mile.

You have two options to return to the parking area. If you retrace your pleasant, leisurely walk along the boardwalk, you'll complete a hike of 1.6 miles. However, if you'd like a more direct—albeit swampy—route back to Russell Landing, walk straight across the field to its far corner, across from the campsite. A rough path carved by maintenance vehicles leads into the hydric hammock. There are no blazes, and the dark, shady hammock can be very mucky with its layer of thick black mud on the forest floor. Follow the tread marks from the vehicles. The trail rises out of the hydric hammock into a much drier oak hammock surrounded by saw palmetto. You emerge behind the rest rooms, pointed toward the picnic pavilion, completing a 1.3-mile hike by this rough route.

50

Bulow Creek Trail

Total distance (1 circuit, 1 one-way):
7.8 miles

Hiking time: 4 hours

Habitats: Oak hammock, hydric hammock,
hardwood hammock, floodplain forest,
saltwater marsh, pine plantation

Maps: USGS 7½' Flagler Beach East,
park map, Florida Trail Association
map NF-2

Following the winding course of Bulow Creek, scarcely 3 miles from the roar of the Atlantic Ocean, the Bulow Creek Trail connects two sites important to Florida's history. At the north end lie the ruins of the Bulow Plantation sugar mill, circa 1831–the largest such complex in the state of Florida. At the south end you'll find the Fairchild Oak, a gargantuan tree thought to be, at two thousand years old or more, one of the oldest oaks in the South. Between them is enjoyable walking through a primeval forest, kept dark by the ancient trees that tower over it.

A hike of the Bulow Creek Trail requires some logistical planning, but there are several good options. If you're hiking with a friend, leave one car at the parking area at Bulow Creek State Park and the other at Bulow Plantation Ruins State Park, where you can leave your car in the small trailhead parking area outside the park gate. If you have only one car and a limited amount of time, hike the 5.2-mile Bulow Creek Loop by connecting the orange-blazed trail with a blue-blazed shortcut. Or, plan a 14-mile round trip from Bulow Plantation Ruins State Park to the Fairchild Oak and back, with or without the use of the primitive campsite available to backpackers. If you plan to backpack, you must pick up a free permit from the ranger's office at Tomoka State Park, located 4.5 miles south of Bulow Creek State Park along Old Dixie Highway.

Take I-95 exit 278, Old Dixie Highway, just north of Ormond Beach. To reach the

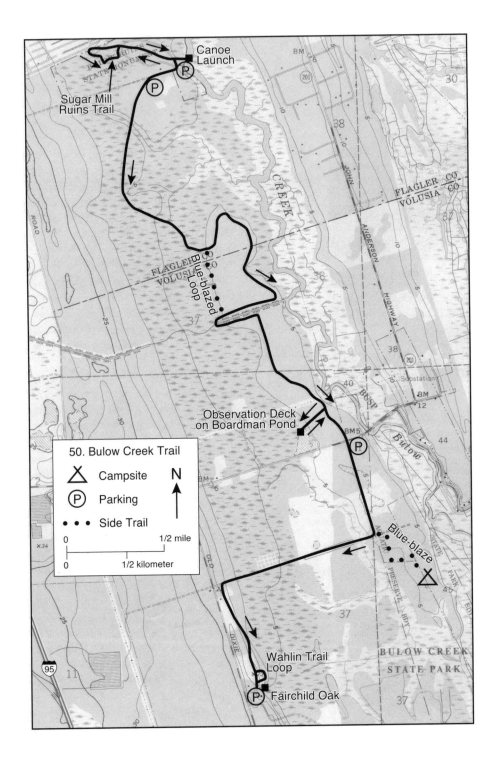

Canoe Launch

Sugar Mill Ruins Trail

CREEK

FLAGLER CO
VOLUSIA CO

Blue-blazed Loop

FLAGLER CO
VOLUSIA CO

Observation Deck on Boardman Pond

Blue-blaze

50. Bulow Creek Trail

△ Campsite

Ⓟ Parking

••• Side Trail

N

0   1/2 mile

0   1/2 kilometer

Wahlin Trail Loop

Fairchild Oak

BULOW CREEK
STATE PARK

northern trailhead, head south on Old Dixie Highway and immediately turn left onto Old Kings Road (CR 2001). Drive 3.6 miles to the entrance for Bulow Plantation Ruins Historic State Park, on the right. Follow Plantation Road, a one-lane sand road, 1 mile to the park entrance. Free parking for the trailhead is available on the right at the BULOW WOODS HIKING TRAIL sign, just before you reach the park entrance. For the southern trailhead, continue south on Old Dixie Highway from I-95 for 1.9 miles, passing Walter Boardman Lane en route. Enter Bulow Creek State Park, on the left, and park in the small parking area in front of the Fairchild Oak.

SUGAR MILL TRAIL

At Bulow Plantation Ruins State Park, the main attraction is the 1821 sugar mill, Florida's largest and most productive sugar mill of its time. Abandoned in 1836 during the Second Seminole War, it was sacked and burned by the Seminoles. Before you start your hike on the 6.5-mile Bulow Creek Trail, take time to explore the Bulow Plantation via the 1-mile Sugar Mill Trail. Drive into the entrance for Bulow Plantation Ruins State Park and pay the self-pay $2-per-vehicle fee.

For a pleasant stroll through the plantation's history, park your car at the first parking lot, next to Bulow Creek. A crisp breeze comes off this brackish marsh. You can rent a canoe to explore the estuary, picnic in bug-free comfort in the screened room, or make use of the rest rooms before starting off on the Sugar Mill Trail, which begins on the opposite side of the parking lot. Entering an oak hammock with scattered southern magnolia, you walk along a footpath of finely ground shells. In 1821 Maj. Charles Wilhelm Bulow acquired 4,675 acres along the creek and used slave labor

to clear 2,200 acres for a plantation of sugar cane, cotton, rice, and indigo. When the major died in 1823, his 17-year-old son, John, took over management of the plantation. You come to the foundation of a former slave cabin, part of a long row of "framed and shingled" cabins that stood within view of Bulow Creek. More than two hundred slaves worked the plantation. When John James Audubon visited Bulow for Christmas in 1831, he noted that Bulow "is now erecting some extensive buildings for a sugar house." Audubon is thought to have painted his *Greater Yellowlegs* during his visit to the plantation, showing the row of slave cabins in the background.

As you walk along, notice the many catfaces on the slash pines. Some are covered in nubs of orange-gold and yellow, from sap leaking out and solidifying. Many trees display only gashes where the trunk has healed. Turpentining continued in this grove up until World War II. Scattered coontie grows in the shade of the forest. You see a live oak on the right with a massive cavity in its base, so big that you can walk right through it.

The trail emerges at a parking lot next to the towering ruins of the sugar mill. Although they look like concrete stained by fire, the rock is coquina—a limestone made up of compressed seashells. Cross the parking lot and turn right to follow the trail around the ruins. Planted in January and February, sugar cane would be harvested in October and brought here to the mill. A steam boiler ran the rollers that crushed the cane, which rode up on a conveyor belt to the second floor to be pressed flat between the rollers. Cane juice ran down to the bottom floor into kettles, which were ladled out into troughs for cooling. After processing, the raw sugar and molasses would be floated on flatboats down Bulow Creek to the Halifax River and on to Mosquito Inlet in New Smyrna, where ships sailed out to the Caribbean and the East Coast with Bulow's products. The town of Bulowville grew up around the mill. In 1836 a Seminole war party burned the town, the plantation, and the mill, causing the settlers to flee. With no guarantee of his plantation's future safety, Bulow did not return.

Behind the mill, a NATURE TRAIL sign points to a trail to the spring house. You pass a large catfaced pine as you walk down into the floodplain forest along the spring, contained by rectangular coquina walls. The perpetual flow escapes through a hole and forms a small run down to Bulow Creek. Small, arching coquina bridges provide a route around the spring as the path winds through the forest and back to the sugar mill. When you reach the sidewalk, turn right. Continue your walk around the mill, taking time to walk down the path to the right to the small interpretive exhibit.

Cross the parking lot to the NATURE TRAIL sign, past the representative plantings of indigo, corn, and sugar cane—the primary crops of the plantation's heyday. Return through the cool shade of the forest to your car, watching for the scurrying of gray squirrels and the fluttering of Carolina wrens, completing this 1-mile hike.

Park hours are 9 AM to 5 PM, so you may want to move your vehicle outside the park gate to the Bulow Creek Trail trailhead to avoid being locked in, depending on the planned length of your hike on the Bulow Creek Trail.

BULOW CREEK TRAIL

At the trailhead, the BULOW WOODS HIKING TRAIL sign shows the loop that comprises the first half of the Bulow Creek Trail. If you are not planning to hike the second half of the trail, the Fairchild Oak Trail, use this map as your guide. Slather on the mosquito repellent; you'll be walking along the edges of marshes and swamps for much of the hike.

The trail starts out in an oak hammock with scattered slash pine; older live oak draped in resurrection fern; tall, thin laurel oak; large southern magnolia; and ironwood, also known as hornbeam. With rich, dark soil underfoot, you're walking along the edge of the floodplain forest of Bulow Creek, and you may find the footpath soggy in places—the forest is full of low spots with standing water. Crossing a bridge, you continue through the dense greenery as the trail winds to the left at a double blaze, continuing to jog left. It narrows down to a single track through a grassy area, passing cracked cap polypores emerging from a fallen cabbage palm trunk. Sporadic interpretive markers explain the trees you walk by. Red bay and red maple grow in the floodplain. The humidity encourages a furry coating of sphagnum moss to envelop the bases of the cabbage palms. A live oak rises more than 100 feet overhead. A thick layer of moss marches up its trunk, providing a soft bed from which sword ferns sprout. As the forest becomes wetter, marsh ferns fill in under the trees.

You cross a bridge over a narrow, slow-flowing clear stream at 0.7 mile, its sand bottom sparkling in the sunlight. The stream picks up speed as it rounds several oxbow bends. Sprouting from the mossy green surface of a downed oak, the spreading forms of artist's conk radiate, each more than 18 inches wide. If a sketch is etched into its easily bruised white surface, it will stand out when these giant fungi dry. As you walk along, take care not to trip over the many roots in the trail. Goldfoot ferns emerge from the top of a cabbage palm. Gigantic live oaks spread their massive limbs, creating the high canopy. A sweet-

Bulow Sugar Mill ruins

gum rains crimson leaves onto the trail; adjoining it, another sweetgum unfolds tiny light green leaves. You cross two planks suspended over the stream as a bridge. Scattered sneezeweed shows off its bright yellow blooms, and lavender-colored violets emerge from the forest floor. The coating of lichen on the trees is so thick it looks like whitewash. As you walk along, the trail squishes.

At 1.5 miles you reach the junction where the loop trail starts. The sign says CISCO DITCH VIA PINE HAMMOCK TRAIL 0.6 to the right and CISCO DITCH VIA MARSH TRAIL 1.6 straight ahead. If you're headed to the Fairchild Oak, the blue-blazed trail to the right cuts a mile off the hike—but the Marsh Trail, straight ahead, takes you through far more interesting terrain. Continue straight, following the orange blazes past a cluster of velvety orange peel mushrooms, their

cuplike insides gleaming like jelly. As you gain a little elevation, you're surrounded with a hardwood hammock of southern magnolia, scattered hickory trees, and sweetgum, with cabbage palm interspersed throughout. Bamboo rises from the forest floor, and the forest crowds closer. You approach a sluggish creek along the edge of a hydric hammock, where enormous giant leather ferns set a primordial scene straight out of the Jurassic period. The trail skirts along the edge of the floodplain; the air is filled with an earthy aroma. You see shimmers in the water, small fish racing upstream.

The trail turns slightly uphill, away from the creek bank and into a forest of pines and young oaks, emerging at a sweeping vista along the edge of the wetlands of Bulow Creek. An osprey swoops overhead, surveying the marsh. Dahoon holly grows along the edge of this salt marsh, showing off its red berries against the black needlerush. You walk through a tunnel of Walter viburnum, their tiny white bell blooms raining down on the footpath. A large southern red cedar stretches its limbs out over a small spot of open water in the savanna. After the trail turns inland, away from the salt marsh and into the hardwood hammock, it's carpeted with a dense layer of loblolly pine needles. In a blur of yellow wings, a palm warbler streaks by. All around you, coontie covers the forest floor. Also known as Florida arrowroot, this endangered plant provided a staple food for the Timucua and the early settlers of Florida, who learned to soak and dry its poisonous roots to create a starch, arrowroot. In the early 1900s biscuit companies descended on Florida's forests, decimating the native coontie population, which does not transplant well. A slow-growing cycad, it continues to be a popular ornamental plant for landscaping. In early spring the glossy orange-red seed pods of the coontie look like miniature bell peppers.

As the trail rounds a floodplain forest on the left, it rises up through a cut and comes to a swiftly flowing canal—Cisco Ditch, its sand bottom sparkling in the sun beneath water the color of iced tea. You've hiked 3.1 miles. The orange blazes follow the water's edge up to your decision point for this hike. At the trail junction, the blue-blazed trail to the right leads back to the main trail along Bulow Creek, where you can turn left and return to your car, completing a 5.2-mile hike.

If you plan to hike to the Fairchild Oak, continue straight ahead, following the orange blazes along the creek. The trail makes a hard left around a side channel, reaching a broad bridge across Cisco Ditch, a scenic spot under the shade of the oak trees. Fossilized seashells gleam with iridescence along the sandy bottom of the stream; flowing tapegrass waves in the current. After you cross the bridge, the trail skirts a floodplain forest and turns to parallel the creek's other shore as it broadens into an old forest road. The remainder of the hike primarily sticks to forest roads. At 3.5 miles turn right at the T intersection. The trail continues down a broad lane edged on both sides by saw palmettos, shaded by massive live oaks thick with resurrection ferns. Carolina jessamine climbs up and over shrubs along the trail, dropping its fading fragrant yellow blooms.

You pass under a power line and can see a stretch of open blue water off to the left in the salt marsh—Bulow Creek. At the BOARDMAN POND OBSERVATION PLATFORM sign, turn right and follow this short spur trail for a close-up look at a brackish inland pond. Jogging through a couple of sharp turns, it reaches a bench on a platform along the edge of the water. The smell of salt rises from the water. Glasswort grows from the remains of a cabbage palm stump. A great blue heron stalks the shallow mud flats, while brown pelicans preen themselves on a tiny island.

Return to the main trail and turn right. Skirt around the park gate and carefully cross Walter Boardman Lane, which cuts Bulow Creek State Park in two. A small parking area off to the left is another possible place to leave a car to create a shorter one-way hike, or to simply hike in to Boardman Pond for bird-watching. On the far side of the road, follow the high-and-dry forest road through a pine plantation until you reach a fork in the road at 5.1 miles. Keep right. You reach a T intersection with the sign GATE B7 to your right. To continue along the main trail to the Fairchild Oak, turn right. However, if you are backpacking, turn left to follow the blue blazes 0.4 mile to the primitive campsite. The blue blazes make a sharp right and meander through the oak hammock until the trail reaches a fire ring under a stand of laurel oaks. If you use this campsite, you must haul in all your water—the water in Bulow Creek and the surrounding wetlands is too brackish for consumption.

From Gate B7 the main trail emerges from the pines onto a long causeway through an open salt marsh teeming with fish. Cross the bridge and continue into the forest on the other side, where incursions of salt marsh seem out of place among the pines. The habitat shifts to floodplain forest, flanking both sides of the trail. Sneezeweed grows on tiny islands in the swamp, adding splashes of yellow to the dark green forest. A clear stream parallels the trail on the right. Although a culvert drains it under the roadbed, the stream manages to overflow its banks in places, creating large puddles across the trail. As the trail rises you can see traffic up ahead, through the gate—Old Dixie Highway, at 5.9 miles. Just before you reach the gate, the trail turns left onto another forest road. Keep alert for the blazes.

The trail rises up out of the floodplain forest into an oak hammock with centuries-old live oaks, a hint of the giant trees to come. When you reach the clearing at Bulow Creek State Park, take a moment to walk down the interpretive Wahlin Trail, which forks off the main trail to the left, along the edge of a fenced-in building. The trail drops down into the floodplain forest onto a boardwalk that circles a small seep spring. Pause and enjoy a rare sound in Florida—flowing, burbling water—as the seepage stream drops down a steep slope. Rising back up, the trail makes a right turn to follow the seepage stream through the floodplain forest, looping back around to the high ground above the spring. Keep to the right, emerging back at the beginning of the trail after this 0.3-mile detour.

Continue straight past the building ruins and rest room to the parking lot, ending your 6.8-mile hike from Bulow Plantation Ruins State Park. The enormous tree in front of you is the Fairchild Oak, the state's largest oak, named for Florida's famed botanist David Fairchild, who decided the tree was a natural cross between a laurel oak and a live oak. It would take at least eight people holding hands to encircle the base of this magnificent tree, which is more than two thousand years old—so ancient that many of the limbs have embedded themselves in the ground and reemerged, healthy and dense with new growth. Resurrection fern stakes a claim in the oak's upper branches. Several other massive oaks lie within this small clearing, a testament to the enduring vigor and beauty of nature when left on its own.

Index

A

Addresses, 26–29
Advice and precautions, 21–25
Agricultural station, 39, 42, 43
Air plant, 72, 119
Air potato, 176, 177
Al Georges Boardwalk, Lower Suwannee National Wildlife Refuge, 82
Alachua, FL, 122
Alachua County, 17, 137
Allegheny Chinquapin tree, 113, 127
Allelopathy, 207
Alligator, American, 21, 155, 158, 160, 161, 264
Alligator Lake Recreation Area, 18, 110–114
Amelia Island, 247
Amelia Island Lighthouse, 240
Amelia Island Plantation, 245
American basswood tree, 68
American beautyberry, 114, 152, 307
American eel, 201
American holly tree, 38, 70, 176, 305–306
American kestrel, 127, 165
American robin, 196
Anastasia Inlet, 308
Anastasia Island, 17
Anastasia limestone, 326
Anastasia State Park, 303–308
Ancient Dunes Trail, Anastasia State Park, 306–307
Anderson Springs Loop, Twin Rivers State Forest, 43–47
Andrews Road, Andrews Wildlife Management Area, 68, 70

Andrews Wildlife Management Area, 64, 66–72
Apex Trail, Goethe State Forest, 162, 165–168
Apple snail, 203
Armadillo, 216, 279
Army Corps of Engineers, 179
Arrowroot, 88, 154, 295
Artesian wells, 24, 177, 320, 326
Artist's conk, 340
Astor, FL, 184, 189, 200
Atlantic Beach Hike, Fort Clinch State Park, 243–244
Atlantic Coast, 15, 285–343
Atsena Otie Key, Cedar Keys National Wildlife Refuge, 92–97
Audubon, John James, 15, 17, 339
Azalea, 19, 174, 176, 177
Azalea Trail, Ravine Gardens State Park, 177, 178

B

Bachman sparrow, 274
Backpacking, 17, 21, 22, 24
Backpacking: One Step at a Time (Manning), 24
Backpacking (Hall), 24
Baker County, 17
Balanced Rock Trail, Suwannee River State Park, 37, 38
Bald cypress tree, 20, 50, 215–216
Bald eagle, 79, 95, 187
Baldwin, FL, 105, 231
Ball moss, 212
Bamboo, 113, 135, 163
Bamboo Springs Trail, Ravine Gardens State Park,

176–177
Banana palm, 176
Banded water snake, 121
Barberville, FL, 184, 189, 200, 218
Barred owl, 18, 176
Barrier island, 19, 92, 245, 311, 314
Bartram, William
    on animal life, 73, 161
    on flora and fauna, 17, 175–176, 281
    on geology, 77, 78, 144, 151, 188
    travels in Florida, 15
Bartram's ixia, 15, 224, 281
Basin, 20
Basswood honey, 68
Basswood Trail, Andrews Wildlife Management Area, 68
Basswood tree, 44
Battle of Horse Landing, 183
Battle of Olustee, 35, 107
Bauldina, 217
Bay, 20
Bay magnolia, 20
Bayard Point Conservation Area, 286–291
Bayhead, 20, 163, 165
Beach Hike, Anastasia State Park, 307–308
Beach morning glory, 244, 249, 251
Beard tongue, 226, 275
Bearded grass-pink, 277, 281
Beargrass, 171, 196
Beaver, 41, 126
Bedrock, 17, 37
Beech tree, 19
Bella Vista Plantation, Washington Oaks Gardens

State Park, 323
Bella Vista Trail, Washington
    Oaks Gardens State Park,
    321, 324–326
Bellamy Road, O'Leno State
    Park, 118, 121
Belleview, FL, 179
Belted kingfisher, 81
Big Gum Swamp Wilderness,
    Osceola National Forest,
    100–104
Big Oak Trail, Suwannee River
    State Park, 33, 39–42
Big Pine Trail, Big Talbot Island
    State Park, 248–249
Big Scrub, Ocala National
    Forest, 192, 194, 200, 204
Big Shoals, 54–60
Big Shoals Trail, 54–59
Big Talbot Island, 245–249
Big Talbot Island Beach Walk,
    Big Talbot Island State Park,
    247
Big Talbot Island State Park,
    245–249
Biking, 23
Bird Blind Loop, Jennings
    State Forest, 274
Bird Key, 92
Bison, 17, 111, 151, 154, 161
Bitter panicum, 95, 299
Black Creek Ravines
    Conservation Area, 18,
    277–283
Black Lake Trail, O'Leno State
    Park, 119, 120–121
Black mangrove, 95, 96, 323
Black needlerush, 80, 81, 249
Black polypore fungus, 203
Black Prong Trail, Goethe
    State Forest, 163, 169–171
Black racer, 24, 154
Black vulture, 78
Blackbeard, 245
Blackberry, 110, 168, 226,
    264
Blackjack oak tree, 109
Blackrock Beach, 223, 248
Blackrock Trail, Big Talbot
    Island State Park, 247–248

Blackroot, 144, 226
Blazing star, 274
Blinds, 141–142, 274
Blockade runners, 90, 96
Blue, Victor, 255
Blue crab, 97, 317
Blue flag iris, 290, 335
Blue Loop
    Goethe State Forest, 163,
        165, 166, 168
    Morningside Nature Center,
        142, 144
Blue teal, 318
Blue Trail
    Goethe State Forest,
        170–171
    Guana River State Park,
        299–301
    Princess Place Preserve,
        318–319
Blueberry, 50
Bluegill, 124, 203
Blue-gray gnatcatcher, 165
Bluejack oak tree, 60, 226
Bluestar, 38, 221, 274
Bluff, 15, 18, 19
Bluff Oak Trail, Andrews
    Wildlife Management Area,
    70, 71–72
Bluff oak tree, 64, 71–72, 77,
    211
Boardwalks, 17, 20, 62–63, 73
Bobcat Crossing, Welaka
    State Forest, 220, 222
Bobcat Trail
    Alligator Lake Recreation
        Area, 114
    Gum Root Swamp
        Conservation Area, 147,
        149–150
Bog buttons, 168, 222
Bolens Bluff, Paynes Prairie
    Preserve State Park, 152,
    155–156
Bouleware Springs Park, 160
Boulogne, FL, 224
Box elder tree, 211, 241
Bracken fern, 48, 53, 102, 104
Bradford County, 17
Bridge of Lions, 303, 308

Bridge to Bridge Trail, Swift
    Creek Conservation Area,
    50–52, 53
British pirates, 15
Broadhead skink, 41, 127, 249
Bromeliad, 136
Bronson, FL, 86, 162
Brown anole, 187, 207, 332
Brown pelican, 81, 97
Browne, Willie, 262, 265
Brown-headed nuthatch, 274,
    288
Bryceville, FL, 231
Buckeye Trail, Andrews Wildlife
    Management Area, 68–70
Buckman Lock, 179, 180, 181,
    183
Bullfrog, 206
Bulow, Charles Wilhelm, 339,
    340
Bulow, John, 339
Bulow Creek State Park, 337,
    339–343
Bulow Creek Trail, Bulow
    Creek State Park, 337–338,
    340–343
Bulow Plantation, Bulow
    Plantation Ruins State Park,
    337, 339
Bulow Plantation Ruins State
    Park, 337, 339
Bulowville, FL, 340
Bunnell, FL, 214, 321, 332
Burial mounds. See Middens
Burlow Creek Loop, 337
Burrowing owl, 274
Bushybeard bluestem, 88, 113
Butterfly weed, 230, 283
Butterfly-pea, 37, 127
Butterwort, 274, 290
Button snakeroot, 121, 230
Buttonbush, 113
Buttonweed, 228

C
Cabbage palm, 17, 19, 20, 45
Cabbage palm flatwoods, 19,
    20
Callahan, FL, 224, 237, 245
Camellia, 326

Camp Finegan, 105
Campfire, 21
Campgrounds
  Amelia River Campground,
    241, 242
  Atlantic Beach
    Campground, 238, 241,
    243, 244
  Bayard Point Campsite,
    289, 290
  Dogwood Campground,
    117
  Lake Eaton Campground,
    206
  Magnolia Campground, 117
  Pug Puggy Campground,
    152
  Suwannee Valley
    Campground, 52
Camping, 21, 22, 25
Campsites, 24
Canadian geese, 318
Canna, 103, 104
Canoe, aboriginal, 146, 149
Canoeing, 58, 63, 73, 93, 110,
  201, 210–211
Cape Francis, Anastasia State
  Park, 308
Capybara Trail, Alligator Lake
  Recreation Area, 113
Cardinal, 64, 142, 269
Cardinal wild pine, 181, 187,
  211–212
Carolina jessamine, 342
Carolina willow tree, 165
Carolina wren, 288
Carr, Archie, 45, 92, 95, 159,
  160
Carr, Marjorie Harris, 179
Cary Nature Trail, Cary State
  Forest, 231–235
Cary State Forest, 231–235
Castillo de San Marcos, 15,
  303, 305, 308
Catface, 18
Catholicism, 15
Cattail, 154
Cattle, 20, 72, 151, 154, 196
Cattle dip, 196
Cattle egret, 112

Cave diving, 43, 45, 73, 124
Caverns, 39, 64, 122, 124
Cedar elm tree, 80, 94, 211
Cedar Key, FL, 63, 79, 86, 92,
  93, 94, 96
Cedar Key Scrub State
  Reserve, 18, 86–91
Cedar Key Seafood Festival,
  97
Cedar Keys National Wildlife
  Refuge, 92–97
Cedar waxwing, 64
Cemeteries, 37, 94–95, 97,
  197, 198, 265
Central Highlands, 99–171
Century plant, 244
Chacala (steamboat), 156
Chacala Trail, Paynes Prairie
  Preserve State Park, 151,
  152, 156, 158–159
Chameleon, 323
Chapman oak tree, 20, 165
Cherokee Lodge, Princess
  Place Preserve, 318–319
Cherry tree, 154
Chert, 119
Chickees, 142, 152
Chicken turtle, 161
Chief Payne, 151
Chiefland, FL, 66, 73, 83
Chigger, 22
Cinnamon fern, 56, 144, 170
Cisco Ditch, 341, 342
Cisterns, 94, 198, 324
Citrus groves, 20, 315, 319,
  323
Citrus industry, 127
Citrus tree, 192
City of Hawkinsville (steam-
  boat), 63
Civil War, 15, 18, 35
  Atsena Otie Key, 97
  Battle of Horse Landing,
    183
  Battle of Olustee, 105–107,
    109
  Fort Clinch, 236–237
  Paynes Prairie Preserve,
    154
Civil Works Administration

(CWA), 174
Civilian Conservation Corps
  (CCC), 117, 201–202, 237
Clay, 19, 20
Clay County, 17
Clay Trail, Manatee Springs
  State Park, 75
Clayhill, 20
Clay's Landing, Manatee
  Springs Park, 75
Climbing hempweed, 295
Clothing, 23–24
Coastal dune, 15, 326
Coastal habitats, 18
Coastal hammock, 15
Coastal savanna, 18, 80
Coastal strands, 18
Coleridge, Samuel Taylor, 188
Columbia County, 17, 110
Columbine (Union gunboat),
  183
Columbus, FL, 35–37, 40, 63,
  105
Common yellowthroat, 46
The Complete Walker IV
  (Fletcher), 24
Conch, 37, 96
Cone's Dike, Paynes Prairie
  Preserve State Park,
  152–155
Coontail, 218, 220
Coontie, 64, 198, 324, 342
Coot, 112, 301
Coquina, 305, 306, 307, 319,
  325, 326
Coquina Beach, Washington
  Oaks Gardens State Park,
  326–327
Coral bean, 60, 124, 137, 279,
  331
Coral-root orchid, 257
Cormorant, 92, 96, 97
Corn snake, 319
Corral, 72, 124
Cotton mouse, 203
Cottonmouth moccasin, 24,
  92, 95
Cougar Trail, John P. Hall Sr.
  Nature Preserve, 289, 290
Cowpea, 137

Index

Coyote, 100
Crab spider, 23
Crabapple tree, 249
Cracked cap polypore, 187, 319
Creeks
  Black, 179, 272–276, 277–282
  Bulow, 328, 331, 337–343
  Cannon, 122
  Dennis, 81
  Dunns, 214–217
  Egan, 240, 241
  Hammock, 262, 265
  Haw, 332–335
  Little Hatchet, 147, 148, 149
  Moonshine, 133, 135, 136
  Moses, 309–314
  Pellicer, 315–319
  Price, 113
  Rose, 122
  Salt, 83, 85
  Sanders, 85
  Shired, 85
  Stiles, 319
Crescent Beach, 311
Crescent Lake, FL, 218, 332
The Cross and the Sword (play), 305
Cross City, FL, 85
Cross Florida Barge Canal, 183, 209, 212
Cumberland Island, 236, 240, 244
Cumberland Sound, 243
Cuscowilla (Seminole village), 151
Cutleaf spleenwort, 132
Cutting, Angela, 315
Cutting, Henry, 315
Cypress dome, 20
Cypress knees, 121, 149, 233

D

Dahoon holly tree, 341–342
Daisy fleabane, 127
Dampier's Landing, Ichetucknee Springs State Park, 128

Davis, Jefferson, 236
Daypack, 23
Deep Creek, FL, 100
Deer moss, 149, 207
Deer Run, Welaka State Forest, 221–222
Deer scrape, 198
Deer Trail, Alligator Lake Recreation Area, 114
Deerberry, 46, 187
Deer's tongue, 199, 279, 313
Deforestation, 21–22
Dehydration, 22
Dennis Creek Loop Trail, Lower Suwannee National Wildlife Refuge, 80–81
Depot Key, 94
Devil's Den, Ichetucknee Springs State Park, 128
Devil's Millhopper Geological State Park, 129–132
Devil's-walkingstick tree, 47, 279
Devilwood. See Evergreen wild olive
Dickison, John T., 183
Dike, 112, 113, 114
Ditch, 50
Dixie County, 17, 63, 83, 85
Dixie Mainline Trail, Lower Suwannee National Wildlife Refuge, 79, 83–85
Docks, 62, 92, 96–97
Doe Bay Road, Dunns Creek Conservation Area, 215
Dog banana, 102, 165
Dog fennel, 138, 154
Dog-hobble, 248
Dogwood Trail, O'Leno State Park, 117
Dogwood tree, 117, 201
Dolphin, Atlantic bottlenose, 17, 82, 97, 323
Dorman, George, 236
Downy woodpecker, 71, 107
Dragonfly, 59
Drake, Sir Francis, 303
Drew, George F., 39
Duck potato, 188
Duckweed, 113, 212

Dunnellon, FL, 17, 162, 163
Dunns Creek Conservation Area, Ocala National Forest, 214–217
Dupont Center, FL, 309
Duval County, 17, 267

E

Eagle Nest Row, Welaka State Forest, 220, 221, 222
Eagle Trail, Alligator Lake Recreation Area, 113–114
Earthworks Trail, Suwannee River State Park, 35–37
East Palatka holly, 176
Eastern box turtle, 177
Eastern coral snake, 24
Eastern diamondback rattlesnake, 24
Eastern fence lizard, 71, 138
Eastern glass lizard, 156
Eastern Loop, Cedar Key Scrub State Reserve, 90–91
Eastern redbud, 112
Eastern towhee, 196, 208
Eberhard Faber Pencil Mill, 94
Ebony spleenwort, 47, 64
Ecotone, 88, 127, 137, 138, 188, 191, 275
Eelgrass, 191
Elderberry, 111, 154
Elephant-ear, 212
Elephant's root, 20
Ellaville, FL, 37, 39, 40, 41, 46, 63
Elm tree, 59, 120, 138
Ephemeral pond, 20
Epiphytes, 119, 212
Equestrians, 23
Equipment, 23–24
Erect dayflower, 226
Estuary, 18–19, 82, 319
Everglades, 39
Evergreen wild olive, 320

F

Fairchild, David, 342
Fairchild Oak, 337, 341, 342, 343

Fannin, Alexander, 63
Fanning Springs, FL, 61, 66
Fanning Springs Hiking Trail, 64–65
Fanning Springs State Park, 61–65
Fargo, FL, 100
Farkleberry. *See* Sparkleberry
Farm and Forest Festival and Cane Boil, Morningside Nature Center, 140–141
Farming, 140
Faver-Dykes State Park, 317
Federal Works Project Administration (WPA), 174
Fence Trail, Manatee Springs State Park, 75, 77
Feral hog, 211
Fernandina, FL, 92, 105, 236, 237, 245
Ferries, 218, 245
Fiddler crab, 80, 323
Field guides, recommended, 25
Field mouse, 56
Finegan, Joseph, 106
Fire, 102, 163, 181
Fire and Water Nature Trail, Jennings State Forest, 272–274
Fire ring, 21
Firebreak, 60, 71
Five-lined race runner, 158, 255
Flag pawpaw, 312
Flagler, Henry, 303
Flagler Beach, FL, 214, 321, 332
Flagler College, St. Augustine, 308
Flagler County, 17, 315, 332
Flame azalea, 50, 52
Flat-topped goldenrod, 290
Flatwoods pond, 20, 330
Floodplain forest, 19, 20, 72
Flora, 17
Florida arrowroot. *See* Coontie
Florida azalea, 58
Florida black bear, 21, 104, 191, 275

Florida box turtle, 177
Florida Champion, 66, 68, 70, 71, 72
Florida Defenders of the Environment, 179
Florida Department of Transportation Ecopassage, 160
Florida Division of Forestry Trailwalker Program. *See* Trailwalker
Florida dogwood tree, 135, 187
Florida elephant's-foot, 217
Florida Fish and Wildlife Conservation Commission, 22, 206, 214, 226
Florida Maple Trail, Andrews Wildlife Management Area, 70, 71
Florida maple tree, 64, 66, 71
Florida National Scenic Trail, 17, 39, 44, 50, 183, 196, 198
Florida Nature & Heritage Tourism Center, 50
Florida Railroad, 92, 236
Florida red-belly turtle, 203
Florida rosemary, 206–207
Florida sand skink, 208
Florida scrub lizard, 15
Florida scrub-jay, 15, 86–90, 196, 326
Florida softshell turtle, 161, 335
Florida State Forests, 25
Florida State Parks, 25
Florida threeawn, 145
Florida Trail Association (FTA), 24, 25
Florida violet, 130
Floridan Aquifer, 18, 20, 38, 41, 184, 200
Flowerpot, 58
Forest ranger, 22
Forests, 19
Fort Caroline National Memorial, 264, 265–266
Fort Clinch Bicycle Trail, Fort Clinch State Park, 238–242

Fort Clinch State Park, 236–244
Fort Clinch Walking Tour, Fort Clinch State Park, 241, 242–243
Fort Fannin, 63
Fort Gates Ferry, 218
Fort George Island, Fort George Island Cultural State Park, 253–259
Fort George Island Cultural State Park, 253–259
Fort George River Walk, Little Talbot Island State Park, 245, 252
Fort George Trail, Fort George Island Cultural Park, 255–257
Fort White, FL, 122, 128
Fossils, 17
Fowler's Bluff, 79
Fox squirrel, 165, 196
France, 15, 259, 265
French Huguenot, 15, 259, 260, 265
Freshwater marsh, 20
From Here to There on the Florida Trail (Roquemore, Hobson), 24

G
Gainesville, FL, 86, 129, 133, 140, 147
Gainesville-Hawthorne Trail Rail, Paynes Preserve State Park, 160
Gallberry, 233, 313
The Gardens, Washington Oaks Gardens State Park, 323–324, 326
Gatorbacks, 64, 285
Geology, 15, 17–18
Georgia, 224, 236
Ghost crab, 250, 251
Ghost towns, 35, 40, 137
Giant leather fern, 320, 324
Giant sword fern, 177
Gilchrist County, 17, 63
Gillmore, Quincy, 105
Glasswort, 18, 95, 308

Index

Godwin Bridge, 56, 59
Goethe, J. T., 162
Goethe State Forest, 162–171
Golden aster, 83
Golden orb spider, 22–23
Goldfoot fern, 211, 324, 333
Gopher apple, 91, 226
Gopher tortoise, 56, 68, 226, 279
Graham Swamp Conservation Area, 328–331
Grand Champion, 41–42
Granite, 53
Grapevine, 39, 142, 177
Gray squirrel, 202
Gray Trail, Guana River State Park, 301
Great blue heron, 269
Great Depression, 237
Great horned owl, 71
Green anole, 333
Green Cove Springs, FL, 286
Green dragon, 19, 38, 47
Green heron, 15, 111
Green Loop, Goethe State Forest, 166
Green needlerush, 104, 112
Green Trail, Princess Place Preserve, 319–320
Greenbrier, 50, 135, 145
Green-crested night heron, 155
Greeneyes, 282–283
Greenfly orchid, 228, 257
Ground skink, 104
Guana Dam, 301, 302
Guana River State Park, 296–302
Guana River Wildlife Management Area, 298, 301
Gulf fritillary butterfly, 233
Gulf Hammock, 86
Gulf of Mexico, 23, 80, 85, 86
Gum Root Swamp Conservation Area, 146–150

H
Habitats, 18–19
Hackberry tree. See Sugarberry tree

Hairy wicky, 281
Hairy indigo, 298
Hamilton County, 17
Hammock Nature Trail, Fort Caroline, 265–266
Hanna Park Fish Management Area, 269
Hardee Plantation, 75
Hardwood hammock, 19
Hardwood Trail, Manatee Springs State Park, 75
Harper, R.M., 209, 211
Hartwrightia, 224
Hatpins, 142, 158, 216–217
Haw Creek Preserve, 332–336
Hay, John, 105
Heat, 22
Heatstroke, 22
Hercules'-club, 127, 268–269
Hernandez, Joseph, 323
Herring gull, 244
Hickory tree, 19, 44, 47
High Springs, FL, 115, 120, 122
Highbush blueberry, 168, 228, 279
Hiking & Backpacking: A Complete Guide (Berger), 24
Hilliard, FL, 224
Historical markers, 39, 175
History, 18
Homestead, 258, 298
Honeysuckle, 39, 181
Hooded merganser, 15
Hooded pitcher plant, 224, 226, 233
Hornbeam. See Ironwood tree
Horned owl, 255
Hornet Trail, Manatee Springs State Park, 75
Horse Landing, 183
Horseshoe crab, 96
Huckleberry. See Sparkleberry
Huguenot Memorial Park, 259
Hunting, 22
Hydric hammock, 20
Hydrilla, 192

I
Ichetucknee Springs State Park, 122–128
Indian Pond Run, Welaka State Forest, 218, 221
Insects, 22
Interpretive, 37
Intracoastal Waterway, 245, 294
Ironwood tree, 19, 126
Island Hiking Trail, Little Talbot Island State Park, 249–251

J
Jack-in-the-pulpit, 132
Jackson's Gap Trail, Paynes Prairie Preserve State Park, 152, 159
Jacksonville, FL, 105, 224, 260, 267, 272
Jacksonville Metro, 223–283
Jai, Anna Madgigine, 259
Jasper, FL, 33
Jellyfish, 23
Jennings State Forest, 272–276
Jesuit priests, 139, 259
Jody's Trace, The Yearling Trail, 196
John P. Hall Sr. Nature Preserve, Bayard Point Conservation Area, 286–291
Johns Landing Trail, Welaka State Forest, 218, 220–222
Jones Cut Trail, Big Talbot Island State Park, 248
Juncus, 251
Juniper Run Nature Trail, Ocala National Forest, 200–203
Juniper Springs Recreation Area, Ocala National Forest, 200–202

K
Karst, 17–18, 37, 62, 115
Karst window, 119, 120, 121
Kathryn Abbey Hanna Park, 267–271
Kayaking, 44, 58, 93, 110,

209–211
Keno (frontier town), 117
Key West, FL, 37, 105
Kingsley, Zephaniah, 258, 259
Kingsley Plantation, Fort
    George Island, 255,
    258–259

L

La Chua Trail, Paynes Prairie
    Preserve State Park, 156,
    159–161
La Natividad de Nuestra
    Senora de Tolomato, 298
Ladder brake fern, 215
Lady lupine, 37, 168
Lafayette County, 17
Lake City, FL, 100, 106, 110,
    113, 122
Lake Eaton Loop Trail, Ocala
    National Forest, 204–207
Lake Eaton Sinkhole Trail,
    Ocala National Forest, 204,
    207–208
Lake Eaton Trails, Ocala
    National Forest, 204–208
Lake George Trail, Silver Glen
    Springs, 191
Lake Trail, Paynes Prairie
    Preserve State Park, 152,
    158
Lakes
    Alachua, 155, 156–158
    Alligator, 111–112
    Black, 120
    Bromeliad, 136
    Eaton, 204–208
    Guana, 296, 302
    Jug, 119, 121
    Lake George, 184–188,
        189–192
    Little Lake George, 218
    Newnan's, 146–149
    Ogden, 121
    Sweetwater, 119, 121
    Wauberg, 152, 156–158
Lantana, 177, 294
Largemouth bass, 179, 193,
    333
Laurel oak, 19, 45, 58

Le Moyne, Jacques, 265, 266
Least tern, 15
Lee, FL, 33, 43
Lee, Robert E., 179
Legacy Trail, John P. Hall Sr.
    Nature Preserve, 289
Leno, 117
Leopard frog, 276, 331
Levee, 41, 44, 45–46, 121
Levy County, 17, 63, 162, 163
Lighthouse, Seahorse Key, 97
Lime Sink Run Trail, Suwannee
    River State Park, 37, 38
Limestone, 17–18, 37
Limestone Trail, O'Leno State
    Park, 117
Limpkin, 203, 301, 335
Linden tree. *See* American
    basswood tree
Little blue heron, 96, 121
Little green heron, 301
Little Shoals, 54
Little Talbot Island, 245,
    249–252
Little Talbot Nature Trail, Little
    Talbot Island State Park,
    251–252
Live Oak, FL, 33, 43
Live oak tree, 41–42, 60, 69
Living-history demonstrations,
    107, 140, 242
Loblolly bay tree, 163, 170,
    216, 274
Loblolly pine tree, 19, 22, 60,
    77
Loggerhead turtle, 251
Logging, 21, 46, 72, 102, 216,
    288
Long, Calvin, 194, 196, 199
Long, Cora, 199
Long, Reuben, 194, 196, 198
Long Branch Trail, Big Shoals,
    54, 59–60
Long Cemetery, 196, 198
Longleaf Lane, Welaka State
    Forest, 221
Longleaf Pine Loop, Jennings
    State Forest, 275, 276
Longleaf pine tree, 19, 143,
    163, 165, 166, 182

Loop Trail
    Anderson Springs Loop, 46
    Manatee Springs State Park,
        75
Louisiana heron, 80, 111
Low panicum grass, 233, 288
Lower Suwannee National
    Wildlife Refuge, 79–85
Lyre-leaved sage, 313

M

Madison, FL, 33
Magnol, Pierre, 307
Maidencane, 318
Mala Compra Trail, Washington
    Oaks Gardens State Park,
    323
Manatee, West Indian, 62, 73,
    78, 79, 97, 179, 323
Manatee Springs State Park,
    73–78
Mangrove swamp, 19
Marine life, 23
Marion County, 17, 163, 212
Maritime hammock, 18, 300
Marjorie Harris Carr Cross
    Florida Greenway, 180,
    209, 211
Marl, 216
Marsh pink, 232
Marsh Point, Stokes Landing
    Conservation Area,
    293–294
Marsh rabbit, 151, 156
Marsh rice rat, 156
Marsh Trail, Bulow Creek State
    Park, 341
Marshes
    Egan, 238
    Round, 262–263
Masonry fortress, 15
Matanzas Inlet, 307, 308
Mayport, FL, 245, 251, 253,
    267
Mayport Naval Station, 251
McIntosh, John, 258
McQueen, John, 258
Meadow, 71, 72
Meadow pink, 305
Menendez de Aviles, Pedro,

265–266, 308
Micanopy, FL, 152
Middens, 79, 82, 191, 221, 260, 263
Middleburg, FL, 277
Milton, John, 236
Milton Light Artillery, 183
Mimosa tree, 145
Mission de Nombre de Dios, 308
Mistletoe, 199
Mockernut hickory tree, 324
Monarch butterfly, 50
Montgomery Trail, Alligator Lake Recreation Area, 110–113
Moon jellyfish, 244, 251
Moorhen, 160
Morningside Nature Center, 140–145
Moses Creek Conservation Area, 309–314
Mosquito Inlet, 340
Mosquitoes, 22
Mount Cornelia, 257
Mount Royal, 221
Mountain bike. See Biking
Mud Spring Trail, Welaka State Forest, 218–220
Mud turtle, 78, 124
Muir, John, 15, 17, 93–94, 96, 214, 240
Mulberry tree, 281
Mullet, 191, 317
Murat Point, 309–314
Musk turtle, 178, 203
Mussel, 307
Mustard-yellow polypore, 144
Myrtle oak tree, 20, 50, 88, 165

N
Narrow-leaf pawpaw, 21, 37, 144
Nassau County, 17
Nature Coast Rail Trail, 66
Naval stores, 18, 90
Needle palm tree, 132, 202
Netted chain fern, 177
Netted pawpaw, 141–142

New Smyrna, FL, 340
Nixon, Richard, 179
North End Trail System, Manatee Springs State Park, 73–77
North Fork Black Creek Trail, Jennings State Forest, 272, 274–276
North Key, 92
Northern waterthrush, 244
Nuthatch, 102, 274

O
Oak hammock, 19, 20
Oak scrub, 16, 20
Oak toad, 233–235
Ocala, FL, 17, 179, 180, 184, 189, 200, 204
Ocala Boat Basin, Ray Wayside Park, 209
Ocala National Forest, 15, 173–222
Ocala Trail, Florida National Scenic Trail, 198
Ogeehee tupelo, 50
Old Canal Trail, Alligator Lake Recreation Area, 112–113, 114
Old Granville Road, The Yearling Trail, 198–199
Old Jennings Recreation Area, Jennings State Forest, 272, 274, 276
Old man's beard, 181, 187, 196
Old Spanish Coquina Quarry Trail, Anastasia State Park, 305–306
Old Spanish Way, San Felasco Hammock Preserve State Park, 135, 138–139
Old Town, FL, 83
O'Leno State Park, 115–121
Olustee, FL, 15, 106
Olustee Battlefield Historical State Park, Osceola National Forest, 105–109
One-flowered hawthorn, 229
Orange jelly mold, 46–47
Orange Park, FL, 272

Orange peel mushroom, 341
Orange Point, Welaka State Forest, 221, 222
Orange Trail
    Goethe State Forest, 166–168, 170
    Guana River State Park, 301
Ormond Beach, FL, 184, 189, 200, 218, 337
Osceola National Forest, 100–109
Osprey, 95, 206
O'Sullivan, Maureen, 212
Otter Creek, 86
Otter Trail, Gum Root Swamp Conservation Area, 147–149
Ottowa (Union gunboat), 236
Oyster, 81
Oyster fungus, 142, 324

P
Painted bunting, 15, 244, 245, 247
Palatka, FL, 174, 175, 180
Pale lilac, 145
Pale meadow beauty, 102, 232
Palm Coast, FL, 321, 328
Palm hammock, 20
Palm warbler, 142, 342
Palmetto, 63
Panhandle, 17, 38
Paraners Branch Trail, O'Leno State Park, 118, 121
Passionflower, 154, 159
Pat's Island, 194, 198, 199
Paynes Prairie Preserve State Park, 151–161
Pelican, 92, 97
Pellicer Creek Conservation Area, 315
Pencil making, 92, 94
Penney Farms, 277
Pennywort, 120, 154
Pensacola, FL, 37, 39, 105
Periwinkle snail, 81
Permits, 21, 25
Persimmon Trail, Andrews Wildlife Management Area, 70–71

Persimmon tree, 66, 70–71
Phosphate mining, 126–127
Pickerelweed, 161, 248
Piers, 40, 56, 59, 212
Pignut hickory tree, 121, 130, 215, 281
Pileated woodpecker, 124, 149
Pine flatwoods, 19
Pine lily, 20
Pine Ridge Loop, Ichetucknee Springs State Park, 126–127
Pine Road, Paynes Prairie Preserve State Park, 159
Pink Loop, Goethe State Forest, 166
Pink meadow beauty, 281
Pipewort, 226
Pithlachocco, 146
Plantations, 105, 255, 257, 258–259
Plants, 23
Pocket gopher, 135, 196, 208
Point Isabella, Fort George Island, 257
Poison ivy, 23, 83
Pond cypress tree, 20, 144, 335
Pond pine tree, 19, 301
Ponds
    Alligator, 264
    Big Savanna, 301
    Blue's, 255
    Boardman, 342
    Chacala, 158, 159
    Graveyard, 77
    Ocean, 106, 109
    Shacklefoot, 75, 77
    Shanty, 185
    Spanish, 264
    Willow, 113, 238, 240
Poppy mallow, 137
Possum haw, 233
Possum Trot Trail, Alligator Lake Recreation Area, 113
Post oak tree, 75, 127
Pothole, 248
Prairies, 15, 19–20, 80
    Alachua Savanna, 77, 151, 175

Paynes Prairie, 17, 151
Precautions. See advice and precautions
Prickly pear cactus, 95, 107–109, 118, 168, 199, 226
Primitive campsite, 21
Princess Place Preserve, 315–320
Puffball mushroom, 217
Purple baldwina, 224
Purple Trail
    Goethe State Forest, 163, 165
    Guana River State Park, 298, 299
Putnam County, 17
Pygmy killifish, 220
Pygmy rattlesnake, 24, 229, 272

Q
Quail, 274, 279
Quarries, 117, 305, 306
Quartz, 305
Quicksand, 202

R
Rabbit tobacco, 264
Raccoon, 21, 191
Raccoon Run Loop, Stokes Landing Conservation Area, 293, 294
Railroad, 92, 126
Rain-lily, 135
Ralph E. Simmons Memorial State Forest, 224–230
Ranching, 72, 151
Ranger station, 35
Rapids, 54, 56, 58
Raspberry, 40
Rat snake, 154–155
Ravine, 15, 18, 19
Ravine Gardens State Park, 174–178
Rawlings, Marjorie Kinnan, 191, 194, 198
Ray, Walter, 212
Ray Wayside Park, 209–211, 212

Red admiral, 275
Red bay tree, 20, 60, 130
Red blanket lichen, 198, 202–203
Red buckeye tree, 137, 191, 217
Red bug. See Chigger
Red chokeberry, 228
Red fox, 119, 151
Red Loop, Goethe State Forest, 163, 164–165
Red maple tree, 20, 142, 228
Red mulberry tree, 293, 323
Red Root Trail, Cary State Forest, 235
Red Trail
    Goethe State Forest, 166, 170
    Guana River State Park, 298–299
    Moses Creek Conservation Area, 312–314
Red-bellied woodpecker, 217
Red-cockaded woodpecker, 15, 167, 168
Red-headed woodpecker, 127, 167
Red/Orange Trail, Princess Place Preserve, 317–318
Red-shouldered hawk, 52, 113
Red-tailed hawk, 100, 326
Red-winged blackbird, 112
Reindeer lichen, 170, 312
Relict dunes, 238, 240
Resurrection fern, 187, 198
Rhesus macaque, 212
Ribault, Jean, 265, 266, 324
Ribault Club, 253–255, 257
Ribault Monument, Timucuan Ecological and Historical Preserve, 265
Ring-billed gull, 252
Ring-necked gull, 243
River Birch Trail, Andrews Wildlife Management Area, 70, 72
River birch tree, 72
River Bluffs Trail, Swift Creek Conservation Area, 52–53
River cooter, 117, 139

River otter, 126, 128, 138
River Rise, 115–121
River Rise Preserve State Park, 115, 118, 119
River Trail, O'Leno State Park, 117–118, 121
Rivers and Runs
Fern Hammock Run, 203
Fort George River, 252, 255, 257, 258
Guana River, 296, 298
Halifax River, 340
Hillsborough River, 45
Ichetucknee Run, 122–128
Juniper Run, 200–203
Lime Sink Run, 37, 38–39
Manatee Springs Run, 73–78
Matanzas River, 308, 309–313, 315, 323
Mud Spring Run, 220
Ocklawaha River, 15, 179, 180. 209
Salt Springs Run, 184–188
Santa Fe River, 115–121
Silver Glen Run, 189, 191
Silver River, 179, 209–213
St. Johns River, 189, 192, 221, 260, 286, 290
St. Marys River, 224–230, 236
Suwannee River, 31–97
Tolomato River, 285, 292–301
Tomoka River, 328
Withlacoochee River, 35, 40, 41, 42
Rodeheaver Boys Ranch, 183
Rodman Dam, 179, 180, 183
Roosevelt, Theodore, 262
Roseling, 127
Rosemary scrub, 20
Roserush, 142, 230, 274
Rosewood, FL, 86, 88
Round Marsh Trail, Timucuan Ecological and Historical Preserve, 262
Royal fern, 48, 56
Royal tern, 97
Russell Landing, 332, 335
Rusty lyonia, 150, 187

S
S. Bryan Jennings Environmental Education Center, Cary State Forest, 231
Sabal palm. *See* Cabbage palm
Salt, 90
Salt flats, 18
Salt marsh, 18–19, 81, 89, 285
Salt Springs, FL, 184
Salt Springs Loop Trail, 184–188
Salt Springs Recreation Area, 184, 185
Salt-making, 90, 96, 105
Saltwort, 95
Samphire, 308, 323
San Felasco Hammock Preserve State Park, 133–139
San Felasco Nature Trail, San Felasco Hammock Preserve State Park, 135
San Francisco Potano Mission, 139
San Juan del Puerto, 259
San Mateo, FL, 214
Sand cordgrass, 113, 318
Sand dune spurge, 308
Sand live oak tree, 144, 198
Sand pine tree, 20, 41, 206
Sandbar, 52
Sandhill, 20, 21
Sandhill crane, 161
Sandhill milkweed, 37, 137, 167, 168, 230
Sandhill wireweed, 102, 144
Sandhills Trail, Suwannee River State Park, 35–37
Sandspur, 124
Sargasso Sea, 201
Sassafras tree, 60, 282
Saturiwa Trail, Fort George Island Cultural State Park, 253
Savanna, 18–19
Saw palmetto, 18, 109, 132, 182, 188, 198

Sawgrass, 113
Sawmill, 40
Scarlet tanager, 250
Scenic Trail, Manatee Springs State Park, 75
Scrub, 20, 21
Scrub buckwheat, 206
Scrub milkwort, 206
Scrub morning glory, 206
Scrub palmetto, 20, 198
Scrubby flatwoods, 19, 50
Sea lice, 247
Sea myrtle, 154, 240
Sea oats, 243, 244
Sea oxeye, 249, 295
Sea pickle. *See* Sea Purslane
Sea purslane, 96, 299, 308
Sea turtle, 79, 251
Seahorse Key, 92, 97
Seaside sparrow, 318
Second Seminole War, 63, 339
Seepage slope, 20
Seminole, 63, 142, 146, 151, 165, 339
Seminole Wars, 18, 63, 339, 340
Sensitive brier, 188, 226
Seymour, Truman A., 105
Shacklefoot Trail, Manatee Springs State Park, 77
Shark, 23
Sheepshead, 78, 218
Shelf fungus, 64
Shell Bluff, Guana River State Park, 299
Shell Mound County Park, Lower Suwannee National Wildlife Refuge, 80, 81, 82–83
Shell Mound Loop Trail, Lower Suwannee National Wildlife Refuge, 81–83
Shell Mound Unit, Lower Suwannee National Wildlife Refuge, 79–83
Shell mounds. *See* Middens
Shell Point, Guana River State Park, 295
Shellcracker, 124

Shiny blueberry, 102, 230
Shiny lyonia, 311
Shired Island, 85
Shoelace fern, 203, 333, 335
Sierra Club, 126
Silk bay tree, 95, 130, 196
Silver Glen Springs, FL, 173
Silver Glen Springs, Ocala
    National Forest, 189–193,
    194
Silver Glen Springs Recreation
    Area, 189
Silver River Connector Trail,
    Ocala National Forest,
    209–213
Silver River State Park, Ocala
    National Forest, 209, 212
Silver Springs, FL, 211
Silver-spotted skipper, 167
Sink Hole Trail Loop, Manatee
    Springs
    State Park, 73, 77–78
Sinkholes, 18, 64, 71, 77–78,
    129–132
Sinks
    Alachua, 156, 157, 160,
        161
    Big, 138–139
    Clay Hole, 122
    Devil's Millhopper, 129–132
    Jim, 121
    Lake Eaton, 204, 207–208
    Lime, 38
    New, 121
    River, 99, 115–121
Six-lined race runner, 91, 181
Slash pine, 19, 20, 48
Slender beard tongue, 127
Slider, 203
Sloughs, 85, 102, 113, 154,
    168
Snags, 64, 70, 75, 102
Snake Key, 92, 95
Snakes, 24
Snapping turtle, 203
Sneezeweed, 343
Snook, 303
Snorkeling, 128
Snowy egret, 269, 306
Sod farm, 20

Solution hole, 45
South Ponte Vedra Beach, FL,
    296
Southeastern five-lined skink,
    127, 187
Southern copperhead, 24
Southern magnolia tree, 64,
    75, 135, 187, 306–307
Southern naiad, 220
Southern pine beetle, 21–22,
    77, 211
Southern red cedar tree, 97,
    124
Southern toad, 203, 249
Southern water snake, 156
Southern woods fern, 177
Spanish, 15, 303, 305
Spanish bayonet, 96, 314
Spanish larkspur, 250
Spanish missions, 15, 139,
    259, 298, 308
Spanish moss, 212, 271
Spanish Pond Trail, Timucuan
    Ecological and Historical
    Preserve, 264
Spanish-American War, 18,
    237
Sparkleberry, 52–53, 121, 288
Spearing, John Nathan, 263
Sphagnum moss, 113, 181
Spider lily, 91
Spiders, 22
Spiderwort, 142, 191, 257,
    323
Spleenwort, 19, 65
Spoil piles, 110, 183
Spoked Flight Bicycle Club,
    238
Spotted fawn, 71
Spring Boils Trail, Silver Glen
    Springs, 189
Spring Grove (ghost town),
    137
Spring Grove Trail, San
    Felasco Hammock Preserve
    State Park, 135–138, 139
Spring vents, 38, 61–62, 122,
    191
Springs, 15, 18
    Anderson, 43–44, 47

Blue Hole, 124, 126
Bouleware, 160, 161
Cedar Head, 124
Fern Hammock, 200, 203
Ichetucknee, 122, 124–126,
    127
Jody's, 191
Juniper, 200–203
Lime, 36, 37–38, 41
Manatee, 17, 73, 78
Mud, 218, 220
Natural Well, 191
Salt, 184
Silver Glen, 173, 189–191
Sulfur, 220, 222
Suwanacoochee, 41
Spruce pine tree, 41
Spur Trail, Manatee Springs
    State Park, 77
St. Augustine, FL, 15, 105,
    265, 303, 305, 308
St. Augustine Alligator Farm,
    303
St. Augustine Amphitheatre,
    305
St. Augustine Lighthouse,
    Anastasia State Park, 307,
    308
St. George Trail, Silver Glen
    Springs, 189
St. Johns Bluff, 265
St. Johns County, 17, 311
St. Johns Loop, 179–183
St. Johns Water Management
    District, 147, 292
St. John's-wort, 295, 312
St. Peter's-wort, 232
Staghorn fern, 326
Star rush, 217, 226
Starke, FL, 231
Steamboats, 35, 40, 63, 155,
    156, 179
Stephen Foster Folk Center
    State Park, 50
Stinging nettle. See Tread
    softly
Stingray, 23
Stokes Landing Conservation
    Area, 292–295
Strapleaf sagittaria, 218

Striped bass, 191, 218
Sugar cane, 339
Sugar hackberry. *See* Sugarberry
Sugar mill, 337, 339
Sugar Mill Trail, Bulow Plantation Ruins State Park, 339
Sugarberry tree, 64, 238, 326
Summer tanager, 274
Sumner, FL, 86, 88
Sun protection, 15–16, 24
Sundew, 15, 216, 274, 281
Sundial lupine, 135, 281
Surface limestone, 45
Suwannee, FL, 85
Suwannee Bicycle Association, 50, 56
Suwannee cooter, 45
Suwannee County, 17
Suwannee River Boardwalk, Manatee Springs State Park, 78
Suwannee River Boardwalk Trail, Lower Suwannee National Wildlife Refuge, 79, 83
Suwannee River State Park, 33–42
Suwannee River Trail, Suwannee River State Park, 37–38
Suwannee River Trail System, Suwannee River State Park, 37–39
Swallow-tailed kite, 79, 165, 329–331, 335
Swamp azalea, 282
Swamp chestnut oak tree, 45, 135
Swamp forest, 20
Swamp hibiscus, 104
Swamp hyacinth, 104
Swamp lily, 102, 149
Swamps
  Big Gum, 104
  Black Point, 90
  California, 79, 83, 85
  Graham, 328
  Gum Root, 146–150

Sweetbay magnolia tree, 102, 158, 216
Sweetgum tree, 142, 228, 333
Swift, Thomas E., 37
Swift Creek Conservation Area, 48–53
Swimming, 124, 128, 189, 190
Sword fern, 176, 326T

T

Tabby, 243, 258
Talahasochte (Creek village), 73, 175
Talbot Islands, 223, 245–252
Tall meadow beauty, 228
Tallahassee, FL, 33, 105
Tampa, FL, 45
Tapegrass, 218
Tarflower, 233
Tarzan, 212
Ten Mile Run, 105
Theodore Roosevelt Area, Timucuan Ecological and Historical Preserve, 262–265
Thistle, 154
Ticks, 22, 66, 73, 196
Tidal marsh, 80, 81
Tidal pools, 248, 303, 307
Tidewater Trail, Goethe State Forest, 163–165
Timber rattlesnake, 24
Timucan Ecological and Historical Preserve, 253, 260–266
Timucua, 15, 139, 191, 255, 260, 265
Timucuan Loop, Washington Oaks Gardens State Park, 324
Timucuan Trail, Timucuan Ecological and Historical Preserve, 262–264
Titi tree, 124, 144, 145
Tomoka State Park, 337
Toothache grass, 224
Trailwalker, 25, 43, 162, 163, 170, 218, 220, 232, 272
Tram Road, Dunns Creek

Conservation Area, 215, 217
Tramway, 85, 102–104, 149, 216
Tread softly, 23
Tree frog, 217, 262
Trestle Point Trail, Ichetucknee Springs State Park, 126
Tri-colored heron. *See* Louisiana heron
Trumpet flower, 111, 126
Trumpet vine, 183, 333
Tubing, 122–128
Tupelo tree, 233
Turkey oak tree, 226
Turkey Track Trail, Andrews Wildlife Management Area, 68, 70
Turpentining, 18, 46, 102, 288, 339
Turtle Trail, Gum Root Swamp Conservation Area, 147
Twin Rivers State Forest, 43–47

U

Union Blockading Squadron, 90, 97, 105
Union County, 17
University of North Florida, 257
Upland hardwood forests, 19

V

Vanilla plant. *See* Deer's tongue
Vehicles, unattended, 24
Violet, 135, 341
Virginia creeper, 38, 47
Virginia willow tree, 88, 111, 154

W

Wacahoota Trail, Paynes Prairie Preserve State Park, 151, 152
Wahlin Trail, Bulow Creek State Park, 343
Wakerobin, 132, 135
Walking stick, 266
Walter viburnum, 342

Warbling vireo, 149
Washington, George
    Lawrence, 324, 326
Washington Oaks Gardens
    State Park, 321–327
Water, 22, 24
Water hyacinth, 161
Water lily, 167
Water moccasin. See
    Cottonmouth moccasin
Water oak tree, 226
Water tupelo tree, 144
Waterfalls, 18, 129, 132, 160
Wax myrtle tree, 137, 142, 266
Weather, 24–25
Weissmuller, Johnny, 212
Welaka State Forest, 218–222
Western Loop, Cedar Key
    Scrub State Reserve,
    88–90
Western Trailhead, Moses
    Creek Conservation Area,
    314
Wetlands, 20
Wheelchair accessible, 107,
    152, 158, 231
White cedar tree, 97
White cheese polypore, 326
White colic-root, 282
White heron, 252
White ibis, 81, 240
White jelly fungus, 127
White jelly tooth mushroom,
    249
White morning glory, 188
White oak tree, 37, 44, 45,
    226
White Sand Landing, Ralph E.
    Simmons Memorial State
    Forest, 227, 228
White Springs, FL, 48, 50, 54
White sulfur butterfly, 96

White Trail, Morningside
    Nature Center, 141
White Trail, Moses Creek
    Conservation Area,
    309–311, 314
White violet, 216
White-tailed deer, 100, 127,
    151
Whitewater, 54, 57
Wild bachelor's buttons, 17,
    91, 142, 233
Wild coffee, 324
Wild horse, 17, 151, 154
Wild indigo, 41, 47, 137
Wild lime. See Hercules'-club
Wild petunia, 216
Wild pine, 72, 212
Wild plum tree, 137
Wild rose, 113
Wild turkey, 276
Wildfires, 21
Wildlife, 18
Willet, 80
Willie Browne Trail, Timucuan
    Ecological and Historical
    Preserve, 262, 264–265
Williston, FL, 140, 146
Willow oak, 83
Willow Pond Nature Trail, Fort
    Clinch State Park, 238
Windmill, 94, 95, 96
Winged Elm Road, Andrews
    Wildlife Management Area,
    70, 72
Winged elm tree, 71
Winged sumac, 257
Wire Road, O'Leno State Park,
    118, 121
Wiregrass, 144, 145, 226
Witch hazel tree, 266
Witchs' butter, 306
Wood stork, 15

Woodbine, 135
Woodlands phlox, 127, 137
Woodpecker Trail, 54
Woods fern, 62, 102, 177
World War I, 18
World War II, 18, 339

Y
Yaupon holly, 240, 269, 299,
    306
The Yearling (Rawlings), 191,
    194, 199
The Yearling Trail, Ocala
    National Forest, 194–199
Yellow aster, 228
Yellow Indiangrass, 113
Yellow Loop, Morningside
    Nature Center, 142–144
Yellow lotus, 206, 212
Yellow pine, 40–41, 46
Yellow sulfur butterfly, 164
Yellow Trail
    Goethe State Forest, 163,
        165
    Guana River State Park,
        299
    Moses Creek Conservation
        Area, 311, 312, 314
Yellow-crowned night heron,
    15, 257
Yellow-eyed grass, 102, 181,
    230
Yellow-star grass, 221
Young, Owen D., 323
Yucca, 196, 314
Yulee, 224
Yulee, David, 92

Z
Zebra swallowtail butterfly,
    104, 109, 230

Let Backcountry Guides Take You There

Our experienced backcountry authors will lead you to the finest trails, parks, and back roads in the following areas:

50 Hikes Series

50 Hikes in the Adirondacks
50 Hikes in Colorado
50 Hikes in Connecticut
50 Hikes in Central Florida
50 Hikes in North Florida
50 Hikes in the Lower Hudson Valley
50 Hikes in Kentucky
50 Hikes in the Maine Mountains
50 Hikes in Coastal and Southern Maine
50 Hikes in Massachusetts
50 Hikes in Maryland
50 Hikes in Michigan
50 Hikes in the White Mountains
50 More Hikes in New Hampshire
50 Hikes in New Jersey
50 Hikes in Central New York
50 Hikes in Western New York
50 Hikes in the Mountains of North Carolina
50 Hikes in Ohio
50 More Hikes in Ohio
50 Hikes in Eastern Pennsylvania
50 Hikes in Central Pennsylvania
50 Hikes in Western Pennsylvania
50 Hikes in the Tennessee Mountains
50 Hikes in Vermont
50 Hikes in Northern Virginia
50 Hikes in Southern Virginia

Walking

Walks and Rambles on Cape Cod and the Islands
Walks and Rambles on the Delmarva Peninsula
Walks and Rambles in the Western Hudson Valley
Walks and Rambles on Long Island
Walks and Rambles in Ohio's Western Reserve
Walks and Rambles in Rhode Island
Walks and Rambles in and around St. Louis
Weekend Walks in St. Louis and Beyond
Weekend Walks Along the New England Coast
Weekend Walks in Historic New England

Bicycling

25 Bicycle Tours in the Adirondacks
25 Bicycle Tours on Delmarva
25 Bicycle Tours in Savannah and the Carolina Low Country
25 Bicycle Tours in Maine
25 Bicycle Tours in Maryland
25 Bicycle Tours in the Twin Cities and Southeastern Minnesota
30 Bicycle Tours in New Jersey
30 Bicycle Tours in the Finger Lakes Region
25 Bicycle Tours in the Hudson Valley
25 Bicycle Tours in Maryland
25 Bicycle Tours in Ohio's Western Reserve
25 Bicycle Tours in the Texas Hill Country and West Texas
25 Bicycle Tours in Vermont
25 Bicycle Tours in and around Washington, D.C.
25 Mountain Bike Tours in the Adirondacks
25 Mountain Bike Tours in the Hudson Valley
25 Mountain Bike Tours in Massachusetts
25 Mountain Bike Tours in New Jersey
Backroad Bicycling in Connecticut
Backroad Bicycling on Cape Cod, Martha's Vineyard, and Nantucket
Backroad Bicycling in Western Massachusetts
Backroad Bicycling in Eastern Pennsylvania
Backroad Bicycling in Wisconsin
The Mountain Biker's Guide to Ski Resorts
Bicycling America's National Parks: Arizona & New Mexico
Bicycling America's National Parks: California
Bicycling America's National Parks: Oregon & Washington
Bicycling America's National Parks: The Northern Rockies & Great Plains
Bicycling America's National Parks: Utah & Colorado
Bicycling Cuba

We offer many more books on hiking, fly-fishing, travel, nature, and other subjects. Our books are available at bookstores and outdoor stores everywhere. For more information or a free catalog, please call 1-800-245-4151 or write to us at The Countryman Press, P.O. Box 748, Woodstock, Vermont 05091. You can find us on the Internet at www.countrymanpress.com.